Robin Barker is a registered nurse, midwife and early childhood nurse with over twenty-five years' hands-on experience with families and babies.

Robin has a great interest in the trickier aspects of babycare such as crying, sleep and strange habits in babies. She also finds the intricacies of breastfeeding an absorbing and challenging part of her work.

She has two delightful children and two grandchildren.

Other books by Robin Barker

Baby and Toddler Meals
The Mighty Toddler

ROBIN
BARKER

BABY
LOVE

Pan Macmillan Australia

NOTE TO READERS

All care has been taken to provide accurate, safe information, but it is impossible to cover every situation, so please consult a competent health professional whenever you are in doubt about your baby's health or behaviour. A book can never be a substitute for an individual professional consultation. The author and the publishers cannot accept legal responsibility for any problems arising out of the contents of this book.

First published 1994 in Pan by Pan Macmillan Australia Pty Limited
This Macmillan edition published in 2009 by Pan Macmillan Australia Pty Limited
1 Market Street, Sydney

Reprinted 2005 (four times), 2006 (twice), 2007 (twice), 2008 (three times), 2009 (twice), 2010

National Library of Australia
cataloguing-in-publication data:

Barker, Robin, 1944– .
Baby love: everything you need to know about your new baby.

Rev. ed.
ISBN 978 1 4050 3910 9.

1. Infants – Care. 2. Infants – Health and hygiene.
3. Infants – Nutrition. 4. Infants (Newborn) – Care.
5. Infants (Newborn) – Health and hygiene.
6. Infants (Newborn) – Nutrition. I. Title.

649.122

Illustrations by Susie Baxter-Smith
Excerpt from 'An Eskimo Baby' by Lucy Diamond, from *The Book of a Thousand Poems*, 1983, reprinted by permission of HarperCollins Publishers Ltd.
Typeset in 11/14.5pt Bembo by Post Pre-Press Group
Printed in Australia by McPherson's Printing Group

Papers used by Pan Macmillan Australia Pty Ltd are natural, recyclable products made from wood grown in sustainable forests. The manufacturing processes conform to the environmental regulations of the country of origin.

For Babe, Adam, Kate, Kim, Sage and Jimmy.

He, she and so on

In this book the mother is she, the father is he and the baby is she . . . (for no particular reason).

Contents

PART THREE

6 TO 9 MONTHS

PART FOUR

9 TO 12 MONTHS

Introduction

Baby Love is the result of the many years I have spent talking to women about their babies. For twenty-five years my job as a child and family health nurse was to help them by providing the technical knowledge they needed to do the job, as well as to help them sort out the vast range of ideas about babycare that drives modern parents mad.

All parenting information reflects the background, the qualifications and the professional experience of the person providing it. *Baby Love* reflects mine. Child and family health nursing is a broad, rather than a specialised, practice where the practitioner is there to see and help all-comers —mothers who breastfeed and those who wean; parents who wish to co-sleep and those who don't; parents who wish to 'wear' their babies twenty-four hours a day and those who don't; parents who use childcare and those who don't; mothers who wish to breastfeed for years and mothers who wish to wean at twelve months, parents for whom routine is important and parents for whom it is not; parents who found it all easy, parents who found it all difficult and so on. Then there are the babies. Some sleep well, some don't; some feed well, others are pernickety; some love food, others turn up their noses; some adore tummy-time, others hate it and so on. The only sane and ethical approach in such a practice was one of providing safe, flexible options to suit the realities of the events and lives of the parents as often as possible. I never saw it as my job to persuade or dissuade parents from following particular child-raising philosophies or methods (unless they were risky or dangerous) especially when in doing so I was likely to further increase their confusion and, sometimes, their distress. *Baby Love* follows this approach.

Baby Love is not meant to be read from cover to cover like a novel (heaven forbid!). It is structured in the manner in which I worked so it is easy to find the information you need at the time you need it by using the index or going to the age-related information. As it is intended to be a parent's working manual some information is repeated when relevant. References to the related subject matter are listed at the end of each chapter to help you find more information on the topic when you need to.

Baby Love has breastfeeding information that covers the whole of the first year. The information is set in the context of the baby's age and development, bearing in mind the extensive range of baby behaviour and the varying lifestyles of women and their families today.

The biggest concerns of parents in the first year after feeding are sleeping, settling and baby crying. *Baby Love* looks at all these topics in a detailed, structured way providing answers when there are answers and options when there aren't. Often just knowing that even the 'experts' don't know and that a particular worry falls into the normal range of baby behaviour is a relief.

Group childcare for the under twos is a dilemma for families in Australia. I think there is ample evidence to suggest that group long daycare does not provide the optimum quality of life for most babies and toddlers. It is unfair to those parents who have a choice to keep giving bland reassurances about the childcare options that are available; they need to be fully informed in order to make the best decision about paid work and non-parental care that is available to them.

I recognise that options for many families are limited as they try to work out how they are going to meet the needs of their children, the economic needs of the family and their own personal needs and it is certainly not my intention to make parents feel guilty. However, it is only by raising everyone's awareness that things on the childcare front are far from rosy that governments and employers might seriously start to consider options other than group-style long daycare for employed parents with babies and toddlers.

Finally, after years of talking to parents I know that most people approach parenthood seriously and professionally and count on the health professionals they seek advice from to provide them with accurate, practical, safe information suited to their baby and their lifestyle. *Baby Love* is written for you with this in mind as the start of your baby's life unfolds.

PART ONE

Birth to 3 months

Chapter 1

Preparing for Parenthood

Babycare information is everywhere. Around the globe there are thousands of books that cover the same information as this book. 'Parenting' magazines are flourishing, along with classes on breastfeeding, sleeping and settling, introduction of solids, discipline and so on and so on. Yet, the most common phrase heard from the lips of new parents, especially new mothers, is still, *'Why didn't anyone tell me it would be like this?'*

How's that for an optimistic start to one of the major events of your life? Please read on—the nice bits are coming.

Most new parents discover that preparing for birth is different from preparing for motherhood, which is different from preparing for fatherhood. Despite all the information available it is common for new parents to be left with the feeling that during pregnancy some information was overlooked—even withheld—that could have made a huge difference to their new baby experiences.

After years of working with families and babies, however, I am convinced that there is no way to totally prepare anyone for the incredible event of the birth of their baby and what follows. An element of mystery remains, which is impossible to anticipate or provide for. No two babies are alike; no two mothers or fathers are alike. This is why, despite the avalanche of information available covering the whole spectrum of babycare from 'attachment-style babycare—never put your baby down' to 'strict routine-style babycare—never pick your baby up', no one can tell you what it will really be like *for you*.

Mothers and fathers and parents

I have not followed the trend to exclusively use the word 'parent' rather than 'mother' throughout *Baby Love*. The change from 'mother' to 'parent' in babycare books during the last decade as a way of recognising that babies have fathers as well as mothers is great, however, the hopeful suggestion implicit in the use of 'parent'—that the work and lifestyle changes related to having babies are now equally shared between men and women—is not the reality for many couples. Surveys consistently show that in 80 per cent of homes the lions' share of the babycare and household administration is still done by women, regardless of whether they are in paid work or not.

For this reason *Baby Love* is often addressed to women, as when children are babies and toddlers the mother and father roles are not interchangeable in the majority of families, so I hope fathers will forgive me for not always referring to them specifically throughout the book. The information is, however, set in a context which regards their participation as absolutely essential.

Baby Love is also intended for same-sex couples. Regardless of their situation, the ideal of a stable and functional family life is something most parents strive for and I strongly believe that it is possible to give children quality care, love and protection in a variety of family structures. I acknowledge that there are tougher challenges for same-sex parents and their children, however, as the majority of same-sex parents in Australia are women, one of the bonuses for them is that the care of their babies and toddlers is more likely to be evenly shared.

Babies

Babies bring indescribable joy. They are funny, they make you laugh. Having a baby makes you feel like you've joined the human race. A baby opens up avenues of communication with other people—you become a member of an exclusive club. Caring for your baby and watching her grow gives you a great sense of achievement and is one of the most creative things you can do. Babies help you appreciate small things (like a good night's sleep). Babies change your priorities in life, develop your tolerance and have the capacity to bring two people closer by sharing an exceptional experience. Caring for a baby is fulfilling, rewarding and exciting. A baby brings unconditional love which motivates you in ways you never thought possible. Babies give us all a reason for living and hope for the future.

Before meeting your baby it is impossible to know how profound the feeling of love is and how intense the anxious feelings about your baby's survival and wellbeing can be.

The hidden surprises about life with a baby are usually centred around unexpected difficulties with babycare and feeding, lack of sleep, unrealistic expectations of the time and attention babies need, and the overwhelming conflict of emotions that are often very hard to deal with and quite unexpected.

I often ask parents to tell me the positives and negatives of life with a baby. Most parents find it much easier to talk about the negatives rather than the positives, even though most find the whole experience overwhelmingly positive. This book, in order to be of assistance, is full of information about the negatives—crying babies, sore nipples, sleep problems, relationship difficulties, stress, fatigue, anger, depression, crying mothers and so on and so on. Is this what babies are all about? How come everyone wants one? Does *anyone* have a nice time with their baby?

The answer is 'yes', but the positive aspects are harder for many parents to express, identify and enjoy when they are trying to adjust to a completely new lifestyle that may place more physical and emotional demands on them than they ever felt possible. And a book like this has to cover the wide range of things parents may experience—including the possible difficulties—so they can get help or reassurance if they need it.

Certainly it's easy to get bogged down by the sleepless nights, the messy moments and the chaos and disorganisation that babies bring, but if life with babies meant only this the human race would have died out. Becoming a parent means learning how to savour and share the joys as well as the stresses and strains.

And the best thing anyone can do for another human is to be a true-blue, loving parent. The benefits flow on for generations. Congratulations for taking the opportunity to grow and to help someone else grow as well.

Part of preparing for life with a baby is about realising and accepting the element of surprise and the unknown, but you can do plenty of practical things beforehand which will help you manage when things don't go according to plan. Here are some suggestions.

Attend childbirth education classes

Most of these classes are primarily concerned with the birth, however there are also many other advantages in attending. Attending puts you in touch with other people who are sharing the same experience. The classes are excellent resource centres which help you find out what help is available in your local community after your baby is born. You will also be taught relaxation skills that prove invaluable long after the actual birth.

Classes are held in maternity hospitals, some child and family health centres, some family care centres and by private organisations, some online. Courses run by government bodies charge a token fee, those run by private organisations charge more.

Is there a parentcraft class near you?

Unfortunately these are few and far between—possibly because it's hard to convince prospective parents that they are very helpful, and people who try to run them give up when no one turns up! Parentcraft classes concentrate on the practical aspects of babycare such as bathing, dressing, nappy changing, equipment to buy, breastfeeding, crying and common worries and queries about the early weeks.

Many maternity hospitals, family care centres and child and family health centres run groups for new mothers after the birth. Some of the topics are also very helpful for prospective parents, so going along *before* the birth, listening to the talk and mixing with new parents can be useful.

Alternatively, if classes and groups aren't your scene, you can select something from the growing range of DVDs, magazines, books and internet resources dealing with parentcraft.

Borrow a baby!

Your baby will be blissfully unaware of your inexperience as a parent, but if you have a few babycare skills it can make the first few weeks more enjoyable for you. Being able to change a nappy, dress and undress a baby, and wrap and handle a baby with confidence helps you feel less nervous.

Of course, it's not always possible to find a baby to practise on. If your friends don't have babies and you feel very unsure of your skills, think about booking into a family care centre after birth. Family care centres are government subsidised places which offer help to mothers and babies. They have a pleasant, homelike atmosphere with an option of spending the day or staying overnight until you feel more confident about caring for your baby.

Family care centres are found in most capital cities but unfortunately residential centres are not available in country areas. Some centres will take mothers and babies soon after birth, others have a waiting time of a week or two. At the time of writing the cost is covered by Medicare.

Never feel inadequate or silly because you need to learn basic babycare skills. Babycare skills don't come naturally to most people—men or women—and usually have to be learnt.

Plan to live with fatigue

Extreme tiredness—both physical and emotional—is the most common problem in the first few months. It's worth taking the time to discuss with your partner what you both imagine will happen after the birth.

Speculate out loud (even if it feels strange).

- What will it be like when the baby cries in the middle of the night?
- What do we do when she cries incessantly and we can't sleep?

- Who will stay up with the baby?
- As the father, will you change nappies, do the shopping, cook sometimes?
- As the mother, will you tell your partner when you want him to do something? This is new to him too and he is not sure what is expected of him.
- As the father, how much time are you able to spend with the baby?
- As the mother, what will you do when you are exhausted, the baby won't stop crying, there's nothing for dinner and there are no clean clothes to wear? Who can you turn to for help?

Talking about these things with your partner may seem trivial and unnecessary, negative even, but imagining the reality together and discussing all possibilities means you will both learn to manage the changes much better.

Here are a few practical things you can do in advance.

- Get as much rest as you can before your baby arrives. If possible, do not continue your paid work until the first contractions—give yourself a few weeks of self-indulgence.
- Stay healthy by eating properly and exercising—this sounds boring and predictable but makes a great positive difference to your energy and stress levels.
- If you are an active superwoman afternoon naps probably aren't your style, but prepare yourself mentally for daytime sleeping after the birth as a stint of night duty is almost always unavoidable. Changing your sleep patterns for a short time is easier than changing your baby's **as there is no safe way of making young babies sleep through the night.**
- Learn about breastfeeding. Breastfeeding is covered in detail in the baby feeding sections of this book. Breastfeeding is not always easy to begin with and the more you and your partner know and understand, the easier it is.
- Give yourself as much room to move as possible. If your life is run on a tight string everything takes on a nightmarish quality the minute the smallest thing goes wrong. Babies are unpredictable; they need time and

peace to adjust to their new world and some need more time and peace than others.

- Avoid moving house and major renovations when your baby is very young. Overseas visitors who arrive at the same time as the baby and stay for months create a great deal of stress. Women often agree to things like this in order to show they are managing well, but it is most unfair of those around her to assume arrangements like this are all right. Make sure relatives invited to help are what and who she wants.
- Any major lifestyle change is harder for you when you have a new baby; for example, your partner changing jobs, starting a new business (especially if you're the one doing the books as well as caring for the baby and doing the housework!) and overseas trips. These things are often unavoidable, but if you talk about them *before* the birth, alternative plans or compromises can sometimes be made.
- Mad shopping expeditions after your baby is born are exhausting. Plan your clothing, bedding and equipment carefully and have it ready and waiting.
- Often women are told to 'forget the housework', yet more often than not the expectation remains that the mother will keep everything on the home front ticking over as well as taking care of the baby, even when she is utterly sleep deprived. Furthermore, many women find that living in a shambles increases their stress rather than the reverse and if they don't attend to the household chores no one else does. Ideally, some sort of system should be worked out in advance. Don't be shy about asking for help. Is your partner prepared to share the housework more evenly? Can your mother or partner's mother help? Is there a possibility of paying someone to do some cleaning for the first few months?
- Going back to your other job raises many important issues which are discussed in detail on page 357, so before you make any firm decisions please read this section carefully. It is vital to give serious thought to the pluses and minuses for babies and toddlers in care under the age of two so you are not locked into a decision you may regret.
- If returning to paid work is unavoidable in the first year, try to limit the hours your baby spends in group care settings (eg, long day care, family day care) by choosing part-time work or sharing care with your partner

or a trusted close relative. If you are planning to use childcare in the first six months, you will need to allow plenty of time to work your way around choice and availability as well as through the tangle of government childcare funding and fee-relief schemes. When you have figured it all out and made a decision, book your baby in as soon as possible as, usually, there are only limited places for babies in the first year in most group childcare settings. In fact, in order to get a place in the first year it is advisable to make bookings before babies are born.

I had intended to spell out the benefits and eligibility requirements of the government childcare subsidies, however, after spending some time researching the topic, I realised that a full coverage would expand *Baby Love*'s size to an unacceptable level. And, as all this information changes at the drop of a hat, I decided it made more sense for me to give you a brief summary of the benefits available and a list of resources for you to get (we hope) comprehensive and up-to-date information without too many hassles.

• Fee assistance

There are two components to fee assistance:

1. The Child Care Benefit (CCB)

There are two parts to CCB:

'Approved' care for long daycare, family daycare, occasional care (see page 357).

Under approved care, a family's income affects the benefit it receives and there is a high income threshold where the benefit cuts out. To access the benefit the childcare service being used has to be an approved Commonwealth Government service and your baby must meet the Government's immunisation requirements or have an immunisation exemption.

The CCB can be received as a lump sum through the tax system at the end of the financial year or you can arrange to have it paid directly to your childcare provider, which reduces your weekly fee.

'Registered' care for nannies, grandparents, relatives or friends who are registered with the Family Assistance Office (Centrelink).

This allows you to claim up to fifty hours a week for each child in registered care if you and your partner are working, studying or looking for work. Your family income is irrelevant but the amount available is miniscule: for each child the rate is 58 cents an hour with a maximum benefit of $29.05 a week.

2. Child Care Tax Rebate (CCTR)

Parents and guardians can receive a rebate of 50 per cent of their out-of-pocket childcare costs up to $7500 (indexed) per child per year paid quarterly, or yearly as a lump sum. Unlike the CCB, the CCTR is not means tested but all the other eligibility requirements are the same as the CCB.

FOR MORE INFORMATION:

Take a look at the *Family Assistance—The What, Why and How* booklet and the *Family Assistance Office Guide to Payments* fact sheet available at www.familyassist.gov.au or by calling 13 61 50.

Visit the Family Assistance Office website at www.familyassist.gov.au (you can send them an email if you want to).

Call 13 61 50 between 8 am and 8 pm (local time) Monday to Friday

Visit a Family Assistance Office near you. They are located in Medicare Offices, Centrelink Customer Service Centres and Australian Taxation Offices.

CareforKids is a privately run childcare resource that aims to help parents through the complexities of the system. The company also publishes a childcare reference book. Go to www.CareforKids.com.au or call (02) 9235 2807.

Knowing how to relax

You are likely to become very irritated at the number of times well-meaning people (usually health professionals) tell you to 'just relax' when you are in situations not at all conducive to relaxing. Knowing how to relax is an art, especially when the going gets tough. It's useful to learn about and practise a few relaxation techniques when you are in a calm frame of mind so you can draw on them when things get tense.

Here is a very simple way to help you relax in a tense moment.

- Whenever you feel stressed or uptight, take a few minutes to regain control.

- Stop whatever you are doing, making sure your baby is safe.
- Clench your fists and close your eyes, taking in a deep breath.
- Breathe in slowly through your nose . . . and breathe out *very slowly* through your mouth.
- As you breathe in, tighten your fists while keeping your eyes closed. As you breathe out, open your fists.
- Shake your arms gently. If you are standing, give your legs a shake at the same time.
- Drop your shoulders and take a few more deep breaths, relaxing your neck, shoulders, chest and abdomen.
- Tell yourself that you will remain calm—that it is all okay.

FOR FATHERS

Being a father is obviously very different from being a mother. Working out precisely why is a little more difficult.

The mother has already started a relationship with the baby during pregnancy and her new work in caring for the baby is quite straightforward. A father, on the other hand, outside of his paid work, can do as little or as much as he chooses and his role in relation to the baby is not straightforward at all. The father has to build a relationship with his baby and keep one going with his partner. Lots of men find that this is a strange experience for which there are no clear and precise guidelines. Unless a man has some previous hands-on experience with a baby, he is unlikely to know what to do with one of his own.

A great opportunity

Many men do now have a more hands-on presence in their children's lives, either from choice or necessity or a little bit of both. The benefits of this, both for the children and the community, are incalculable. But, understandably, men feel there is no recognition of the fact that the provider role is still mostly theirs. They have to single-handedly take care of the mortgage and can feel locked into an inflexible work role from which there is no escape.

Very often, after the euphoria of the birth fades, the mother disappears into the mother world and the father disappears into the father world with a general lack of understanding from both about each other's worlds. This seems to happen to many couples despite the best-laid intentions beforehand to share the load, so the housework and babycare ends up belonging to the woman while the man dedicates himself to paid work. Women often feel disappointed, tired and alone, while men are often concerned about money, feel they have no leisure time and that life is no longer any fun.

Is this unavoidable? Yes, to some extent, depending on how much the couple want to avoid it. Often, fathers don't know what to do or how to change the way things are and many mothers don't know how to separate from their babies and include their partners in their new lives. Research shows that these are probably the main reasons most relationships go through a difficult patch during the first six months after a baby arrives.

When you're a new father, chances are you need some information and ideas to help you become a family man instead of the distant, non-participating breadwinner. Granted, there will be times when the latter role is more attractive and indeed a handy escape from the daily humdrum of domestic life, but the men who become hands-on fathers discover a profound dimension to their lives, difficult to describe but never to be missed. Many men over fifty express disappointment about not having helped more and not having spent more time with their children throughout their lives, especially when the children were babies. Older men who become fathers the second time around frequently become participating fathers the way they never were the first time.

Don't let the opportunity pass you by!

Some inside information

In general

The last thing I want to do is alienate fathers, especially the ones who do share the care, but I think it's important to let you all know that surveys still show most blokes don't do enough during the labour-intensive, sometimes boring, sometimes tedious first few years. To put it bluntly, selective help is not enough—cooking the odd meal, changing the occasional nappy, playing in the bath with the baby or toddler or reading a story before bed are all relatively enjoyable tasks which don't contribute in any sustained way to the nitty-gritty, down-on-your-knees care of babies and toddlers in the first three years. The only way to get some equity is to draw up a detailed list of jobs, make a roster and stick to it, regardless of whether your partner is in paid work. It's vital during evenings, at weekends and during holidays that the care is shared and both partners, rather than just one, have some reliable time off (more than an hour here and there) to pursue sport or some other activity. Inadequate help during these years leaves many women with a wafting thread of resentment that never quite fades and has the potential to detract from an otherwise solid relationship.

After the birth

- Help your partner have a peaceful, pressure-free home after the birth, free of unwanted visitors and relatives.
- Try not to have unrealistic ideas about your baby. She will amaze and delight you, but she will also cry, throw up, poo everywhere and disrupt your life. Your partner will not instinctively know what to do a lot of the time, so don't expect this or make her feel she should know. On the other hand, she might know. Either way, if you can gain some understanding of normal baby behaviour and give some practical help rather than advice, you will be doing a lot to support her.
- Accept change. Burying your head in the sand and pretending life will go on as before means the changes will be for the worse, not the better. A lot of the changes are temporary but some are permanent, and to keep on waiting for things to get back to 'normal' creates friction and makes the time with your baby much less satisfying. What is 'normal' in your life with a baby is not at all what it used to be.
- Some of the temporary changes are things like less or no social life and maybe less or no sex for a while. Babies are very good at creating chaos in the evenings, so being prepared to come home and take over until this stage has passed will mean an enormous amount to your partner.
- It's very good for your baby to have lots of physical contact with you as well as her mother. Dressing and undressing her, changing her nappy, bathing, cuddling and playing with her is a great way to get to know her and for her to get to know you. Don't worry if she cries in the early

weeks whenever you do anything with her—this stage is only temporary and passes quickly. Lying with her on your bare chest and stroking her back will help calm her and you will both enjoy the skin-to-skin contact. Carrying her in a front-pack at home, or when you are out and about, and bathing and showering together are other ways of enjoying each other.

- Sleep deprivation is always an issue. I find parents, and fathers in particular, think there is some way very young babies can have their sleeping and crying patterns changed so adults are able to sleep the way they did before the baby arrived. This is not possible and as no one, father or mother, can exist indefinitely on little or no sleep, co-operation and planning will make living with broken sleep easier until the baby is older.

  For example, if your baby is waking a lot at night, your partner will be under a lot more stress if you constantly complain about your lack of sleep. She then feels she is dealing with two babies, not one (or three if you have twins). Talk things over. It may work better if you sleep in another room on some nights so you can remain lucid at work the next day. At the weekend you can help by bringing your baby to your partner for a breastfeed, or feeding her yourself if she's bottle fed, and then taking the responsibility to settle her after the feed (which might mean walking the floor if she's not ready to sleep).

  When your partner is up a lot at night she will have to rest when the baby sleeps during the day, which means you may come home to no dinner at times. If you are prepared for this and for sharing the household tasks more evenly, especially the shopping and the cooking, your family life will be much more harmonious.

- The first few months after giving birth is a very teary, emotional time for many women. While that great scapegoat, 'hormone imbalance', possibly contributes to a minor degree, many other reasons exist for these erratic feelings and these mainly centre around the shock of motherhood. The shock of motherhood affects every woman's self and lifestyle and is a mixture of a sense of gain, a sense of loss, intense joy, intense fatigue, intense worry of the sort never felt before (which fades but never quite goes), boredom, wonder, delight and lingering fears that the former body she once occupied has gone, never to return. You don't have to find solutions—listen, comfort and give her practical help.

- The shock of fatherhood means you will feel some of these things too, as well as other feelings particularly related to fatherhood—like a mixture of jealousy towards and overwhelming feelings of love for your baby. A sense of losing an exclusive relationship with your partner as well as enormous respect for her for enduring the mystery and pain of childbirth, plus confusion about re-establishing a sexual liaison with a woman who is now a mother are all strange new feelings you might have to work through. It helps to acknowledge them and talk about them together.
- Give your partner some time to herself whenever you can. Take your baby for some long walks—don't come back in ten minutes. Offer to care for your baby while she has some time out with friends or goes to the hairdresser. If you can come to reliable arrangements about timeout without constantly having to be reminded, she will have something to look forward to and plan for each week, even if it's only a couple of hours. Don't worry—healthy breastfed babies who won't take bottles can last two to three hours without a breastfeed.
- Last but not least, support your partner's care of your baby. Many options are possible when caring for babies, which gets a bit confusing at times. A co-operative approach works best, so help and encourage her decisions.

  Breastfeeding, for example, works much better when those around the mother have a basic knowledge of how it works and show confidence in the mother and baby's ability to breastfeed.

Finally

Having a baby is one of the most wonderful events in life. The next twelve months are the beginning of an extraordinary adventure and you will find it is a moving, loving, fearful, exciting, boring and muddling time. You probably don't think you know much or you might think you know everything—either way you're likely to be surprised by the extent of your ignorance or knowledge.

In the past the extended family supplied a lot of help and information and, in many families, still does. The advice of years gone by was by today's standards often rigid, but it supplied consistency and structure, unlike today, where the plethora of baby and childcare information provides an endless supply of conflicting advice.

The sweeping lifestyle changes over the past forty years have not only given new parents more independence and freedom, but more uncertainty and soul-searching about what they should and shouldn't do.

Being a parent is not always easy and is certainly not simple, but when sifting through the maze of information it's important to remember that babies' and children's basic needs have never changed. **They need buckets of love, the right food, a safe place to grow, lots of cuddles, the chance to learn the skills they need to take their place in the world and constant interest in their progress through life from the same one or two adults in a peaceful home.**

It's possible to give your baby all this in your own way according to your own particular beliefs, culture and lifestyle. Safe options are usually available—the trick is working out the best plan for you and your baby and not getting too bogged down by preconceived ideas or completely impractical theories which sound great 'pre' baby but fall apart in the realities of life after birth.

FOR MORE INFORMATION

Chapter 6: Breastfeeding Your Baby For the First Two Weeks, page 58
Chapter 16: For Parents (*childcare/returning to paid work, page 357*)

FURTHER READING

From Here to Paternity: A User's Manual for Early Fatherhood, Sacha Molitorisz, Pan Macmillan, Australia, 2008.
I am aware that many fathers feel left out at times, particularly during the birth and what comes after. Father books were once unheard of but in the last decade they've begun to creep onto the market. If you are looking for a father book for the roller-coaster first few months this is the one I recommend. It is hip, honest and from the heart, and provides a host of things new fathers wonder about in a straightforward, engaging way.

Child Care Guide Sydney/Melbourne (with plans to expand this to a national guide soon).

Chapter 2

More Than One Baby

They've shared the womb, they've been born together.
They're on their journey together.

HELEN TOWNSEND, *BABY CRAZY*

Twins occur in about one in sixty births. Exactly why multiple births occur is something of a mystery but it is more likely if there is a strong family history or, in recent times, because more women are taking infertility drugs, turning to in-vitro fertilisation (IVF) and delaying conception. Women who conceive between thirty-four and thirty-nine are more likely to give birth to twins.

Twins may be identical (monozygotic) or fraternal (dizygotic). Identical twins occur when one egg and one sperm join and then split into two halves. Each half has identical genetic make-up and both halves are usually joined to a single placenta by two cords. Identical twins are the same sex and look very similar.

Fraternal twins are more common. They come from two separate eggs being released instead of one. Each egg is fertilised by a different sperm so there are two placentas and two cords. Non-identical twins are just as different to look at as any two children of different ages with the same parents.

It's more common for women over thirty-five to release two separate eggs at the same time when they ovulate so non-identical twins are more common when the mother is older.

It's rare for twins to arrive unannounced these days—most are diagnosed well ahead of time. A twin pregnancy is like a single pregnancy but with both the delights and discomforts somewhat magnified. Women having twins need plenty of rest—and this is often difficult when there's another toddler in the house. A premature birth is more likely, as are minor complications, which means one or both babies might need special care for some time after birth.

Knowing twins are on the way evokes a joy difficult to describe and most parents with twins are irritated and annoyed by the generally negative comments which are commonly expressed by people who only have one at a time. It is certainly a surprise, but the initial feelings of shock are quickly replaced by feelings of excitement and delight with the anticipation of the arrival of two little people.

Like having one baby, there are negative aspects about having twins. These are perhaps most noticeable during the first year, but parents of twins find the rewards and sense of achievement for 'twice the work' give 'twice the pleasure'. Here are some thoughts from parents of twins:

- *It's a great ego trip to have two beautiful, healthy babies.*
- *Two babies keep each other entertained, especially when they're in the bath together. I love watching the two of them—it makes me melt inside.*
- *There's an enormous feeling of accomplishment and pride watching them grow. The pleasure of seeing two of them smile and talk and having two of them hug you is indescribable.*
- *Twins attract an enormous amount of attention, which can be a nuisance, but also makes you feel very special and part of an exclusive club.*
- *My girls are a joy that is impossible to describe—starts at the toes and works its way right up to my heart.*

If you are having twins it's a good idea to get in touch with friends who have twins and the Australian Multiple Birth Association for clues on what to buy as well as some enlightened information and reassurance. Few health professionals have any personal experience to offer in the realm of day-to-day management of twins.

Everyone chooses slightly different equipment and everyone ends up managing in their own way, so it's important to be flexible. You may feed simultaneously, you may feed separately. Options for prams include the traditional pram (difficult to get through doors), tandem style (where the babies sit one behind the other), or the side by side lightweight stroller, which is the choice of most parents. Some of your equipment and clothes can be borrowed, hired or bought secondhand.

Obviously any useful help should be snapped up if offered voluntarily, or paid for if you are financially able to do so.

While life with twins and triplets varies widely from family to family there are some common difficulties during the first year. Here is a brief look at three of the most common:

Breastfeeding

Most women start out with every intention of breastfeeding their twins and triplets. While it can be a struggle for the first three months, as can breastfeeding one baby, breastfeeding twins is certainly achievable and often easier than bottle feeding if there are no overwhelming problems. If you are reading this before your twins are born, learn all you can about breastfeeding before the birth. If possible, visit someone who is breastfeeding twins who can talk to you about the practicalities and show you how she does it. An optimistic approach is to be encouraged; however, bear in mind that a considerable number of women find the reality of breastfeeding twins beyond them after the first six to eight weeks, even with the best intentions and the right advice. It's sensible to be prepared for other outcomes so that you are not totally devastated if things don't go to plan. These may include using expressed breastmilk in bottles, combining breast and formula feeding or fully formula feeding earlier than you planned. Breastfeeding triplets requires some bottle feeding which may be expressed milk or formula. Occasionally triplets receive mostly breastmilk for extended periods, but most mothers of triplets find the demands of such a strategy too hard to meet and use formula (with my blessing).

Small differences

Remember that the normal variations in eating, sleeping, crying, behaviour and development will occur with twins as they do with any two babies.

Sleep

Sleep information is the same for twins as singles, however, two babies complicate matters when their sleep patterns vary. This is particularly difficult in the first six months when it can be hard to get the babies synchronised. 'Yo-yo' crying, where the babies take turns to cry and sleep, means there are periods of the day and night where they never seem to be asleep at the same time. This is often a problem around three to six months. As usual there are no easy answers. It's important to stay flexible. Some parents find things work better by separating the babies for some periods of the day and night, others find it useful to sleep them together. Residential mother and baby centres can provide good respite care in the first six months if needed.

And here in some parents' own words are some of the difficulties of caring for twins in the first year:

- *The first year is hectic. It's easy to get completely bogged down by the chores and miss the good bits—the playing, the laughter, the cuddles and the amazing way they learn about the world.*
- *It's isolating because it's very often hard to motivate yourself to go anywhere; it's such a hassle and so difficult doing simple things—like catching a bus, getting up and down stairs and so on. I know how disabled people feel.*
- *It's exhausting having two babies crying and wanting attention at the same time. It's essential to learn to tune out and deal with them one at a time.*
- *Two babies means two of everything and costs more.*
- *The safety factor is more of a concern, especially when the babies become more mobile. Keeping them safe is constant hard work and exhausting at times. Long bouts of sickness are very difficult.*

Triplets

Caring for triplets is an exaggerated version of caring for twins. Every mother is a working mother, but a mother of twins or triplets works very hard indeed. While much of *Baby Love* is as relevant to multiples as to singles, I recommend the following book for brilliant inside information: *Twins* by Katrina Bowman and Louise Ryan, Allen & Unwin, 2nd edition, 2005.

Chapter 3

Premature and Small Babies

The baby's limbs are like threads. They do not bend at angles as older babies' do, but lie curved like pieces of apple peel.

KATE LLEWELLYN, *DEAR YOU*

A 'small' baby is one who weighs less than 2.5kg (5lb) at birth. Babies may be born small because their parents are small, because they are born before the expected forty weeks' gestation or because they are born smaller and frailer than would be expected for the number of weeks they were in the womb.

A full-term 'small', healthy baby born to small parents does not need any special care.

Babies born before thirty-seven weeks' gestation are called premature babies and may need help with some important body functions such as breathing, eating, digesting and maintaining body temperature and sugar levels. The earlier a premature baby arrives, the more help she is likely to need.

The survival rate for premature babies is three times higher than what it was in the early seventies. Because of improved technology and skilled staff care the chance of a positive outcome for even very premature babies has doubled in the last decade. Babies born up to eight weeks early have about the same chance of survival and normal development as babies born at full term. About one in every 130 babies born prematurely weighs less than 1500 grams (3lb) at birth (the average birthweight for thirty weeks) and with expert care 90 per cent of these babies grow up fit and healthy and only about 5 per cent have major handicaps. Even babies born at twenty-eight/twenty-nine weeks now have an 85 per cent chance of a fit and healthy life although there's often a long, hard haul in the beginning.

Premature babies needing specialised care have a much better chance when they are cared for in the biggest and best centres and are transferred to these centres when necessary by a special transport service with highly trained teams giving intensive treatment along the way.

If you know in advance there is a possibility of a premature birth do an intensive care nursery tour if one is available at the hospital where you expect to give birth. Doing this can help prepare parents—but make sure you have plenty of tissues and a sympathetic health professional with you.

'Small for dates' babies may be full-term or premature babies who have not grown as much as they should have during the pregnancy, usually because the placenta did not function efficiently during the last few weeks before birth. A 'small for dates' baby needs extra attention as well—the amount depends on the number of weeks she is at birth and how much she weighs. Some babies can stay with their mothers where their breathing, body temperature, heart rate and blood sugar levels are regularly checked by midwives. Others may need to be in an incubator for a short time.

Healthy, full-term 'small for dates' babies usually have a good appetite, suck well and put on weight appropriately in the first three months.

What causes prematurity and/or 'small for dates' babies?

- About half are unexplained. Some women just seem to give birth a little earlier. This may happen with all their pregnancies, so knowing an early birth might happen can help the mother and her family prepare for the event.
- Medical problems such as an infection, kidney trouble, high blood

pressure, high blood pressure of pregnancy, or bleeding during the pregnancy can contribute to an early birth and/or a small baby.

- Waters break early (ruptured membranes).
- The chances of an early birth and/or smaller babies are increased when twins or triplets are expected.

Who is more likely to have premature babies?

- Teenagers having a baby for the first time.
- Older women (over thirty-seven) having their first baby.
- Smokers—10 per cent of all premature births can be attributed to smoking and it is recognised that smoking during pregnancy also contributes to babies being born 'small for dates'.
- Excessive alcohol or other drugs of addiction also contribute to giving birth to small/premature babies.

When babies are very small, premature or sick, they need special care in a neonatal intensive care unit.

The care is aimed at keeping the baby alive and well while her body matures. Immaturity of heart and lungs, nervous and digestive systems as well as problems with breathing and temperature control and the possibility of infection require skilled one-to-one nursing combined with highly sophisticated technology.

The atmosphere of a special care nursery can be daunting, but hospital staff try hard now to care for families as well as babies. You will be encouraged to spend as much time as possible with your baby, but if you find everything completely overwhelming take it slowly until you feel more comfortable about being in the nursery.

Ask lots of questions—write them down as you think of them no matter how 'silly' or frightening they seem. Every parent wants to ask things like, 'Will she live?' or 'Will she be normal?' and 'How long before we can take her home?'

Feeding

If your baby is too premature to suck and digest food, she will be fed either by a fine tube directly into the stomach or by a tiny direct drip into the vein. The staff will show you how to express and store your milk which can be used for your baby straight away or once she is able to tolerate milk feeds depending on her condition.

You can participate in the care of your baby by changing her and tube feeding with instructions from the staff as soon as you feel up to it. Many mothers say the 'out of control' feeling is one of the hardest things to deal with and caring for their babies while they are in the intensive care nursery helps them feel more in control.

Feelings

As well as dealing with the practical issues, you might find yourself overwhelmed by some unexpected emotions.

Feelings of numbness, of being out of control and in a dream-like state are very common. Sadness, anxiety and guilt are also very powerful emotions that parents feel when their baby has a problem after birth and those feelings may make you angry with each other, the staff at the hospital and even, perhaps, the baby. All these hurt feelings are part of the accepting and healing process which will happen in time. Some parents benefit from debriefing with a skilled counsellor.

You might find that people, even close friends, don't congratulate you or send the usual gifts and flowers, which can be distressing. Jealous feelings towards other mothers with their full-term babies and pregnant women obviously due soon are often felt by mothers of premature babies. Leaving your baby behind when you go home is sad and very hard to come to terms with, but nowadays every effort is made to get babies home as soon as possible.

Going home

There isn't likely to be a predetermined age or weight at which your baby is allowed to go home. Various factors are considered, such as her general condition and how well she is feeding and putting on weight. Some babies are discharged quite early when there is a follow-up team from the hospital who can visit the family at home. Babies may be discharged even though they still need oxygen for lung problems.

Follow-up support varies throughout the country. Capital cities always seem to have more resources and more help available for parents who have sick and/or premature babies. Some major maternity hospitals continue to give specialised care from staff who come to your home for a time. This is a great help. Apart from this you can seek assistance from your paediatrician, your family doctor, your child and family health nurse and community nurse. And in the immediate weeks following your baby's departure you can continue to call the medical staff who can answer your queries about her care.

Nervous feelings about taking your tiny baby out are normal for a while. When you do take the plunge you will find everyone stops you to comment on how small she is. One mother told me it made her feel as if she never fed her baby.

Premature babies who are born healthy follow the same range of crying, eating and sleeping patterns as healthy full-term babies.

Very low birthweight and sick premature babies may be erratic and tense and can be a great challenge to care for until they become more settled and predictable. Very low birthweight babies may also need extra care throughout the first year for wheezing conditions and gastroenteritis. Surgical repair of an inguinal hernia is also common.

Premature or sick babies benefit from a specific way of positioning and handling and by avoiding the use of bouncers, walkers and doorway jumping seats. Good help with this can be obtained from physiotherapists and occupational therapists (see Further Reading at the end of this chapter).

A premature baby has to spend the first weeks or months of life making up for lost time in the womb, so naturally she'll reach developmental milestones later. By the time most premature babies reach their fourth birthday, four out of five have caught up with their peers and many catch up long before this, some in the first twelve to fifteen months.

While it's wise to bear in mind your baby's prematurity when assessing development, it's also a good idea to start to treat your baby normally as soon as you can and encourage those around you to as well. All the information in this book is as applicable for babies who have been premature or sick as it is for any other baby. In areas where I think mothers of premature babies need a little reassurance or extra information I have included it.

FOR MORE INFORMATION

Chapter 8: Breastfeeding Your Baby After the First Two Weeks (*expressing and storing breastmilk, page 114*)

FURTHER READING

Hold Me, Sally Brown (occupational therapist) and Janet Pickering (physiotherapist), produced by the Children's Hospital at Westmead, Sydney, 1989. (A very useful small booklet which provides suggestions for parents to assist and promote development of babies who have required the services of newborn intensive care.)

Handling Your Prematurely Born Baby—A Physiotherapy Approach, Kim Morris, Copyright Publishing, Brisbane, 1993.

Premature Babies: A Guide for Parents, 2nd edition, Dr W.H. Kitchen, Dr M.M. Ryan, Dr A.L. Rickards and Dr L.W. Doyle, Hill of Content Publishing Co Pty Ltd, 1998.

All books are available from Kids Health at the Children's Hospital at Westmead, NSW 2145. Phone (02) 9845 3585.

Austprem is an incorporated, non-profit organisation in Australia available to help parents and caregivers of premature babies and children. All those involved in Austprem have experienced or been closely involved with the experience of prematurity. Go to www.austprem.org.au

Chapter 4

Doing it Alone—Single Parents

This baby is society's future and resources need to be given to assure this future is sound.

NORMA TRACEY, *MOTHERS AND FATHERS SPEAK ON THE DRAMA OF PREGNANCY, BIRTH AND THE FIRST YEAR OF LIFE*

I'm sure one of the irritating things about being a single parent is the constant assumption in pregnancy and baby information that there are always two doing it. Pictures of mothers and babies in magazines and TV series always depict smiling, happy, well-groomed mothers who invariably have smiling, well-groomed, caring men sitting beside them. The reality is that nearly a quarter of Australia's parents live on their own with their children and many more parents are on their own a great deal of the time because of absent partners.

I am guilty myself of not mentioning single parents specifically throughout this book, mainly because of the difficulties in constantly referring to the total range of parenthood experiences. In my work I often talk to single parents, who range in age from as young as fourteen to as old as forty-eight. They are usually women, less occasionally men. All of their stories and reasons for being on their own are different. Some women choose to be pregnant alone so they don't miss the experience, but for most not having a partner is not their option of choice;

rather, the result of an unplanned pregnancy or relationship problems.

The lovely things that babies bring are there for everyone whether they have a partner or not, but not having anyone to share the physical and emotional demands of babycare with makes the job harder. Thankfully our society has largely moved away from the moral judgements and harsh treatment of single mothers so prevalent for most of last century. There is more help available today from government agencies and community support networks than ever before.

A few tips just for you

- Contact the Family Assistance Office on 13 61 50 to make sure you get all the government assistance you are entitled to.
- Try to arrange to have someone with you for the first three weeks or so after the birth as this is usually a physically and emotionally draining time (a weird combination of exhilaration, extreme fatigue, relief and anxiety).
- Make sure you know where to go or phone for help, for example, the Australian Breastfeeding Association, the nearest children's hospital, the child and family health nurse, a mother and baby centre, a family doctor and so on. Put all the numbers into your mobile and/or have a list by the landline.
- Take up all offers of practical help. When it is offered give the helper specific ways in which they can be of assistance.
- It is of huge benefit for all parents to have access to a network of reliable friends and family but this is particularly so for single parents. If you don't have this support it is crucial for you to establish contact with other mothers, single or otherwise. Obviously having contact with other single parents means you are spending time with people going through the same experience as you but you'll also find that you'll have a lot in common with all mothers so don't limit your options here. Mothers' groups can be invaluable for this or you can find out via your local council or community health centre what might be available for you to tap into. Most local areas have a range of resources available for mothers and babies.

- Make staying sane and healthy a priority. It's normal to feel apprehensive about raising children, most of us do. This is one time when you really do need to live one day at a time until you adjust to your new life. Eat well, do some simple exercise and catch up on sleep whenever you can.
- Never lose sight of the fact that the main things babies and children need are love and security which you can give in bucket loads. There will be times when you find the going hard but very few women—or men—regret having children.
- You may need childcare during the first year for social and/or work purposes. For short periods occasional childcare centres are available to give you time off for shopping, dental appointments, study, social events and many are approved for government subsidy of their fees. To find out what's available in relation to the whole spectrum of childcare go to the links and resources on page 11.
- As you emerge from the first year, start to make plans for an optimistic future. Working for a qualification part-time or part-time work is a great morale booster and will give you confidence and help you meet new people. It's a good way to move back into the wide world again.
- For a summary of resources for single parents try www.community.gov.au or call 1300 653 227.

Chapter 5

Choosing Baby Products

Away in a manger, no crib for a bed.

MARTIN LUTHER

Part of the excitement of preparing for your baby is deciding what clothes and equipment to buy and this chapter is to help you buy the things you need before your baby arrives. The range of products is endless and it's often hard to sort out useful and essential items from those that are merely decorative or simply duds. Buying for babies is flavoured with emotion. It's easy to get completely carried away gazing at a quaint cradle or a tiny, elaborate nightie and end up spending more than you can afford on something that is of no use at all, so it's worth taking your time and doing some research.

The Australian Consumers' Association's magazine, *Choice*, publishes their book, *The Choice Guide to Baby Products*, every year and it is an excellent resource if you are full of doubt about what to buy. It's also handy to know about the Australian Standards Mark. Standards Australia is a non-profit, Australia-wide organisation which publishes and promotes safety standards for products used in Australia.

The Australian Standards Mark is owned by the Standards Association of Australia and when the Association has established a standard for a particular product the manufacturer can put this sign on the product if it complies with the standard. It's always worth looking for the mark because it means the product has been manufactured according to sound quality assurance programs and if used according to the manufacturer's instructions will do what it is meant to do.

Clothes

It's a good idea to wait until late in your pregnancy before buying clothes for your baby. As friends and relatives tend to like to give clothes as presents you may only need a set of the basic clothing items.

A useful list follows. Variations can be made to allow for hot or cold climates.

- 4 to 6 singlets or body suits. Body suits have little sleeves in them and do up between the legs—they are cosy for the winter months.
- 6 to 8 nighties/jumpsuits and other outfits. Stretch jumpsuits are incredibly practical, summer or winter, which is why you see so many babies wearing them, but it's nice to have one or two other outfits for special times or a morale boost when you need it. The simpler the clothes the better. Cotton is best next to your baby's skin, but there are many artificial fabrics or combinations of natural and artificial fabrics which are soft and easy to wash and dry, so it's not essential to go for pure cotton or wool fabrics for the rest of her wardrobe.
- 4 cardigans or jackets.
- 3 brushed cotton wraps (cuddlies).
- 3 cotton or gauze wraps (cuddlies) for summer babies.
- 1 shawl or sleeping bag (for outings).
- Hats, socks and leggings.
- Bibs.

Tips on clothing

- Sizes are a bit confusing because there is no standard way that manufacturers use to work them out. A small size for a particular age in one garment may be a large size in another; some go by chest measurement and some go by length. Generally 000 supposedly fits from birth to three months, 00 is for three to six months and 0 up to one year; however, it seems 000 size is too small for most full-term babies so buy 00 to begin with and move on from there.

- It is compulsory throughout Australia to label children's nightwear with an indication of fire hazard. Small babies are not at risk of fire danger the way active, older babies and children are, but it's a good idea to start reading and understanding labels on baby clothes which define the fire hazard of the fabric. Labels indicate whether a garment is a low, reduced or a high fire danger. Best to stay away from anything labelled 'high' right from the start.

LABELLING OF CHILDREN'S NIGHTCLOTHES FOR FIRE HAZARD

Classification	Description	Wording, typeface style and minimum character and symbol size
Category 1	Garment made from domestic apparel fabrics of the low fire hazard type	LOW FIRE DANGER
Category 2	Garment design to reduce fire hazard	STYLED TO REDUCE FIRE DANGER
Category 3	Garments which comply with the requirements given in section 4, AS1249 but which do not comply with the requirements given in Section 2 & 3 AS1249	WARNING HIGH FIRE DANGER KEEP AWAY FROM FIRE

- Cuddlies are sometimes called bunny rugs. Some babies like to be wrapped, others don't. Either way a cuddly is an inner lining that keeps them secure when they are in bed or in their stroller. A shawl or blanket goes over the top, when needed in cooler weather.
- Hats, socks and leggings. Winter babies need beanies, bonnets or helmet-type hats when they are out and about. Ribbons on bonnets are a nuisance, sometimes irritating and can also be dangerous so it's better to go for a beanie or a helmet. Babies need cotton hats once they are exposed to the sun, even on cloudy days. Hats should provide shade for face, ears and neck.

  Leggings are obviously for winter babies. Socks are useful most of the year round. Mittens are not needed unless you live in a very cold climate. Babies prefer having their hands free.
- Avoid frills and ribbons on bibs, clothing (especially around the neck), shawls and cuddlies, and avoid open weave fabric that small fingers can get caught in. Loose threads in socks, mittens and clothing can wind around fingers and toes, sometimes causing serious injury.
- Bibs are often more decorative than useful. Bibs need to be large and absorbent. Most babies throw up and some do it all the time. Just about all of them dribble a lot until they are at least a year old.

  Soft towelling bibs are absorbent and soft on baby skin. Plastic-backed bibs stop clothes from being constantly wet but are not as efficient at mopping up and are harder on skin. Pull-on bibs with T-shirt-type ribbing around the neck instead of ties are easier to use than fasteners and ribbon ties. Gauze squares are wonderful to use as mopper-uppers and bibs or a range of different-sized squares are great. You can make them yourself or buy them from specialist baby shops or department stores.

Nappies

Years ago nappies were a major consideration. No liners, no nappy soaking solutions, no nappy service, no decent pilchers and no disposables! Modern ways have managed to eliminate most of the hard work and inconvenience associated with baby bowels and baby bladders. There are several choices.

Cloth

You need between twenty-four and thirty. Terry towelling are the most effective type of cloth nappy and need the following accessories.

PILCHERS: If you don't have some sort of covering over your baby's nappy the washing and inconvenience is endless. A faint message from another era still exists that 'good mothers don't use plastic pants'. Ignore this. Pilchers do not have to be the old-style hard plastic pull-ons with tight elastic around the waist and legs; many types are available now made of soft plastic with a webbed fabric lining and fasteners on either side. Using pilchers does not cause nappy rash as long as the nappy is changed regularly.

Non-plastic thick cotton pilchers are an alternative if you prefer not to use plastic, but as the baby grows, leakage and dampness can be a problem with this style.

NAPPY LINERS: Nappy liners can be disposable or made of cloth. Nappy liners make washing the nappies easier because they collect the poo which can be neatly disposed of into the toilet. They also help prevent friction on the skin from a wet nappy. If you're using cloth nappies it's probably worth buying one box of disposable liners to start with and see if you think they are needed. Avoid cheap brands—I have noticed they seem to cause red bottoms on some babies.

Non-disposable nappy liners are made from a soft fabric that allows moisture to pass through and so keeps the skin dry. They are relatively expensive and not needed by most babies, but for babies with extra-sensitive skin who are prone to nappy rash they are a boon. It's important to follow instructions for correct use.

FASTENERS: The use of safety pins for fastening nappies has become a thing of the past but if you're an old-fashioned girl (and you can find nappy pins) go for the self-locking variety. Alternatively there are a range of fasteners to choose from, which are easier and quicker than safety pins and hold the nappy tighter as well.

TWO NAPPY BUCKETS: You need two good-size buckets with secure lids. Always try the lids in the shop first—they must be difficult for you to open.

If you wash your nappies in a water temperature of 65°C or hotter and dry them in the sun there's no need to worry about using a nappy soak solution—just soak them in water or water and detergent. Stubborn bright yellow baby poo stains will come out if soaked in a bucket of very hot water with some powder bleach added.

If you are a cold water washer and/or generally use a tumble drier then it's advisable to use one of the nappy treatments available or try the following for a more environmentally sound method (it saves money as well).

Scrape any solids off with a brush. Wash the soiled area with soap. Dissolve one handful of salt in a bucket of very hot water. Soak nappies in this solution overnight.

Tailored nappies

Tailored nappies are another nappy option. They are expensive initially but fit snugly from birth until after toilet training, need no pins or folding (so can be easier to use than standard squares) and can also last several children. Tailored nappies make ideal gifts from fond relatives. Drying them quickly can be a problem. They are available from selected pharmacies, babycare shops or by mail order from baby/parent magazines or the Australian Breastfeeding Association.

Nappy service

A nappy service brings you a couple of plastic bags full of clean nappies as well as a bin with a liner bag for the used nappies. You decide how many you need—up to seventy or eighty a week is standard for one newborn baby. On an agreed day each week (or twice a week if needed) the used nappies are taken away and the clean nappies left. At the moment nappy services are not widely available outside capital cities and are expensive compared to looking after nappies yourself, though some firms offer long-term discounts, so the longer you subscribe, the cheaper the weekly cost becomes. A nappy service is an ideal gift and, for those who can afford it and have access to it, an alternative to disposable nappies. If you only use it temporarily, you need to consider what to do when you have finished using it.

Disposable (single-use) nappies

Disposable nappies are convenient and easy to use. The single-use nappy market has expanded to include sizes and shapes according to age and sex, the toddler 'pull-up' and the swimming nappy. Because of their convenience 90 per cent of Australian parents now use disposables most of the time.

In many respects the efficient disposable nappy is a dream come true, especially for women in paid work and for all sorts of other situations—multiple births, close births, overseas trips, holidays, long bouts of illnesses and so on. I'm sure if they'd been available when my children were babies I'd have used them.

But there are problems with disposables. Apart from the ongoing expense that must be budgeted for, the two main ones are environmental and behavioural.

ENVIRONMENTAL: Single-use nappies are not disposable and pose a growing solid waste disposal problem that is still to be satisfactorily resolved.

- Disposables take years to decompose; conservative reporting estimates 100 years, other sources claim up to 500 years. 'Biodegradable' single-use nappies are a recent innovation. Potentially they decompose more rapidly than conventional disposables but the process requires oxygen and water lacking in landfill operations. And biodegradable disposables retain the plastic component that other disposables have which is not compostable.
- The manufacturing process required for disposables consumes more raw materials and energy than the manufacturing process for cloth nappies. Studies analysing the extent of these environmental costs conflict with some claims made that the use of resources in the after-use care of cloth nappies (water, energy, equipment and chemicals) cancels out the difference unless nappies are washed in cold water and dried outside in the sun. Other studies claim that single-use nappies use up to five times more energy than reusable nappies.

BEHAVIOURAL: Single-use nappies have changed our behaviour. Toddlers are in nappies longer, increasing the number of disposables being used, and normal rules of hygiene seem to have faded into the past. Human poo now gets dumped in places that would once have been unthinkable where it eventually makes its way into landfill. There it is left untreated, seeping into groundwater supplies with the potential to contaminate and transmit disease.

SENSIBLE USE OF DISPOSABLES

- Limit use by combining cloth with disposables. Bypass swimming nappies and daytime use of 'pull-ups'. 'Pull-ups' delay potty training and the reusable swimming pants that are available are excellent.
- Whenever possible put most of the poo in the toilet where it belongs. I know this is difficult when it's a liquid embedded poo, however a good flush significantly reduces the amount going into the garbage.

Nappy-free

There is a tiny group of parents who are dramatically minimising nappy use by holding their babies out over a pot (or the laundry sink or the lawn) at regular intervals from birth. Potty training fashion in the last thirty years has swung strongly in favour of waiting until the toddler is 'ready' and not putting on too much pressure for fear of causing long-lasting psychological problems. And there's no doubt there is a risk that poo catching from a young age for the wrong reasons or taking a militant potty training stand with a reluctant toddler will cause problems.

Nevertheless, in many cultures nappies are still not used—babies are held out from birth and by a year many are happily trained. In our own culture, in another era when nappies were a burden, it was common to hold babies out, have nappy-free times during the day and start more formal potty training well before the second birthday.

In the cloth-nappy era, toddlers were much more likely to be trained soon after their second birthday in contrast to today where nappy time seems to be getting longer and longer—the convenience of single-use nappies are almost certainly making a major contribution to this trend.

Parents taking the nappy-free route need to be united in the decision, have a great deal of commitment and tolerance for some mess, and a lifestyle to accommodate their choice. If it is done with the right attitude (relaxed not competitive), for the right reasons (suits the family rather than to impress the neighbours) it can be a very rewarding, self-sufficient way to go. For more information go to www.sarahjbuckley.com

Nappies—the choice

Cost, convenience and baby comfort all have to be considered. Individually, some babies' bottoms do better with disposables, some with cloth. A small number of babies are allergic to disposable nappies. The skin in the nappy area turns bright red and the redness follows the exact line of the nappy.

Cloth nappies need water and, ideally, a washing machine. Disposables are the most convenient, an understandably major reason for their popularity, but cause skin problems for some babies. Nappy services are limited to major cities.

The most economical and environmentally-friendly option is thirty good-quality cloth nappies that are washed in cold water, and as often as possible, dried in the sun. Good quality cloth nappies will also last several children. The most expensive option is either exclusive use of 'super absorbent' single-use nappies or a nappy service.

Sleeping equipment

- Six or more bassinet and/or cot sheets: You can't have too many of these. They can easily be made up from larger sheets. A pillowslip works well over some small mattresses while your baby is in a bassinet.
- A mattress protector for bassinet and/or cot: These are available from any stores that sell baby goods. A mattress protector is made of suitable material with a waterproof backing. Alternatively a piece of blanket is an option during the first three months.
- Two blankets and a quilt (plain, no fringes).
- A fitted mosquito net.
- Something to sleep in: Most parents prefer to have their baby in a small bed (bassinet) in the first three months but there is no reason not to put your baby into a cot from the start if you are happy to do this. Parents with triplets, for example, put their babies into cots from birth so they don't have to buy two lots of beds.

  If you are looking for a small bed for the first three months don't overspend. The bassinets in maternity hospitals are ideal but a cheaper version of them is not available for the home. Look for something that's not too narrow or too heavy. If it's on a stand make sure it's stable. It's important to have the bassinet at the right height for you so you don't have to lean over your baby—there may be times when you have to pat her to sleep and it's essential that you can do this comfortably.

Cute, colonial wooden cradles are quite impractical but if you do buy one check the security of the pin. If the pin comes out, it may force the cradle on an angle which can cause suffocation. Sadly, this has happened in Australia in recent years.

Mattresses

Mattresses are sometimes sold with an indirect message that they are 'safer' and protect against cot death. This message is implied, not stated outright, but parents do buy these products believing they give protection against sudden infant death syndrome. A conclusive link between SIDS and any nursery product has not been established, so do not be misled by manufacturers' claims when buying your baby mattress.

Babies are easier to settle and do seem to sleep better on a firm mattress. Dense latex mattresses such as used in maternity hospitals are preferable to softer 'wobbly' type mattresses—purely from a practical view of helping babies to sleep better, not in relation to cot death.

Cots

It's essential that cots are safe, but a lot aren't. The Australian Consumers' Association's magazine, *Choice*, does not have a lot of good things to say about many cots, so for advice on specific cots I would recommend checking out the range covered in their book *The Choice Guide to Baby Products* before buying either a new or secondhand cot. Another resource to use if you are unsure of the safety features to look for when buying furniture or equipment is the Department of Fair Trading in your state. In some states this is also known as the Department of Consumer Affairs. Look for the phone number in the *White Pages*.

Cots with an adjustable mattress position (two positions) are very useful. When your baby is still very young she will be up high at an easy reach for you; as she gets older the mattress goes lower so she can't fall or climb out.

Here are a few things to look for, especially if you are buying a secondhand cot:

1. Smooth, rounded edges—no sharp bits sticking in or out of the cot.
2. Decorative transfers, counting beads or cutouts in the headboard or footboard are all potential hazards.
3. The cot should have high sides so your older baby can't fall out. The recommended measurement from the base of the mattress to the top of the cot side is 600mm (2 feet).
4. The dropside catches should be child resistant and work smoothly and efficiently.
5. The mattress should fit snugly in the cot—less than 25mm between the mattress and the cot all round (especially important if you are going to use a secondhand mattress).
6. The space between the bars should be between 50–85mm (2–3 inches).
7. Old paintwork on secondhand cots may contain lead. This can be a problem if the paint is peeling so stripping and repainting will be necessary. Take care when disposing of the leaded paint that has been stripped.
8. Older, secondhand cots may have a cross bar which can be used as a step by an older baby, so don't buy one of these unless you can fix it safely.
9. If wheels are fitted, two should be removed.

Cot mattresses

Once again, a firm mattress is preferable, so look for innerspring or dense latex. Make sure the mattress cover is completely sealed so your baby can't get her head stuck between the cover and the mattress. Nothing should be tied or attached to the mattress with tapes or elastic.

A good quality secondhand mattress is fine—give it a couple of days in the sun before you use it. Despite media reporting from time to time (bless the media, anything to give parents more to worry about) that secondhand mattresses are dangerous because of certain bacteria that may lurk within, Sids and Kids say there is no evidence to show an increased risk of sudden unexpected death in infancy (SUDI, an umbrella term now used that refers to all unexpected deaths, see page 213) for babies who sleep on secondhand mattresses provided the mattress is firm, clean and well-fitting.

There's no need to use pillows until your baby moves into a bed—usually some time between eighteen months and three years.

Cot bumpers

A cot bumper is a fabric liner about 30cm (12 inches) high which surrounds the inside of the cot above the mattress. It is held in place by ties or elastic. Cot bumpers are designed to prevent babies from banging their heads against the cot or getting their legs caught between the bars.

They are no longer recommended as their use poses significant safety risks of strangulation and suffocation. Sids and Kids has also registered concern about the decrease in air flow in cots when bumpers are used. To date no evidence exists to show that babies have ever come to harm because they bang their heads on the cot sides or get their legs caught between the cot bars, so give cot bumpers a miss.

Staying mobile

In the car

It is compulsory in Australia that all babies up to the age of one year travelling in a car must be protected by an approved infant restraint suitable for the baby's age and weight. In NSW this also applies to taxis. If you are travelling in a taxi without a restraint (in states other than NSW) sit in the back seat with the seat belt around you but not around your baby. Legislation and penalties vary across the states. To find out the law in your state, contact your local authority. It is anticipated that there will soon be a complete overhaul of child car restraint laws that will make it mandatory for all toddlers and children (not just babies from birth to twelve months) to be restrained in suitable car seats according to their ages. See page 57 for information on the new laws (2010).

An Australian Standards-approved infant restraint labelled AS 1754 must be used. Many brands are now available and all restraints in Australia meet the Australian Standards pass mark. The Australian Standard is recognised internationally as the most stringent child restraint standard in the world.

Single-purpose (non-convertible) capsules are for babies weighing up to nine kilos (from newborns to about six months old).

Dual-purpose (convertible) car seats are for babies weighing up to nine kilos in the *rearward-facing* position, but can be converted into a *forward-facing* child car seat and used for babies who weigh between nine and eighteen kilos (from about six months to about four years of age). Select the car seat that most suits the size and type of your car (convertible car seats sometimes do not fit very well into small cars).

All car seats/capsules should be attached to the restraint anchorage points in your car. Sedans manufactured before 1976 and some station wagons, light passenger vans and four-wheel drives may not have anchorage points. Anchorage points can be attached to any car—ideally by an authorised restraint fitter. If you fit them yourself or if you are unsure who did the job, have them checked. Telephone the road safety authority in your state for the nearest Restraint Fitting Station.

Remember this will have to be organised before leaving hospital with your baby!

New car seats/capsules cost from around $130 (non-convertible) to $270 (convertible). You can also hire them from maternity hospitals, local councils and specialist retail outlets. Again, call the road safety authority in your state for the nearest approved baby restraint rental plan.

If you acquire a secondhand one, check that it has the Australian Standard label AS 1754. **Those marked AS E46-1970 must not be used and are illegal.** Make sure you have all the necessary parts to install the restraint according to the manufacturer's instructions. If in doubt, have it checked by an authorised restraint fitter.

If possible check the background of the restraint. If it has been in an accident or shows any sign of wear, for example, cracks, frayed strapping or faulty buckles, don't buy or borrow it.

Baby car seat accessories: A lot of the accessories available are not approved and can compromise the safety features of child restraints. Nothing should be placed between the capsule liner and your baby. Accessories such as head supports, lambskin liners and padded mattresses are not approved, are not necessary for the baby's comfort and may interfere with the safe working of the restraint.

Sunshades over the restraint can reduce the airflow, trap heat and increase body temperatures. It's much safer to attach sun screens to the car windows.

Dashing about

As well as buying or hiring an approved baby car seat, you need to make some decisions about what you will use for baby transport when you are on foot or on public transport.

CARRIERS: SLINGS, FRONT-PACKS AND BACKPACKS

Slings and front-packs are a very useful way of keeping your baby next to you and your hands free. They are excellent for trips to the supermarket, on public transport and for times when carrying her next to you is the only way to calm her during an unsettled period. They are not so practical for any situation where you have to carry your baby for long stretches of time. If you buy a sling or carrier you are unlikely to use it much after six months when your baby becomes heavy. Also, they may not be a good idea for those with back problems.

- **Slings**

  A sling is a simple device that slips over one shoulder across the chest. Your baby lies inside the sling across your body so her head is on your chest. Some women find slings a great breastfeeding aid when breastfeeding in public. Slings are more for newborns and up to the first three months, although some parents use them for the whole of the first year. Most babies, however, find slings too restrictive after the early months and prefer to be upright, watching what's going on. And many parents find slings uncomfortable as the baby gets bigger because the weight tends to be distributed unevenly.

- **Front-packs**

  A front-pack is more complicated and it can be tricky getting one on and off until you get the hang of it (it won't take long), but they are designed to distribute the baby's weight more evenly.

  There are many varieties to choose from. Some hold your baby facing inwards until she is around four to six months, at which time she can be turned outwards to face the world. Others convert to a backpack when the baby is between six and nine months.

TIPS FOR FRONT-PACKS

- Look for one that's easy to adjust (especially if different people are using it) and get on and off on your own. Also, a wide bottom and padded shoulder straps are more comfortable for both baby and parent.

- Make sure your baby's head is still supported securely when both your hands are free.
- Try to find a front-pack that is strong without being bulky and hot.
- **Backpacks**
  Backpacks are designed for babies from about six to nine months who have good head support and are sitting (or close to sitting) on their own. A baby/toddler backpack is similar to a hiking/camping backpack. If you plan to use it a lot it is worth getting a more expensive model with a frame that stands on its own, a waist belt and weather protection. Backpacks are more for the hardy. They can be very useful for older babies and toddlers who refuse to sit in strollers.

PRAMS AND STROLLERS

Selecting a carriage or stroller can be confusing, as there is now a wide variety to choose from. Take your time and do some research so you can work out what is best for your lifestyle and your budget. You will need some sort of transport system from early babyhood to around age three. Here is a sample of what's available:

- **Traditional prams (heavy, can be more than 13kg, 28lb)**
  Prams are becoming a thing of the past, especially for people who live up flights of stairs, in crowded cities or anywhere where there is rough terrain to negotiate. Prams are very comfortable for young babies and protect them well from the elements. They also have a springy, rolling motion that can calm fussy babies, and usually have a removable carry bed that can be used as a bassinet. Sometime between six and nine months you will need to change to a stroller, which means making an extra purchase.
- **Prams/strollers**
  These models convert from a pram (so young babies can lie flat) to a stroller (once they are old enough to sit up or be propped up). Some models have a removable carry bed that can be used as a bassinet. They are expensive and relatively heavy (compared to the lightweight strollers) but do grow with your baby.

- **Umbrella strollers (5.5kg, 12lb)**
  These have curved umbrella-like handles. They are easy to manoeuvre in tight spots and easy to store. Step-up models include a canopy, an adjustable seat and padding. Durability is often poor, you may need several for one child, and the wheels (like the wheels on supermarket trolleys) may not perform well on bumpy terrain (or sometimes even on smooth terrain).
- **Lightweight strollers (5.5kg, 12lb)**
  These models are the most sophisticated (and often the most expensive) on the market. They feature smooth folding mechanisms, thick padding, a reclining seat, weather protection extras and built-in shock absorbers in the wheel assemblies. Some models of these strollers are large and while they are easy to push and manoeuvre, great for weather protection and for putting baby to sleep, there is a growing criticism of them because of their size. 'Monster' strollers, as they are often called, do take up a lot of space in shopping centres and coffee shops, on narrow streets and in public transport. Also, they sometimes don't fit through supermarket check-outs. Judging from media reporting on the topic, I suspect increasing numbers of mothers are getting harassed when out and about with their monster strollers. Much as I deplore this baby unfriendliness in our community, if you live in the city it might be an idea to consider a smaller version that has similar function and convenience to the larger models. More and more stroller varieties are arriving on the market; look around and take your time when selecting. If you are planning on a second baby it is also worthwhile considering buying a stroller that will accommodate a toddler and a baby.

  N.B.: Take care when hanging bags on the handles of umbrella strollers and lightweight strollers as heavy items can make the stroller tip backwards onto the ground.
- **Jogging strollers**
  Jogging strollers have three large wheels mounted on a lightweight frame. They are perfect for rough terrain and for taking your child on runs or hikes. The bigger the wheels, the more space taken up in the boot of the car and jogging strollers can be difficult to manoeuvre around small spaces.

Strollers have become smaller, lighter and easier to push around in the last ten years, but the perfect design to suit every purpose remains to be invented. You may have to make a compromise.

ESSENTIAL REQUIREMENTS

- **Seat belts**

  Many strollers have inadequate restraints (for example, too loose, no shoulder straps, non-adjustable). Ideally the stroller should have a shoulder harness and a waist and crotch strap (especially for jogging strollers), however, most models only have waist and crotch straps. The buckle should be easy for you to operate but impossible for your baby/toddler to unfasten.
- **Brakes**

  The wheels should lock when you engage the brake.
- **Leg holes**

  Pram/strollers that can fully recline must have leg holes that close so an infant can't slip through one of them.
- **Sturdiness and flaws**

  Shake the stroller and check that all the mechanics work smoothly and efficiently, remembering you will often be opening and folding your stroller while holding your baby. Look for flaws such as malfunctioning wheels, frames that are likely to bend out of shape, faulty locking mechanisms, loose seat belts, flimsy buckles.

MANOEUVRABILITY

Can you push it and turn it with one hand? The best wheels are the swivel type that move in all directions and can be locked when you are going over rough surfaces.

STORAGE AREAS

How big is the storage bin under the stroller? Check how strong it is—it shouldn't drag on the ground when loaded. Storage nets fastened onto the handles are suitable only for lightweight articles.

WARRANTIES AND RETURN POLICIES

Purchase your stroller from a store, catalogue or website that offers a 100 per cent satisfaction guarantee.

A FINAL CHECK LIST

- What is your price range? The range is $40 (umbrella strollers) to $800+ (top of the range). Bear in mind that high price and good quality don't always match up. *Choice* tests have shown that some economical strollers can perform as well as highly priced models.
- Do you have back problems? Think about the weight of the stroller and how much you might have to lift it.
- Will you be lifting the stroller in and out of the car a lot?
- Do you have many stairs to climb up and down daily?
- What sort of terrain will you be pushing your stroller over?
- What is provided for shopping? What happens to your shopping when you want to collapse the stroller to get onto the bus?
- Is it the right height for you and your partner? Can you push it without damaging your shins? Do you need adjustable handles?
- What extras do you need for weather protection?
- Check the width; some strollers are much narrower than others. Extra width can be useful.
- Don't forget, there are strollers that can accommodate a toddler and a baby.

Baby cosmetics and baby baths

Most baby cosmetics are unnecessary products. Here's a short list of essentials:

- Cotton wool balls and tissues.
- A mild, simple soap.
- A moisturiser—combined sorbolene and glycerine is excellent.
- Disposable wash cloths or baby change lotion for when you are out. Pump pack sorbolene and tissues are fine when you are at home.
- A small jar of petroleum jelly.
- Two soft bath towels and two washers.
- Small blunt-ended scissors for cutting your baby's fingernails.

The use of bath lotions instead of soap is common practice. As well as commercial lotions designed specifically for your baby's bath time, oils such as jojoba or almond oil can be used. All of these products are fine but not essential. Simple soap, water and some sorbolene and glycerine is sufficient for most babies unless they have a dry skin condition such as eczema (see page 411).

Buy small quantities until you know for sure which products suit your baby. Wait until you need specific items before buying out the pharmacy.

Baby baths: The range is many and varied. One of the problems with baby baths is emptying them when they are full without causing yourself injury or making a terrible mess everywhere. Here are some possible, convenient baby baths:

- A large plastic wash bowl.
- Any plastic baby bath designed for the purpose. Make sure it gives you easy access to your baby. Baths with a moulded back support for young babies are helpful.
- The model that sits across a bath solves the problem of emptying but will not fit on all baths.
- Other bathing devices such as sling baths and cradling bath seats make bathing easier initially and are helpful for parents with back problems, but have to be replaced as the baby grows.
- Bathing in the laundry sink is another option, providing your baby can't bump against the taps or get burnt on the hot tap.

Child safety products

In keeping your baby safe nothing can replace constant vigilance, planning and commonsense, and making sure your basic equipment is not hazardous. However, at each age and stage you'll find there are some items worth buying to help make your baby's life safer. Safety 1st make a range of child safety products at a good price and are available at World for Kids, Toys R Us, Target and KMart.

During the first three months babies are fairly immobile, but there are a few basic items worth considering, such as:

- A low-power night-light in your room, your baby's room and the hall.
- An efficient torch.
- A childproof lock or handle to the baby's room.
- A childproof lock on the laundry door.
- A child-resistant cabinet for medicines.
- Power point covers.
- An emergency telephone number listing.
- Curly cords for electrical appliances in the kitchen.
- A non-slip mat in the bath and shower.
- An automatic doorstop.
- A chair for you: A suitable chair for you to breastfeed your baby is essential. In general, low, soft lounge chairs or rocking chairs are not great to learn to breastfeed in. You need a reasonably wide, firm chair with good back support that is about 40–45cm (14–16 inches) from the floor.

Optional extras

Change tables

Change tables are specially constructed tables to put babies on while you change them, dress them and so on. It's much easier for you and kinder to your back to be able to attend to your baby without bending over all the time. A variety of change tables are available, some with storage space and many with restraining straps. As babies can fall off, safety is an important consideration when a change table or any high surface is being used.

The change table should be stable and strong, especially if there are small children in your family likely to try climbing it. It should not be on wheels. Some mothers couldn't manage without change tables; others feel they are a waste of money. If the change table can double as a place to store nappies, nappy-changing equipment, clothes and so on it's a lot more useful.

Do you have room for one? Maybe a changing mat on a table or chest of drawers would suit you better.

A portable baby chair

Most parents find these useful. They come in a soft, bouncy style or in a stable, moulded plastic style. The stable style are preferable to the bouncy ones (made of mesh) as they do not move when the baby moves and so encourage better posture. This is especially important for premature babies or babies with developmental problems.

Specialist baby bags called change bags, nappy bags

Important if you're the sort who likes to be highly organised; alternatively, any large bag will do. Make sure it is cleanable and fits over the handles of your stroller or buggy (remember heavy bags tip strollers over).

Breast pumps

I find this is the most common piece of equipment that is never used or rarely used, so don't rush off and buy one early on. For more on breast pumps see page 117.

Lambskins, sheepskins

Sheep and lambskin products for babies were such an 'in' product at one time that mothers believed they were an essential item. Promoted as being warm in winter, cool in summer, absorbent, cosy and comfortable, they are certainly handy—and useful as an all-purpose changing, sleeping blanket when travelling.

On the negative side there are some concerns that sheep and lambskin products may cause allergic reactions in babies who come from families where there are allergies.

Baby products in lambskin and sheepskin come as liners for child safety car seats and strollers as well as versions for bassinets, cots and single beds.

Baby Monitors

- **Sound monitors**

  Sound monitors allow you to hear your baby cry when you are not within immediate earshot. They work like a one-way walkie-talkie so you can hear your baby's noises but your baby can't hear yours. There is a variety of styles which cover a range of distances—room to room, up or down stairs or out in the garden.

Sound monitors are becoming more widely used, and in certain circumstances, may be useful. Many parents who attempt to use them routinely overnight find that they increase rather than decrease their baby-stress and, because their baby's amplified snorts and snuffles fill the room, prevent them from sleeping. Sound monitors are for reassurance only. They do not monitor baby breathing or movement. They are not protective safety devices, particularly in relation to sudden unexpected deaths in infancy and shouldn't be used as such.

- **Breathing (apnoea) monitors**

Breathing monitors aim to detect slow or absent breathing. The baby sleeps on a sensor pad under the cot sheet and if her breathing stops for more than 20 seconds the light on the alarm box (attached by a wire to the sensor pad) turns from green to red and the alarm starts. Similarly to the sound monitor there is a variety of styles.

There is no evidence that breathing (apnoea) monitors protect babies from sudden unexpected deaths in infancy. Many breathing monitors drive parents mad with frequent false alarms rather than giving them peace of mind.

They are not recommended for general use and are only advised for babies in specific situations—a previous SIDS death, a very premature baby and/or a very ill baby who has spent a long time in an intensive care unit. They can be obtained from large public maternity or children's hospitals or hired from some manufacturers. Sids and Kids will help parents who have had a previous SIDS death obtain breathing monitors. It is important to get advice from a paediatrician about how to use a monitor; what to do should the alarm go off; how to do heart–lung resuscitation (all parents should learn this skill, see page 225); and who to call in an emergency.

If you decide to use a breathing monitor simply to keep your mind at ease you will also need to know the above.

- **Sleep position monitors**

Sleep position monitors work by a button that is attached to the front of the baby's clothing which sets off an alarm if she rolls over onto her stomach (for stomach sleeping in older babies see page 214).

In my opinion sleep position monitors are yet another commercial response to parental anxiety. There is no research to show whether they have any benefits other than a commercial benefit for the manufacturers. These monitors are not recommended by Sids and Kids.

Dummies

A dummy is not an essential item and before you start using one it's worth looking at the advantages and pitfalls.

ADVANTAGES

- Relieves baby and parent distress in the early months.
- Allows the baby to fulfil her need for non-nutritive sucking without being constantly on the breast.
- Dummies can be useful in helping establish some sort of routine with feeds so mothers have a more predictable day.
- Dummies are very useful for calming sick babies, premature babies or babies under lights who are jaundiced.

DISADVANTAGES

- Can interfere with initiating and establishing breastfeeding.
- May increase the incidence of thrush. At times causes contact dermatitis around the baby's mouth under the plastic shield which surrounds the teat.
- Dummies contribute to sleep problems in some older babies.
- Hazards such as tooth decay and safety risks are associated with improper use.
- Statistically, the use of dummies causes a higher incidence of ear infections, gastroenteritis and respiratory infections.

Into the future—prolonged use:

- There is a slight risk that dummy-sucking, similar to some thumb-sucking (see page 409) will push teeth up and out to a degree that will require orthodontic treatment. This seems to depend on the strength and frequency of the sucking and in a tiny number of children, unusual sucking habits.

- When toddlers have dummies in their mouths twenty-four hours a day it can inhibit speech and communication. Speaking clearly around a dummy is difficult especially when a toddler is in the speech-learning phase. A dummy also hides facial expressions so if it is never out of the toddler's mouth it's hard to know exactly how she might be feeling.
- Occasionally the prolonged use of the dummy during the toddler years interferes with optimum muscular development around the mouth and encourages tongue thrusting, resulting in excessive dribbling as the saliva pools under the tongue and falls out instead of being swallowed.

THE PERPLEXING QUESTION OF SIDS AND DUMMIES

Some studies suggest that dummies may have a protective effect against SIDS. However, the downsides to dummies have to be weighed up against this possibility.

As the evidence that dummies are protective against SIDS is inconclusive, Sids and Kids do not recommend their routine use at this time. You can obtain their information statement, *Pacifier/dummy use* from the Sids and Kids website or by calling their office on 1300 308 307 to request a copy via snail mail.

IF YOU DECIDE TO USE ONE WHICH TYPE SHOULD YOU BUY?

Choices centre around material and shape:

Shapes are either the bell shape or the more recently developed orthodontic shape which manufacturers claim resemble women's nipples and is in some way advantageous to babies. This is based on very flimsy evidence. Orthodontic dummies are not pliable and responsive like women's nipples so it is misleading to make these claims.

Bell-shaped dummies come in a variety of sizes ranging from small to large. There are no advantages to any particular size apart from your baby's personal preference. If she prefers a small size there's no need to change the size as she grows.

The material is either rubber or silicone:

Rubber is softer, cheaper and more flexible. Concerns were raised in 1986 about the level of nitrosamines in rubber dummies and teats. Nitrosamines are formed from chemicals added during the manufacturing of rubber to give it elasticity, strength and durability, features which are desirable in a dummy or teat. Nitrosamines are known to cause cancer in animals so the fact that there are levels of nitrosamines in rubber dummies and teats was widely publicised.

Interestingly, after an initial outburst this whole issue died down and rubber dummies and teats continued to be sold and used. Rubber has been used for most of this century and it is hard to find any evidence that it has caused medical problems. Rubber dummies or teats which contain less than sixty parts per billion of nitrosamines are considered safe by the National Health & Medical Research Council.

Silicone is the other option. Silicone dummies are more expensive, harder, less flexible, more durable and contain only negligible levels of nitrosamines. Because they are less flexible they are more prone to tearing and being bitten through so choking is a possible risk you should be aware of.

Washing baby clothes

Baby clothes can be washed with the rest of the family clothes. They do not need to be washed separately unless there is a medical reason for doing so.

To buy or borrow—basic equipment for the first three months

Clothes

4–6 singlets or body suits
6–8 nighties and/or jumpsuits
4 cardigans or jackets
3 brushed cotton wraps (bunny rugs or cuddlies)
3 cotton or gauze wraps (for summer babies)
Hats, socks or tights
Bibs

Nappies

Cloth (terry towelling) squares
Tailored
Disposables

Liners, disposable or cloth (optional)
Nappy buckets with lids

Sleeping

Bassinet and stand (optional) and firm mattress
Cot and mattress
6 or more bassinet and/or cot sheets
Mattress protector
2 blankets
Fitted mosquito net (optional)

Staying mobile

Sling, front-pack or backpack (optional)
Pram or stroller
Baby bag (optional)

Car safety

A standards-approved baby restraint

Baby bathing and cosmetics

Bath
Basic toiletries
Blunt-ended scissors
Change table (optional)

Miscellaneous

Child safety products
A comfortable chair for you
Portable baby chair

FOR MORE INFORMATION

Chapter 12: Safety, page 223 (*for safe use of equipment, including car safety and safe use of dummies*)
Chapter 11: Daily Care (*SIDS, page 213, use of baby cosmetics, page 221*)
Chapter 16: For Parents (*SIDS, page 361*)
Chapter 17: Equipment (*portable cots, page 368*)

Chapter 15: The Crying Baby, page 285
Chapter 28: Sleeping and Waking Six Months and Beyond, page 480

FURTHER READING

The nappy-free bible is *Diaper Free! The Gentle Wisdom of Natural Infant Hygiene*, Ingrid Bauer, Plume, 2006. Available from www.sarahjbuckley.com

If you would prefer to try a DVD: *Nappy Free!* Available from Moore Pictures, PO Box 50, Repton, NSW, 2454, MoorePictures@excite.com

UPDATE: CHILD CAR RESTRAINT LAWS

On 1 March 2010 new national child car restraint laws were announced. The following is a summary of the new laws. For more information contact the traffic authority in your state.

- Children younger than six months must be secured in a rearward-facing restraint.
- Children aged six months to under four years must be secured in either a rearward- or forward-facing restraint.
- Children aged four years to under seven years must be secured in a forward-facing child restraint or booster seat.
- Children younger than four years cannot travel in the front seat of a vehicle that has two or more rows of seats.
- Children aged four years to under seven years cannot travel in the front seat of a vehicle that has two or more rows of seats, unless all other back seats are occupied by children younger than seven years old in child restraints or booster seats.

Evidence from Swedish research strongly suggests the rearward-facing position is the safest for children up to age three. However, at the present time Australians do not have access to rearward-facing restraints for children over six months. It is hoped by many child safety experts that in the future the restraints, and the law, will be upgraded to accommodate this. In the meantime, if your baby is under nine kilos, leave her facing rearward until she is twelve months (or older).

For more on this issue go to www.caradvice.com.au and search for 'rearward-facing restraints'.

Chapter 6

Breastfeeding Your Baby For the First Two Weeks

As usual, pedagogy has brought us to the point where new mothers view breastfeeding as a skill, a schedule, a kindly kingdom of motherly feelings. It will surprise her to find that breastfeeding is above all a relationship, and that it occupies the mind in a way you don't even realise until you step outside that tired dreamy bubble.

MARNI JACKSON, *THE MOTHER ZONE: LOVE, SEX AND LAUNDRY IN THE MODERN FAMILY*

Breastfeeding is the normal way to feed babies. Breastfeeding and the benefits of human milk have been promoted much more vigorously in the last thirty years as research reveals more and more about the special qualities it has, how they benefit babies and impact on adult health.

People who support, protect and promote breastfeeding do not do so to make women who struggle with breastfeeding and wean feel guilty—some of them bottle fed their own babies. Their information and efforts to change our society's approach to how babies are fed is aimed at the product (human milk and formula), not the person.

If an interest had not been taken in breastfeeding by passionate individuals and groups, breastfeeding may well have disappeared from our culture. If the art and act of breastfeeding is lost, it is reasonable to assume there will be far-reaching negative effects on the human race in the same way irresponsible use of the environment is a potential threat to us all.

Think about the implications of our babies being completely reliant on manufacturers to provide, indefinitely, safe artificial baby milk without having the blueprint of the naturally-occurring biological milk that has sustained human babies for thousands of years. Producing a suitable substitute for the few babies who need it is a very different proposition to completely replacing a superbly adapted evolutionary system which has stood the test of time and demonstrated, unequivocally, its superiority over anything else we have come up with—and are likely to come up with—to replace it. One of the spin-offs of the renewed interest in breastfeeding research has been a great improvement in the manufacture of formula, which has made bottle feeding safer, so the protection of breastfeeding is also about the protection of baby feeding.

Unfortunately, in the rush to promote breastfeeding, the ease and enjoyment of it is at times unrealistically portrayed and the practicalities of life as we live it overlooked. A woman's decision to keep breastfeeding is always influenced by support systems and we have not reached a stage where appropriate support, resources, education and community awareness is in place in Australia to have most babies breastfed for six months. We also need to recognise that very few women 'choose' not to breastfeed. When breastfeeding is abandoned it is usually not a matter of choice, rather it is because the circumstances surrounding the breastfeeding make it impossible to continue. The few women who do *choose* to formula feed usually do so because circumstances make it impossible to continue or because a previous breastfeeding experience was painful and stressful and/or their babies did not thrive.

To help overcome the difficulties that can occur in the first six to eight weeks it helps enormously to know what the advantages of breastfeeding and breastmilk are for you and your baby. Doing what you can to prepare yourself and your partner and having access to accurate information to solve the solvable problems when and if they occur makes a great deal of difference during the early weeks. **Not all breastfeeding problems are solvable,** but the ones that aren't can often be overcome with good support, the right advice and a little time.

Feeding your baby cannot be seen as separate to other aspects of her life or yours. Bear in mind that many of the difficulties with babycare have nothing to do with feeding but simply with the way babies are, which most of us find a challenge, and sometimes a trial, especially when we are doing it for the first time.

Why breastfeed?

It's the normal way to feed babies

Breastmilk is perfectly balanced and contains everything your baby needs to grow and develop the way she is meant to. It's easy to digest and contains antibodies to protect her from illness and foster optimum brain growth. Breastfeeding is good for your baby's jaw development and speech and breastmilk enhances her eyesight.

Exclusive breastfeeding for about six months delays the onset and reduces the severity of conditions such as asthma, eczema and food intolerance. Breastfed babies rarely get constipated when they only have breastmilk and no other food or milk. Their poo is always soft. Current research also suggests that breastfeeding may reduce the risk of heart disease in later life and that breastfed children may have a lower risk of developing juvenile diabetes and coeliac disease.

And, finally, in these current times of rising obesity amongst our children, early research looking at breastfeeding and obesity suggests that children who are breastfed have a lower incidence of overweight and obesity—the longer the duration of breastfeeding the less the chance of too much weight gain in childhood and adolescence. Obviously there are other significant factors involved in the current obesity epidemic, but breastfeeding has the potential to get things off to a promising start in the weight stakes. Reasons suggested by some studies include less exposure to unnecessary calories, the presence in breastmilk of a special protein thought to act as a satiety factor inhibiting overeating and the ability of breastfed babies to adjust their own intake. And one study found mothers of breastfed babies to have a more relaxed attitude to their toddlers' eating habits.

It's good for you

The hormones your body secretes when you breastfeed keep you calm. Many women find the hormones also help with weight loss by making their bodies work more efficiently.

Breastfeeding helps your uterus return to normal size after birth and speeds up the blood loss so the bleeding after the birth is over quicker.

Breastfeeding delays the return of menstruation. Exclusive breastfeeding without use of dummies, bottles or any other food is effective, natural contraception.

Once you and your baby are breastfeeding well it is easy, convenient and, of course, freely given and freely obtained, so it is easy on the family budget.

A possibility that breastfeeding may reduce the risk of pre-menopausal cancer of the breast, cervix and ovaries is indicated in some research. It also suggests that women who breastfeed have a lower risk of osteoporosis and heart disease in later life. Research in areas like this is difficult and there are no guarantees, but they are an added bonus which you should be aware of.

Breastfeeding is potentially sensual and pleasurable for mother and baby alike. Skin on skin, close body contact—it is a richly emotional and physical time, a delicate balance of nature and a wonderful way for you and your baby to get to know each other.

Women's experiences of breastfeeding are as diverse and individual as everything else to do with babies. The issues surrounding baby feeding are emotional, psychological, social and political. The concepts are complex and a challenge for all of us to deal with whether we are parents, health workers, baby food industry workers or bureaucrats who set policies on infant nutrition.

The following are letters written to me about breastfeeding. I am including them because I think they reflect the thoughts and experiences of women generally and it may be comforting to read them if you are going through a few dilemmas yourself.

A POSITIVE ATTITUDE

I guess I've been very lucky in that I grew up with very positive attitudes on breastfeeding. I am one of nine children and my mother breastfed all of us for about nine months each. When I had my first child I had no doubts about my ability to breastfeed. To me, choosing to breastfeed in preference to formula feeding is like choosing to feed the family fresh food as opposed to tinned and frozen food. Many women are not given a 'real choice about baby feeding' due to a lack of knowledge on the subject.

WHY AM I DOING THIS?

I am currently breastfeeding my two-month-old son. If I were to give my expecting friends any advice regarding this topic, it would be to breastfeed. My rationale for this is as follows:

When you have a baby such as mine that wants to be fed every two and a half hours, could you be bothered, screaming child in hand, heating the bottle only to find that the baby has fallen asleep on you after five minutes and the bottle has gone to waste?

You are portable. I can't imagine what a pest it would be to go out if you are bottle feeding. Have you got enough bottles? Are they sterilised? How can you keep them cool? When you breastfeed wherever you go your milk goes in a nice simple package. It is cheap. I have not had to buy formula but I can imagine that it becomes very expensive.

Breastfeeding also helps you lose weight, or so I am told. Personally I think you lose weight due to all the walking up and down the hall pacifying the little gem.

Bonding? Well I am sure bottle-fed babies bond just fine too, but I am the one feeding him. For the moment I am his lifeline. It is one hell of a responsibility and perhaps one of the only times in your life when you are truly useful.

Breastfeed just for the experience of it. I mean, we go back to our animal forebears when we bear the child and breastfeeding is another one of those experiences you do simply because you can. I am a bit vague on this point, but in the same way people go parachuting for the sensation, breastfeeding, while not as dangerous, is still done for the experience and sensation.

Off the top of my head these are the issues I find to be most important. However, let's not kid ourselves—why don't any of the books ever describe the associated hassles with breastfeeding?

I think that we should all accept that there are people who want to bottle feed for their own very good reasons. I think there are far more potentially harmful things in store for our children; whether it be an electrical fault, some misplaced medicine, or an accident when they get their driver's licence.

I mean, if I could have more than two hours of consecutive sleep I would be the happiest person in town right at the moment.

WAY OF LIFE

My belief is that unless a comfortable breastfeeding relationship is established within the first two to four weeks, many mothers quickly opt for the bottle. It seems many problems arise in those first few days of a baby's life. This is particularly distressing as every hospital, birth centre, clinic sister and Australian Breastfeeding Association counsellor appears to have different and often conflicting ideas. Without the support of loved ones it's not surprising the number of women who turn to formula feeding to help them cope.

Probably the greatest thing I have learnt about breastfeeding is that it is a 'way of life'. Much of our parenting skills are a direct spin-off of the 'breast is best' attitude. I am grateful to be parenting in this manner as my son is a delight.

ENCOURAGED TO BREASTFEED

The lack of breastfeeding is a sad affair, but it slowly seems to be coming back. I was encouraged to breastfeed my son which I did happily for a year. He was ten weeks premature and I expressed my milk for eight weeks until he was strong enough to feed from the breast. It was quite an ordeal at first, expressing milk by hand and electric pump, but all worthwhile. My son took to the breast as if it was what he was waiting for. It was a great experience for both of us.

A NON-BREASTFEEDING EXPERIENCE

I am writing to let you know of my experience of not breastfeeding. I am aware that there are pressures on women who decide to either breastfeed or not to breastfeed. These are discussed in many publications and books for pregnant women and new mothers.

There is almost complete silence on the subject of those women, like me, who fail to produce milk at all. Does this indicate almost complete ignorance about this problem? My experience indicates that it does.

My husband and I were in Canada for the birth of our son. Despite help from a doctor, La Leche League, a lactation consultant, and tests from an endocrinologist (which showed my hormone levels were normal), there was no reason any of them could come up with for my lack of milk.

This time was very upsetting for my husband and me and we are still upset and disappointed that breastfeeding information for prospective parents does not make it clear that some mothers (if only a small number) are unable to breastfeed. After telling friends of my problem they related stories of people they know with similar problems. Thus I know I am not alone in having this problem.

DIDN'T CONNECT WITH BREASTFEEDING

While I was pregnant with my first child I had every intention of breastfeeding. I read all the appropriate information. Unfortunately there isn't enough literature stating that not all mothers and babies can connect with breastfeeding. This is agonising for a new mother as she is constantly told to persist. Meanwhile her child is losing weight and crying continually with hunger.

Sadly, I will never have the first seven weeks of my son's life back to enjoy; instead it was misery for this time due to so much emphasis being put on breastfeeding. I don't think I'll breastfeed again because the experience was far from fulfilling for me or my baby.

LET'S PREPARE WOMEN FOR THE DIFFICULT ASPECTS OF BREASTFEEDING

To some first-time mothers the pain and stress involved in breastfeeding comes as a total shock. The literature aimed at them only talks about the pleasurable, positive aspects. Breastfeeding promoters need to realise that talking about the difficult aspects of breastfeeding will help mothers overcome the initial and subsequent hurdles to experience the positive and pleasurable aspects. If health professionals cannot be realistic about the difficulties of breastfeeding then how can emotional and sleep-deprived mothers remain positive about the advantages breastfeeding offers themselves and their babies?

THE PERFECT PRODUCT

My baby is now fifteen weeks old and I am breastfeeding her. Both she and I are thriving. In the beginning I found breastfeeding painful and stressful for both my husband and myself. I thought I wanted to give it up. My health worker gave me lots of sensible advice and loads of encouragement to continue. When I complained about breastfeeding she pointed out two important facts:

- *Breast milk is the perfect food for babies*
- *If I hang in there it will get easier.*

She was right on both points.

THE DREADED FORMULA

I enjoyed the twelve months I breastfed my first baby. With my second baby I had feeding difficulties from day one. He was placed in special care because he was a low weight. Once my milk came in and we thought he was feeding okay we went home to what was to become hell on earth. The next six to eight weeks consisted of a screaming baby who was not gaining weight. Eventually my family doctor (who was very supportive of breastfeeding) was concerned that my son needed to gain weight so I ventured to the chemist and bought the dreaded formula which I then fed to my son. He not only drank it happily but then slept for five hours, the longest he had ever done. It suddenly dawned on me that through my stubborn desire to breastfeed and the feeling that mothers who bottle feed weren't really 'good' mothers I had probably done my son a disservice who, in hindsight, had probably been hungry most of his life.

He went on to thrive on artificial milk and I think I have recovered from my guilt and have tempered my feelings about breastfeeding. If I had another child I would still do my utmost to breastfeed as it is ideal, but I no longer look down on mothers who bottle feed.

BREASTFEEDING WORTH THE STRUGGLE

I am breastfeeding my six-month-old son and would not have it any other way—now. However, feeding was a nightmare for the first eleven weeks of his life and a desolate time for me. I so wanted to breastfeed and I'd read about the techniques to use, but 'your nipples may feel a little tender at first' was the understatement of the year. I wanted to lob a hand grenade at those whose books had given me the expectation that breastfeeding would be warm, comfortable and pleasurable. It is now, but it wasn't then.

After struggling through sore nipples and recurrent mastitis, almost weaning then having to re-establish my milk supply, I finally did it by the time my baby was twelve weeks old. A supportive husband helped me stay sane.

Establishing breastfeeding can be a lengthy, demoralising process. It's no wonder some of us, used to snapping our fingers to deal with difficulties, reach for formula to solve the problems. I can still recall being amazed that I, a 'tough' high school teacher who'd been able to maintain discipline in all sorts of school situations, should be so beaten by a tiny baby who simply needed to be fed.

I don't think we should back away from saying 'breast is best'. It is a scientific fact that formula only approximates breastmilk, but we need more realistic education about what can go wrong. We need it given in detail so we can be prepared.

BREASTFEEDING IS SENSUAL AND PLEASURABLE

My son was born by caesarean section. Breastfeeding him was and is a natural experience that is convenient and economical. The staff at the hospital were very encouraging and actively promote breastfeeding through lactation consultants giving presentations on the ward and providing all the support needed.

I'd like to address some aspects about baby feeding. Firstly, mothers who bottle feed feel at odds with breastfeeding mothers.

When I learned that some of my friends weaned at two to five weeks I asked how they found it in an attempt to learn of their experience. Their responses were consistent— 'it's great', 'more convenient'. I did become aware of some minor conflict between the two methods from the mothers' view point. I feel that breastfeeding mums feel compelled to defend their position.

Secondly, breastfeeding is sensual and pleasurable.

I found it interesting and comforting that you wrote of breastfeeding being frequently sensual and pleasurable. I certainly found it to be both. It's something one feels inhibited to express but it does feel quite nice. This aspect, I believe, is not made known by health workers.

What's in breastmilk?

I think we sometimes lose sight of what it is the baby is getting and why it's worth persevering through the hard bits to make sure your baby doesn't miss out, so let's look briefly at what it is.

Breastmilk is a living substance. Despite the wealth of information now available, lots of things about breastmilk remain elusive and unanswered so we are still a long way from manufacturing a substance that is an exact equivalent.

One of the reasons precise breastmilk analysis is so difficult is because human milk changes constantly. Breastmilk components vary from woman to woman, from breast to breast, during the course of a feed and over time. Human milk adapts to babies' ages and needs and to climatic conditions. Its taste varies, so breastfed babies are exposed to a variety of interesting tastes from feed to feed. Women are usually aware of the difference in the way their milk looks when it changes from the first milk, colostrum, to the later milk known as mature milk. Colostrum is rich-looking and yellow while mature milk is a fine fluid often with a bluish hue. Milk from different women can look quite different, and all variations are fine. Human milk doesn't look like formula which is uniformly thick and white. They are different substances so this is to be expected.

Everything your baby needs is in her own special milk made by you. There are over one hundred known ingredients. Let's look at the main ones and some of the amazing features of human milk.

Water

There's lots of water in breastmilk. Water quenches your baby's thirst and during the early weeks helps make up for the water she loses from evaporation from her lungs and skin. This evaporation is normal and is one of the reasons new babies lose body heat quickly, so breastfeeding contributes to maintaining your baby's body temperature after birth. Even in very hot climates babies get all the water they need from breastmilk, clean and uncontaminated—your baby doesn't need extra water in a bottle.

Fat

Fat makes up the next biggest part of breastmilk after water. The fat in breastmilk is very well absorbed because of a special enzyme present in the milk which makes the fat instantly ready to digest without having to be broken down in your baby's liver. Fat satisfies her hunger and is the main way she gets her calories and puts on weight. The special fats in breastmilk are quite different to fats in any other food or milk, and so far unable to be replicated. These fats give your baby energy and provide essential nutrients in the correct amounts and proportions that are needed for growth and development of her central nervous system.

Breastmilk also has plenty of cholesterol, needed by babies for optimum brain development at this time of their lives.

Protein

Protein is important for growth and development of every part of the body, down to the tiniest cell. Humans grow slowly compared to other mammals so the protein in their milk exactly suits the growth rate of human babies.

The two types of protein are casein and whey. The casein, or milk curd, is soft and small and easy to digest. The whey, which is the clear fluid left when milk clots, is also easy for your baby to digest. The whey protein contains a lot of the antibodies that protect your baby from disease.

Carbohydrates

The main carbohydrate is lactose. Lactose makes it easier for babies to absorb calcium—which compensates beautifully for the relatively small amounts of calcium in breastmilk. Lactose also supplies energy to your baby's brain and contains a special carbohydrate known as 'bifidus factor' which helps stop harmful germs from growing in your baby's gut.

Some other special things about breastmilk

Breastmilk contains living cells like those found in blood. They have complex functions but are important in protecting your baby from illness and delaying the onset of possible allergies.

Many hormones are found in breastmilk. Hormones are substances the body produces which have a specific effect on a particular part of the body. One of the hormones found in breastmilk is a growth hormone. The exact role of many of the hormones found in human milk is still to be discovered. It is reasonable to assume they all play some part in the growth and development of babies. Breastmilk also contains vitamins, minerals, iron (which is very well absorbed) and trace elements.

Breastmilk is an intriguing, living substance—the real benefits of which are only just beginning to be understood. Breastfeeding is an extension of birth and part of nature's grand plan to help babies adjust to life outside the womb.

Getting ready for breastfeeding before the birth of your baby

Getting ready to breastfeed doesn't mean doing things to your nipples and breasts. Past ideas of toughening your nipples or pulling them out have now been found to be unnecessary and even harmful. Preparation is about learning how breastfeeding works, getting an idea of the best things to do to make it work the way it should, and doing a little bit of flexible planning.

Learning to feel comfortable handling your breasts by gentle massage (using a technique similar to that advised for self breast examination) is also helpful. If you are curious to see what your milk looks like or tastes like express a little, gently, and see.

Here are some planning suggestions:

- Read the early breastfeeding parts of this book before your baby is born.
- Breastfeeding is usually part of childbirth education classes so make sure you go the night it's on. Alternatively, many maternity hospitals conduct breastfeeding classes.
- The Australian Breastfeeding Association (ABA) is a national voluntary organisation whose members help mothers and babies with breastfeeding in numerous ways. ABA has trained breastfeeding counsellors who you can talk to before the birth and help you afterwards; making use of this wonderful resource is strongly recommended.
- Maternity hospitals have lactation consultants on their staff—midwives whose job is specifically to help with breastfeeding. If you feel very unsure about breastfeeding, an appointment to see a lactation consultant before the birth will give you confidence before you start and will help with any difficulties that may arise once your breastfeeding is under way.
- Plan to rest more than you usually do during the first six weeks until your body adjusts to your new life and breastfeeding. The matter of housework rears its head again and can't be ignored—talk to your partner about possible strategies.
- Having someone you can call on who believes in breastfeeding and on whom you can rely for consistent advice and encouragement is a great boon. Research has shown that breastfeeding support from your baby's father is a tremendous help in getting breastfeeding started and continuing through the first year and beyond. Other supporters might be a child and family health nurse, an ABA counsellor, a lactation consultant, a midwife or a close friend or relative who has breastfed.
- Think about ways of avoiding the three Ss which are smoking, stress and supplements. Women who *smoke* often find they don't have quite enough milk to keep their baby happy, especially after the first two or three months. Constant *stress* that makes you feel unhappy and ill means your body doesn't work as well as it is able to, so try to change stressful areas in your life before the birth. Learning relaxation techniques also helps. *Supplements*, which are fluids given in bottles to babies, may mean

the end of breastfeeding if they are given in the first six weeks, so avoid them. Water and juice are not necessary.

When breastfeeding problems occur

Baby Love covers the main problems women may encounter when they breastfeed, but there are often many variations on the theme, some of which respond to standard advice and some of which don't. It's always advisable to consult a breastfeeding adviser if you run into difficulties you can't manage yourself.

I think it is wise to bear in mind that despite the fact a lot more is now known about breastfeeding problems and how to manage many of them, not all problems are solvable, even if you are seeing a knowledgeable health professional. There is a great tendency nowadays to use a medical model (diagnose and treat) to solve all breastfeeding difficulties, which is great when it works (as it will for clear-cut problems). There are, however, times when definitive diagnoses and treatments are given for problems that may not be clear-cut. Subsequently women are sometimes put through exhausting regimes and end up feeling let-down and frustrated when they do not work, or even worried that they and/or their babies are different from everyone else.

I think it is unfortunate that some health professionals involved in breastfeeding are reluctant to acknowledge that there is not always a guarantee of a successful outcome for the treatment or course of action they are advising.

Things such as mastitis, blocked ducts, nipple dermatitis, nipple thrush and low milk supply are eminently diagnosable and treatable. However, things like breast refusal, ongoing mastitis, breast pain, some cases of low milk supply and some cases of painful/damaged nipples may not respond to a specific diagnosis and treatment.

Why am I telling you this? Because I am aware that it happens, and it may be a comfort, if you are going through a difficult breastfeeding experience, to know that the breastfeeding experts do not know everything. While we do know a lot more than we did, there remain times when particular problems can't be solved. Often with good support and when they can see light at the end of the tunnel, many women continue to breastfeed through the problem. Sometimes weaning is the only option (see page 95).

A word about flat or inverted nipples

Flat nipples are nipples which do not stand out when they are stimulated by touch or cold. Flat nipples usually start to stick out once the baby is feeding well and drawing the nipple out, but feeding can be tricky in the early weeks.

Inverted nipples turn into the breast, so there is a dip instead of a nipple standing out. It is more difficult to breastfeed if your nipples don't stand out as it makes it harder for your baby to get a good mouthful of the breast tissue around your nipple. Inverted nipples provide a real challenge, but women can succeed with patience, perseverance, help from a skilled adviser and a baby who sucks well. Having said that, it must be acknowledged that inverted nipples often present a considerable hurdle which prevents some women from breastfeeding. In these cases breastmilk can be expressed and given in a bottle.

Having flat or inverted nipples might discourage you from breastfeeding. If you are concerned, check it out with someone reliable like a midwife, a child and family health nurse, an Australian Breastfeeding Association counsellor or a lactation consultant.

Special exercises and wearing breast shells (devices made of rigid plastic that are placed over the nipple and held in place by a firm bra) during pregnancy have been shown to be of little benefit, however, the use of a nipple shield after the milk comes in for the first six to eight weeks after birth can be a worthwhile strategy if the baby has trouble taking the breast because of flat or inverted nipples. For more on nipple shields see page 91.

How breastfeeding works

Breastfeeding involves not only your breast but your areola, nipple and several hormones which are released by the brain. The areola is the area of coloured skin which surrounds your nipple. The size and colour of the areola varies a great deal between women and has nothing to do with the way breastfeeding works. Dark hair on or around the areola is common and doesn't interfere with breastfeeding in any way.

Milk production

Milk production is inhibited during pregnancy by the hormone progesterone which is produced by the placenta. Once the placenta is expelled after birth the progesterone levels in your body fall. During the next thirty hours as the progesterone decreases, milk production increases and while this is happening your baby takes in small amounts of colostrum. Colostrum is rich in good things which protect her digestive tract, respiratory tract and urinary tract against infection, as well as helping her gut and bowel to function efficiently. After this time milk production rapidly increases to meet your baby's needs.

Recent research suggests that breasts can produce more milk than required by the baby and that within a few days of birth each breast begins to regulate its rate of making milk according to the amount of milk the baby removes at each breastfeed. Feeding well and often in the first days and early weeks means your breasts get a clear message to keep making milk. As your baby and your body become more skilful at breastfeeding, the milk supply and release becomes very efficient, which is why sucking time decreases as your baby grows, not increases as you may imagine.

Releasing the milk

After the milk is made, the breast has to release it. As your baby sucks, the nerves around your nipple send a message to your brain to release another hormone called oxytocin. Oxytocin contracts the muscles around the milk-producing sacs in the breast, squeezing the milk down towards the nipple. Oxytocin is the same hormone that contracts the muscles of the uterus, drawing it tight—a feeling ranging from pleasant to painful. Painful contractions of the uterus while breastfeeding are not permanent and only last for a short time after birth. The contraction of the milk sacs by oxytocin is called the 'let-down', a feeling that may range from not being able to feel anything, to tingles, to pins and needles, to a needle-sharp sensation which is painful for some women for a while. Some women who breastfeed well never feel a let-down. Let-downs occur in between feeds, from one breast while you are feeding from the other, at times when you are thinking about your baby or if you hear her cry. Feeling sexy can also start a let-down or alternatively a let-down can make you feel sexy—the latter doesn't happen to everyone, so if it happens to you, half your luck—enjoy!

Getting started—the first two weeks

Breastfeeding is natural, but not something all mothers and babies know how to do. There's no doubt that a lot of babies and breasts go well together right from the start and the whole experience is a smooth operation that just happens. For others it's a skill to be learnt like riding a bike or learning to swim. The learning is made more complicated because there's two learning together, a bit like learning to have good sex.

There are two important things to remember when you start breastfeeding:

- Frequent good sucking removes the milk, which tells the breast to make more milk and stops the milk from banking up. Banked-up milk causes painful breasts, sore nipples, much less milk and a hungry baby.
- When your baby takes the breast the right way everything works well. Good sucking and comfortable feeding depends on you both being in the right position.

Let's look at getting the position right

Getting both your posture and your baby's position right each time you feed is sometimes not easy in the beginning, although the basics are fairly simple. Like any practical procedure, learning how to breastfeed from written instructions is difficult—imagine learning to drive a car from a book! It's of great benefit to get help from an experienced person who can guide you and your baby for the first several feeds. This is likely to be a midwife or a lactation consultant. The following basic guidelines are suitable for most mothers and babies. However, as all breasts and babies are different, a number of women find they need specific help tailored to their requirements. Most hospitals and communities in Australia have lactation consultants available who are skilled at working out what changes individual mothers and babies need to make to help their breastfeeding become more effective and comfortable. If you find you are having difficulties after you leave hospital, ask your child and family health nurse how to contact an experienced lactation consultant. She/he can closely watch you feed and help you by making recommendations adapted to you and your baby.

While the ideal time for the first breastfeed is within a few hours after birth, there are times when this can't happen, so don't panic if something delays the first feed. Breastfeeding can work at any time after birth, even weeks later.

Here are the main things to think about and do when you breastfeed your baby:

- When your baby is awake and ready to feed, make sure you are both comfortable before you start. In the beginning you need to think things through step by step. Empty your bladder, wash your hands and have a glass of water close by (breastfeeding makes you thirsty). Have a footstool or telephone book handy in case you need something to put your feet on. Don't worry about changing your baby at this stage if changing her is going to result in a distressed, screaming baby (unless there is poo everywhere).
- Finding a comfortable position for yourself is easier if you are not holding your baby at the same time. Ask someone to hold her if she is crying or leave her somewhere safe within easy reach until you are ready.
- While you are getting used to handling your baby and getting the position right, sitting in a straight-backed chair (like a dining room chair) that gives you good back support is best.
- Lying on your side may be a better way to feed after a caesarean or if your bottom is sore, but as it is difficult to see what your baby is doing, ask for help.
- Most women find it easier to use a pillow to support their babies while they are learning to breastfeed. Your lap needs to be almost flat, your trunk facing forwards and your back straight (not tilted back or leaning forwards). Sit so your legs are down with your feet flat on either the floor, a footstool or a telephone book.
- Feeding babies unwrapped has many advantages. It lessens the likelihood of the baby becoming too warm and sleepy to feed well, there is more direct skin contact and the baby's hands on the breast help stimulate the milk supply. You may find, however, that you prefer to wrap your baby until you are more used to handling her and your breast (it won't take long). Make sure if you do wrap that your baby's hands are wrapped either down or up and *not* across the front of her chest, as this forms a barrier between her and your breast.

- Hold your baby so she faces you, her chest against your chest. Support her behind the shoulders with her body flexed around your body so that her nose (not her mouth) is level with your nipple. You may find it helpful to tuck both her legs into your armpit area, holding them firmly in place with the top of your arm (like a set of bagpipes—forgive the comparison).
- There are various ways to support your breast and you may try several before you find one that suits you both. For starters, try placing your palm and fingers flat on your rib cage, bring your fingers forwards along the side of your breast and cup the breast between the fingers and thumb.
- She needs to take a good mouthful of breast, so wait until her mouth is wide open before you bring her to the breast. When your baby's cheek is touched, a reflex called the rooting reflex makes her turn her head in the direction of the touch and open her mouth to suck. You can help her open her mouth by gently brushing your nipple against cheek and lips or by running your nipple lightly over her nose and lips.
- When her mouth is wide open, move your baby quickly up to your breast. Her chin should reach the breast first and tuck well into the breast with the bottom lip curled back. Support your baby's head and shoulders so the nose and forehead can extend slightly, allowing for good air circulation while your baby feeds. When the position is correct you do not have to press the breast with your finger so she can breathe. If her nose and forehead are pushed into the breast it becomes more difficult for her to suck and breathe and she may go to sleep after only a short suck.
- A lot of the areola will be in her mouth but you will still see some of it above the nipple—the bigger the areola the more you will see.
- When she starts to suck, take a deep breath, make your shoulders go floppy and feed away. Once your baby gets going she will suck deeply and strongly at a regular pace. You will see her jaw moving and her ears moving slightly.
- You may experience a drawing sensation at first; some women find this painful for about thirty seconds. If any discomfort or pain persists after this or if your baby sucks quickly and lightly all the time and is sucking

her cheeks in, take your baby from the breast. To do this place your finger in the corner of her mouth to break the suction, then gently remove her. Try again. Sometimes it takes several tries before it feels right.

- Every time you feed think carefully about how you are doing it. This may seem tedious, especially in the middle of the night, but it is the best way to prevent sore nipples. After the first six to eight weeks you will find you and your baby are such an efficient team you won't have to think about what you are doing, where you are sitting or even have to use a pillow.

A good mouthful of breast

A good mouthful of breast means your baby takes in part of the breast tissue around the nipple as well as the nipple and draws the nipple right back past her hard palate. This protects the nipple and is a major factor in preventing painful feeds.

Think about the difference between sucking the skin on your forearm and sucking your finger. To suck the skin on your forearm you need to open your mouth wide to get a good mouthful of skin and it is a similar action to what your baby does at the breast. Sucking your finger, however, does not require an open mouth or a big mouthful. When babies suck like this to feed, nipples quickly become sore, the breast is not well drained and no one has a nice time.

A summary of the most important points

- Sit with a straight back and flat lap with good support for your back.
- Hold your baby so she faces you, her nose in line with your nipple.
- Bring your baby up to your breast. Let her take a good mouthful. Don't lean forwards and give her your nipple.
- Her chin should be tucked well into the breast, her nose and forehead slightly extended.
- Take a deep breath and make your shoulders go floppy.
- If it hurts after thirty seconds gently take her off. Avoid pulling. Try again.

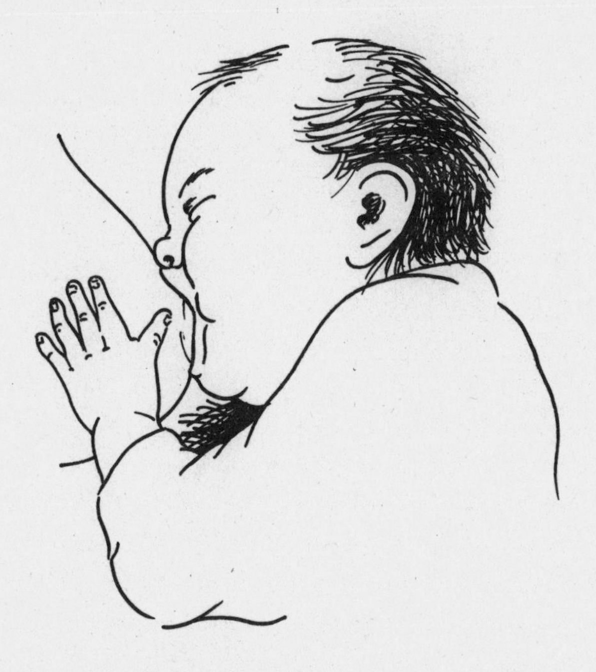

What about twins?

Women's marvellous bodies respond to the stimulation of two babies sucking and can produce enough milk for more than one baby.

The basics are the same. The decision has to be made whether the babies will be fed separately or together. In the early weeks it is probably better to feed one at a time until you become more confident and the babies are feeding well. After a while it is usually easier to feed them together. You will need help to master this as well as privacy and peace and quiet.

Trying different positions, feeding one at a time and two at a time while you are in hospital with the support of the staff, is a good idea. I find that everyone who breastfeeds twins does it slightly differently, so don't get bogged down by 'rules'.

Eventually it is a good idea to swap breasts as some twins become so attached to one breast they will not use the other one, which may cause great inconvenience further down the track.

Weighing babies

Some health workers, both in the past and present, have been obsessed by the issue of a baby's weight. This is seen as disadvantageous to breastfeeding by many mothers and people involved in supporting breastfeeding. Constant weighing of breastfed babies with an unsympathetic health professional who makes incorrect assumptions from the baby's weight can indeed be most unhelpful and work against successful breastfeeding. Test weighing (weighing a baby before and after a feed to see 'how much she gets') is a pointless, stressful exercise which should never be inflicted on a mother—so if it's ever suggested to you, change your adviser.

When a baby is breastfeeding well, has six to eight pale, wet nappies and a good soft poo either frequently or every so often, and there are no problems, weighing is unnecessary apart from the nice buzz it gives a mother to see a tangible sign of the great job she's doing. It can also be a very positive, reassuring thing for women who are breastfeeding for the first time.

If problems arise there are times when weighing the baby to assess weight gain (as opposed to static weight or weight loss) is necessary to give the mother appropriate guidance, particularly when the problem is a crying, unsettled baby. Certainly, many problems can be sorted out without weighing, so whenever I suggest weighing in this book it is because I think the baby's weight is very useful information on which to base advice in that particular instance.

How long and how often to feed?

There are no set rules about the length of time babies need to suck to get the milk they need. Some babies get all they need quickly, others take longer. In the past problems were caused because the general guidelines suggested short rather than long feeds; now some women have problems with the current standard advice which suggests leaving the baby to decide when to come off the breast. There is also a lot of unnecessary advice about foremilk and hindmilk.

Many women are being needlessly worried by the whole concept of foremilk and hindmilk so let's get it out of the way now so you can forget about it.

The composition of breastmilk changes as milk is removed from the breast at a feed. Usually the milk at the beginning of a breastfeed (the foremilk) has a fine blue appearance which changes to a whiter appearance (the hindmilk) as the breast becomes emptier at the end of a feed. The change in appearance of the breastmilk occurs because the fat content of the milk increases as the breast is emptied. However, these changes vary greatly as the baby rarely removes all the available milk at any particular feed. The important point is that the changes in breastmilk even out over each twenty-four-hour period and you do not have to be concerned about it. It is not possible to change your baby's energy intake by altering your pattern of feeding—your baby cannot consume consistently either low fat foremilk or higher fat hindmilk.

In my opinion, the role of foremilk/hindmilk imbalance in what is called 'colic' is minimal, if it exists at all. I have seen no clear evidence in my work that it is a reason or answer for crying, unsettled breastfed babies. The main thing for you to be aware of is that you don't have to worry about foremilk and hindmilk: just think of your milk as breastmilk.

It would be nice if breastfeeding just happened and there was no need to offer advice to mothers, but if you're doing it for the first time you may be looking for something to hang your hat on in the early weeks. Some women breastfeed in whichever way suits them and never have a problem, so if you're doing just that, for goodness sake don't change a thing. **Others find the current standard advice is fine; again if you and your baby are happy, carry on.**

However, if you are looking for a little more structured breastfeeding advice to help you through the first six to eight weeks, here are my guidelines.

- The longest babies need to get enough milk and comfort is around twenty minutes or so of good sucking on one or both breasts. **Lots of babies finish in under twenty minutes, which is fine. If you are happy to leave your baby sucking longer than twenty minutes, keep going.** If you would sooner finish the feed, gently take her off and offer the second breast. It's quite all right for you to end the feed after about twenty minutes rather than wait for her to come off the breast by herself.

- Always offer the second breast—there are no advantages to 'one-breast feeding' apart from times when there may be temporary difficulties with an oversupply (see page 131). Before you offer the second breast, wake your baby up so she is alert and ready to feed. Change her nappy if you have to or tickle her feet. If she is not interested in the second breast she is getting all the milk she needs at this time from one breast. This is rarely a permanent arrangement and may vary from feed to feed and over time. As babies grow they usually take both breasts at most feeds.
- When your baby only takes one breast you may need to hand express the other breast for comfort. If the breast is comfortable don't worry about expressing.
- The number of times you feed your baby in the first week or two varies from six to eight every twenty-four hours. After your milk is flowing, six to seven feeds suit most mothers and babies. Less than six feeds over twenty-four hours usually lessens the milk supply over time, more than six is fine as long as you are both happy. Some of the feeds will be two hours apart, some three to four, and your baby may have one long sleep of five or six hours. Stay flexible about feed times. If you are looking for some sort of pattern, it is better to think in terms of the number of feeds every twenty-four hours rather than three-hourly and four-hourly feeds. Expecting a set four-hourly feeding routine is unrealistic for most babies.

Lying down

Sitting in a chair

Sitting on the floor

Here is one way to feed twins

Front hold

Underarm (twin) hold

How can you tell if the baby is hungry?

Working out whether babies are hungry or not is confusing as babies cry, suck their fists and make mouthing signs when they are over-tired, over-stimulated or generally distressed, as well as when they are hungry. Feeding breastfed babies to comfort them for any of the above—rather than because they are due for a feed—is not harmful to the baby in any way, but being worn out from too many feeds and an unsettled baby is a common problem for many women in the first three months. If this is happening to you here are two simple things to check:

- Your baby's position at the breast and sucking technique. If you have an adviser to call on, so much the better.
- That your baby is getting enough milk. The best way to do this is a quick weigh with a sympathetic adviser who uses the weight as a guide to help you and your baby—not worry the life out of you.

Most of the time, endless feeding and an unsettled baby fall into the broad range of normal baby behaviour and are not breastfeeding problems, so there is rarely a quick, easy answer once hunger and poor positioning are ruled out. If your baby is bright-eyed and alert, sucks well, is gaining some weight and is wetting and pooing, but is never 'off the breast' and you are feeling very tense, see if you can limit some of her feeds. Limit the time at each breast to about twenty minutes and wait two to two-and-a-half hours before feeding again. Try other ways of settling her. This advice is for your sanity, not because endless feeds will harm her—you cannot overfeed a breastfed baby. You may also find it helpful to refer to other sections of the book that deal with low milk supply, crying and sleeping and the crying baby (see the index).

Very few women breastfeed in exactly the same way. What works for another mother and baby may not work for you, so stick to your own style and ignore unwanted, uncalled-for advice. On the other hand, you can always change what you're doing if someone suggests something that suits you and your baby better.

Common difficulties in the first week

Your baby won't suck

FULL-TERM HEALTHY BABIES: Recommendations for getting breastfeeding off to a good start include offering the baby the breast as soon as possible after the birth. And while many babies do take the breast well soon after birth, others are simply not interested. It can be very stressful for the mother when those around her keep trying to encourage a reluctant baby to take her breast. When the birth is a normal one and the baby is full-term and healthy it is best to stay relaxed about the early breastfeeds. Some babies do not start sucking well for two or three days. Remember that newborn babies have quite a lot of food in reserve.

SLEEPY BABIES: Babies may be sleepy if they are jaundiced, a few weeks premature or if they are recovering from a long or difficult labour. Sometimes it can take two to five days before they start to suck well. Try to stay relaxed and patient. Sleepy babies start to feed very well when they 'wake up' two to four days after birth. Unwrap your baby when you put her to the breast as skin-to-skin contact helps stimulate her senses.

BABIES WHO FIGHT THE BREAST: Some babies thrash about, move their head from side to side and scream. Like a lot of things babies do, it's often difficult to know exactly why they do it because they can't tell us. If this is happening to you it can turn into a cycle where your baby becomes more and more tense and you become more and more distressed, dreading the thought of putting your baby to the breast. Happily, this sort of situation is usually short-lived. The cycle can be broken by having a third person, not as emotionally involved with the baby, to help. If there is no professional help available a calm neighbour or friend could fit the bill.

Here are some tips for your helper:

- Separate mother and baby. Calm the baby and see if you can help her go to sleep.
- Nurture the mother. A cup of tea, a bath or a shoulder massage all help.
- When the mother and baby are calm and comfortable, try another feed. The mother should express a little milk before starting the feed to

encourage the baby to suck. This softens the areola, making it easier for the baby to take the breast.

- Skin-to-skin contact can be very helpful or, if the mother is comfortable with the idea, feeding the baby in the bath helps.
- Expressed milk or boiled water may be given by bottle and teat if necessary. This is usually not required as these babies do tend to start feeding well before any extra fluid is needed.

Engorged breasts

What are engorged breasts? Engorgement refers to painful, swollen breasts usually caused either by the milk not flowing well or because the breasts are temporarily producing far more milk than the baby needs at each feed. It can happen in the early days or later.

- In the first two to four days your breasts may feel full and heavy because of the increased blood supply to your breasts as they get ready to make milk. Discomfort is variable and passes quickly as long as your baby feeds frequently and she is positioned so she can suck well to drain the breast.
- Later engorgement—painful, swollen breasts persisting after the first few days—means too much milk is stored because too much is being made and not enough is being removed. The areola is stretched and distended which makes it difficult for your baby to get a good mouthful.

WHAT CAN YOU DO?

- Feed often, eight (or more) times in twenty-four hours.
- Waking babies to feed often doesn't work, so put your baby to the breast whenever she is awake and ready to suck.
- Ask for help if it's available to make sure your baby is in the best position to suck well.
- Avoid giving any fluids from bottles.
- Gently hand-express a small amount of milk before the feed to soften the areola to make it easier for your baby to take the breast.
- Stand with your back to the shower so the hot water spraying down doesn't increase the discomfort. To relieve the pain and full feeling

express a little milk in between feeds under the shower. Placing cold packs on your breasts also helps them feel better. To make a cold pack soak a clean face washer in cold water. Wring out hard and place in a plastic bag in the freezer.

- If it all becomes unbearable, the cycle can be broken by completely draining both breasts with an electric pump after a feed. This brings relief and makes it easier for your baby to take the breast at the next feed. It should be done once only, preferably at the end of the day and with some help from a breastfeeding adviser.
- Take some anti-inflammatory medication for pain if you need to, it won't hurt your baby.

Not enough milk/fluid

Occasionally babies become dehydrated in the first week because they are not getting enough milk. The reasons for this vary. Sometimes it is because the baby is not sucking efficiently; sometimes the milk supply is late coming in; sometimes it is a combination of both. This can sneak up on new mothers especially if it is their first baby. I must stress it is unusual, nevertheless it's useful to know the signs and symptoms of dehydration:

- A floppy and sleepy baby not waking to feed at least six times every twenty-four hours.
- Sucking weakly or only for a short time before falling asleep.
- You may be aware that your breasts are not full and feel the same before and after feeds.
- Nappies are dry or only damp.
- Splats of khaki or black poo.
- Increased jaundice (yellow colour of skin and whites of eyes).
- Loose skin around your baby's neck, back and tummy.
- There may be pink/orange staining in the nappy (see page 191).

You need to see a health professional (family doctor, paediatrician, lactation consultant, child and family health nurse, children's hospital casualty) as soon as possible.

STRATEGIES TO TREAT DEHYDRATION INVOLVE:

- Frequent short feeds alternating each breast after three to five minutes.
- Setting the alarm and waking your baby during the night.
- If necessary extra fluids (water or formula) via a supply line (see page 128) or bottle can be used on a temporary basis.
- Twice-weekly weighing until things are back on track.

Baby won't burp

Burping babies is more tradition than necessity. For some reason it is indeed very satisfying to hear a baby burp (I enjoy it too), but medical problems don't happen because babies don't burp and in many cultures it is an unknown practice. An unnecessary emphasis is placed on 'getting the wind up' in our culture, which is unfortunate as it worries the life out of new mothers. Whether a baby burps or not is not related to unsettled behaviour, vomiting or interesting coloured poo. It's fine to put your baby to bed without hearing a burp first. Babies won't always oblige with a burp no matter how experienced the burper, so don't think everyone in the world knows how to burp a baby better than you. No secret tricks exist! Try for a few minutes then forget about it.

Sore nipples

Sore nipples remain one of the most troublesome aspects of early breast-feeding for many women. Past theories on sore nipples dwelt on the necessity of having to toughen up the nipples and making sure babies didn't suck for too long. Current research shows that neither of these things are relevant in avoiding and treating nipple problems; rather, the way the baby takes the breast is the crucial factor.

This is why there is now so much emphasis on getting the mother's and baby's position right for a feed. If positioning is right for all the early feeds, nipple problems can be avoided a lot of the time. However, despite current knowledge and the best efforts with correct positioning, sore nipples are still with us. This may be because the damage can be done during only one feed in the early days when the mother is tired or uncomfortable and the baby doesn't quite take the breast in the best way. Once nipples become sore, comfortable feeding is difficult so the problem gets worse.

Sometimes nipples get sore even when the feeding position seems to be right. This may be because the nipple and areola are being used constantly in a new way which causes temporary discomfort.

Nipple discomfort, pain and damage can be experienced in a number of ways.

- Many women find their nipples are sensitive when hormonal changes take place—for example, pre-menstrually, during early pregnancy and the first few days after having a baby. If you have sensitive nipples you may initially find breastfeeding uncomfortable or painful at the beginning of a feed. The discomfort should only last up to thirty seconds. Sensitive nipples become less sensitive as the weeks go by, but a small number of women have sensitive nipples for up to three months while they are breastfeeding.
- Sore, grazed or blistered nipples are all signs of a damaged nipple. The nipple looks red and raw and sometimes there may be a blister which is filled with blood or clear fluid. See if you can get help as soon as possible to position your baby.
- Cracked nipples: A split appears which may be on the nipple or areola or both. A common place is where the nipple joins the areola.

WHAT CAN YOU DO?

- Get help to get the position right. If you are in hospital, ask for help from the staff.
- In the community you can visit your child and family health nurse, talk to an Australian Breastfeeding Association counsellor or in some areas there are community nurses/lactation consultants who help with breastfeeding problems at home.
- Remember to think carefully at every feed about your posture and position as well as your baby's. Don't leave your baby sucking if it continues to hurt after the first thirty seconds. Gently remove her and try again. Sometimes in the early weeks you might find you have to do this three or four times before it feels right.
- Fresh air and a little reflected sunlight helps.
- Gently hand express for about thirty seconds before feeding to soften the areola, draw out the nipple and start the milk flowing.

- Much as it would be nice to apply a magic cream or cure, there is no consistent evidence that any of the commonly used creams, sprays and ointments make any difference. Other cures such as grated carrot, geranium leaves and so on all appear at regular intervals, often hailed as the long-awaited answer to sore nipples. I have never seen any evidence that these things fix the problem either. Nevertheless, some women do find comfort in using some of these preparations. They can make the nipple feel better, which in turn stops breastfeeding from being abandoned even if they don't actually hasten the healing process. Gently massaging some expressed milk onto the nipple at the end of a feed appears to be as useful as anything else and has the added advantage of being free, safe and non-allergenic.

  If you do use something other than breastmilk on your nipples, be careful. Some preparations make things worse. Avoid nipple sprays in aerosol packs. They have ingredients which interfere with natural lubrication and the normal protective barrier of the nipple which prevents infection. They also contain a local anaesthetic which prevents you having any idea from the level of discomfort whether the baby's position is right.

  Cortisone, antifungal or antibiotic creams should not be used unless a specific skin problem is diagnosed. Most sore nipples are related to the way the baby takes the breast, not to skin conditions.

For most women with sore nipples, getting the position right, fresh air, a little indirect sunlight plus massaging expressed milk into the nipple is all that's needed. Most nipples improve rapidly in the first few weeks.

For those who find feeding painful beyond the first few weeks there are other things to try. Unfortunately all of these suggestions involve doing things which might upset the supply and demand system of breastfeeding and so cause more problems. These strategies include such things as using a nipple shield, limiting feeds or temporarily stopping breastfeeding from one or both breasts. Trying any of these tactics is best done with help from an experienced person who will help you get your baby back on the breast as quickly as possible. Such help, however, is not always available, so please go ahead and try them yourself if the thought of another breastfeed fills you with despair.

LIMITING FEEDS AND SUCKING TIME: It's often difficult to separate hunger from other aspects of baby behaviour when you're breastfeeding for the first time. Lots of normal, healthy, well-fed babies cry a lot, wake frequently or have endless fussy, unsettled times when they don't sleep. It's easy to see this behaviour as a breastfeeding problem and fall into a pattern of endless, frequent feeds which seem to run into each other all day and all night.

Very long sessions at the breast in the early weeks can contribute to sore nipples. When babies are left on the breast for a long time and mothers are tired the position can go wrong during the feed and nipples get hurt. Twenty minutes or so is all babies need to get what they need and drain the breast. If there are no nipple problems and you are happy, it's fine to feed as long and as often as you like, but if your nipples are sore or damaged, try limiting your feeds to twenty minutes or less (depending on your baby) and to about six every twenty-four hours until your nipples are feeling better.

TEMPORARILY STOPPING BREASTFEEDING ON ONE BREAST: Sometimes only one nipple is sore. This may be the right one if you are right-handed or the left one if you are left-handed because you are not as skilled at positioning your baby with whichever arm and hand you don't use as much.

Stopping feeding from the breast with the sore nipple and only feeding from the other breast for twenty-four hours works well for some mothers. Express the unused breast (by hand for comfort) if your baby is content on one breast, or express enough for top-ups (by hand, or electric pump if hand expressing is too tedious) from a bottle or cup if she needs extra. If you can't express enough for top-ups and your baby is not content with one breast, use formula when necessary.

After twenty-four hours put your baby back to the breast with the sore nipple, paying a lot of attention to your posture and her position. You may like to try the gradual approach, where you put her back to the breast by introducing one feed daily until you are fully breastfeeding again.

TEMPORARILY STOPPING BREASTFEEDING ON BOTH BREASTS: If both nipples are very sore you might consider stopping breastfeeding for a period of time until they feel better. You will need to express every three to four hours during the day to keep your supply going. Hand expressing is often advised in this situation. If you can hand express easily go ahead, but many women find it easier to use a hand pump or an electric pump. The expressed milk and/or formula is given to your baby from a bottle or cup. Complications can arise from doing this which you need to be aware of:

- Your milk supply may decrease.
- Expressing and feeding from a bottle or cup is tiring and time-consuming.
- Some babies are reluctant to go back to the breast after having bottles.
- Some babies will not drink from a bottle and miss the sucking if they drink from a cup, which makes them unsettled.

NIPPLE SHIELDS: A nipple shield is a soft rubber or silicone cap which fits over the nipple and areola. Using a nipple shield helps some women to breastfeed more comfortably until the nipple pain or discomfort gets better. It sounds great but there are disadvantages to using a nipple shield:

- A nipple shield forms a barrier between your breast and the baby's mouth so, as your breast doesn't get as clear a message to make milk, using a nipple shield can gradually reduce your supply.
- When you become used to using a nipple shield it is often hard to stop using it when you need to—that is, if your supply starts to decrease.
- Babies beyond the newborn stage often object to nipple shields, so starting to use them after about three weeks of age is not highly successful.
- Many women find feeding just as uncomfortable with a shield as without.

But a number of mothers and babies do find a nipple shield very useful and for them, using one stops breastfeeding from being abandoned. Occasionally nipple shields are used successfully for long periods of time.

- Choose a thin silicone shield.
- Remember to keep following the guidelines for your posture and your baby's position when you feed.
- Dry your nipples and areola gently. Lubricate the shield with a little breast milk so it will stay in place. Hand express a little milk into the nipple part of the shield before bringing your baby to the breast.

- Let your baby suck longer than she normally does to compensate for less stimulation to your breast.
- Plan to use the nipple shield as a short-term strategy only—try some feeds without it.
- If possible, stay in touch with an adviser who can help you try some feeds without the shield and make sure your milk is flowing.

On the positive side, nipples always get better, most in the first two to six weeks. Think of all the wonderful benefits of breastmilk and try to see sore nipples as a short-term problem in relation to the whole time you will be breastfeeding. Support from family and friends and help and encouragement from health workers do make an incredible difference.

Nipple problems are not inevitable but they are common. Everybody's pain threshold varies, so some women decide to wean. This is quite understandable when life is a constant round of painful feeds which never seem to improve and neither you nor your baby are happy.

Tongue tie and breastfeeding

Tongue tie refers to a condition where the baby's tongue is attached to the floor of the mouth rather than floating free. Mild tongue tie is very common in newborn babies and does not cause breastfeeding problems. Serious tongue tie is rare and more likely to be found in babies where such a condition runs in the family. A tiny number of babies have a degree of tongue tie that interferes with successful breastfeeding, resulting in damaged nipples and low milk supply (the baby is unable to adequately extend the tongue under the nipple). The incidence of this happening is unknown and surgical release of the tongue for breastfeeding problems in selected situations is occasionally performed. Case studies where this has been performed report successful outcomes, but it should only be considered after a full assessment of the baby and the breastfeeding problems. (See also Tongue tie, page 182.)

Needle-sharp pain

A few women experience a piercing, stabbing breast pain which may happen while the baby is sucking or in between feeds. Apart from these spasmodic pains the breast feels fine. Needle-sharp pain is different to mastitis or a blocked duct, where discomfort or pain is felt all the time. Needle-sharp pain is possibly due to the release of oxytocin (which tightens the muscles around the milk sacs in the breast). As it is spasmodic and gradually fades it is something women learn to live with. It usually disappears some time in the first three months. It's possible for a woman to experience it with one baby and not another. Needle-sharp pain is often diagnosed as a fungal infection of the nipple or breast, but may not respond to treatment either because there is no fungal infection or, rarely, because the fungus is a species resistant to the anti-fungal medication being used (see page 138).

Delays in getting breastfeeding started

Sometimes it is not possible for babies to go straight to the breast; for example, premature babies or babies who have problems at birth and need to be in an intensive care unit for a while. Many women and babies breast-feed well after difficult beginnings. Your milk flow can be stimulated and kept going by massage and expressing until your baby is able to take all her feeds from the breast. Here's a guide:

- It's a good idea to start expressing as soon as possible after birth but don't panic if there are delays. If you are very tired, distressed or in any discomfort, wait until you feel you can handle learning how to express. When you are ready, a midwife can show you how to hand express. Hand expressing is best to begin with. After the milk is flowing a hand pump or electric pump can be used. Keep asking for help after you are shown what to do if your technique doesn't seem to be working. See How to express and store breastmilk, page 114.
- Regardless of the amount of milk you express, don't give up. In the beginning you might only express a few drops of colostrum—don't throw it away, even tiny amounts are good for your baby to have. Once the mature milk is flowing, try not to compare how much you express with how much someone else expresses. Remember, babies stimulate and remove the milk much more efficiently than expressing does; once your baby is sucking regularly your supply will build up.
- The transition from tube feeding or bottle feeding to breastfeeding is a challenge. Many premature or sick babies take the breast well and suck

strongly, others take quite a long time to learn what to do. When this happens, expert help from the midwives and lactation consultants who work in maternity hospitals is needed for a while.

FOR MORE INFORMATION

Chapter 16: For Parents *(contraception and breastfeeding, page 353, health professionals you may come in contact with, page 337)*
Chapter 13: Growth and Development *(rooting reflex, page 252; weighing babies, page 249)*
Chapter 14: Sleeping and Waking in the First Six Months *(settling techniques, page 270)*
Chapter 15: The Crying Baby *(wind, page 294)*
Chapter 10: Early Worries and Queries *(blue around baby's mouth, page 170)*
Chapter 8: Breastfeeding Your Baby After the First Two Weeks *(Candida albicans (thrush), page 138)*

FURTHER READING

The Politics of Breastfeeding, Gabrielle Palmer (Co-ordinator, Baby Milk Action Coalition (BMAC), Rivers Oram Press, 1993. Available in Australian bookshops, this book is a fascinating look at the growth of artificial feeding over the last century. Read it with an open mind—it can give you a whole new perspective on infant feeding.

Breastfeeding Matters, Maureen Minchin, Alma Publications, 4th edition, 1998. A breastfeeding classic. As with the above book, much of the information gives a fresh perspective to many of the dilemmas surrounding infant feeding. Available direct from Alma Publications, PO Box 1569, Business Mail Centre, Gheringhap St, Geelong, Victoria, 3220 or The Lactation Resource Centre, 1800 032 926, www.breastfeeding.asn.au

Breastfeeding with Confidence: A do-it-yourself guide, Sue Cox, Finch Publishing, Australia, 2008. A detailed guide for getting breastfeeding started and established by an experienced hands-on lactation consultant which, if you are having early difficulties, you may like to refer to in addition to *Baby Love*.

Chapter 7

Bottle Feeding Your Baby For the First Two Weeks

Bottle or breast, there are some wonderful aspects of feeding a baby and terrible ones. Feeding is a very basic function, an integral part of mothering, and as such, immensely satisfying. But it can also be frustrating, and, at times, unbelievably disgusting.

HELEN TOWNSEND, *BABY CRAZY*

Breastfeeding and formula feeding are very emotional issues for lots of reasons. There may be feelings of disappointment when breastfeeding doesn't work out and a sense of loss or even anger that something promoted as easy and pleasant turned out to be problematic and stressful.

Women usually wean because breastfeeding problems arise which either seem impossible to solve *or are* impossible to solve any other way. (See page 154 for more on weaning.)

It's as important for women who are bottle feeding to have accurate, detailed information about formula feeding as it is for women who are breastfeeding.

Bottle feeding babies is so much a part of modern living it is very much taken for granted. Safe bottle feeding, however, depends on a healthy water supply, enough money to meet the costs, refrigeration, clean surroundings and satisfactory arrangements for cleaning and storing equipment. Parents without literacy skills or parents who do not speak English need extra help to make sure their bottle feeding is done safely.

If you are unsure of whether you want to breastfeed or not, remember that weaning and formula feeding is an option at any time. Breastfeeding isn't, and once you start to wean it can be difficult to go back to breastfeeding.

When babies are not breastfed or have a combination of breastmilk and formula it is very important to make sure that the substitute milk they are receiving meets as much of the baby's nutritional needs as possible. It is also important to make sure it is mixed, stored and handled properly so the baby does not get sick.

What's in formula?

It's good to have an idea of what's in formula so you know what you are giving your baby.

Commercial artificial milk for babies has been around since 1900. Early attempts to mimic breastmilk were disastrous. Apart from no one having any idea what the ingredients should be, poor bottle and teat design, unhygienic practices and surroundings and unhealthy water all contributed to a high infant mortality rate. During last century general improvements in the standard of living, better-designed bottles and teats and the growing realisation of the complexity of breastmilk has helped make formula feeding safer.

Infant formula is made from either cow's milk, goat's milk or soya beans. Formula made from cow's milk has been around the longest, suits most babies and is considered to be the safest. The cow's milk, goat's milk or soy liquid is altered to overcome the dangers of giving babies these substances unmodified. Formula is being constantly changed to try to get nutritional profiles closer to that of breastmilk.

Infant Formula Standard

Food Standards Australia New Zealand is responsible for the Infant Formula Standard, which consists of an acceptable *range* of macronutrients and micronutrients. All infant formulas sold in Australia must meet the Standard.

Choosing a formula

All infant formula varies but there is no 'best' formula. The variations between brands and types of formula mostly centre on the balance and types of fat, protein and carbohydrates that are used; however, there are ingredients that are found in some products and not others. (See next page.)

'STANDARD FROM BIRTH' FORMULA

The recommended choice is a cow's milk formula labelled 'standard from birth'. Cost is as good a criterion as any when selecting a brand—price and whether formulas are sold in supermarkets or pharmacies bear no relation to their quality or nutritional value.

FOLLOW-ON 'MILK'

Follow-on 'milk' has no advantages over 'standard from birth' formula unless it is cheaper. However, as it is higher in protein and electrolytes it should **not** be given to babies under six months. This preparation is not necessary for most babies as, ideally, extra protein comes via food from a spoon. By twelve months babies should be offered a variety of foods including cow's milk and as soon as possible be drinking both milk and water from a cup.

Features of 'standard from birth' formula made from cow's milk

PROTEIN: Human milk protein consists of 65 per cent whey ('soft' protein) and 35 per cent casein ('hard' protein); however, cow's milk contains only 18 per cent whey and 82 per cent casein. Cow's milk protein in formula is altered so the proportion of whey to casein is like that of human milk. Most formula for use from birth has a proportion of 60 per cent whey/40 per cent casein.

CARBOHYDRATE: Lactose is the carbohydrate found in mammal's milk. Human milk has a higher lactose content than cow's milk, so extra lactose is added to formula. The carbohydrate in standard formulas is 100 per cent lactose; in 'anti-reflux' formula it is maltodextrin; and soy and low-lactose formulas contain carbohydrates in the forms of corn starch, corn-syrup solids, dried glucose syrup or sucrose.

FAT: Over half the calories in breastmilk and formula are derived from fat. The fat in cow's milk is different to that in human milk, so formula also contains a blend of vegetable oils (palm, coconut, oleic safflower and soy) to get a fatty acid profile more like breastmilk.

Formula is supplemented with vitamins, minerals and trace elements.

New ingredients in formula

The following ingredients are all relatively recent additions to formula in Australia, though they have been in use in formulas overseas for some time.

[ALPHA]-LACTALBUMIN (BOVINE): [Alpha]-lactalbumin is the major protein in breastmilk. Apart from its nutritional value it has antibacterial and immune-boosting properties that protect against infection, and is a major source of tryptophan, which plays a part in neurological development. Cow's milk also contains [alpha]-lactalbumin and some formulas are now supplemented with bovine [alpha]-lactalbumin.

NUCLEOTIDES: Nucleotides are the basic building blocks of RNA and DNA, and are important in periods of rapid growth. They are found in higher amounts in human milk than in cow's milk and are thought to enhance the immune system, improve iron absorption and help maintain 'good' bacteria populations. Nucleotides used in formula are purified from plant yeast.

LONG-CHAIN POLYUNSATURATED FATTY ACIDS (LCPUFAS): LCPUFAs are essential fatty acids obtained through the diet. Breastmilk has many unique LCPUFAs, among them DHA (docosahexaenoic acid) and AA (arachidonic acid), which contribute to cognitive and visual development. Some 'standard from birth' formulas contain DHA and AA extracted from various sources such as fish oil, egg yolk lipid, fungus and marine algae.

PROBIOTICS: Probiotics are live, active, 'good' bacteria such as are found naturally in yoghurt and fermented milk. Unlike cow's milk, breastmilk contains a high proportion of non-digestible sugars that feed 'good' bacteria in the gut. These bacteria are important in immune development as well as providing a barrier to intestinal infections. The probiotics organisms found in formula are *similar* to those in the guts of breastfed babies, though not the same.

NEW INGREDIENTS: THINGS YOU NEED TO KNOW

- At time of writing (January 2009) none of these new ingredients have been used for long enough or have been tested in sufficient depth to confirm their claimed benefits.
- It remains uncertain, doubtful even, whether they function in a similar way to their counterparts in breastmilk.
- Comparisons between formulas containing various combinations of these ingredients and formulas that contain none of them are limited and so far have not yielded anything conclusive.
- If there is conclusive evidence that a formula ingredient is beneficial and/or essential for baby health—for example, iron—then it is mandatory for it to be added to all brands and types of formulas. As there is not enough accumulated evidence to show that these ingredients are essential, their addition to all formulas is not mandatory. This explains the confusing situation at the moment where the inclusion of all or some of them varies between formulas. To find out, read the labels carefully.
- While there is no conclusive proof of their benefits nor has there been any proof of harm for healthy, full-term babies.
- Formulas with these ingredients are more expensive. Bear in mind if you use one you are paying extra for a *potential*, not a proven, benefit. There is no formula on the market that is 'closest to breastmilk' even if advertising on the side of the tin gives you the impression this might be the case.

Specialised formulas

These formulas (described below) are not advantageous for most babies and may cause problems. Using one of these formulas or changing to one from a standard cow's milk formula because your baby is unsettled, a fussy feeder, a happy regurgitator or has a rash is unlikely to make any difference.

HYPOALLERGENIC (HA) FORMULA

The cow's milk protein in hypoallergenic formula is partially artificially broken down with the aim of minimising food allergy and intolerance. Recent research from the CSIRO suggests that whole-milk proteins broken down naturally by digestion may play a significant role in growth, preventing infections, developing immunity and supporting mineral transport. Ideally whole breastmilk proteins are the best, but when breastmilk is not available a standard cow's milk formula is preferable to HA formula **unless** there is a high risk of allergy (where both parents or one parent and a sibling have a confirmed allergy). See Allergies and food intolerance on page 384.

SOY FORMULA

There is no role for soy formula any more and it is anticipated that it will eventually be phased out. There have long been concerns about nutritional and other problems with its use. These include the presence of plant hormones and high levels of aluminium. Some research has shown a higher incidence of infection in babies fed on soy formula. Soy formula does not help babies with 'colic', excessive crying or sleep problems. Babies at high risk of allergy (as per HA formula) should, ideally, be breastfed, or seek professional advice regarding which formula to use. Formula-fed babies with a proven diagnosis of lactose intolerance can usually be given a low-lactose cow's milk formula.

LOW-LACTOSE FORMULA

Low-lactose formula is a cow's milk formula with reduced levels of lactose, used for babies with lactose intolerance (see page 299). The most appropriate use of this product is in older formula-fed babies recovering from gastroenteritis.

'ANTI-REFLUX' (AR) THICKENED FORMULA

This formula aims to lessen the amounts of milk regurgitating babies bring up (see page 188), and is primarily designed to ease parent anxiety. There is rarely a medical requirement for 'anti-reflux' formula.

GOAT'S MILK FORMULA

There are no benefits or medical indications for using this formula.

GENETICALLY MODIFIED (GM) FORMULA

The use of genetically modified components in formula has not been prohibited by government regulations. The constituents most likely to be affected are those of soybean origin, but any formula may contain GM protein as other constituents derived from soybean products, such as lecithin, are used in cow's milk formula. For information, call formula hotlines.

Safe bottle feeding

If you start breastfeeding and then decide to wean, talk to your midwife or, if you have left hospital, your child and family health nurse about the best way to do this. Gradual weaning is much more comfortable than stopping breastfeeding suddenly. Unless there's an emergency there's no need to do anything quickly. Medication is no longer used owing to risks associated with its use.

A word about 'sterilisation'

Sterilisation is somewhat of a nonsense word we use in relation to caring for babies' feeding utensils at home. Sterilisation is an operation theatre technique where the aim is a complete absence of all micro-organisms. This is not only an impossible feat in the average kitchen but not necessary for the baby's wellbeing.

Cleanliness is next to godliness and is a vital component of bottle feeding and expressing and storing breastmilk. Thorough cleaning and disinfecting of equipment as well as close attention to hand washing to make sure any harmful bacteria are destroyed is what is required.

HERE'S A BASIC LIST OF EQUIPMENT

- **4–6 large bottles**

  A large variety is available. Bottles are made of clear glass (heavy, breakable) or polycarbonate (rigid plastic, light, unbreakable). Concerns were raised in 2008 in Canada about the chemical Bisphenol-A (BPA) used in the production of polycarbonate plastic. Studies on animals suggest that BPA can affect neural development and behaviour when animals are exposed to this chemical in early life. Canadian scientists involved in the study of BPA do not believe, at this time, that there is a link between BPA and obesity and breast and prostate cancer, as has been claimed by some sources.

  While BPA used in the manufacture of bottles and cups is a concern in relation to babies and toddlers under eighteen months, exposure levels are below those that could cause health effects, so don't panic. There are also no adverse effects reported as a direct consequence from the use of baby bottles/cups with BPA in the past. Nevertheless since exposure rates are close to levels where potential ill-effects could occur in the vulnerable population of babies and toddlers, it is advisable to avoid or reduce their exposure to BPA. Some governments are looking at banning the import/manufacture of polycarbonate baby bottles and cups.

Here are some steps you can take to minimise the very small risks of BPA:

- Choose BPA-free products. Glass is the obvious alternative but as it is heavy and breakable it is nowhere near as convenient. Several alternatives to polycarbonate exist, and more will be arriving on the market as the word gets out. Polycarbonate products usually have a 7 in the centre of a recycling symbol on the base, often with a PC beside it.
- If you are using polycarbonate bottles do not put boiling water into the bottles as very hot water causes BPA to migrate out of the bottle at a much higher rate. Water should be boiled then cooled in a non-BPA container before transferring it to baby bottles.
- Bottles can be disinfected in the normal way and washed in dishwashers. Make sure the bottles have cooled down before you use them.
- When heating made-up formula aim for room temperature, no hotter (in fact, many babies don't mind cold milk). Heating polycarbonate bottles in bottle warmers or microwave ovens is risky as it's too easy to overdo it and, in the case of bottle warmers, there's a risk of contaminated milk if the bottle is left in the warmer for too long. (I don't recommend either heating method regardless of the type of bottles).

Other bottle tips

Many bottle manufacturers offer a range of different shaped bottles, bottles with 'handles' and bottles with anti-colic devices. These are all marketing ploys, not science. Decorations and odd-shaped bottles make bottles hard to clean. There's nothing clever about encouraging babies to clutch at handles and 'feed themselves', and strange shapes do not prevent 'wind' or 'colic' so stick to plain bottles.

- **Several teats**

  Teats are either made from rubber, also called latex (brown coloured) or silicone (clear coloured).

  Latex teats cost less, are softer and preferred by some babies, and there is the issue of nitrosamines to consider (see page 55). Companies that manufacture latex teats manufacture silicone teats as well, so if the thought of nitrosamines bothers you, try silicone. Silicone teats are harder and cost more, but last longer. Less elasticity means they are liable to tear and that bits can break off, which makes them a possible choking hazard. Inspect them frequently by holding them up to the light. If they look faulty throw them away.

  Shape variations have no particular advantages (as in orthodontic teats) unless your baby prefers that shape. There are no superior bottles and teats. Some babies may prefer one system to another but, in general, constantly changing bottles and teats is a needless expense.
- **A knife for levelling the powder**
- **A bottle brush to clean the bottles and teats**
- **Disinfecting equipment**

  It's advisable to disinfect bottle feeding equipment until your baby's immune system is mature enough to protect her against nasties. If you live where there is clean water, clean surroundings and refrigeration you do not need to keep disinfecting after your baby is six months old.

  Rinse everything in cold water straight after use. Before disinfecting wash carefully in hot, soapy water. Rinse well again. Washing is important—disinfecting doesn't work if old milk is left on bottles and teats. Give teats and dummies an extra good scrub.

When you disinfect choose between:

(A) BOILING

Place utensils in a large saucepan.

Cover with water.

Bring to boil and boil for five minutes, adding teats for the last two minutes.

Please take care when boiling equipment to avoid scalding yourself or children. One way to reduce this risk is to allow the equipment to cool in the saucepan until it is hand hot before moving it and, as often as possible, to do your boiling when the children are not around.

Store equipment you are not going to use straight away in a clean container in the fridge.

Boil clean equipment every twenty-four hours.

(B) DISINFECTING USING CHEMICALS

A chemical sterilant is an anti-bacterial solution which comes in liquid or tablet form. The chemical used is a bleach which is diluted with water to a safe solution so it will not harm your baby although it does kill harmful bacteria.

Follow the manufacturer's instructions carefully when you make up the solution. The instructions will tell you how to dilute the tablets or liquid. After a twenty-four hour period discard the used solution, thoroughly scrub the container and equipment in warm, soapy water and renew the solution.

Make sure all your equipment is plastic or glass, not metal, as metal corrodes when left in chemical sterilant.

Completely submerge everything and leave it all in the solution for the recommended time before using. Equipment may be left in the solution indefinitely when it is not in use. Store the concentrate and solution well out of the reach of children.

(C) STEAM STERILISERS

Steam sterilisers are automatic units which raise the temperature quickly to the range which kills harmful bacteria. To use, place clean equipment into the unit, add water according to the manufacturer's instructions and switch on. The unit switches itself off when the job is done.

(D) MICROWAVE STEAM STERILISERS

Sterilising units for use in microwave ovens have recently appeared on the market. They are suitable to use as long as the manufacturer's instructions are followed.

Using formula

When formula powder or liquid formula is combined with water, all of your baby's food and drink needs are being met. The finished product is only as good as the manufacturer claims if the formula is reconstituted properly.

Here's some important information

- The strength of formula is designed to remain constant so you never have to strengthen or weaken the mixture. As your baby grows it is the amount that increases, not the strength.
- Always use the scoop that comes with the particular brand of formula you are using. Scoops are not interchangeable between brands. Never use half scoops of powder.
- If you use concentrated liquid formula, use equal proportions of formula and water unless otherwise stated.
- If you change brands of powdered formula remember to check the number of scoops per ml of boiled water. The proportions vary between brands.
- When in doubt, check with a pharmacist, child and family health nurse or doctor.

Making your baby's feeds

Prolonged boiling of water has been found to be unnecessary when making up formula. To prepare water for making up formula, the electric jug should be emptied, refilled with tap water prior to use and brought to the boil. Jugs with no automatic 'cut off' should be switched off within thirty seconds of boiling.

Always allow the water to cool before adding the powder or liquid.

The preferred and safest method for making formula at home is 'in the bottle', one at a time, because:

- It reduces contamination.
- It reduces the amount of equipment needed.
- It reduces the possibility of mistakes when mixing the water and scoops of formula—if a mistake is made it is only for one feed.

- If you prefer preparing formula for a twenty-four-hour period it is safer to prepare five to seven individual bottles than prepare the formula in a jug.

To prepare the bottles

- Measure the amount of cooled, boiled water required into individual bottles.
- Using the scoop from the formula tin, measure the required number of scoops into the bottles. Use a knife to level off each scoop.
- Seal the bottle with a cap and disc and shake gently to mix it.
- Store all made-up formula in the centre back of the fridge where it is coldest, not in the door where it is warmer.
- Throw out any formula not used after twenty-four hours.

To prepare formula in a jug

Many parents do prepare formula in a jug for use over a twenty-four hour period. This is acceptable when refrigeration is available and as long as the correct proportions (scoops to ml of water) are calculated.

- Double-check the proportions needed for twenty-four hours with someone else if you are unsure. If there is no one to ask, it is better to make up the formula one feed at a time, in the bottle.
- Measure the cooled, boiled water into a measuring jug with clear levels marked on the side.
- Using the scoop from the formula tin, measure the required number of scoops into the measuring jug. Use a knife to level off each scoop. Avoid distractions when counting the scoops. Take the phone off the hook and turn off the radio. Have pen and paper handy to jot down the number of scoops you are up to if you are interrupted.
- Store the mixture in the centre of the back of the refrigerator in either the covered jug or individual feeding bottles.

Safety tips

- Always wash your hands and work surfaces before preparing formula.
- Put formula straight into the fridge as soon as it is made.
- Storing half-empty bottles for future use is risky as they quickly become

Safe bottle feeding steps

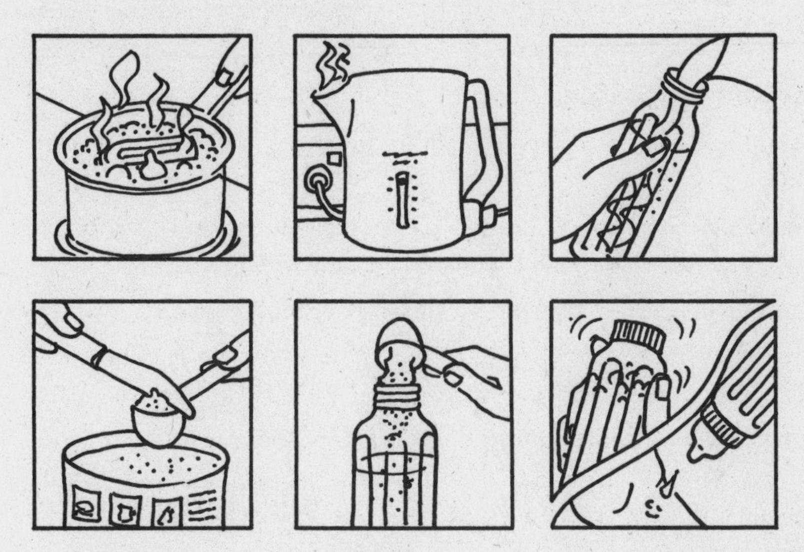

contaminated once they have been heated and sucked on. Throw away the contents of used bottles after an hour.

- Check the expiry date on tins of formula and discard them if they are out of date.
- Discard any opened tin of formula after one month.
- The safest way to transport formula is to take the cooled, boiled water and the powdered formula in separate containers and mix them when needed. If transporting prepared formula or expressed breastmilk it must be icy cold when you leave home and carried in a thermal baby bottle pack to keep it cold. If you cannot heat the bottle when you reach your destination it's quite all right to give it as it is.
- Never leave bottles warming for more than about ten minutes. Bacteria multiply rapidly in warm milk—this is a common cause of diarrhoea.

Giving the bottle

Giving babies cold formula is not at all harmful and at times may be safer than trying to heat it quickly (for example in a microwave oven in a busy restaurant). Warming to room temperature is the generally acceptable way

Giving the bottle

to give it but if your baby is flexible about the temperature of her milk it does make it easier for you when you are out and about.

Standing the bottle in warm to hot water is the traditional way (and remains the safest) of heating bottles. Bottle warmers are convenient and safe as long as they have a thermostat control, but remember not to leave bottles warming in them longer than ten minutes. Microwaves are not recommended because of the safety aspects—babies end up with burnt mouths because the temperature of the milk is misjudged or because of hot spots in the milk.

Teats and getting the formula to flow right

Initially it's often tricky getting the milk to flow just right. You may find you have to try several types of teat before your baby is happy. To test the flow, hold the bottle upside down when it is filled with the milk mixture at room temperature—the milk should drip steadily. If you have to shake it vigorously it is too slow and your baby will go to sleep before she drinks what she needs. The milk should drip easily at a steady rate without pouring out in a great stream. A little leakage at the corner of her mouth while she feeds is nothing to worry about; as she gets older this will stop. If you have difficulty finding the perfect teat, always go for a faster teat rather than a slow one.

Feed time

Before giving the bottle, always check the temperature of the feed by shaking a little from the teat onto the inside of your wrist.

Make yourself comfortable and cuddle your baby close to you, holding her gently and firmly. If she feels secure and cosy the feeding will be more enjoyable for you both.

Put the teat against her lips. She will open her mouth and start to suck. Keep the neck of the bottle at an angle so the neck of the bottle is filled with the milk mixture. When she stops sucking strongly or when she drinks about half the milk, gently remove the bottle and see if she wants to burp (see burping, page 87).

If she has gone to sleep, unwrap her, put her over your shoulder, rub her back and stroke her head, legs and tummy to wake her up. Wait until she is in an alert state before offering her the rest of the milk.

How long does it take to drink the bottle?

This varies tremendously between babies but roughly it takes between ten and thirty minutes. Less than ten is too fast when they are young as they are not getting all the sucking time they need to feel contented. More than thirty is too slow for most babies and means they are probably falling off to sleep before drinking quite enough. Adjust the flow as best you can to suit your baby; either by screwing the plastic attachment on the neck of the bottle tighter or by trying different teats. As babies grow older they take a lot less time to drink their bottles.

Safety tip

It is dangerous to 'prop' a bottle and walk away, leaving baby to manage on her own. The milk may flow too quickly and cause her to splutter or even choke so she can't breathe. As well, babies who feed a lot on their own are at greater risk of ear infections. Babies need to be held, cuddled and talked to when they are fed.

Bottle feeding twins

When one baby is asleep and one awake, you can nurse and feed. When they are both awake and hungry at the same time change them both, give each one a cuddle, then sit them in either portable baby chairs or propped up together on a lounge. Sit in front of them and feed one baby with one hand and one with the other. Make sure you are comfortable and not straining your back, neck or arms while you feed.

Of course, hold them for feeds whenever possible, but when it's not, sit them close together and chat away while you give them their bottles. Don't worry if one drinks more than the other—twins are like any other two individual babies and may drink different amounts.

Bottle feeding premature babies

When premature babies are very young and/or sick the volume of milk is restricted and monitored closely, but by the time they go home they are ready to follow the same guidelines as for full-term babies. Premature babies do better with faster teats or teats that have a cross-cut rather than a hole.

How much milk?

Bottle fed babies, like breastfed babies, drink variable amounts and may have some feeds close together and others further apart. Your baby needs 150–200ml per kilo of body weight per day until she is three months old, then 120ml per kilo of body weight. These amounts are divided into six to seven feeds every twenty-four hours and offered on demand.

Please remember there are many individual variations on these amounts and number of bottles. Information about the quantity for age on formula tins is a guide only and may not necessarily suit your baby. Many babies never drink the 'required amount' for their age and size, others need more.

(Note: Number of feeds relates to the volume in the bottle, i.e. less volume, more bottles, and more volume, fewer bottles)

Age	**Weight**	**Volume**	**Feeds**
Birth to one week		30–60ml	6–8 bottles every 24 hours
One to four weeks	150ml per kilo of body weight	60–120ml	5–8 bottles every 24 hours
Four to eight weeks	150ml per kilo of body weight	120–150ml	5–8 bottles every 24 hours
Eight to twelve weeks	150ml per kilo of body weight	150–210ml	5–7 bottles every 24 hours
Three months to six months	120ml per kilo of body weight	150–240ml	4–5 bottles a day
Six to nine months		120–180ml	2–4 bottles a day or drinks from a cup as well as 3 meals a day*
Nine to twelve months		120–180ml	2–3 bottles a day or drinks from a cup and 3 meals

**Babies who are breastfed and/or use cups rarely drink the volume of liquid consumed by babies who drink from bottles—this is not a problem.*

Plenty of wet nappies, consistent weight gains that are not excessive and a thriving, active baby mean all is well.

FOR MORE INFORMATION

Chapter 15: The Crying Baby, page 285 *(lactose intolerance, protein intolerance, 'wind', 'colic' and the relationship of formula)*
Chapter 14: Sleeping and Waking in the First Six Months, page 265
Chapter 24: Feeding Your Baby *(introduction of whole cow's milk, page 452)*
Chapter 9: Bottle Feeding Your Baby After the First Two Weeks *(early weaning, page 154)*

Chapter 8

Breastfeeding Your Baby After the First Two Weeks

Your diet

Sometimes so much is made of 'the mother's diet' that women choose to use formula because they incorrectly believe they have to make unacceptable changes to their diet. Breastfeeding is a body function and like any body function works better if you are well nourished. Eating well helps you enjoy your breastfeeding and your baby more and helps your body adjust to the extra work.

On the other hand, women who live where there is never enough food manage to breastfeed well—so even when diets fall short of the ideal your baby will still thrive. It is only in extreme cases that the mother's diet affects the quality of breastmilk. After all, breastfeeding ensured our survival 40,000 years ago when humans had very little in the way of food reserves. Let's dispel a few myths:

- You do not have to eat enough for two. Women's bodies seem to conserve energy when they breastfeed. As well, fat stores laid down during pregnancy provide extra energy. Regular meals are the best way to go, so try not to skip meals. Alternatively, frequent snacks throughout the day might suit you better until you are used to your new life and worked out who is going to prepare the meals!

- You do not have to drink heaps of any sort of fluid to 'make milk', including cow's milk. You will notice that you are often thirsty when you feed, so drink what you need to, to relieve your thirst.
- There is no food or beverage that 'makes more milk'.
- Baby rashes, baby poo, baby crying and all the strange and wonderful things babies do in the first three months are rarely anything to do with what their mothers are eating. Eat your normal diet, experiment with food you don't normally eat—if you think it upsets your baby don't eat it again for a while. Restricting your diet while breastfeeding (avoiding peanuts, for example) to prevent sensitisation by the baby and thus future allergy problems is no longer recommended. See page 384 for more on food allergy and intolerance.

  Take no notice when well-meaning people around you suggest something you're eating is upsetting your baby or giving her a rash. Think about women from other cultures who have been eating 'spicy' food and breastfeeding for thousands of years as you enjoy a chocolate after dinner.

Feeding patterns

Breastfeeding is not like bottle feeding, where the volume taken per feed increases and the number of bottles every twenty-four hours decreases as the baby gets older. Most women need to keep breastfeeding six times or more every twenty-four hours to maintain the milk supply; however, the sucking time usually decreases, often quite dramatically, between six weeks and three months. Breastfeeding around this time becomes easy, often sensual and pleasurable without having to worry any more about the all-important 'position'. This pattern of breastfeeding continues until a reasonable amount of food from a spoon is going down (between six and eight months), at which time **if you want** to or if **your baby decides** to, you can start to decrease the number of breastfeeds. For breastfeeding tips on what to do if your baby sleeps all night from a young age see page 276.

How to express and store breastmilk

Expressing isn't an essential part of breastfeeding, but being able to express your breastmilk is a very handy skill for a few different reasons, for example:

- When breastfeeding is delayed after birth.
- To relieve engorged breasts in the early days. Hand expressing helps soften the nipple and areola so it's easier for your baby to get a good mouthful of breast.
- To remove a little milk before feeding if your supply is abundant and your baby is being overwhelmed by a sudden rush of milk.
- For your comfort if your baby refuses one breast or goes through a phase of breast refusal. (See Breast refusal, page 142.)
- To remove a little milk if your breasts still feel lumpy and uncomfortable after a feed.
- For times when you won't be around for a feed—study, returning to paid work or a night out.

Learning how to express can be messy and tedious and, like whistling or riding a bike, some women find it easier than others. Many women breastfeed and never express. If you can't express much milk it does not mean you have a low supply. Your baby can stimulate and remove the milk much more effectively than you can. Whichever expressing method you use, you will find switching breasts frequently increases the amount you express and relieves your fingers (if hand expressing) and arms. Switching frequently also lessens the chance of hurting your breasts by trying to express milk after the flow has slowed down.

N.B.: Expressing is different from breastfeeding. When breastfeeding, the baby is not rapidly swapped from one breast to another.

Expressing can be done by hand expressing, by using a hand pump or by using an electric pump.

Hand expressing

There are lots of good things about hand expressing.

- It's convenient and free.

Expressing by hand

- Skin-to-skin contact stimulates milk production more efficiently and makes the let-down easier.

Hand expressing seems awkward and slow in the beginning, but many women find it becomes easy and efficient with a little practice. When you express, the aim is to stimulate the let-down reflex, then, by putting pressure where the milk is stored (under the areola), removing the milk. Gentle pressure is applied to the areola, not the nipple or the breast.

Wash your hands before you start. There are a few different ways of hand expressing and once you know the basics you will probably find your own style.

Here's one way. Think of expressing as two separate actions.

(A) ASSISTING THE LET-DOWN: Support one breast from underneath with the opposite hand. Massage your breast gently but firmly with your free hand. Use a circular motion similar to that recommended for self breast examination, paying particular attention to the underneath part and the part along the side of your breast near your arm as this is where most of the glands where the milk is made are located. After massaging, stroke the breast with a feather-light touch using all your fingers. Stroke from the top of your breast to your nipple.

This technique for helping the let-down is used for whichever method of expressing you are using.

If there is going to be a long time before your baby can go to the breast because she is premature or sick and you are expressing every three hours or so, thinking about your baby and looking at her photo can help stimulate your milk. A quiet place and some relaxation techniques help too.

(B) EXPRESSING THE MILK: Until you get used to hand expressing don't worry about collecting the milk. Practising in the shower or bath is relaxing, or simply squirt the milk into a towel.

Support your breast in one hand. Place your thumb and first two fingers of the other hand on the edge of the areola—the thumb is above, the fingers below. When hand expressing the aim is to move the milk along the ducts in the breast and empty the stored milk under the areola so you use your fingers in the same way a baby sucks.

Here's the tricky part. Push your thumb and finger into your breast then compress your thumb and fingers together. Repeat the action. Push in, compress, push in, compress. Rotate your fingers and thumb around the areola to express all the stored milk. Swap hands when the position of your thumb and fingers becomes awkward.

Avoid pinching or squeezing the nipple as this closes up the milk ducts and the milk won't flow—it also hurts!

Until you are used to hand expressing it's easier to use a clean wide bowl held between your legs or on a low table to catch the milk so both your hands are free; leaning forward means gravity helps the let-down. Have a towel handy. Later, when you can do it better, hold a clean container near your breast and express into it.

Expressing milk for storage takes twenty to thirty minutes in the early weeks. After your milk is flowing well it takes less time. Try expressing each breast for five to seven minutes, three to five minutes then two to three minutes. These times are just a guide—when the milk dwindles, change breasts. Never try and force milk out when it's not coming easily. Handle your breasts gently, as putting pressure on them can cause bruising and discomfort.

Expressing with a hand or electric pump

Some women find it easier to express using hand or electric pumps. There are now many types of hand, battery-operated and electric pumps available. Breast pumps have improved out of sight in relation to efficiency, comfort and ease of use but there are still some duds out there so do some research before you buy. Ask your friends for recommendations, the ABA or try this website devoted to breast pump research—www.babylovesyourmilk.com It is American, however, many of the brands are available here.

HAND PUMPS

Hand pumps are more economical to buy but more tiring to use if you are expressing regularly several times a day for any length of time. The technique for using a hand pump is similar to hand expressing. Use the same massage and stroking techniques to stimulate the let-down, arrange for privacy and go slowly and gently.

ELECTRIC AND BATTERY-OPERATED PUMPS

Battery-operated pumps suit some people as they are easier to use than hand pumps and cheaper than electric pumps. Do your research before buying (see above). Electric pumps are more efficient and less tiring when expressed milk is needed for any length of time. Electric pumps are also useful occasionally to increase the milk supply. Electric pumps are expensive to buy and may be hired to use at home from pharmacies, Australian Breastfeeding Association (ABA) or specialist retail outlets. ABA only has limited supplies and gives priority to mothers with sick or premature babies. If you don't have anyone to show you how to use an electric pump, follow the instructions for use carefully to avoid infection or getting bugs in your milk.

When is the best time to express?

When to express depends on *why* you are expressing:

- When your baby can't go to the breast for a long time. If your baby is sick or premature, most of the time you will need to express about eight times every twenty-four hours. You can be flexible about the length of time in between—expressing does not have to be done every three or four hours. The more you express, the more milk you will make; however, it is also important that you look after yourself as well. Six hours of undisturbed sleep at night is good for you.

- Returning to full-time paid work. (See Paid work and breastfeeding, page 389.)
- For times when you won't be there—regular absences for study, part-time paid work or voluntary work or for occasional absences.

While they are fully breastfeeding as well, most women find it difficult to express enough for one feed in one expressing session, so don't be surprised if it takes several days to express enough for one feed. It is quite normal to only be able to express 30–40ml a day. Think ahead, express daily and store the expressed milk in the freezer until you have enough so you are not under pressure to produce enough milk for a feed on Saturday morning before going out on Saturday night—very stressful! If you expect to have regular absences it is a good idea to express and freeze milk daily.

The best times to do this are:

- After a feed when there is likely to be extra milk available. Early morning feeds after you and your baby have slept are often a good time.
- In between feeds when you are pretty sure your baby is going to sleep for three or more hours—try pumping after she has been asleep for two hours.
- Any time when your supply is abundant and your baby fills up on one breast. Feed on one breast and express the other.

How much to express?

A guide is 150ml per kilo of body weight for each twenty-four hour period when babies are under three months. This may be anything from 60ml to 240ml depending on your baby's age and size. When it's for an occasional bottle a rough estimate is fine.

FOR EXAMPLE: 0–4 weeks, 60–120ml
4–8 weeks, 120–150ml
8–12 weeks, 150–240ml

If for some reason all your baby's feeds are going to be expressed breastmilk given in a bottle, please refer to the section on bottle feeding for more information. When expressing for occasional feeds, be kind to your babysitter and leave a little extra when you can, as babies can often drink faster from a bottle than the breast then look around for more.

Storing breastmilk

Breastmilk can be stored in plastic containers, plastic or glass bottles or disposable, sealable plastic bags. Plastic bags take up much less space but need a label with volume as well as the date. Double plastic bags are more secure. If most of your baby's feeds are to be given in a bottle, avoid freezing her milk in a glass container as there is some loss of antibodies when breastmilk is stored in glass.

Wash the containers, rinse and disinfect them. After you express the milk, pour it into the prepared container and put it in the fridge. If you intend to freeze the milk, wait until it is cold then pour it into another container in the freezer. Each time you express fresh milk, wait until it is cold and add it to your frozen supply until you have enough for a feed, then start a new lot. It's quite all right to keep adding fresh milk to frozen milk as long as you cool it first. This avoids lots of little packets of frozen breastmilk all over the freezer. Freezing breastmilk in ice cube trays is not practical once your baby is old enough to drink substantial amounts. Apart from that, a cube might go into your gin and tonic by mistake!

Storage of breastmilk for home use

Expressed breastmilk looks quite interesting because it freezes in layers which may be different colours and at times there appears to be little specks in it. This is normal and as long as you have followed these guidelines for storing the milk, don't worry.

HOW LONG CAN BREASTMILK BE STORED AND STILL USED?

The guidelines below are for healthy babies at home. If you are collecting and storing milk for a premature or sick baby in hospital ask for advice from the staff in the nursery.

Breastmilk	Freezer	Refrigerator	Room temperature
Freshly expressed breastmilk (in a sealed container)	• 2 weeks in freezer compartment inside refrigerator • 3 months in freezer section of refrigerator with separate door • 6–12 months in deep freeze (–18°C or lower)	• 3–5 days (4°C or lower) N.B. Store in the back of the refrigerator on the top shelf where it is colder—not in the door.	• 12–24 hours (colostrum) 26°C or lower. • 6–10 hours (mature milk) 26°C or lower. It is always advisable to use a refrigerator when one is available.
Previously frozen breastmilk (thawed in refrigerator or under running water)	• do not refreeze	• 24 hours	• 1 hour

IN GENERAL

- Use fresh milk whenever possible.
- Breastmilk has a good shelf life, but it is always advisable to refrigerate it soon after expressing when a refrigerator is available.
- Freeze milk that will not be used within two days.
- Use the oldest milk first; date the container at the time of collection.
- When adding cold, unfrozen milk to stored frozen milk, don't leave more than a week between additions.

Using the stored milk

If the milk has not been frozen, stand the bottle in a container of warm water to warm it before feeding or give it as it comes. The person feeding your baby should always test the temperature of the milk by shaking a little from the teat onto the inside of their wrist.

If the milk is frozen, defrost it gently. Here are two ways:

- Defrost just before feeding by running cold water over the container. Gradually increase the water temperature until it is warm to hot. Keep the container in the water until the milk defrosts. It's similar to the way you defrost frozen prawns.
- Alternatively, you can prepare in advance by taking the frozen milk from the freezer and leaving it in the fridge until it defrosts. It must be used within twenty-four hours—if it hasn't fully defrosted when it's needed use some warm water. This method has the advantage of having milk available instantly for a feed but it may be wasted if your baby doesn't use it. Breastmilk should never be refrozen.

Microwaves shouldn't be used to defrost or heat breastmilk as they are a safety hazard.

Is there enough milk?

You may find yourself worrying if you have enough milk. Worrying about milk supply is one of the main reasons women stop breastfeeding, yet a lot of the time the worry is unfounded.

How can you tell if there is enough milk?

Mothers and those around them mistakenly think there is not enough milk at times. All is likely to be well if:

- Your baby has six to eight pale, wet nappies every day.
- She has a good poo every so often or at every feed.
- She grows steadily—which is easy to see as she grows out of her clothes, her bassinet and fills up the space in her car safety restraint. Weighing her from time to time also gives you an idea of how she is growing.

Here are some common reasons for believing there may not be enough milk. If all the signs mentioned above are present it is unlikely the following things are signs of 'not enough milk'.

- **Your baby keeps turning her head and opening her mouth as if**

she wants to suck on something even after several good feeds: This is called the rooting reflex and is present in all babies from birth, usually disappearing by three to four months of age. Babies do this when they are hungry, but they also respond like this when they are awake for any length of time, restless, over-stimulated, bored or over-tired. Often wanting to suck on something is a sign of needing sleep, not food.

- **No sensation of a let-down:** Some women never feel a let-down, others find the let-down sensation fades or disappears as their baby grows older, so not feeling a let-down is not a sign of low supply unless there are other indications.
- **Your baby is very unsettled a lot of the time:** The reasons why some babies cry a lot and have trouble falling asleep and staying asleep are complex and varied. If your baby is taking the breast well and growing and developing as she is meant to, it is unlikely her unsettled behaviour has anything to do with your breastfeeding.
- **You can't express much milk:** Many women who breastfeed well can't express. Your ability to express isn't a reflection of how much milk your baby takes.
- **Your baby starts to suck her fists all the time:** Between eight and twelve weeks babies' hands are never out of their mouths. 'Hands in the mouth' is a normal part of their sensory/motor development and not a sign of hunger.
- **Your breasts change; they stop leaking, become softer and smaller and the full feeling goes:** Breast changes like this are normal and happen between six and twelve weeks. Breastfeeding becomes easy and efficient, the fullness and leaking which happens in the early weeks is only temporary.
- **Your baby stops pooing a lot and only goes once every few days:** Most breastfed babies don't poo nearly as much after the first six weeks—a big soft poo less often does not mean your supply is low.
- **Your baby takes a lot less time at the breast:** Breastfeeding is a body function and like all body functions, the more you do it the better you get. It's a bit like running around the park—after you've been doing it for a few months it's much less tiring, you enjoy it more and do

it faster. As your baby grows she becomes more skilled at removing the milk and your body responds, so you become an efficient team.

- **Your baby wakes a lot at night or suddenly starts waking a lot at night:** Night-time waking is dealt with in detail in Sleeping and Waking in the First Six Months, page 265 and The Crying Baby, page 285. In general, unless there are obvious signs of 'not enough milk', night waking in itself is not a sign that babies need more food.

How do you know there is a problem?

Sometimes, of course, the feeling that your baby is not getting enough milk is correct. It is not clear-cut. Obsessions with weight gains in the past meant many women weaned when they didn't have to or want to, but if you are unsure of what is happening, weighing and measuring your baby is still the best guide. Weighing is best done with an experienced health professional who is as interested in breastfeeding as you are and can use the weight as a guide to work with you to resolve the problem—if one exists. Weighing is not a test to determine whether or not formula should be given.

INTERPRETING WEIGHT

It's quite likely your baby is not getting enough milk if:

- there is a constant, gradual weight loss;
- she is still below her birthweight at four weeks or older;
- she keeps gaining less than 500 grams a month.

Other signs which *may* indicate there's not enough milk:

- a sudden change from a reasonably content baby to increased fussiness and more unsettled times;
- a sudden increase in the number of feeds which don't seem to satisfy your baby as much as they used to;
- fewer wet nappies. You may also notice some nappies are damp rather than wet (it's difficult to judge nappy wetness with the latest hi-tech disposables as they absorb fluid very efficiently);
- Infrequent poo is fine as long as there's a good big soft one when it comes. Infrequent green 'splats' are often a sign of underfeeding.

When your baby is healthy and well, temporary underfeeding is rarely an emergency situation but there are times when prompt medical attention is needed. It is unusual for these things to happen simply because of a low milk supply but here are some signs something more serious is wrong:

- your baby is floppy and pale and won't suck;
- your baby is not waking for feeds;
- most of her nappies are dry or just damp, rather than wet;
- she has a sudden, major weight loss over a short period.

Why isn't there enough milk?

Here are the most likely reasons:

- **Difficult start:** If your baby is premature, sick or jaundiced, your birth complicated, or your baby sleepy, you may find breastfeeding takes longer for everything to start working so there may not be enough milk for a while.
- **Your position, your baby's position:** If your baby is not in the best position for breastfeeding, she can't suck well enough to make everything work as well as it can. If you are uncomfortable or ill at ease, your body can't respond and this affects the amount of milk you make.
- **Not enough feeds:** If your baby doesn't take the breast often enough your body doesn't get a strong message to keep making milk, so the amount of milk available gets less than your baby needs.
- **Strategies for sore nipples:** Temporarily stopping breastfeeding or using a nipple shield can decrease the supply.
- **Hormonal changes:** Sometimes hormonal changes in your body alter the balance slightly so less milk is made, for example, pregnancy or menstruation. Concerns are also often raised about the mini pill interfering with the milk supply. In theory the mini pill (which is progesterone only) should not diminish milk supply, unlike oestrogen which does. Two researchers in Australia have been unable to demonstrate in controlled studies that the mini pill diminishes the milk supply; but to be absolutely sure, a study would have to be done with larger numbers of women over longer periods of time. Overseas researchers claim that the mini pill demonstrates no consistent alteration of breastmilk

composition, volume or duration of lactation. Occasionally there are times in my work when I suspect that the mini pill may contribute to fussy feeding and a diminished milk supply, but it is usually very hard to be certain whether the problem is caused by the mini pill or other reasons. However, there are times when stopping the mini pill seems to help increase the milk supply.

- **Smoking:** Smoking affects the milk supply for some women and not for others. When it does, the supply tends to start out all right but gets less as the baby grows. Lots of low milk supply difficulties can be solved, but if you smoke and your supply gets low the chance of increasing your milk to meet all your baby's food needs for any length of time is unlikely. Reducing the number of cigarettes you smoke to as few as possible, not smoking in the hour before feeding and not smoking while you feed reduces harmful effects. The relationship between smoking and low milk supply is unclear, but it is well documented. However, it must be emphasised that if you are a smoker who can't stop, all the advantages of breastfeeding are still there for your baby, so breastfeed for as long as you can (which may turn out to be a long time).
- **Illness:** If you or your baby become sick you might find there is not enough milk. Again, this should only be a temporary situation until you recover. If your baby is sick and not sucking as often or as well, you need to express for comfort and to remind your body to keep making milk.
- **Lifestyle, stress and/or exhaustion:** Lots of women find their breastfeeding works well even when they lead busy lives, get very tired, work outside the home, have stressful days or come through a major upheaval. For others, breastfeeding is a fine balance and doesn't work well unless they adapt their lifestyle to breastfeeding. Lifestyle adjustments are often only temporary, but some women find that for the period that their baby is exclusively breastfed they have to limit their activities, avoid major upheavals and make sure they are always well nurtured and rested.
- **Breast reduction and other breast surgery** may hinder milk production.
- **The way the baby sucks:** Breastfeeding takes two and occasionally the baby's technique just doesn't do what's needed to keep the milk flowing. The baby is usually healthy and well and sucks on a teat quite

happily but when it comes to the breast, feeds in a way that does not stimulate the mother's supply. This is sometimes temporary and by expressing to increase supply, use of a Supply Line (see page 128) and a little formula the problem can be overcome until the baby sucks more effectively. Occasionally it is impossible to resolve and either expressed breastmilk or formula has to be given in a bottle.

- **Unknown:** It is very distressing when you and your baby are doing everything right and yet your baby does not thrive. This does not happen very often, but there are times when there does not seem to be a definable cause or solution for a low milk supply. Some researchers believe that a small number of women do not have the metabolic capacity to produce enough milk for their babies, however, to date there is little work being done to investigate the reasons for this.

Apart from the possibility of underlying metabolic problems the following things may play a part sometimes for some women:

a) Unresolved grief for the loss of another baby (cot death, stillbirth or a baby given up for adoption).
b) A sudden emotional shock (such as the sudden death of a parent).
c) Intense homesickness (having a baby miles away from familiar faces and places).

It must be emphasised that these things do not mean breastfeeding won't work. Successful breastfeeding can be a beneficial healing process in times of emotional trauma, but occasionally the emotional trauma gets in the way of the breastfeeding.

What do you do when there isn't enough milk?

Fortunately, there are things you can do to increase the amount of breastmilk your baby is getting without using extra food or weaning. Low supply is usually a *temporary* difficulty.

Occasionally it is a *longstanding* problem and the breastmilk has to be supplemented with formula or food from a spoon. This can often be done carefully so breastfeeding continues.

Here's a general guide for a *temporary* low supply. Ask your partner and other family members around you to read this as well.

- Support and encouragement from those around you makes an enormous difference. Comments which constantly undermine your confidence don't help. For example, 'The women in our family have never been able to breastfeed'; 'Are you sure she's getting enough?'; 'Your milk is too watery'; 'Put her on the bottle—it doesn't matter'.
- If possible, get help from an adviser who knows how to check your position and your baby's position during a feed.
- Feed your baby whenever she's hungry or awake and alert. Try not to keep using a dummy to extend the time in between feeds. Remember, she needs seven to eight breastfeeds every twenty-four hours.
- On the other hand, don't let your feeds go on forever in an attempt to give your baby 'the hindmilk'. Endless long feeds are exhausting and aren't an effective way to increase your supply. Frequent feeding has to be balanced with rest and relaxation for you. As long as the position is right, ten to twenty minutes of effective sucking does the job.
- Always offer both breasts every feed. Try to make sure your baby is offered the second breast when she is in an alert state. Change her nappy and tickle the soles of her feet to wake her up if she is asleep. If she still doesn't take the second breast, don't worry, offer both breasts again at the next feed.
- Plan a few days of complete rest. See if you can arrange help with the household chores as resting while everything around you is in a state of chaos is not very relaxing for most women. Take your baby to bed. Feed her as much as you can while you watch the soapies, listen to music and read the latest Mills & Boon.
- There is no special food which makes more milk, but if you stop eating properly your body doesn't work as efficiently, so make sure you stay well nourished.
- Avoid strenuous exercise programs and dieting rigorously to lose weight.
- If you are using a nipple shield, try as many feeds as possible without it; if you are giving bottles to rest sore nipples try to let your baby take your breast again as soon as possible.
- Express to make more milk, but with caution. When there are difficulties with the position and your baby's sucking technique needs a little

time to develop, expressing a few times a day after feeds can be useful. A full-service electric double pump is easier and more efficient. When the positioning is better and your baby's sucking is stronger you can stop.

If your baby's position at the breast is good and she sucks well then let nature take its course. Frequent feeds and rest should solve the problem without expressing as well. Expressing to increase the milk supply is not always useful as it has a tendency to make a stressful situation even more stressful, which doesn't do a lot to help the milk flow. If expressing as well as feeding makes you tense and hassled then it is unlikely to be of much benefit.

When low supply becomes a *longstanding* problem:

- If you have access to one, a residential mother and baby centre where you can rest and get help may suit you. Or, going home to your mother might be a solution.
- If after a period of time you have to give some extra food because your baby is not gaining enough weight, start with a small amount of formula (30–60ml) once or twice a day after a good breastfeed. Continue to feed frequently, rest and make sure you are both comfortable at feed time. A small amount of formula does not mean all is lost!
- An option instead of a bottle and teat is a Supply Line. A Supply Line consists of a container similar to a bottle which contains either expressed breastmilk or formula which is worn in a pouch around the mother's neck. A piece of fine tubing which carries the milk from the container to the nipple is gently taped to her breast so the end of it lies near the nipple. When the baby sucks at the breast the milk is drawn through the tubing into her mouth at the same time as milk from the breast. For some mothers use of a Supply Line helps while they build up their supply and keeps their baby at the breast. Supply Lines don't suit everyone. Some mothers find them difficult to use, especially in front of anyone, and some babies won't suck with a Supply Line in place while others quickly get used to it and won't suck without it. Two brands of Supply Lines are currently available—the Australian Breastfeeding Association Supply Line available from the Association and the Medela Supplemental Nursing System available from some Family Care Centres.

It's essential to have a person experienced in using a Supply Line to help you when you start.

- Medications and herbal treatments (galactagogues) are frequently prescribed to increase breastmilk supply and may be beneficial for some women in some circumstances.

  Prescription medications that are used for this purpose are drugs that are used for other reasons, for example, nausea and vomiting, depression, tranquillisers and blood pressure reducers, all of which may produce milk as a side effect. Obviously only some of these drugs are considered safe to use to increase the milk supply in otherwise healthy women.

  The use of herbs to increase milk supply has been around for centuries and anecdotal reports of success are widespread; however, there is no research in the medical literature to support or refute these claims. I never see enough overwhelmingly positive results in my work to urge women to try herbal remedies.

  Galactagogues should not be used until all the common reasons for low supply have been explored and the basics, as outlined on the previous pages, have been tried. Galactagogues should always be used in conjunction with frequent feeds, rest, emphasis on correct attachment, and attention given to issues such as smoking, the health of the mother and the way the baby sucks. They are not a miracle cure for low milk supply, do not work for all women and can have unpleasant side effects.

Here are the commonly used galactagogues:

— **Metoclopramide (Maxolon, Pramin, Reglan, Maxeran):** These are used for nausea and vomiting and are the most common drugs prescribed to increase milk supply. Side effects include 'spacing out', drowsiness, fatigue, stomach pains and diarrhoea. They need to be taken three times a day for no longer than two weeks.

— **Domperidone (Motilium):** A similar drug to above, normally used for nausea and vomiting and gastro-oesophagael reflux but causes fewer side effects.

— **Herbal Remedies:** Traditionally herbs such as fenugreek, garlic, caffeine, fennel seed, blessed thistle and alfalfa have been used but it is important to make sure they come from a reputable source and must be used according to directions. I don't recommend any of them; however, if you are keen to give a herb a go, best to talk to a lactation consultant.

- From four months onwards babies can be supplemented with food from a spoon instead of formula in a bottle—an option which can work well when it seems unlikely the milk supply is going to provide all your baby needs. When your baby is not getting quite enough breastmilk and you have done all the best things to do to increase your milk, she can get extra food from rice cereal, fruit and vegies. Trying food from a spoon instead of formula in a bottle means your baby still gets all the milk you do make because:
  a) It takes time to increase the amount she manages to eat from a spoon, which means she is still keen to take the breast. Large amounts of formula in bottles go down quickly, the baby loses interest in the breast and bottle feeding takes over.
  b) Food from a spoon is not an alternative food source taken by sucking, so she eats from a spoon and sucks from the breast.
  c) The extra calories from the food helps your baby gain weight, you gain confidence and often the milk supply improves.

  Remember this is an option. It doesn't suit all mothers and babies when low supply is a problem and your baby should be at least four months old before you try it.

'Not enough milk'—summary

Not having enough milk does not happen nearly as often as everyone thinks it does. Check carefully why you think there is not enough. If you can, talk it over with an experienced breastfeeding adviser.

IF IT DOES SEEM TO BE A PROBLEM

- Check your position when you are feeding;
- Check your baby's position—she may need tucking in closer to you;
- Feed your baby seven or eight times every twenty-four hours;
- Always offer both breasts;
- Try to get some extra rest;

- Can you stop smoking or cut down?
- Delay taking the mini pill for contraception;
- Expressing after some feeds may help.

IF IT BECOMES LONGSTANDING

- Offer some formula (a small amount to begin with) or any expressed breastmilk you might have after two or three breastfeeds every twenty-four hours; OR
- A Supply Line might suit you and your baby; OR
- Give one bottle of formula or previously expressed breastmilk once a day in the evening. Give the appropriate amount for age. Let your partner give the bottle while you have a complete break. Continue giving seven or eight breastfeeds the rest of the time, taking care with positioning. Stop the supplements if your supply increases; OR
- Consider medication, with caution; OR
- Start food from a spoon when your baby is four months old (see page 373). Continue breastfeeding. Slowly build up the food to two to three meals a day. Give the food after the breast and continue seven to eight breastfeeds every twenty-four hours.

Lots of milk

Some women find they have so much milk it causes temporary difficulties. If you have lots of milk you might find your breasts always feel full and leak all the time. Your baby will probably have big weight gains, poo heartily and everywhere and may gasp and pull off the breast because the flow is fast at times. She is also likely to have some good vomits. Some of these things are distressing, but they are harmless. As your baby grows and the milk flow settles you will find the leaking, pooing and vomiting gets less.

What can you do?

- At first, do nothing as the milk flow often adjusts to the baby's needs quite quickly.
- If the milk flow continues to be abundant, try feeding your baby only

one breast each feed for a while. Put your baby back on the first breast instead of offering the second breast. For comfort only, hand express the breast your baby doesn't take—just express until the full feeling stops.

- Hand expressing a little milk just before a feed sometimes makes it easier for your baby to manage when she goes to the breast.
- Sometimes changing positions helps. The underarm hold (see page 82) sometimes seems to stop the choking.
- You might find the leaking is embarrassing. Try using the non-disposable breast pads made from a soft fabric that allow moisture to pass through and keep your skin dry. Multi-coloured tops are a good disguise.
- Remember, this is temporary and will not go on for the whole time you breastfeed. In the meantime take pleasure in watching your baby thrive on all your wonderful milk!

For a small number of women, oversupply is a distressing situation which causes constant breast problems such as blocked ducts and mastitis (see page 134). The baby may also be very unsettled and become a fussy feeder, pulling away from the breast after only sucking for a short time. Like many breastfeeding difficulties these things will usually resolve in time. (It's unusual for oversupply problems to continue past three months.) Here are some suggestions to manage:

- Try to feed your baby when she is sleepy on a softer breast and leave her on the same breast until it is fully drained (very soft). Hand express the other breast for comfort if you need to.
- Avoid skipping feeds until the supply has settled. If your baby starts sleeping longer than five hours at night you may need to express at the time of the missed feed if you wake with painful, bursting breasts. (It's very unfair when the baby lets you sleep and your breasts don't.)
- Continue to make sure you follow the guidelines for positioning so your baby can drain your breast efficiently.
- Check your breasts frequently for hard, painful or red segments. Use massage and hand or pump expression to relieve the troublesome spot.

Fast flow

Milk often spurts out when you let-down at the beginning of a feed or halfway through. Babies find this upsetting when they are young and often choke and cry and pull off the breast. Fast flow is not necessarily associated with an oversupply of milk so care has to be taken that any strategies used for a fast flow do not diminish the milk supply. If your baby is generally settled and you are not having the difficulties described in the previous section (see Lots of milk, page 131), just try hand expressing a small amount of milk before the feed. You may also find changing the position from across your front to under your arm halfway through the feed helps avoid choking on the second let-down. As your baby grows and the let-down intensity decreases the problem rights itself.

Clicking noise when breastfeeding (the baby, not you)

Sometimes babies click while feeding. If your baby is thriving, the feeding is comfortable and your nipples are not sore (apart from some discomfort for twenty to thirty seconds at the beginning of the feed) ignore the clicking noise. If your nipples are hurting throughout the feed or if your baby is very unsettled and perhaps not gaining weight, the clicking in this instance is a sign that the position is not right. If you have an adviser, ask for help to check your feeding. If not, go back to the basic guidelines for positioning and go through them step by step. Changing position from front to underarm (twin style) might help.

One breast bigger than the other

Some women find when they are breastfeeding one breast is bigger than the other. It may be because the baby prefers one breast and sucks longer and more efficiently on that breast or because one breast just makes more milk. If this happens it is much more noticeable in the first six to eight weeks and then tends to settle. At times the breast size will continue to be different for the whole time the baby is breastfeeding, but the breasts do go back to being similar after weaning—so if this is happening to you, don't panic about being lopsided forever.

Blocked ducts

When you are breastfeeding, the milk is carried from the glands deep inside the breast to the front of the breast by a network of tiny tubes called ducts. If one of the tubes becomes blocked the milk can't flow as well and you are likely to notice a lump which at first may not be painful. The lump is thickened milk. One or more can form at any time but this is more common in the first three months.

Why does it happen?

Something holds up the milk flow. Here are the usual causes for a blocked duct, but sometimes it is difficult to pinpoint a reason.

- If your baby's position at the breast is not quite right, the breast won't be well drained after a feed so there's more chance of milk banking up in one of the ducts. Pain or discomfort throughout the feed is a sign the position is not right. This should not be confused with the toe-tingling discomfort many women experience for the first thirty seconds before and after a feed in the early weeks. (Opinions vary as to the cause of toe-tingling discomfort, but it is not due to positioning when the feed is comfortable apart from the uncomfortable sensation at the beginning and end of the feed.)
- Sometimes the way breasts are handled harms the ducts. Try not to grip them tightly when you feed your baby. Using a finger to hold the breast away from your baby's nose while she feeds is unnecessary when the position is correct. When you massage and express, try not to squeeze or slide your hands on your breasts.
- Tight bras or clothing putting pressure on breasts can stop the milk flow.
- If the normal pattern of your breastfeeding is interrupted, ducts may become blocked. Things like delayed or hurried feed, going back to paid work, stopping night feeds, travelling or giving up breastfeeding suddenly can contribute to problems with the milk flow.

What can you do if you feel a lump anywhere in your breasts?

- Feed frequently and offer the lumpy breast first for two feeds in a row. Try changing the way you feed. If you normally sit, lie down on your side. If you usually feed with your baby's body under your arm, try holding her in front of you. If you can do it so you are both comfortable, feed her so her chin points towards the lump.

- Massage the lump firmly with the same technique used for self breast examination. It's important not to squeeze your breast or slide your hands down the breast. The lump may be painful and red. Sometimes it helps if the lump is massaged by your partner, lover or friend with some nice oil.
- Massaging and hand expressing while sitting in a warm bath helps if the breast is still lumpy and uncomfortable after a feed.
- Arm exercises similar to breaststroke movements also help.
- Make a point of putting your feet up and resting whenever you can, especially when your baby is sleeping during the day.

Mastitis

Mastitis is a medical term for a red, swollen breast. If mastitis happens while you are breastfeeding, it is very painful and usually caused by bacterial infection. The Royal Hospital for Women in Sydney estimates that 10 to 20 per cent of women develop a breast infection in the first few weeks of breastfeeding.

Why does it happen?

- An abundant supply in the early weeks while the milk supply adjusts to your baby's needs.
- A blocked duct which doesn't resolve.
- From damaged nipples when bacteria enter the duct through a graze or a crack in the nipple.
- Mastitis is more likely to happen if you become ill or exhausted; smoking may also contribute.

Sometimes the cause is unknown. Mastitis can strike like lightning and is often mistaken for influenza as sometimes at first there is only minimal breast tenderness and no sign of a blocked duct. When this happens the breast symptoms do appear later.

What are the symptoms?

- You feel hot, feverish and depressed.
- Your breast may be red, swollen and exquisitely tender.
- There are often red streaks on the sore breast.

With prompt treatment you may be able to avoid antibiotics through the use of warm packs, massage, rest, anti-inflammatory medication, arm exercises and frequent breastfeeds.

Whatever you do, don't stop breastfeeding. Let your baby suck—your milk will not harm her in any way.

If this works you will know, because the influenza symptoms will go away and the pain will be gone from your breast.

On the other hand, if after six to eight hours there is no improvement and you feel very ill and depressed, you need medication.

Antibiotics are the most effective medication for treating infective mastitis and preventing the risk of an abscess, so visit your family doctor. The antibiotics will not harm your baby.

Continue frequent breastfeeding while you take them. Disregard advice to stop breastfeeding temporarily—this is wrong advice and can lead to added discomfort and unplanned weaning.

It is important to take a ten-day course of antibiotics. Take the whole course even though you will feel like a new woman in forty-eight hours.

A few women seem to get one bout of mastitis after another. Recurrent mastitis is very wearing and the precise reason for the problem varies between women and for the same women between bouts. Finding the exact cause and fixing the problem so the mastitis doesn't keep recurring is difficult and different things may work (or not work) for different women. The Australian Breastfeeding Association can be of great help in this situation as word-of-mouth remedies from women to women can sometimes offer potential solutions unavailable from other sources.

Breast abscesses

An abscess is a collection of pus (like a boil) which happens in a breast either because mastitis has not been quickly and effectively treated or because of an infection from cracked or grazed nipples. If it's because of damaged nipples the abscess is likely to be near the nipple; if it is because of mastitis it forms where the red infected area of the breast is. An abscess is keenly painful.

Breast abscesses are rare, but if one forms, medical attention is needed immediately. Treatment involves antibiotics and usually surgical drainage. Breastfeeding should continue even if you are losing pus from your nipple—it will not hurt your baby. If for any reason you can't feed from the infected breast or it is too painful, express it until you can put your baby back to the breast.

If you have to go to hospital, see if you can arrange to take your baby with you or get help to express your milk regularly. Continuing to breastfeed from both breasts during and after treatment is recommended, but milk often continues to leak from the incision following drainage of an abscess, which can be hard to deal with. Nevertheless, although it is messy and aesthetically a problem, there is no harm in it. If you continue breastfeeding you may find that the breast with the abscess doesn't produce as much milk as it did before the abscess appeared. Interestingly, research shows that the bulk of the milk supply is found in different parts of the breast with each baby, so with another baby it is likely that the breast will function as if there has never been a problem.

Persistent sore/damaged nipples

Most damaged nipples heal well in the first six weeks, but unfortunately some women find feeding is not particularly enjoyable (an understatement some would say) for up to three months because of ongoing sore nipples and breast pain for which there may not be a solution other than time. If you reach a point where you cannot bear the thought of another breastfeed, it is advisable to take your baby from the breast and express for a week before putting her back. Hand expressing is often advised in this situation, but is unrealistic for many women who find it easier to use an electric pump or hand pump. Give your baby the expressed milk in a bottle. When your nipples (or nipple; it is often only one nipple that is a problem) are healed, start to put your baby back to the breast once or twice every twenty-four hours, slowly building up to full breastfeeding again. If possible, get help from a child and family health nurse or lactation consultant the first time you put her back to the breast.

Sometimes ongoing nipple soreness can be diagnosed as specific medical conditions, which means they can be helped by treatment. The range of conditions follow.

CANDIDA (COMMONLY KNOWN AS THRUSH) OF THE NIPPLES

Candida causes a common fungal infection known as thrush. It is able to infect the deep organs of the body as well as the skin, and particularly affects mothers and babies. The most common species that causes the infection is known as *Candida albicans*; however, there are other species of Candida, which while much rarer also cause human fungal infections. The significance of this is that the rarer species are resistant to commonly used medications for *Candida albicans*, which may explain some of the times when thrush doesn't appear to respond to treatment.

Nipples may become infected with Candida in a number of different ways:

- Candida infections occurring in women are common in the mucous membrane which lines the vagina. If this is present when a woman gives birth her baby will be born with the same infection in the baby's mouth and digestive tract.
- Candida can occur in a baby's mouth whether her mother has a vaginal infection or not.
- Women who are breastfeeding sometimes find the combination of their baby's sucking, the constant dampness and friction of breast pads and bras leads to thrush on the areola and nipple.

A fungal infection of the areolas and nipples may happen at the same time as cracked and/or painful nipples in the early weeks after birth, following a course of antibiotics for mastitis, or out of the blue at any time when there is no history of sore or damaged nipples or mastitis. A definite diagnosis is sometimes difficult and I feel there is a tendency for thrush to be over-diagnosed as a cause of sore nipples and breast pain, however, when the signs and symptoms are clear, thrush can be treated effectively with miconazole (which comes in an oral gel). The treatment should be continued for a week or more to be effective. The baby should also be treated, even if there is no sign of thrush in her mouth, to avoid the infection passing back and forth between mother and baby. At the current time, oral antifungals are also often given to the mother for at least two weeks.

The following things strongly suggest a fungal infection of the areola and nipples:

- Dry, red ('sunburnt') nipples that suddenly start to hurt where previously they didn't.
- Pain before, during and after a feed, even when the baby is well attached to the breast.
- A burning pain radiating up the breast from the nipples, especially after a feed.

(See also Needle-sharp pain, page 92.)

DERMATITIS

Dermatitis is caused by something irritating the nipple and areola such as creams, sprays, clothing or soap which makes the nipple and areola red and sore. Women who have sensitive skin and suffer from eczema are more likely to develop nipple dermatitis.

Expose your nipples as much as possible, taking care outdoors if it's windy and/or sunny. Wear cotton near your skin. Be very careful about what you put on your nipples as lots of products are likely to make things worse, not better. A hydrocortisone ointment (ointment is better than cream on a moist surface) will relieve the inflammation if the diagnosis is definite.

Hydrocortisone will not help if the problem is caused by the way your baby is taking the breast.

SMALL, WHITE BLISTER

Occasionally milk collects in a spot on the nipple, just under the skin, and looks like a whitehead. The skin around the spot is swollen and painful. As the collection of milk causes a blockage in the milk flow there may be associated lumps further back in the breast.

The discomfort doesn't last for long. Usually the baby's sucking removes the collection of milk but if it is very painful, try having a warm bath or shower then gently apply some pressure behind the spot and see if it will pop out. Sometimes removal with a sterile needle by a family doctor or midwife who is skilled in the area is advisable.

WHITE NIPPLE (NIPPLE VASOSPASM)

Primary vasospasm (vasospasm that happens without any evidence of nipple damage or infection) is similar to chilblains of the nipple. It is not common, but does happen to a small number of women who may also have a history of experiencing numbness, tingling and pain in their fingers and toes, but not always. The pain, mostly in the nipple, sometimes in the breast as well and usually only on one side, can start soon after birth or as late as eight weeks afterwards, and is nearly always associated with a breast-feed. The nipple goes white, tight and hard and becomes extremely sensitive. A severe jabbing pain is experienced at the time the nipple goes white and again when the blood returns, changing the nipple colour from white to blue and back to red. The pain and blanching of the nipple may continue in intervals over one or two hours. The nipple blanching and pain often disappear in six to eight weeks but occasionally some women experience pain and blanching for the whole time they breastfeed.

Secondary vasospasm is vasospasm that occurs as a reaction to nipple pain caused by an infection—thrush or bacterial—or painful feeding from nipple damage caused by attachment problems.

Treatment

- It is important to diagnose and treat any damage or infection of the nipple, and ensure that your baby is taking the breast in the best way to avoid damaging the nipple (see pages 87–92 for suggestions on how to manage sore nipples). In this instance, cover your nipples instead of airing them, as exposure to cool air intensifies the pain of vasospasm. If possible contact an ABA counsellor, a lactation consultant or your child and family health nurse.
- Avoid chilly environments and getting cold while you breastfeed. Wear warm clothes and apply a warm compress to the breast before and/or after the feeds.
- Smoking and caffeine exacerbate this condition by further constricting the blood vessels.

- Magnesium and calcium supplements *may* be helpful for some women—evidence supporting this is contradictory.
- A medication, nifedipine, has been found to be safe and often beneficial (not always, but is definitely worth a try). However, you will need to find a family doctor who is familiar with the condition and the medication. Lactation consultants cannot prescribe nifedipine, but if you're having trouble finding a doctor, a lactation consultant can either pass on the information about the medication as well as the correct dosage or refer you to a suitable doctor.

Breast pain

Persistent breast pain that is not related to an obvious condition such as mastitis or referred pain from damaged nipples is a problem for a small number of women. It is perhaps more common in women who experience troublesome breast pain prior to pregnancy or who have very sensitive skin. If you feel the pain is unusual, please see your family doctor. Here are some suggestions that have been found to be helpful:

- Reduce the caffeine in your diet. Apart from coffee, caffeine is found in many other drinks and processed foods.
- Reduce the salt in your diet. Again, check processed foods.
- Take vitamin B1 and vitamin B6 tablets—50mg a day.
- Wear a firm, well-fitting cotton bra day and night.

Aching upper back and shoulders

This can be a problem for some women while they are learning to breastfeed, especially if there is an old injury or a past history of problems in that area. Take care to sit square on with a straight back. Try not to lean over your baby—bring her to your breast not your breast to her. Use a firm pillow to support your baby.

Warmth around your upper back and shoulders helps (a shawl or soft blanket). Heat to your back and shoulders (a hot water bottle) after feeding is soothing. Physiotherapy and/or massage can be beneficial. Back and shoulder discomfort gradually improves as you and your baby become more skilled in this breastfeeding business.

Should I wean?

You may find yourself in a dilemma where you feel breastfeeding is the pits but the thought of weaning also fills you with dismay. I find that most women get through this time as long as their babies are thriving and they have good support from family and a health professional. The problem will not last forever and you will almost certainly be delighted that you carried on.

It is very difficult, however, to keep going when there is the added problem of a low supply which cannot seem to be resolved especially if your baby is not thriving. In this situation you may need to talk to your health professional about combining breast and bottle feeding or slowly starting to wean.

Combining breast and bottle feeding

Combining breast and bottle feeding is an option when, despite all efforts, there is not enough breastmilk. Many babies in this situation will happily take both. Even though the amount of formula may indicate that most of the feed is via the bottle, there are still benefits from giving your baby the breast before each bottle and perhaps at other times, such as in between feeds, for comfort or to get her off to sleep. Give your baby ten minutes or so at both breasts then offer the bottle with the amount of formula required for your baby's age (see chart, page 111). Combining breastfeeding and formula feeding in this way can continue for as long as you are both happy.

Breast refusal

Breast refusal is a broad term used to describe a range of behaviour at the breast where the baby, for reasons that may not be clear, fusses and fidgets, screams or gets distracted and refuses to feed. There is often no satisfactory diagnosis of the problem or a solution although you'll find suggestions below. Often the most comforting thing to know is that this behaviour is quite common for many normal, healthy babies. The most common age when it becomes a problem is between eight and sixteen weeks, but there are variations on this—sometimes it starts soon after birth. It often happens out of the blue although some babies who refuse the breast have always been fussy feeders.

What happens?

When you try to feed your baby she might suddenly cry, suck, pull off the breast then keep crying or simply fidget and squirm and refuse to take the breast. You might find she refuses every feed for twenty-four to forty-eight hours then takes the breast again as if nothing has happened, or she might take some feeds well and refuse others. The on-again-off-again feeding may go on for three weeks. Often the night and early morning feeds are fine with each feed during the day becoming more and more difficult. By evening everyone is very tense.

If this happens to you, you are bound to feel devastated, wonder what on earth you're doing wrong and even lose confidence in yourself and your breastfeeding. Don't panic. Be aware that it is not your fault; it happens to lots of mothers; it is nearly always temporary; with the right advice and moral support you can get through this dilemma and continue breastfeeding.

Why does it happen?

The following reasons are possibilities. You may find one that applies to your situation and provides a solution; however, much of the time a definitive cause and treatment remains elusive.

BABY CAUSES

- Illnesses such as coughs, sore throats, ear infections or blocked noses. Rare occasions crop up when refusing the breast is a sign of something more serious so if your baby is floppy, pale and not wetting her nappies, please see your doctor straight away.
- Frequent regurgitation and/or heartburn—to be honest this is a handy diagnosis and rarely likely to be the reason for the breast refusal. (See pages 188, 295.)
- Distractions, especially around three to five months, can cause a few breastfeeding hassles including breast refusal. At this age babies become fascinated with the world around them. Feeding is not as important as what is going on elsewhere. Even though it seems like they are having days and days where it seems they don't feed much they continue to look the picture of health.

- Shorter sucking time. Don't confuse breast refusal with a shorter sucking time. Breastfeeding is a body function and the process becomes more efficient as time goes by. Your baby learns to feed very competently and your body responds so the feeds become much shorter. Avoid trying to keep her at the breast longer than she wants.

MOTHER CAUSES

- A change in perfume, talcum powder or a radical change in diet.
- Early mastitis which leads to salty-tasting milk.
- Any illness or stress which may deplete the breastmilk supply or inhibit the let-down.
- Medication which may alter the taste of the breastmilk.
- Hormonal changes which may alter the taste or amount of the breastmilk, for example, the progesterone-only pill, early pregnancy or menstruation. Usually any problems caused by hormonal changes are temporary—the fussy feeding stops when the baby and breasts adjust. Some women find that breast refusal occurs when a period is due and stops when it is over.

BREASTFEEDING CAUSES (FOR REASONS WHICH MAY BE UNKNOWN)

- Low milk supply (see pages 121–130.)
- A slow let-down response—there are no useful explanations for this apart from illness or stress, as noted on the previous page. Relief of stress and extra rest can help.
- A rapid let-down response that frightens the baby, who then gets a temporary mental block about the breast.

What can you do about breast refusal?

Most episodes of breast refusal are not related to ill-health (mother or baby) but if you are concerned see your family doctor to make absolutely sure and to set your mind at ease.

Check that there is enough milk if you suspect there may not be. Breast refusal is usually not related to low milk supply but in this instance weighing and measuring your baby with a competent health professional is the best way to be absolutely sure and put your mind at rest. Extra rests for you and company from a calm person during the day and evening helps.

HERE'S A BASIC PLAN OF ACTION TO FOLLOW:

- Try not to see what's happening as a personal rejection (easier said than done, I know). As mentioned before, breast refusal is not uncommon, usually temporary and not because you are doing anything wrong.
- When your baby cries, pulls off and refuses the breast, stop the feed. Trying to make her take the breast usually makes things worse.
- Change tactics—go for a walk, hand her over to a calm person or see if she will sleep.
- When possible pick your baby up and feed her when she is still drowsy after a sleep, before she fully wakes.
- **Sometimes the following strategies work:** Let your baby suck on a finger then try slipping the nipple in; calm her by singing and rocking before the feed; try alternative feeding positions (see pages 80–2); hand express some milk into your baby's mouth; try breastfeeding in the bath.
- Usually the night feeds are good so try to enjoy them and bear in mind that your baby is probably making up for the fussy day feeding by feeding well at night.
- Avoid bottles and formula as much as possible. Mostly when breast refusal happens extra fluids in bottles are not needed. If your baby refuses the breast for twenty-four hours or if she is sick, you might need to use a bottle or a small cup. Giving a bottle has the potential to cause more stress—either because the baby won't take it or because she decides she prefers it to the breast. Sometimes, though, a bottle can provide a welcome opportunity to ease the tension.
- Express for comfort and to keep the milk flowing if you need to.

Breast refusal is usually only temporary, lasting from two to three days to two to three weeks, but occasionally a baby cannot be persuaded to return to the breast. The problem becomes permanent instead of temporary. This doesn't happen very often but when it does some of the pleasure of breastfeeding goes and weaning becomes an attractive alternative. It is important for you to have a nice time with your baby so this is certainly reasonable in these circumstances.

Juice, water and vitamin drops

Your baby doesn't need daily water (even in hot weather), juice, vitamin supplements or fluoride. Premature babies do need extra supplements for the first three to four months after birth as they do not arrive with stores of iron and vitamins.

Breastmilk contains all of the above apart from fluoride, which is not needed until the third year and only then if you live somewhere where there is none in the water supply.

Some mothers do give their baby water in a bottle for a few reasons that have nothing to do with nutrition. Here they are—you may decide yourself if you think it's a helpful thing to do. When your baby is very unsettled and you've just done the twentieth feed of the day, letting someone else give her some water in a bottle may give you a rest and break the unsettled cycle—if she'll drink it. Babies often won't drink water.

Regular drinks from a bottle might (no guarantee) prevent potential difficulties caused by bottle refusal at a later date when it would be very useful for her to drink from a bottle.

If you become ill

It's certainly no picnic when you are unwell and you have a baby or young children to look after. Mothers can rarely take sick leave.

When you are breastfeeding the milk supply might be less than it is when you are well. Babies manage quite well when there is less milk for a while without anything alarming happening. Is your partner able to take time from work and/or go to your baby at night, change and settle her so all you have to do is feed? When your partner is around or anyone else who can help, take your baby and go to bed. Your baby is unlikely to catch coughs, colds, the flu, or a tummy bug through your breastmilk. Being breastfed protects her from these things to a large extent, especially gastroenteritis, but don't forget to wash your hands carefully before feeds and stick to all the rules of good hygiene.

Occasionally a medical condition arises and hospital admission is required. Make sure you tell your doctor you are breastfeeding as sometimes it's possible to take your baby with you. You may have to express or get help to express for a short time if you are not well enough to feed so someone else can feed your baby. If there is short-term use of problematic drugs the milk can be discarded until the drugs are out of your system and previously stored breastmilk or formula used for a while—there is no need to wean.

Staff in general hospitals are usually not familiar with breastfeeding, expressing or the distress of weaning suddenly, especially when the mother doesn't want to, so ask someone to contact the nearest maternity unit where there should be a midwife available who can help you and act as a spokesperson for you.

Drugs and medications in breastmilk

It's wise not to take any unnecessary drug or medication while you are breastfeeding. This includes alcohol, tobacco, cannabis, cocaine, methadone and heroin. Women who can't stop using tobacco, methadone or heroin can continue breastfeeding, as long as the milk supply doesn't diminish to a stage where the baby is malnourished. We do not have safe levels for cocaine and cannabis so don't take a risk. Alcohol is harmless in small quantities but not in any greater quantities than a small drink every so often.

When it's necessary to take drugs for an illness or a medical condition it's important to get the most appropriate drug and correct information about possible effects on your baby. It's also important to take what you need in order to maintain your health or to help you get better as quickly as possible. Tell your doctor you are breastfeeding so he or she can choose the best drug. You also need to know if your baby may be temporarily upset, get diarrhoea or be at risk of a fungal infection while you are taking the medication.

Drugs can cause problems either because they are harmful for the baby or because they interfere with the body's ability to make milk. It is now recognised there are relatively few drugs that can't be taken while breastfeeding but unfortunately the reference which is widely used at the current time still contraindicates most drugs. This means that women are sometimes not treated adequately or babies are removed from the breast unnecessarily. It's impossible in this book to provide detailed information but I would like to make the point that drugs for postnatal depression, epilepsy, diabetes and anti-coagulant drugs such as heparin and warfarin may be safely given as misinformation about these particular drugs is common.

The best people to check with are lactation consultants or child and family health nurses as they have detailed references.

Breastfeeding from one breast

When there is only one breast to feed from because of the removal of all or part of a breast, breastfeeding can still work well providing the remaining breast is normal. If you only have one breast to use you may feel apprehensive about breastfeeding when you are doing it for the first time. Here are a few tips:

- Confidence is everything. Think about all the women who breastfeed twins. Encouragement from those around you and help when you need it from an interested breastfeeding adviser makes an incredible difference.
- Difficulties and problems that might arise when feeding on one breast are exactly the same as for women who feed from two breasts. The two most likely to worry you in the first four to six weeks are thinking you may not have enough milk and a sore nipple. The advice about these is the same whether you feed with one breast or two.

Feeding after implants or breast reduction surgery

Being able to fully or partially breastfeed after augmentation or breast reduction surgery varies a lot according to the way the surgery is performed, so it is best to decide to breastfeed and wait and see what happens. While an optimistic and positive approach is desirable, I am aware of the heartbreak involved when women are given completely unrealistic expectations by well-meaning breastfeeding enthusiasts. Some women do breastfeed well but others only manage to breastfeed to a small extent. Nevertheless, they find the experience fulfilling, and not disappointing, as long as they haven't been led to hope for the impossible.

- Breast implants: As there is usually little disruption to the ducts or nerves in the nipple or breast, breastfeeding proceeds normally for many women who have had implants, but care needs to be taken to drain the breasts well, so let your baby have the breast frequently. Research suggests there may be problems related to breastfeeding after *silicone* implants. More research is needed to verify this. At this stage it seems wise to take further advice if you wish to breastfeed following breast implant surgery that involves the use of silicone implants.

- Breastfeeding following breast reduction surgery is also possible and it never should be assumed that it won't work, but it is much harder to establish and maintain breastfeeding for any length of time. Most women who breastfeed following breast reduction surgery also use some formula. The formula can be given by bottle or Supply Line (see page 128). When this is carefully done breastfeeding can be maintained and often the use of formula stopped when food from a spoon is introduced.

Jaundice and breastfeeding

(See Jaundice, page 171.)

Phenylketonuria and breastfeeding

Phenylketonuria is an 'inborn error of metabolism' and a rare condition affecting one in 10,000 births in Australia—in which the baby cannot tolerate normal amounts of protein. Special milk and a diet supervised at a metabolic clinic in a children's hospital is essential but it's important to know that breastfeeding can usually continue as well, under supervision.

Human Immunodeficiency Virus (HIV) and breastfeeding

Research around the world strongly suggests that HIV, the virus which causes Acquired Immune Deficiency Syndrome (AIDS) is passed in breastmilk sometimes. It is still not clear why some babies are infected from breastfeeding and others aren't. Many women who are HIV positive breastfeed without infecting their babies, however, when formula feeding is a safe option it is now considered wise for women who are HIV positive not to breastfeed. When formula feeding can't be done safely, it is best to breastfeed.

Hepatitis B

Women who are Hepatitis B carriers may breastfeed safely once the baby has been immunised; immunisation is commenced straight after birth.

Hepatitis C

Evidence at the time of writing this book does not suggest that Hepatitis C is transmitted through breastmilk, so breastfeeding is safe for the babies of women who are Hepatitis C carriers.

Baby won't take a bottle

Many breastfed babies are understandably not keen on using bottles. Some babies obligingly drink from breast or bottle which makes life easy, especially for times when mothers aren't there.

Others will drink some things from bottles and not others—for example, expressed breastmilk but not formula.

A few make life interesting for their mothers by drinking from a bottle at some times but not at others and give no clue as to why or when they are likely to oblige or refuse. An appreciable number adamantly refuse a teat and bottle no matter what's in it. Sometimes this happens even when the baby has been having regular bottles from a young age so making an effort to avoid bottle refusal by giving a bottle a week from an early age doesn't work for everyone but it might help.

Lots of women breastfeed and never use bottles. **Bottles are not an essential part of baby feeding.** Their main value is convenience and the first thing to do is work out why you want your baby to take a bottle then decide what your options are if she keeps refusing. Here are some reasons why you might want your baby to drink from a bottle:

- Pressure from those around you who tell you a few bottle feeds will make your baby sleep better at night (not a valid reason—it won't make any difference);
- A rest from the breast;
- Occasional times when you're not there (a night out, shopping, the dentist and so on);

- Regular times when you're not there (part-time paid work, voluntary work, study and so on);
- Full-time paid work;
- Early weaning because of breastfeeding difficulties.

What can you do when your baby refuses to drink from a bottle?

- Changing bottles, teats and brand of formula hardly ever makes any difference. When babies are ready to accept a bottle in general, any type of bottle or teat and any brand of formula will be accepted. You might like to try a few different products, but it's not worth buying out the pharmacy.
- Try once a day, at the same time every day, when your baby is hungry but not overtired and hysterical. Make sure it's several hours since her last breastfeed.
- Starting to give the bottle while she is half asleep might help.
- When possible, have someone other than you offer the bottle. Persist for as long as you or they can, even if it means trying on and off until the next feed—if you succumb and give a breastfeed quickly you are unlikely to get anywhere.
- Changing the position from the breastfeeding position helps. Try sitting your baby in a portable baby chair opposite you or feed while you walk and talk to her.
- Warming the teat might help.

PAINFUL OPTIONS—THE LAST RESORT

If time is running out and it is absolutely essential that your baby uses a bottle, the only way left, unfortunately, is to not feed your baby until she is so hungry she takes a bottle. Naturally this is painful for you and your baby, but there are rare times when there is no other choice. There are several ways of tackling this:

- As long as your baby is well and healthy try leaving her and the bottles with your babysitter. Obviously you need a skilled babysitter willing to give it a go. Grandmas are sometimes the answer. Fathers can also be invaluable for this as they are often more consistent and persistent so the baby responds.

- If this does not work, unfortunately the only other thing to do is to withhold the breast until she drinks from the bottle—this might take up to twenty-four hours and usually means weaning as giving some breast and some bottle simply won't work.
- When there is absolutely no other option, a mother and baby centre can help by being with you, making sure your baby is all right and assisting you with weaning if weaning is necessary. If you do this at home, please have someone with you for moral support and practical help. It is advisable to give your baby some fluid during the process, either from a cup, spoon or dropper or go back to the occasional breastfeed if you have to.

AVOIDING THE PAINFUL OPTION

When you are faced with this dilemma it's a good idea to reassess things and work out how essential it is that your baby uses a bottle. A rest from the breast, occasional absences and regular times when you're not there can be managed by using a cup, teaspoon or dropper and letting your baby wait until you come home. Healthy breastfed babies can wait five to six hours for a feed. You are likely to find your baby is not looking for a feed nearly as often when you're not around. Alternatively, when your baby is very young you might decide to take her with you.

Trying to make a well-fed, healthy, breastfed baby drink from a bottle when she doesn't want to so she'll sleep better at night is a pointless, stressful exercise which will make no difference to her sleeping patterns, so ignore suggestions like this. Once your baby is old enough to eat food from a spoon, breastfeeds can be replaced with food and a cup. A breastfed baby never needs to be forced to use a bottle after five or six months of age unless there's some sort of unavoidable emergency (rare) or for nutritional requirements because the milk supply is very low and the baby refuses food and a cup.

FOR MORE INFORMATION

Chapter 9: Bottle Feeding Your Baby After the First Two Weeks, page 154
Chapter 10: Early Worries and Queries *(heat rash, hormone rash and so on, page 163; poo variations, page 186; regurgitation and vomiting, page 188; Infant Newborn Screening Test, page 173)*

Chapter 13: Growth and Development *(rooting reflex, page 252; hands in mouth, page 258)*
Chapter 14: Sleeping and Waking in the First Six Months *('unsettled period', page 269)*
Chapter 15: The Crying Baby *(normal crying patterns, page 286)*
Chapter 16: For Parents *(contraception and the mini pill, page 353)*
Chapter 18: Feeding Your Baby *(starting new food, page 370)*

Chapter 9

Bottle Feeding Your Baby After the First Two Weeks

Weaning

Weaning means stopping breastfeeding or expressing breastmilk into a bottle, and using other food and/or fluid instead. Infant formula is the best and safest substitute for breastmilk when babies are under twelve months of age.

Early weaning when breastfeeding doesn't work out

Weaning is often accompanied by feelings which you may find unexpected. Breastfeeding is an extension of birth—the powerful physical and emotional responses are very similar. When women plan to breastfeed and are subsequently unable to do so for reasons outside their control they can feel intense grief, guilt, anger and a great sense of loss. Alternatively other women may find that not having to continue through insurmountable problems and endless ineffective regimes brings great relief.

Intense grief and loss is experienced especially by women committed to breastfeeding, who have access to good knowledge and support but who unexpectedly experience problems no one can help them with. The decision to wean comes after weeks and sometimes months of perseverance and endless consultations with a range of breastfeeding experts.

A common complaint is that as soon as they make the often agonising decision to wean they are dropped like hot cakes by the experts they have been seeing.

I'm not sure what the answer to this is, but it seems to me that those involved in breastfeeding have an ethical responsibility to:

- Prepare women in the ante-natal period for the possibility of breastfeeding not working out as they plan (I believe this can be done without setting women up for breastfeeding failure).
- Ensure breastfeeding information is accurate, positive *and* realistic. This means avoiding making promises that 'everyone can breastfeed' and that 'all problems are solvable as long as you have access to the right health professional'.
- Learn better ways of supporting women through their grief over weaning. It's not good enough to say, 'Well, never mind, you did your best, the baby will be fine.' If this is so, these women wonder, why is the importance of breastfeeding stressed to the degree it is?

If you feel sad and/or angry about weaning it's important to let it out by talking things over with a sympathetic person who understands your anger and grief. For some women the anger and grief last a long time and it is crucial to have some appropriate support during this time.

How to wean

Weaning is often referred to as 'drying up the milk'. This is an inaccurate term as it implies weaning means a complete absence of milk. In fact, many women find they can still express some milk months after they finish breastfeeding. What you are aiming for when weaning is not an absence of milk but avoiding hard, painful breasts which may lead to mastitis.

The time it takes to do this varies from woman to woman. If lactation is not well established weaning may only take a few days, if the milk supply is abundant it's a good idea to plan on four to five weeks. Gradual weaning is the most comfortable way to wean for most women; both physically and psychologically. It also gives you a chance to think about things and perhaps combine bottle and breastfeeding rather than completely weaning (see page 142).

Start by missing one breastfeed and replacing it with formula. When you do this you will notice your breasts become quite tender. Continue to breastfeed as usual for the other feeds. When your breasts feel comfortable again, drop another feed. See page 157 for a guide to when to substitute the bottle for a breastfeed. The feeding times on the guide are only approximate. Feed at the times you normally feed. Go to each stage when your breasts are comfortable. As your milk diminishes you will need formula top-ups for some of the breastfeeds. Medication is not used to help the weaning process any longer as there are health risks associated with its use.

Weaning straight after birth

Some women decide not to breastfeed at all. Resulting levels of discomfort and breast inflammation vary a lot from woman to woman. Engorgement and pain can be helped by oral analgesics and cold compresses or cabbage leaves placed on the breasts.

The use of cabbage leaves is somewhat controversial as there is no reliable research supporting their beneficial effects or any scientific explanation as to how they work. However, there is plenty of anecdotal evidence that the use of cold cabbage leaves reduces inflammation and pain. Cabbage leaves also reduce the milk supply so care has to be taken if they are used for engorgement or oversupply not related to weaning.

USING CABBAGE LEAVES

Thoroughly washed and dried cold cabbage leaves are applied to the breast and held in place with a bra. Fan the leaves around your breast avoiding any contact with the nipples. Change leaves frequently when they become limp and warm. When using cabbage leaves for weaning continue using them for as long as they are needed for breast comfort. Obviously, do not use cabbage leaves if you think you may be allergic to cabbages or if the idea is distasteful. Stop using them immediately if you develop a rash or itchy skin.

Sudden weaning after a period of breastfeeding

It is not always possible to wean gradually for a few different reasons. When stopping breastfeeding quickly, you may experience full, hot painful breasts unless your milk supply is low or not well established.

MANAGING SUDDEN WEANING

- Wear a well-fitting firm (not tight) bra day and night.
- Take analgesics (such as paracetamol) when you need to.
- Apply cold compresses or cabbage leaves.
- Gently hand express three times a day for four to five days, twice a day for two to three days, then once a day if you need to. Whenever possible, hand express under a warm shower. You do not need to express much milk—the expressing is for comfort only.
- An intensely painful breast accompanied by illness and fever is a sign of an infection. See your family doctor as soon as possible.

Once your baby is having formula for all her feeds you may have lumpy breasts for some time. As long as they are not painful ignore them.

TIME	STAGE 1	STAGE 2	STAGE 3	STAGE 4	STAGE 5	STAGE 6
6 am	breastfeed	breastfeed	breastfeed (+ top-up)	breastfeed (+ top-up)	breastfeed (+ top-up)	W
10 am	breastfeed	BOTTLE	BOTTLE	BOTTLE	BOTTLE	E
2 pm	breastfeed	breastfeed	breastfeed (+ top-up)	BOTTLE	BOTTLE	A
6 pm	BOTTLE	BOTTLE	BOTTLE	BOTTLE	BOTTLE	N
10 pm	breastfeed	breastfeed	breastfeed (+ top-up)	BOTTLE	BOTTLE	E
2 am	breastfeed	breastfeed	BOTTLE	breastfeed (+ top-up)	BOTTLE	D

Your hormones may take some time to return to normal. Some women begin to ovulate as soon as they wean, others find the return of ovulation and menstruation is delayed by several months. If you are taking the mini pill (progesterone only) you should be aware that the chances of conceiving increase as the breastfeeding decreases so it's advisable to use alternative contraception if you wish to avoid pregnancy. It is safe to start the combined pill (oestrogen and progesterone) while your baby is still having some breastfeeds. The combined pill also helps diminish the breastmilk.

The decision to wean is yours. Try not to let anyone pressure you either way. If breastfeeding is important to you, try every avenue before you start weaning. The correct advice at a sensitive time can make the world of difference. Avoid hasty decisions. A nutritional emergency in a healthy baby that requires sudden change is very rare.

Feeding patterns

As your baby grows, the amount of milk taken at each feed increases and the number of bottles gets less. (See the chart on page 111.)

When your baby is emptying all her bottles go to the next recommended amount. Remember there is a range of variation on amount of milk and number of feeds at any age. Giving your baby what she wants, when she wants it, works well most of the time but occasionally small problems arise which need a slightly different approach.

Babies who drink too much

A number of babies seem perpetually hungry, rapidly increasing the amount they drink until they are having a lot more than what is recommended for their age and weight.

You might find that she drinks a lot between three and eight weeks of age then the amount she drinks gets less and she doesn't seem as hungry. Alternatively, she might continue to want endless bottles of 240ml without any sign of slowing down. What can you do?

- Check that you are making up the feeds correctly. If the formula mixture is too strong your baby might be thirsty, not hungry. If the mixture is too weak your baby is needing extra because she is hungry.
- Is your baby really hungry? Babies who don't sleep much want to suck

a lot for comfort, not food. Settling techniques, instead of constant bottles, can help to cut down excessive feeding. Don't forget, crying and sleeping difficulties in a baby are usually separate issues to feeding, whether the baby is breastfed or bottle fed.

Babies who drink too little

Some babies are small eaters who are invariably healthy and developing normally but exist quite happily on half the recommended amount for their age and weight.

If your baby is like this, you are probably finding that once her immediate appetite is satisfied she loses interest and starts to cry when you try to keep giving her the bottle. She may have been like this from birth or has gradually become more fussy as time goes by. When you're a mother, you can have a deep emotional investment in feeding your baby. If your baby fusses and doesn't drink what she's 'supposed' to drink, it's very easy to start thinking it's your fault and feel anxious, guilty and even angry. It's normal to feel like this but unfortunately it adds to feeding-time stress. As well, you may be contending with people around you urging you to make her drink more which doesn't help. What can you do to save your sanity? Here are a few options.

- Check that the hole in the teat is not too small.
- Check you are preparing the formula correctly.
- Look at your baby. Is she bright-eyed, alert and vigorous? Is she having six to eight pale, wet nappies a day and having a good poo every so often? If so:
  a) Take it easy—accept that she is a fussy eater. You cannot make your baby drink when she doesn't want to.
  b) Try to have relaxed feeds. When she starts to cry and refuses the bottle stop the feed, don't keep trying to make her drink when she is upset.
  c) Offer her the bottle three- to four-hourly as much as possible rather than little snacks every hour or so. Waiting until she's really hungry means she'll drink more.
  d) When you can, feed her when she is sleepy.
  e) Avoid endlessly changing the formula, the bottles and the teats. Whenever you make a change you will notice that for a day or two

things seem to improve, then go back to how they were. This tends to increase everyone's anxiety and make things worse.

Babies who drink less may put on less weight. This is not a problem for your baby as long as she is well and keeps gaining around 500 grams a month. If she has no weight gain for a month or so or loses weight, a visit to a paediatrician is a good idea.

Starting food from a spoon early (around three months) usually doesn't make a lot of difference as fussy drinkers are often fussy eaters so you end up with double trouble. Occasionally a fussy drinker loves food from a spoon which is a great relief for everyone because the amount she eats from a spoon makes up for what doesn't go down by bottle. If you try food from a spoon, make sure you give the bottle first as one or two little mouthfuls of food may mean she drinks less from her bottle than usual.

Hard poo

Generally babies who are having formula produce poo which is something like plasticine or play dough in texture and is a khaki sort of colour, but there are a few variations on the theme so don't worry if your baby's poo doesn't quite fit this description. These babies tend to go only once every day or two.

Constipation is not *how often* your baby goes but what it's like when she does go. If her poo is hard and dry like a 'rock' or small pebbles it means she is constipated. Some babies having formula do get constipated for a while until their bodies adjust.

No brand or type of formula can guarantee that your baby won't get constipated. Because all formula varies slightly, some babies may become constipated on one brand and not another. Constipation problems are hardly ever prevented or solved by using or changing to a particular brand of formula. When your baby is having formula it is nice to see a poo every day or so as that's a way of keeping check of what's going on. If she hasn't been for several days or if she does a hard, dry rock, action needs to be taken! This might happen in the early weeks if she has been having formula since birth; however, with improvements to formula this is less likely to happen now than once was the case.

What do you do?

- Remember plasticine or play dough poo is normal—no need to do anything.
- Make sure you are making up the formula correctly. Formula that is too strong causes constipation—don't forget, water first, then add the powder.
- First, try offering your baby extra drinks of cooled, boiled water a couple of times a day. This will help—if she will drink it.
- Here is an option for you to follow, **for a maximum time of twenty-four hours only,** if extra water doesn't do the trick:
  a) Put one small teaspoon of sugar into every bottle of formula until your baby does a good poo. When she poos, stop the sugar. Stop the sugar anyway after twenty-four hours—she will probably do a poo soon after the last bottle in the twenty-four hour period. A little sugar is a good way to stimulate her bowel and get things moving and far better than resorting to medications and suppositories.
  b) After the sugar regime, give a little diluted prune juice every day for a while until your baby is pooing well.
  c) Prune juice is a fruit juice made from dried plums which has an ingredient that stimulates the bowel. It is available in the supermarket or alternatively you can make your own by gently boiling about twelve prunes in 600ml of water; don't add sugar. When the mixture is a nice dark brown, strain off the water. Dilute it half and half with cooled, boiled water—try 30ml of prune juice with 30ml of water. This may be strengthened or weakened or you may give more or less according to what you think your baby needs.
- Occasionally, before you know it a crisis situation happens and your baby is so distressed immediate action is needed. If this happens it is necessary to give an infant suppository to bring quick relief. After the event start one of the regimes suggested here or see your family doctor or child and family health nurse for advice.

Sudden bottle refusal

If your baby suddenly refuses her bottle it might be a sign she is not well, especially when it is accompanied by floppiness, fever, diarrhoea or sudden unusual vomiting. Even when none of these symptoms are present see your family doctor to rule out a sore throat or an ear infection.

Bottle refusal can be caused by the smell and taste of chemical sterilant, so if your baby is well and you can't think of any other reason for her to refuse the bottle, try boiling the bottles and teats instead of using a chemical.

Changing the formula

Formula is constantly changed, often at the advice of health professionals, but changing formula will rarely change your baby's health or behaviour—it simply gives you something else to think about for a day or two. Changing the type of formula once may sometimes be warranted in special circumstances where there are clear indications for doing so (standard to hypoallergenic to low lactose and so on) but constantly swapping *brands* is pointless apart from a cost advantage.

Juice, water and vitamin supplements

Full-term babies having formula need none of the above unless constipation is a problem or the weather is very hot in which case you might like to offer extra water between feeds. Vitamin supplements are unnecessary as formula contains adequate amounts of all nutrients. Premature babies are given supplements for the first three to four months after birth to make up for their lack of stored vitamins and iron.

FOR MORE INFORMATION

Chapter 8: Breastfeeding Your Baby After the First Two Weeks *(hand expressing, page 114; mastitis, page 135)*

Chapter 16: For Parents *(contraception, page 353)*

Chapter 14: Sleeping and Waking in the First Six Months *('growth spurts' or the six weeks change, page 275; the unsettled period, page 269; options for settling, page 270)*

Chapter 18: Feeding Your Baby *(starting new food, page 370)*

Chapter 10

Early Worries and Queries

I could still remember how having a two-day-old baby makes you feel faintly sorry for everyone else, stuck in their wan unmiraculous lives.

MARNI JACKSON, *THE MOTHER ZONE, LOVE, SEX AND LAUNDRY IN THE MODERN FAMILY*

Small things cause anxious moments for parents in the early weeks after birth. Most of these things are normal and have a simple explanation—or are easy to treat if treatment is needed. If you are ever unsure of what is happening, ask for help from your child and family health nurse or family doctor.

Baby skin

Babies rarely have a flawless complexion in the first three months, so don't be alarmed when your baby breaks out in a variety of rashes and blotches. Strange rashes and dry skin during this time are usually due to your baby's body adjusting to her new world and to hormones which are passed from you to your baby just before birth. They are unlikely to be caused by allergies, breastmilk or formula, your diet or in fact anything you are doing.

Dry skin

Most newborn babies have patches of dry, flaky skin ranging from barely noticeable to what looks like a shedding of the whole outside layer of skin. Dry skin on young babies is not a dry skin condition—it is the layer of skin that came in contact with the fluid inside the womb. A moisturiser helps the appearance of the skin, but eventually the flakiness disappears whether you use a moisturiser or not.

Peeling skin is common in the groin of newborn babies. It won't worry your baby at all so don't confuse it with nappy rash. Peeling skin in the groin doesn't need treating, but if you would like to smooth on a soft cream until it goes, that's fine.

Newborn rash

The newborn rash appears soon after birth and is a blotchy red rash which is all over the baby's body. Some of the blotches have a white spot in their centre. The newborn rash is caused by things being next to your baby's skin that she is not used to such as clothes, cuddlies and nappies. It comes and goes and is more obvious when your baby cries. The blotches won't worry your baby and disappear quickly so no treatment is necessary.

Heat rash

Heat rash refers to those tiny red dots that are mostly over your baby's head and neck but you may notice it anywhere on her body, especially where two lots of skin come in contact. The tiny red dots often join up to form red splotches. Heat rash is common in babies and toddlers up to the age of three, especially when the weather gets hot; however, it appears in most newborns regardless of the weather while their bodies adjust to the relatively hot, humid environment after life in the temperature-controlled womb. As your baby's body sweats less and her skin gets used to having sweat on it, the rash fades. Overdressing sometimes contributes, but many babies of this age get heat rash no matter how they are dressed or what the weather is like. It does not cause itchiness or distress in young babies and does not need treating.

Sweating

It is normal for babies to be sweaty little people. Their bodies overcompensate for their new environment, so you are likely to notice your baby's head gets very damp while she is feeding and that the sheet in her bed is quite damp at times when you pick her up. Sweaty heads and bodies are common up until three years of age.

Hormone rash

Hormone rash is the rash still sometimes known as the 'milk rash', which is unfortunate as the rash has nothing to do with your baby's diet. The exact cause is unknown but thought to be due to the high levels of hormones passed from mother to baby during labour, stimulating the oil-producing glands (the sebaceous glands) and causing pimples. Your baby's skin may feel crusty and there may be crust on her eyebrows, head and ears.

Hormone rash and heat rash are usually around at the same time all mixed up together and the combined effect can be a bit alarming when there's a lot of both. Unless it's very severe, which is unusual, it needs no treatment as it won't bother your baby at all—she's too young to look in the mirror! The rash disappears like magic at around three months, leaving behind the fine, clear baby skin you see in advertisements in magazines or on TV.

Neither of these rashes has anything to do with your baby's crying and sleeping patterns.

Cradle cap

Cradle cap refers to the formation of crusts on the scalp, eyebrows and behind the ears. The exact cause is unknown, but cradle cap is an oily skin problem not a dry skin problem. The underlying cause can't be treated so treatment of cradle cap involves softening the crusts as they form so they can be painlessly removed. Crusts can persist on the scalp well into early childhood for some children, but for the majority of babies it stops happening between six and eight months, and often before.

Suggestions for softening and removing the crust are many and varied. Here are the ones I find easiest to use and most effective:

- For eyebrows and/or behind ears try frequent applications of sorbolene and glycerine. When you're at home, massage a little into your baby's eyebrows and behind her ears every time you change her nappy so it becomes part of your routine. At bath time wipe her eyebrows and ears gently with a flannel to remove the softened crust.

- For a crusty scalp try petroleum jelly. This is very effective for babies who don't have much hair but trickier for those with a lot of hair. Massage some petroleum jelly into your baby's scalp before bed, leave in overnight and wash out with soap the next day at bath time, removing any crusts that are soft enough to remove easily. You have to remove the crusts—they don't just float out. After the bath brush your baby's head with a soft brush.

Make sure you massage the petroleum jelly into your baby's scalp, not her hair, and don't overdo it or there'll be a terrible mess!

If there are a lot of crusts building up and it's very difficult to soften and remove them ask your chemist to mix you a combination of 2 per cent acid sal and 2 per cent sulphur in sorbolene and glycerine. Use in the same way as the petroleum jelly.

Cradle cap is a nuisance because it can't be prevented and time is the only cure. If it is mild and you don't mind the look of it you needn't do anything—it is harmless. If a lot of crusts are building up, softening them and removing them regularly prevents a build-up which looks unsightly and can get quite smelly.

Bright red rash around the anus

Most breastfed newborns poo a lot, especially in the first six weeks. Lots of poo is quite normal, but you might find your baby gets a bright red rash around her anus. Occasionally there may even be a little bleeding. It is unlikely this rash will bother your baby and once she stops pooing so much (around six weeks) the rash goes away. Until this happens a good barrier cream helps protect the skin. Put a generous dob on the anal area at every nappy change.

Baby impetigo

Occasionally newborn babies develop blisters or pimples filled with thin pus—usually on the lower part of the abdomen under the navel and/or in the nappy area. They burst and leave a raw area. The blisters and pimples are caused by a staphylococcus infection and spread if they're not treated so see your family doctor. In the early stages they can sometimes be treated successfully by applying povidone-iodine or an antibiotic ointment but often oral antibiotics are needed.

Tiny movable lumps

Tiny, movable lumps are sometimes felt under the skin anywhere on a baby's body, including the head. They are harmless and are likely to be either a small sebaceous cyst or a lump caused by burst fat cells. Neither needs treating.

Nappy rash

Nappy rashes don't happen because mothers do the wrong thing, although I'm sure many are made to feel this way when they ask for help to treat a rash.

'Do you use plastic pants?' 'What sort of nappies do you use?' 'How often do you change her nappy?' are all questions you're likely to become familiar with in the next year. Advice to stop using plastic pilchers or to leave your baby out of nappies for long stretches of the day and night is impractical and unnecessary and usually offered by experts who have never looked after babies for any length of time.

WHAT IS NAPPY RASH?

Nappy rash is a general term which refers to the variety of red, blotchy and sometimes spotty skin conditions babies get in the nappy area. Nappy rash may appear on the genitals, around the anus, on the buttocks, on the lower part of the tummy which is covered by the nappy, in the groin and on the thighs. Sometimes the whole nappy area is affected and sometimes the rash may only appear on one of the above areas.

WHAT CAUSES NAPPY RASH?

The combination of wetness, friction and heat that is generated inside a baby's nappy makes the risk of a nappy rash ever present. The chafing and sogginess damage the protective layer of skin causing an area of rough, red, hot blotchiness. Once the skin becomes damaged it often becomes infected. The most common infection in the nappy area is Candida, which is a fungus. Most nappy rashes have a fungal infection as well as the original rash within seventy hours if the treatment to remedy the red bottom is not successful.

Nappy rash can also be caused by medication, viral diarrhoea or occasionally when a new food is introduced into the baby's diet. Sometimes rashes are caused by creams, washing powders or disposable nappy liners.

No miracle cream or powder exists which prevents or cures all rashes. Frequent nappy changing helps avoid red bottoms but some babies are prone to nappy rash no matter how often the nappy is changed and will not be free of nappy rash until they are out of nappies.

Claims are made by disposable nappy manufacturers, and supported by some dermatologists, that disposable nappies have a place in preventing and treating persistent nappy rash. Good quality disposable nappies use modern materials that keep the skin dry and as they are thinner than cloth nappies are less likely to result in overheating. However, I cannot say that in my work I notice any great difference between the incidence of nappy rash whether cloth or disposable nappies are used. Successful treatment of nappy rash is most likely when a correct diagnosis of the rash is made. So if your baby's bottom doesn't respond quickly to simple measures it's a good idea to seek help from a nurse or doctor before buying out the pharmacy.

SOME GENERAL NAPPY RASH TIPS

- Frequent nappy changing helps avoid prolonged skin contact with urine and poo and so minimises wetness, friction and overheating.
- Washing of the skin in the nappy area at every change to 'keep the skin scrupulously clean' increases wetness, is irritating to the baby's skin and wipes away the natural protective secretions. If you are not treating a nappy rash, routine use of a moisturiser to both clean and keep the skin supple is recommended. Combined sorbolene and glycerine or aqueous cream in a pump pack is ideal. Use with a tissue to clean up after a wet or pooey nappy.
- If your baby has a rash and you are using a prescribed medicated cream, discard all other powders, moisturisers or creams. When your baby is just wet, pat dry with tissue. If she does a poo, clean using a damp tissue then pat dry. Use only the medicated creams for seven to ten days or until the

rash is gone. If the rash does not improve markedly in three days then let your nurse or doctor know.

- Pre-moistened baby wipes are convenient to use when you are out and about but avoid them if your baby develops a nappy rash until the rash is better because they sting and tend to dry the skin out even more. Always pat the skin dry after using baby wipes as they leave the skin very wet, causing extra friction.

NAPPY RASH IN THE FIRST THREE MONTHS

Nappy rashes in the first three months mostly cure themselves or respond to simple treatment. Newborn babies often have a heat rash in the nappy area and on the lower part of their tummy which is covered by the nappy. This usually clears quickly of its own accord. Cornflour or zinc and starch powder helps. When using powder, put some in a saucer then apply with your fingertips rather than shaking it out of the container—your baby might inhale the powder.

Many red bottoms respond well to one of the barrier, healing creams available. When one of these preparations doesn't work it often means a fungal infection is present and needs an anti-fungal cream to clear it up. When you use medicated creams make sure there is no other cream or powder on the surface of the skin as this stops the medicated cream from working.

Red patches

Red patches are often present on babies' eyelids, between their eyes on the bridge of the nose or on the forehead and on the nape of their neck. Occasionally they are also on the nose or top lip. The official name for red patches is 'storkbeak marks' and they are caused by collections of tiny blood vessels, highly visible underneath babies' fine skin, which is half the thickness of adult skin.

Storkbeak marks fade slowly, taking up to a year to finally disappear, and are always much more visible when your baby cries.

Birthmarks

Birthmarks come in a variety of colours and shapes. The common ones are listed below. Unusual birthmarks need a trip to a skin specialist to have a name put to them and to discuss the likely outcome.

MOLES

Moles are brown marks, come in a variety of shapes and sizes and often don't appear until the baby is six weeks old. Some are coffee-coloured and look as if they are painted on, others are dark brown, some are raised and sometimes they are hairy. Moles may be anywhere on the body and they are permanent.

STRAWBERRY MARKS

Strawberry marks are very common and are caused by red blood cells escaping from the blood vessels. Strawberry marks are not present at birth but appear some time in the first six weeks. They are bright red, soft swellings with often a blue appearance around the edges of the larger ones. After they first appear they have a period of growth until the baby is about nine months old then they just sit there until some time late in the second year when they begin to disappear. Most strawberry marks completely disappear by three years of age. Strawberry marks surface anywhere on the body—sometimes in the most unlikely places like inside the mouth, eye or on the genitals.

MONGOLIAN SPOTS

Mongolian spots are caused by accumulations of pigment under the skin and look like bruises. Mongolian spots are harmless and found on the skin of babies who have olive or dark skin. They are present at birth but occasionally appear as late as three months. They fade during the first three years.

Milia

Small 'whiteheads' often found on babies' noses at birth are called milia. They are caused by blocked sebaceous glands and are usually gone by four to six weeks. Don't squeeze them!

Blue patches and veins under the skin

Your baby's skin is very thin, which makes the veins under the skin very easy to see. You may notice a blue vein across the bridge of her nose and small blue patches on her body. Fine baby skin is also the reason for the blue tinge around her mouth where there is an abundant blood supply and has nothing to do with 'wind'—goodness knows where that piece of folklore came from. It's time health professionals stopped perpetuating the myth.

Blue baby hands and feet

Blue hands and feet are nothing to worry about as long as your baby is otherwise well. Tiny extremities often feel cold even in a warm atmosphere and are due to an immaturity in your baby's circulation. You will find her hands and feet quickly turn pink again when she wakes up, cries and moves around. Baby hands and feet are often very sweaty because the large numbers of sweat glands on the skin surface of the hands and feet are all over-reacting to the new environment.

Mottled skin

Mottled skin with a blue hue is quite normal and due to immature circulation of the blood. Premature babies frequently have very noticeably mottled skin.

Hairy bodies

You may be astonished at the fine fuzz of hair on your baby's body, found mostly across her shoulders, on top of her arms and on her back. Hairy ears are also common. Called 'lanugo', this hair grows while your baby is in the womb and usually disappears in the first four to six weeks after birth.

Jaundice (yellow skin)

Jaundice means that your baby's skin and the whites of her eyes look yellow. In most cases, jaundice in newborn babies is different to the jaundice children and adults get, which is usually related to illness.

A newborn baby is born with an overload of red blood cells which she needs while she is in the womb but doesn't need once she is born, so her liver starts working immediately to break down the red blood cells and excrete the left-over product which is called 'bilirubin'. Bilirubin is one of the breakdown products of blood and is normally processed in the liver then eliminated from the body in the bowel motions and urine. For some time after birth a baby's liver doesn't work as well as later, so the bilirubin builds up inside the baby's body and causes the yellow colour on the skin and eyes.

In most babies jaundice is not harmful and the colour fades by the end of the first week. Frequent feeding in the first days of life helps reduce this jaundice. Occasionally, however, the amount of bilirubin gets very high and the baby needs special treatment. As high levels are dangerous, care is taken to make sure the bilirubin levels are within a safe range. Bilirubin levels are checked by placing a special device on her skin or, if a more accurate check is needed, by a blood test. Jaundice can be made to fade more quickly by placing the baby naked under a shining bright light with her eyes protected. The light breaks down the bilirubin in the skin and takes the load off the liver.

Some jaundiced babies who are breastfed remain a pale yellow for many weeks (up to twelve weeks sometimes). This type of jaundice is referred to as 'breastmilk jaundice' or 'late onset jaundice'. Breastfeeding jaundice in otherwise healthy babies is harmless but in order to exclude other harmful forms of jaundice a blood test will be done to confirm the diagnosis. Once it is confirmed that it is breastmilk jaundice no treatment is required; it is rather a matter of waiting for the pale yellow colour to fade and disappear. *There is no need to stop breastfeeding.* Women are sometimes put through needless stress and inconvenience when they are asked to 'take the baby off the breast for forty-eight hours and give formula'. Ask for a second opinion if you don't want to do this as the only reason to stop breastfeeding for forty-eight hours is to reassure the parents and the doctor that the jaundice is in fact breastfeeding jaundice and nothing more serious.

Occasionally prolonged, worsening jaundice in the early weeks is a result of underfeeding (see page 86). On rare occasions, the jaundice is caused by something serious such as an infection, a blood disorder or a liver problem in which case the baby is cared for by a paediatrician. Again, breastfeeding can continue either from the breast or by giving expressed milk by tube, dropper, syringe or bottle.

Vitamin K

Vitamin K is offered routinely to all newborn babies to prevent a rare but potentially fatal bleeding disorder in babies in the first six months. Vitamin K is best given by a single injection soon after birth.

Infant newborn screening

Shortly after your baby's birth she will have a heel prick to collect some blood. The blood test is done to detect medical disorders which may be present in apparently normal babies. The four main disorders tested for are phenylketonuria, hypothyroidism, cystic fibrosis and galactosaemia. Some laboratories routinely test for up to thirty other rare disorders.

Phenylketonuria (PKU)

This is a rare condition (affecting one in 10,000 births in Australia) in which the baby cannot tolerate normal amounts of protein. Late diagnosis has devastating results because high levels of phenylalanine (an amino acid) circulating in the blood cause progressive brain damage which in the past was not diagnosed until the problem was obvious, by which time nothing could be done. A special milk and diet, plus supervision at a metabolic clinic in a children's hospital to frequently measure blood phenylalanine levels during early childhood means these children can now grow and develop normally. Breastfeeding can usually continue under supervision.

Hypothyroidism

This condition is caused by a lack of thyroid hormone being produced. The incidence in Australia is one in 3800. It is extremely difficult to diagnose hypothyroidism in young babies because the symptoms are very subtle and easy to miss. A delay in diagnosis results in both growth and intellectual retardation. Early treatment with thyroid hormone leads to normal mental and physical development. Treatment can be started as early as three weeks of age.

Cystic fibrosis

Cystic fibrosis is a disease which causes the intestines and lungs to produce thick mucus and affects one in 2500 babies. There is still no cure for cystic fibrosis, but the outlook has improved tremendously in the last few years, mainly due to an early diagnosis which is now possible because of the Newborn Infant Screening Test.

Galactosaemia

Galactosaemia is an extremely rare disorder caused by the accumulation in the blood of one of the sugars (galactose) found in milk. Galactosaemia is one of the few times breastfeeding is contraindicated. Babies with galactosaemia who receive breastmilk or cow's milk for any length of time will develop liver and kidney damage fairly quickly and may die. Once galactosaemia is diagnosed the baby receives a special milk which does not contain galactose and so prevents serious illness and possible death.

Parents are not informed of negative results, only positive. Sometimes a second sample has to be taken. Naturally this causes anxiety but it is usually because the first sample was not satisfactory or because of an ambiguous result at the laboratory. The overwhelming number of these repeat tests are negative and parents are informed of the result (negative or positive) as soon as possible.

Heads

Your baby's head is about a quarter of her total length so you will probably think it looks enormous in proportion to the rest of her body. The bones of her head are not joined together firmly at birth so her head can shape or mould to fit through the birth canal during labour. This means babies who are born the usual way (head-first through the vagina) often have odd-shaped heads for a while—especially noticeable when there's no hair!

Babies who are born by caesarean section or who come bottom-first usually have more rounded heads.

Sometimes babies' heads have swollen areas caused by pressure from labour. When it is just the skin involved it is called a 'caput'. Swelling caused by a caput disappears in a few days. If the bone also becomes swollen it is called a 'cephalhaematoma' and takes longer to disappear. About 20 per cent of cephalhaematomas take up to twelve months to disappear—this is nothing to worry about and again is much more noticeable on bald-headed babies.

Your baby's head has two spaces where the bone is missing, called 'fontanelles'. The fontanelle at the back of the head closes quickly and is often not noticed by parents. The fontanelle at the front of the head is diamond-shaped and fairly visible in most babies so parents are aware of its existence and are sometimes nervous about touching it or washing their baby's head. You won't hurt your baby by touching the 'soft' spot or by washing her head as the space in the bone is covered by very tough material. The size of the fontanelle varies tremendously from baby to baby and can close any time from three to eighteen months. It is quite normal to see the fontanelle pulsating and, at times, sunken. A sunken fontanelle is not a sign of impending illness in a healthy baby unless there are other signs and symptoms that something is wrong.

The joints in your baby's head are movable to allow her head to adjust to the birth canal during delivery. This is called moulding and the reason why baby heads are bumpy and sometimes a funny shape. Strange shapes usually right themselves during the first few months.

Lopsided heads

Many babies' heads grow in what appears to be a lopsided way. Head shape is a common concern for many parents, particularly as the incidence of flatness at the back of babies' heads has increased with the practice of placing babies on their backs to sleep as recommended by Sids and Kids.

Here is some basic information, but I must emphasise that if you are concerned about the shape of your baby's head please see your child and family health nurse or family doctor who will advise you if you need to see a specialist doctor. It sometimes takes an expert to differentiate between the causes of lopsided heads. The vast majority of asymmetrical or flat heads either need no attention or simple changes as to how the baby sleeps or is held, however a small number need surgery or time in a special helmet.

There are four main reasons why babies' heads look lopsided. Sometimes the flattening or asymmetry will be a combination of one or two of the following:

- As mentioned above, the joints of your baby's head are movable to allow her head to pass through the birth canal during birth. This is called moulding and is the reason why newborn heads can look lumpy and bumpy and have a funny shape. Strange shapes due to moulding usually right themselves during the first few months.
- Some heads are lopsided because the bones of the skull are soft and

when babies sleep continually on their backs as is now recommended the back of their head flattens. As the baby grows and becomes more mobile and rolls around in the night, the head shape becomes more regular. If your baby's head is very flat as a result of her sleeping position—and please get a professional opinion if there's any doubt about the exact cause of the flattening—here are some tips to help:

— Alternate your baby's head position from left to right each time she goes down to sleep.

— When your baby is awake, minimise the time she spends lying or sitting with pressure on the flattened back part of her head. Give her 'tummy time'—see page 260—when you can. Hold her upright as much as possible (without driving yourself bonkers).

- The joints of the skull (called suture lines) gradually join and become fixed by around six months of age, but are not solidly fused until late in childhood. When one of the suture lines joins more quickly than the others do, the head looks asymmetrical (lopsided). The flattening that occurs due to this process is most common on the right side of the back of the head. Most of these asymmetrical heads improve by themselves. A very small number may need surgery or special helmets to correct the shape or to allow for proper brain growth.
- Sometimes the head looks lopsided because the baby holds her head constantly to one side while looking at the other (see below).

Holding head to one side

Parents are often aware that their baby constantly holds her head to one side while always looking to the other, especially noticeable around three months when the baby has good head control. This is called 'torticollis' and varies from a mild degree of asymmetry, which is common, to a severe degree which is not nearly so common. In the past, surgery was often performed in late childhood to correct torticollis because the significance of a baby constantly holding her head to one side was not understood. Nowadays a severe degree of torticollis is almost always fully correctable with early diagnosis followed by exercises and muscle stretches under supervision of a physiotherapist.

The exact cause for torticollis is unknown but is thought to be a combination of the position of the baby in the womb, some damage to the neck muscle during birth and a lack of blood supply to a small part of the neck muscle pre-birth.

MILD DEGREE

Opinions vary as to whether any treatment is needed but a visit to a paediatric physiotherapist is useful to assess the movement of your baby's neck and to get some information on a few simple exercises and things to do to encourage your baby to hold her head to the other side and look the other way.

SEVERE DEGREE

A severe degree may be caused either because the baby has a very tight muscle in her neck or because a lump is present in the muscle. The lump is called a 'sternomastoid tumour' and is usually not present at birth but appears some time later. It gets bigger for a while then disappears at about six months. Physiotherapy treatment is the same for both and consists of exercises and muscle stretches as well as advice about the best ways to carry and lie your baby to enhance the benefit of the stretching exercises.

Hair

Your baby may be born with a thick crop of hair or she may have almost none. Thick hair tends not to fall out while fine, wispy hair falls out in patches and is gradually replaced by a new lot. Babies who sleep on their back can have a shiny bald patch on the back of their head for a long time.

It may take months or even years for hair colour to become apparent.

Eyes

Your baby can see clearly from birth and will be very interested in human faces, especially yours. Babies are short-sighted so as well as staring at your face you will notice she is attracted to light and movement.

Eye colour is a fascinating topic of conversation. Eyes that go brown stay brown so if this happens early you know what the colour will be. All other colours can change and it may take up to a year or longer to know what the final colour will be. Green eyes are unusual in the first year so it may take even more than a year before the colour is obvious. I have seen very blue eyes go brown as late as nine months.

Red streaks are often seen in babies' eyes and are due to tiny blood vessels bursting from pressure during birth. They disappear in a few weeks and are nothing to worry about.

Young babies sometimes look endearingly cross-eyed because their eye muscles are not strong enough to keep them straight (not a sign of 'wind'). Cross-eyes are usually fleeting, not constant, and stop happening at around six months of age. If it is constant or persists beyond six months the eyes need checking by an ophthalmologist or an optician.

The whites of babies' eyes look coloured, usually a bluish hue, and often stay this way until the age of two or three years. This is because the sclera (the tough white covering) is half the adult thickness for a couple of years and the blood vessels behind the sclera are easily reflected.

One eye looks bigger than the other

You might think one of your baby's eyes looks bigger than the other—lots of parents ask about this! Generally, if you look closely at photographs of anyone you will notice eye size is not identical and that most people of any age have a slight variation in the size of their eyes. It seems to be more noticeable in babies and is often because one of the eyelids falls a little lower than the other adding to the impression that one eye is bigger than the other. A mild 'droopiness' of one eyelid is very common and usually fixes itself in the first year.

Foreign body in eye

Babies occasionally collect a small foreign body in their eye such as fluff or a speck of dust which just seems to sit there not causing any irritation or distress the way it would in an adult's eyes. The best way to remove it is to float it out by squeezing some water from a saturated cotton wool ball over the eye. If this doesn't work or if your baby is distressed, see your family doctor.

Tears

Tears can be present when your baby cries as early as four weeks or might not appear until nine months.

Blocked tear duct (sticky eye)

About half of all babies develop 'sticky eye' some time in the first three months after birth. Because it is so common parents are not given a clear explanation of what the cause and possible consequences of sticky eyes are.

Most sticky eyes in young babies are caused by a blockage in the ducts which drain the eye. Sometimes the eye just waters without crustiness or discharge but often there is a yellow discharge which is worse when the baby wakes after sleep.

'Sticky eyes' in babies are usually a plumbing problem, not infectious, and don't harm the eye, so don't confuse this with the highly infectious conjunctivitis which older babies and toddlers sometimes get (usually from rubbing mucus from their noses into their eyes during the course of a cold).

WHAT SHOULD YOU DO?

Bathe the eyes when they need it. Use one clean cotton wool swab for each wipe. Start near the nose and gently wipe out. Dry the eye in a similar manner. You don't need to buy sterile, normal saline from the chemist—tap water is fine.

Breastmilk is also a useful fluid to clean sticky eyes with. If the eye is very swollen and crusty, and bathing can't keep it in check, antibiotic drops or ointment are needed. Drops are easier to put in the eye but they increase the watery effect which sometimes causes dermatitis around the eye or on the baby's cheek. Ointment is harder to administer but marginally more effective. The antibiotic ointment or drops clear away the discharge and make the eye more socially acceptable, but don't unblock the duct, so the eye often continues to water even after antibiotic treatment. If antibiotic treatment is used it is limited to a week as blocked tear ducts can take a few months to resolve and it is not necessary to continue to use antibiotics for the entire time they are blocked. On very rare occasions the blockage is so extreme oral antibiotics and attention from an ophthalmologist is required.

Mothers are often advised to massage the tear ducts. Massaging involves pressing gently but firmly up on the inside of the top of the nose where the two small ducts from the eye meet the duct which runs down the inside of the nose. For this to have any effect at all you need someone to show you how to do it.

Massaging tear ducts several times a day is something mothers find difficult to do because their baby objects and they end up feeling guilty about 'not following instructions'. Stop feeling guilty and don't worry about massaging your baby's tear ducts. After many years of observing lots of blocked tear ducts I have come to the conclusion that massaging the ducts rarely makes any difference. The tear ducts unblock spontaneously regardless of antibiotic treatment or regular massage. Most ducts clear by six months of age if not before. A few older babies need the duct probed by an ophthalmologist to clear the blockage. In an adult or older child this is a simple outpatient procedure but as babies can't lie still they need a general anaesthetic. Probing the duct is left as late as possible but usually done around twelve months of age when the blockage is still easy to fix.

Ears

Sometimes baby ears fold forward or look creased and out of shape because the ear tissue is very soft. It's best not to try sticking the ear back as doing this makes no difference, is uncomfortable for your baby and irritates her skin—most ears correct themselves in time but if you are unduly concerned about the way an ear sticks out have a consultation with a paediatric plastic surgeon.

After a while you will notice your baby's ears secrete a lot of wax. This is quite normal—it's the way the ear cleans itself.

Noses

Babies breathe rapidly, often irregularly and at times sound as if they have a blocked nose. As they cannot blow their nose or clear their throat, and their tiny airways are very narrow, normal mucus and milk accumulates which makes their breathing sound weird to adult ears. Inhaling the fluff and dust in the air is another reason babies sound blocked up and noisy when they breathe. If your baby shares your room you'll find the way she breathes very noticeable in the middle of the night. Noisy breathing accompanied by strange squeaks doesn't mean your baby is at risk in any way or she has an allergy. Ignore it if you can—there is no need to use drops or any device to extract things from your baby's nose.

Continual noisy, rattly breathing

A small number of babies who are otherwise healthy have continual noisy, rattly breathing which doesn't cause distress for the baby—only the mother who has to live with constant comments from well-meaning people around her. The reason for the noisy breathing is a temporarily 'floppy' voice box which causes the strange sounds as the baby breathes. When the vocal cords tighten some time in the first two years the noisy breathing stops.

Hoarse cry

Parents sometimes notice a hoarseness present when their baby cries and feel guilty for 'letting their baby cry for ten minutes'. In fact, babies are prone to a certain amount of hoarseness because the tissue on the area below their voice box is susceptible to swelling when they are young which makes them sound hoarse at times when they cry. In a well baby this has no significance.

Sneezing

You are probably aware that your baby sneezes a lot. Baby sneezing is due to fluff and dust in the air and sneezing is a good way for her to clear her nose.

Hiccoughs

Adults find hiccoughs uncomfortable and tedious but babies don't seem to mind them at all. A top-up at the breast or some cooled, boiled water helps if your baby's hiccoughs are worrying you but there's really no need to do anything. By the way, hiccoughs aren't caused because of the way you are feeding or burping your baby!

Sucking blisters

You might notice small blisters on your baby's top lip. These are called sucking blisters and are normally present when babies are getting all their food from sucking. Sucking blisters are a natural condition which do not cause discomfort.

White tongue

Babies do not make a lot of saliva until they are eight to twelve weeks old so they frequently have milky-looking tongues when they are very young because there's not a lot of saliva to clean the tongue. When they are having formula the white tongue looks quite thick.

N.B.: White tongue and sucking blisters are often confused with thrush. Thrush in a baby's mouth appears as patchy, white spots on the inside of the lips and cheeks. The patchy spots cannot be removed by wiping. Thrush rarely causes babies discomfort unless it is left untreated for a long time and gets to the inflamed, bleeding stage. If you are unsure whether your baby has thrush or not, see your child and family health nurse or family doctor.

White spots on gums

Raised, white pearly spots are sometimes seen in the roof of babies' mouths and on their gums where they are often mistaken for teeth. These small cysts tend to pop out on the side of the gum, are not related to teeth in any way and are not the reason why your baby is going through an unsettled stage. Raised white spots appear on and off during the first year and disappear as mysteriously as they arrive.

Tongue tie

Tongue tie refers to a condition where the baby's tongue is attached to the floor of the mouth rather than floating free. Mild tongue tie is very common, tends to correct itself and is unlikely to cause any problems with sucking, eating or talking. Babies or children with more severe tongue tie who have difficulties with sucking, eating or talking may need surgical release of the tongue after careful evaluation of the anatomy by a paediatric surgeon. It is important that severe tongue tie is released. As well as problems with sucking, eating and talking, serious tongue tie causes tooth decay from a young age because the anchored tongue is unable to clean the mouth and teeth effectively. Severe tongue tie needing surgical intervention is not common and more likely to be found in families where there is a history of the condition.

(See Tongue tie and breastfeeding, page 92.)

Lumps in the jaw

You may feel lumps under the skin on your baby's jaw or cheekbone. These are due to fat cells bursting during labour and more likely to present after a birth with forceps. The lumps are harmless and disappear in a few weeks.

Lumps like small peas on the back of the neck

Small, movable lumps behind a baby's ears or on the back of the neck are common and normal. They are enlarged lymph nodes and are not significant unless they are large, tender or warm to touch, in which case see your family doctor.

Lots of saliva

Between eight weeks and twelve weeks you are bound to notice that your baby starts to have a very wet mouth with lots of bubbles. 'Teeth!' everyone around you exclaims, but constant dribbling from the age of three months is unrelated to the growing of teeth. All babies froth and bubble from this age whether they grow their first tooth at three and a half months (earliest apart from the rare baby who is born with a tooth) or seventeen months (the latest).

Eight to twelve weeks is the time the human body starts to make saliva. Babies don't know how to swallow their saliva and sit around with their mouths open all day so it all falls out! When your baby learns to shut her mouth and swallow her saliva (some time around the age of fifteen months) the dribbling stops.

Bodies

'Poddy' tummies (pot bellies)

It is normal for babies to have poddy tummies. As long as they are healthy, well-fed and not showing any other signs of illness, poddy tummies are not an indication of 'colic', 'wind', 'overfeeding', 'underfeeding', 'lactose intolerance' or anything other than a normal lack of muscle tone, a state of affairs that lasts well into toddlerhood.

A dimple at the base of the spine

This is called a sacral dimple and looks like a tiny hole the size of a pinhead in the centre of your baby's back just above her buttocks. Close examination will reveal it isn't a hole but a dimple. Sacral dimples are very common and most grow out in time.

Fingernails

Staff in maternity hospitals may advise you to bite, peel or file your baby's fingernails; this is fine when she is very young but after the first week feel free to cut them with a pair of scissors. Buy a small pair of blunt-ended scissors, wait until your baby is relaxed, gently pull away the skin from behind the nail and cut the top off the nail. When you are not used to cutting baby fingernails it's a bit scary at first, but you'll be amazed at how quickly you become good at it.

Toenails

Baby toenails look as if they are ingrown as they are very short and embedded in the nail bed. Toenails grow up and out during the next three years so there is no need to worry about this.

Blisters around fingernails and toenails

Sometimes the skin around the fingernails and/or toenails becomes red and swollen and may form blisters. This doesn't bother the baby and can usually be treated by dabbing on some povidone-iodine. Occasionally more severe infections need antibiotics.

Scratching

Small babies scratch their faces and it's impossible to cut their nails short enough to prevent this happening. Mittens aren't a great idea as babies prefer their hands free and the scratches heal very quickly. Most scratching stops when the baby's movements become a little more co-ordinated, usually around three months of age.

Grunting

You are probably amazed at the strange noises your baby makes, especially as you lie awake in the middle of the night unable to sleep as snuffling, snorting, squeaking, grunting and groaning sounds fill the air. Grunting seems to be the one that bothers most parents as there is the fear there is a 'blockage' or that their baby is in some sort of pain and needs treatment. All babies make noises in the night and all babies grunt to some degree, some more than others—premature babies do it all the time!

Red, swollen breasts

The same hormones, passed from mother to baby at birth which cause the hormone rash, also cause enlarged breasts in many babies (boys and girls). It may happen to one or both breasts and varies from being hardly noticeable to extremely obvious. Occasionally the breasts excrete a little milky fluid. They will take six to eight weeks to go back to normal, are not uncomfortable for your baby and rarely need treatment.

Umbilical cord

Your baby's cord will eventually shrivel and fall off. The time it takes to do this varies from a few days to three weeks, occasionally longer. After the cord falls off, expect a little discharge and bleeding to come and go for up to three weeks. If needed, clean the navel with cotton wool and water. Alcohol is unnecessary once you leave hospital and in fact the use of alcohol on cords for full-term healthy babies is being stopped in many maternity hospitals throughout Australia. Cord infections are rare but a very strong smell and shiny, puffy red skin around the navel is an indication all is not well. See your family doctor.

Navels that stay moist

Sometimes a collection of cells, called a 'granuloma', remain after the cord has fallen off. Until these cells die a continual, sticky discharge keeps the navel moist. The discharge is usually not a sign of an infection and won't harm your baby but may irritate the skin around the navel and cause a red rash. Granulomas can persist for several months. Your family doctor can touch the granuloma with some copper sulphate which helps it dry up, but don't be tempted to do this yourself as there are rare times when a granuloma is a sign of something more complicated.

Bowel motions

The first motion your baby passes is called meconium and is a greenish, black sticky substance which gradually changes until the amazing, unpredictable array of bowel motions start to appear.

Mothers are often amazed at the number of times their baby does a poo in the early weeks. It's quite normal when you're breastfeeding to feel as if you are putting food in one end only to have it immediately returned from the other. Frequent runny poo doesn't mean your baby has diarrhoea or your milk is too sugary or rich.

You may find your baby's bowel motions vary a lot. They can be bright yellow (like pumpkin), seeded dark yellow (like French mustard), dark green and mucousy or a lovely lettuce green. None of these variations are significant in a healthy, thriving baby.

Breastfed babies generally poo many times a day in the first six weeks. This gradually decreases in the second six weeks until some only do a big poo every so often. Every so often may be once every two or three weeks. When your baby is only having breastmilk and no other food or fluid this is absolutely nothing to worry about. Don't compare it to adult bowel habits and feel you have to do something to make your baby 'go' if she is in this sort of a pattern.

A breastfed baby who doesn't poo much in the first six weeks may not be getting enough milk, although this is certainly not always the case. The best way to check is to weigh your baby and get an idea how much weight she has been gaining weekly since birth.

Babies who have formula usually do dark, sticky poo that looks like plasticine.

BLOOD IN THE POO

Occasionally an otherwise healthy baby passes a mucousy blob of blood in her poo. This can happen whether the baby is breastfed or having formula and although it is rarely a sign of anything significant you should always check with your family doctor or paediatrician. Unless it persists or unless other symptoms are present your baby should not need treatment or investigation.

Cracking joints

Many parents notice their baby's joints crack, most noticeably the knees and shoulders. Clicky hips may need treatment (see below), but cracky knees and shoulders are quite normal.

Clicky hips

A clicky hip means that the hip joint can be moved around easily. Most new babies have clicky hips at birth because the ligaments around the joint are loose which means the head of the thigh bone moves out of place easily. The ligaments are loose because they have been softened by the same maternal hormones that also cause the temporary hormone rash and enlarged breasts. Clicky hips due solely to stretched ligaments are also temporary, improve rapidly and need no treatment.

CONGENITAL DISLOCATION OF THE HIP

This means the head of the thigh bone does not fit properly into the socket because the socket is shallow. It doesn't happen very often but when the socket is shallow it is important the treatment to form a deep socket for the head of the thigh bone to fit into is started as soon as possible.

Congenital dislocation of the hip (CDH) can be diagnosed by a skilled health professional moving the baby's legs in a special way to see if the thigh bone can be moved out of the socket. It is tricky and sometimes X-rays or ultrasound is used when CDH is suspected or a baby is in the high risk group for CDH. Early diagnosis is vital to prevent lifelong problems. The modern treatment is usually a 'Pavlik harness', which holds the hips at right angles to the body and stops the baby stretching her legs out so a deep socket is formed for the head of the thigh bone to fit into. The harness is worn for about three months and is a highly successful way of treating CDH. The use of double nappies for treating either clicky hips or CDH is no longer recommended.

Feet

Baby feet often turn in and out in a funny fashion. Most of the time this is because of the way the baby lies in the womb. These are called postural deformities and always correct themselves either spontaneously or with simple exercises or the use of a plaster for a short time.

A club foot points downwards and inwards and is usually a structural deformity where the foot has limited movement. It needs immediate attention from birth. Treatment is long-term and involves physiotherapy, splinting and possibly surgery to get a more normal foot position.

Regurgitation and vomiting

Terminology has become a complicated issue in relation to the subject of the throwing-up (a nice simple term accessible to everyone) that most babies do to some extent during their first year—and occasionally beyond.

Here are some definitions to make it clearer.

REGURGITATION (FORMERLY REFERRED TO AS REFLUX VOMITING)

It is normal in humans of all ages for food from the stomach to flow back up into the gullet, especially after meals. This back-flow is called 'reflux', the technical name of the stomach is *gastro*; of the gullet, *oesophagus*; hence the term gastro-oesophageal reflux is used to describe this action. In childhood and adulthood we are unaware of it unless it causes heartburn or other problems (nasty taste in the mouth, sore throats, coughing, sleepless nights).

The reason the food flow goes up and down unnoticed in adults and children is because the gullet is large enough to hold the churned up food (isn't this disgusting?) from the stomach and because the muscle, known as the oesophageal sphincter, at the top opening of the stomach works efficiently to keep the food down where it's supposed to be.

Babies, on the other hand, because of small gullets, inefficient oesophageal sphincters and a few other highly technical things I won't bother you with tend to lose the gastric contents when reflux occurs. The fact that babies' diets are liquid, they are kept horizontal rather than vertical a lot of the time and have their legs pushed up at nappy change time doesn't help.

This loss of milk and later food in the first year in otherwise healthy babies is viewed as normal and is now referred to as regurgitation, not vomiting. Regurgitation is, by and large, harmless even when it looks like your baby is regurgitating every skerrick of milk from the last feed.

Now we've sorted that out, let's look at the regurgitation problem. It is normal for healthy babies to regurgitate their food. Some do it a lot, others only occasionally. Sometimes it is quite dramatic and will frighten the life out of you as your baby returns milk in a great gush from both nose and mouth. If the milk is returned straight after a feed it comes up the way it went in. If it comes up sometime later when it is partly digested it is lumpy and a trifle smelly. About half of all babies regurgitate enough to worry their parents and complicate normal living, whether it's a great gush or continual splats of curdled, partly digested milk with its own distinctive aroma, often deposited on a shoulder. Almost all babies bring up some milk along with a burp in the middle or at the end of a feed.

The regurgitation may start soon after birth or may not start until your baby is nearer to three months. It is often an on-again, off-again sort of thing—just when you think it's over it starts again. A small number of babies have problems associated with regurgitation such as heartburn—a rare, over-diagnosed condition—lung problems and very occasionally, poor weight gains. See Gastro-oesophageal reflux disease, page 295.

All these things need special attention; however, the majority of regurgitating babies have no ill effects from their regurgitating, apart from the constant aroma and mess which doesn't bother them at all. Needless to say, being regurgitated on all day does not do much for mothers' self-esteem and it is a great relief when it stops happening—at about a year for lots of babies, earlier for others.

Here are a few tips:

- Regurgitation happens equally to breastfed and bottle fed babies, although the amount of spilt milk is less from breastfed babies. Most families with more than one baby will have one baby who regurgitates all over the place, nearly always a happy baby with no other complications.
- There is no treatment that is outstandingly successful, so if your baby is

otherwise happy and well there is no need to worry or do anything. Weaning or changing to a soy formula is a pointless exercise. The smell of breastmilk returned is far more pleasant than formula and soy formula smells the worst.

- If you are bottle feeding it may be tempting to try the 'reflux' formula kindly offered by thoughtful formula manufacturers in response to the normal anxiety constant regurgitation brings. Thickened formula does decrease the volume of milk being returned by otherwise happy babies, so it makes the parents of regurgitating babies happy too. In view of the fact that the baby is happy anyway, the use of thickened formula is more for social reasons and a clean carpet than health. Thickened formula tends to make babies constipated. Because of what I see as their limited use I do not recommend them unless the amount of milk being regurgitated is causing the parents a great deal of grief.
- Don't change your feeding to accommodate the regurgitation—that is, don't feed less often or for shorter periods if you're breastfeeding (posture feeding is not recommended) or dramatically cut down the amount in the bottle if you're using formula. It is not your method of feeding or your technique that is making your baby regurgitate, so feed away as if it wasn't happening.
- Helpful relatives and health professionals may advise starting on solids to help stop the flow of milk up and out. Early introduction of food from a spoon makes no difference, it just makes for interesting coloured regurgitated stomach contents, especially if your baby eats avocado!

Should the milk be replaced after a lot comes back?

If your baby seems content don't worry about replacing the milk. If she seems to be hungry or wanting to suck some more, put her back to the breast or give her another 60ml of formula.

NOW LET'S LOOK AT VOMITING

Vomiting, as opposed to regurgitation, technically refers to a heaving ejection of food by the stomach because of illness. Vomiting is not normal and may be harmful. Vomiting can be caused by illnesses such as pyloric stenosis, an upper respiratory tract infection, a urinary tract infection or gastroenteritis. These illnesses cause signs and symptoms such as fevers, significant weight loss, sniffles and mucus, loss of interest in feeding, dry nappies or diarrhoea. It's wise to get vomiting checked out unless it's a one-off and you're pretty sure what's caused it. Regurgitation is unlikely to have any of these symptoms, but if in doubt always seek a professional opinion.

BLOOD IN REGURGITATED MILK

Healthy babies who regurgitate milk with blood in it are usually breastfed babies whose mothers have sore nipples. The colour of the blood can vary from pink to a dark, almost black colour. When the nipples are cracked and bleeding the reason for the blood in the regurgitated milk is quite obvious, but sometimes there may be no visible signs of a bleeding nipple, just tenderness. This does not hurt your baby but you will need help with your breastfeeding.

Pink urine

A pink stain in the nappy is a substance called urates (not blood). This is often present in the urine of young babies until the kidneys become mature enough to filter it out. Urates in the first seventy-two hours after birth are viewed as normal, after this time, especially if accompanied by green 'splat' poo, urates are indicative of dehydration. In this situation seek advice as quickly as possible, especially if your baby is not sucking vigorously (see page 86).

Transparent 'crystals' in urine

If you see tiny balls of clear white jelly in your baby's urine and she is wearing a disposable nappy it is the filling that is used in disposable nappies to absorb moisture. It is harmless.

Genitals

The genitals of both boys and girls often look larger than life, which is partly due to hormones and partly due to the birth process (particularly babies who are born bottom-first).

BOYS

It's quite common for a baby boy's scrotum to have fluid in it which makes the scrotum look large and swollen; this is called hydrocele. As the fluid is gradually absorbed the scrotum subsides—it may take several months.

Normally there are two testes in the scrotum which are quite easy to feel. Testes travel from the abdominal sac into the scrotum during late pregnancy. If the opening through which they travel doesn't close off, one of the testes can appear and disappear from the scrotum, especially when the scrotum is exposed to the cold. Eventually the opening from the abdominal sac closes and the testicle remains in the scrotum.

Occasionally one or both of the testes never descend and so are never felt in the scrotum. If the testicle doesn't descend into the scrotum after one year of age surgery is performed some time between one and three years. The operation involves bringing the testicle into the scrotum and securing it there. Penises come in a variety of shapes and sizes. If you are worried about the size or shape check with your family doctor.

Circumcision: In most baby boys a piece of skin, known as the foreskin, covers the tip of the penis. Surgical removal of the foreskin is called circumcision. Twenty to thirty years ago circumcision was performed routinely on most baby boys in Australia, often without discussion with the parents! At one time baby boys were subjected to this procedure in the labour ward straight after delivery.

Most medical opinion now views routine circumcision as an unnecessary, risky operation. From time to time media reporting suggests that routine circumcision prevents Human Immunodeficiency Virus (HIV) and sexually transmitted diseases (STDs). And, indeed, there are some health professionals who claim this to be the case and favour routine circumcision for this reason. This is controversial as the studies supporting this claim are conflicting and have mostly been done in poor countries with high HIV rates, where, owing to living conditions, there is poor personal hygiene, inadequate medical services and dodgy safe-sex education. In industrialised countries primary prevention of HIV and STDs centres around sound safe-sex education and appropriate public health measures (eg, condom use) not routine circumcision. To see the Royal Australasian College of Physicians *Policy Statement on Circumcision* go to www.racp.edu.au The current policy was last updated in 2004 and is under review at the moment. The updated policy will be released sometime before the end of 2008. If you would like a parent's brochure on the topic email paed@racp.edu.au or call (02) 9256 5409. If you want your son circumcised for non-religious reasons talk it over with a few people so you are clear about why you want it done.

Things like cleanliness, a matching set with father or to avoid future problems are not valid reasons either medically or aesthetically.

If you decide to go ahead, the safest and kindest way is to wait until your son is over six months old and have it done under a general anaesthetic.

Newborn circumcisions are still performed and if this is your choice you will probably have to make private arrangements with your doctor, as circumcisions are hardly ever done in maternity hospitals. Newborn circumcisions are done rapidly without any anaesthetic, usually in the doctor's surgery sometime in the first two to four weeks after birth. Your baby should be full-term, healthy, gaining weight and not jaundiced. It is normal for the tip of the circumcised penis to often look bluish in colour.

Uncircumcised penises need the same care as the elbow—none! The foreskin should not be pushed back. It will retract eventually of its own accord, often around three years of age. Forcing the foreskin back before it is ready causes pain, bleeding and scarring that may cause damage resulting in a circumcision having to be done.

GIRLS

Baby girls occasionally have a small amount of bleeding from the vagina, caused by the withdrawal of some of the maternal hormones they receive at birth. When you part the labia you will see a white discharge around the vagina and inside the labia. This is a normal secretion—you do not have to clean it. If the labia can't be parted on a baby girl of any age check with your family doctor. The labial skin on babies and toddlers is often paper thin so the edges of the labia adhere to each other. This is a benign condition which usually resolves without treatment so the previous practice of applying oestrogen cream has been abandoned unless there are complications (unusual).

Minor medical problems common in the first three months

Hernias

A hernia in a young baby happens because a special structure needed by the baby when she was growing in the womb doesn't close off the way it is supposed to after birth. One of the internal parts of the body then bulges through the opening. The two most common places this happens are the navel and the groin.

UMBILICAL HERNIA (NAVEL)

An umbilical hernia is a soft swelling on the navel which becomes noticeable when the cord drops off. Some are small, others are almost alarmingly large.

If your baby has one you will notice when she is quiet the navel is flatter than when she cries, at which time the bulge pops out looking like a 'cherry balloon'. Gently pushing it shouldn't worry your baby and makes a squelchy sound.

An umbilical hernia is caused by an abnormal opening between the abdominal wall and the abdomen which is present before birth to allow nourishment to pass to the baby by the umbilical cord. Sometimes it does not completely close as it is supposed to after birth and a small part of the intestine protruding through is well covered with skin and tissue, so the condition is usually harmless and rarely needs treatment. In time the tummy muscles grow close so the bulge decreases slowly and goes away, usually by the age of three years, if not before.

Rare conditions do exist where an umbilical hernia is partially or fully strangulated. More rarely, abdominal protrusions in young babies can be a sign of an abdominal defect which needs urgent repair, however, unless these abnormalities are present even large umbilical hernias are usually left untreated.

Applying sticking plaster or binding to the navel causes a rash, is uncomfortable for the baby and makes no difference to the bulge.

INGUINAL HERNIA (GROIN)

An inguinal hernia appears as a lump in the groin. The swelling often comes and goes according to whether the baby is sleeping or crying. It's a good idea to check for the presence of a lump in the groin if your baby is having sudden screaming attacks for no apparent reason, especially if your baby is premature, as inguinal hernias happen to premature babies more often than full-term babies.

This kind of hernia is caused by an abnormal opening between the abdominal wall and the groin which is present before birth to allow the passage of the testicle into the scrotum. The opening is present in boys and girls (even though girls don't have testes or a scrotum) and normally closes a month before birth, which is why an inguinal hernia is more common in premature babies.

Unlike an umbilical hernia, an inguinal hernia always needs an operation to prevent complications. This is because the opening through which the intestine protrudes is small and the muscles in the groin tight, so the blood supply to the intestine may be cut off. Even if the lump can be pushed back or doesn't cause distress, it should be repaired as soon as possible. It may repeat on the other side so both sides are repaired. Surgery is very successful and involves one or two days in hospital.

Head colds

Colds are not common in the first six to twelve weeks because the antibodies mothers pass to their babies protect them to some extent. Remember, snuffling and sneezing in the first three months is not a sign of a head cold unless there are other symptoms. Head colds are caused by viruses which damage the mucous membranes of the nose and throat. This is what causes the runny nose, the sore throat and eyes, the cough and sometimes a headache and fever.

Complications from head colds such as ear or chest infections are more common in babies and young children than in adults. As well, the extra mucus generated by a cold seems to hang around forever, even after the cold gets better.

There's not a lot you can do to prevent your baby from catching a cold. Breastfeeding helps, but breastfed babies can still catch colds. It's difficult to keep a spluttering toddler with a streaming nose away from her baby brother or sister, but you can ask friends and relatives with head colds not to come too close.

HERE ARE SOME HEAD COLD TIPS

Head colds without a fever are rarely helped by any of the various medications commonly suggested. The decision whether or not to use antibiotics can be difficult. Most head colds are caused by viruses so antibiotics (which fight bacteria) are unlikely to do a lot. Antibiotics can cause diarrhoea and fungal infections so their use often complicates head colds in babies rather than having any beneficial effect. Babies with head colds aren't helped much by drugs which dry up the mucus. Some have a sedative effect which is best avoided, especially in babies under six months. Constant use of medicated nose drops increases the mucus and may damage the lining of your baby's nose—which leads to other problems later—however, used occasionally, can help if your baby is too blocked up to feed properly.

If your baby is sleeping and eating as well as can be expected given that she is somewhat miserable and uncomfortable, there is no need to medicate. Noisy, 'bubbly' breathing is acceptable as long as she is not struggling to breathe. It's normal for a baby with a head cold to do poo which contains mucus and have a few mucus-filled vomits too.

Unfortunately there is no magic potion which makes colds get better quicker. Treatment always involves relieving the symptoms. If your baby has a badly blocked nose here are some helpful hints:

- Try a vaporiser. Despite the fact that recent research shows a vaporiser makes very little difference, lots of the parents I talk to find a vaporiser helps. Some pharmacies have vaporisers for rent which means you can try before you buy.
- A little Vicks dabbed onto the sheet in your baby's cot, well away from her mouth, will help her to breathe more easily. It's best not to put it directly onto a young baby's skin and to test a small amount before rubbing it onto the chest of an older baby.
- Weak saline nose drops can be used freely to wash out her nose. If you use medicated drops try to only use them occasionally before a feed if her nose is so blocked she can't suck. Once the worst of the cold is over (about a week) and your baby can suck reasonably happily again stop using them.

If your baby has a head cold with a fever (37.5°C or above), dress her lightly and give extra breastfeeds or other clear fluids. See page 469 for more information regarding fevers.

Coughing accompanying a head cold is usually caused by the mucus trickling down the back of your baby's throat. If there is a lot of coughing, check with your doctor to make sure there is no chest infection. If her chest is clear, try some of the suggestions for blocked noses. Cough suppressants shouldn't be given to babies.

It's wise to consult your doctor if you are worried or if she has a fever when she is under three months. Other symptoms which need medical attention are breathing difficulties or wheezing and feeding problems in young babies who suddenly refuse to suck.

Bronchiolitis

Bronchiolitis is an infection caused by a virus that babies can get and is similar (but not the same as) an attack of bronchitis in adults. It often occurs in epidemics, especially during the winter months. The virus causes coughing, wheezing and cold symptoms and the younger the baby, the more potentially serious the condition, especially if the baby was born prematurely. An attack of bronchiolitis can range from being mild to severe. No drugs are available to destroy the virus so antibiotics are not appropriate and treatment involves making sure the baby's breathing is adequate, and that the baby is eating enough to stay well nourished.

Mild cases are treated at home while moderate to severe cases need admission to hospital, sometimes to an intensive care unit.

Bronchiolitis usually gets worse for three to four days, stays the same for another three to four days then starts to get better, taking about two weeks for full recovery. The cough is the last thing to go. An attack of bronchiolitis does not mean the baby will become an asthmatic later on.

Medicating babies

A wide range of baby medications is available and large numbers of healthy babies are given some sort of medication before they are three months old. Most of the time the use of medication is inappropriate, not needed and doesn't cure the problem.

Why are drugs used so much?

Part of the delight and frustration of babies is their mystery. They can't talk and tell us what the matter is or how they feel, and unfortunately part of the way we look after babies is to regard everything they do as a curable medical condition even when what they are doing is related to their behaviour, not their health. Parents become very anxious when their baby is either not well or does puzzling things (like crying a lot) and often, on the advice of a health professional, use some sort of medication in the hope of a miraculous cure or a change in their baby's behaviour.

Most of the time the commonly used drugs or herbal remedies have little effect on the health and behaviour of otherwise healthy babies. At best they are a waste of money—at worst some may be harmful, particularly when they have a sedative effect.

There are times when medication is vital because of a chronic or serious health problem and this should be taken care of under a doctor's supervision and monitored regularly; however, giving well babies drugs is often unnecessary so here's a few things to think about before you do:

- Try to think through why you are giving the drug. Is it for a clearly defined physical symptom or is it because of the way your baby is behaving? For example—a fever is a clearly defined physical symptom. Grunting, going red in the face and drawing up legs is a normal way for babies to behave. These are not clearly defined physical symptoms of a medical problem.
- If you are advised or prescribed medicine for your baby ask the following questions: What's in the drug?; What are the possible risks and side effects?; What condition are you treating and how does the drug work?; What are you hoping to achieve by giving my baby this drug?; What are the chances of a positive response?; Is this drug really necessary?
- Read the label. Find out what is in the medication. Generally, medication which contains a single drug is preferable to those which combine several.
- Give the medication from a dropper or a teaspoon—not in your baby's bottle or in her food.

As your baby grows and you learn more about her normal development and behaviour, you will become more confident and manage without relying on unnecessary medication, especially when you have seen her through one or two minor illnesses.

When to call the doctor

Often new parents don't have a doctor as having a baby usually happens at a time in life when people are generally well and have no need of medical care. Once a few babies start to arrive, however, a doctor you know and trust is a very worthwhile investment. Lots of doctors have special areas of interest that they have given extra time, attention and study to, so look for one who has an interest in paediatrics and family medicine.

Deciding when to take your baby to the doctor because she is unwell or behaving strangely is a dilemma for most new parents (and often for those not so new). A few guidelines follow.

There are often times when a baby has slight behaviour changes or mild symptoms which do not need urgent attention. Frequently the problems resolve themselves quickly or you find out they are not problems at all but normal features of babyhood.

Babies in the first twelve months have a whole range of interesting strange habits which adults try to interpret, often coming up with quite inappropriate conclusions. Similar strange actions and habits are common to all babies and are usually reflexes, part of normal development or a baby's way of practising skills. For example, playing with and pulling ears is one of these actions and not a sign of 'teething' or an ear infection.

If your baby is thriving, active and wetting and pooing normally it's unlikely there's anything wrong, but always seek help when in doubt. Sometimes situations do arise that need immediate medical attention. Here they are:

- A sudden loss of interest in feeding, especially when it's a young baby who won't suck.
- A constant high fever that doesn't respond to paracetamol and taking off some of the baby's clothes. Any fever in a baby under three months.
- Sudden vomiting and diarrhoea for any length of time.
- Persistent screaming—'crying around the clock'.
- Difficulty breathing.
- Any abnormal discharge, especially from the ears.
- A convulsion or fit.
- Any strange posture or unusual eye or body movements.

- A sudden outbreak of a strange rash you can't identify.
- Any unusual swelling or lump, especially if it is painful to touch.
- Loss of interest in surroundings and/or abnormal sleepiness or floppiness.
- Thick, smelly urine.

Helping your doctor to help you

Find out about house calls and what service is available out of hours.

If several things are worrying you about your baby, make a list before you see your doctor. Try to give her or him a clear message about the problem without introducing a whole range of irrelevant issues. Ask for a clearer explanation, if you don't understand something.

Second opinions are useful, but if you keep shopping around no one will be directly responsible for your care and you may not get the best help when you really need it. Give your doctor time to get to know you and your baby so she or he can give you individual care which is suited to your needs.

Finally, babies and young children often behave in quite unpredictable ways which are well within the normal range. They also get funny things wrong with them when no one really knows what the matter is. Don't push your doctor for a diagnosis and medication for the sake of it. If she or he is honest enough to admit they don't know what's wrong, respect this honesty. Far too many normal babies and children are put through a barrage of unnecessary and invasive diagnostic tests and given inappropriate medicine because of pressure from parents for a precise answer when there is none.

FURTHER READING

All About Kids' Skin: The Essential Guide for Parents, Dr Phillip Artemi and Tina Aspres, ABC Books, Australia 2008. Great detailed information by an Australian paediatric dermatologist and a pharmacist.

Chapter 11

Daily Care

If you were an Eskimo baby
You'd live in a bag all day.
Right up from your toes
To the tip of your nose
All in thick cosy furs tucked away.

LUCY DIAMOND, 'AN ESKIMO BABY', *THE BOOK OF A THOUSAND POEMS*

Unless you are used to handling small babies you are likely to feel awkward and a bit nervous for the first few weeks when you dress and undress your baby, change her nappy and bath her. Feeling like this is normal. Your baby is blissfully unaware that you are learning and you will be amazed how quickly you become efficient at babycare skills.

Changing the nappy

If you are using cloth nappies it really doesn't matter which of the folding methods you use as long as the nappy goes on firmly and does what it's supposed to do. The same size cloth nappies fit your baby until she no longer needs them. Adjustments are made to allow for her size as she grows by the way you fold the nappy. You will need to use double cloth nappies at night once your baby starts sleeping longer. Most brands of disposables last all night without leaking, but if there are problems try poking holes in one nappy with a fork, put it on then put a second one over the top.

How often?

Expect to use eight or more nappies every twenty-four hours. Nappies need changing once or twice at most feed times and at other times when your baby is awake.

There's no need to change your baby before a feed when she's ravenous unless there's a leaky mess. Likewise, if she's been changed before and during a feed it's fine to put her down without changing her again. If your breastfeeds are close and frequent don't worry about changing her every time you feed—just pop her on the breast and put your feet up.

What do you do?

Take off the used nappy using the front of the nappy to wipe off any poo still on your baby. Fold the nappy so the poo can't fall out and put it to one side. Gently wash her bottom, front and back, with damp tissues or tissues and pump pack sorbolene and glycerine, paying attention to wiping in between creases. To clean the back part lift her legs, holding both ankles together in one hand with a finger between her ankles and raise her bottom slightly.

After washing, pat dry. Apply cream or powder if you are using any. Put on a clean nappy. If you are using disposables, wipe your fingers clean of any cream otherwise you'll have trouble getting the adhesive tabs to stick. The part of the disposable nappy with the tab goes to the back—the part of the nappy the tab adheres to goes to the front.

Girls do not need the labia separated to 'clean inside'. Boys should never have their foreskin pushed back.

Dress your baby and leave her somewhere safe while you deal with the used nappy. Whether you use a cloth or a disposable scrape the poo off the nappy into the toilet before either soaking it or putting it in a plastic bag and throwing it out.

Don't forget to wash your hands.

Dressing and undressing

Make sure the change table or bench top you are going to use to dress and undress your baby is flat, firm, stable and the right height for you to work comfortably. It's much easier to use a change table or a bench top than to use your lap or bend over a bed.

When dressing or undressing you'll probably find it's the top half that's the trickiest until you become more skilled.

Undressing

Leave the nappy till last. Undo all the fasteners. Gently slide her legs out of the jumpsuit or pull off any tights. Roll the jumpsuit to shoulder level and gently pull the sleeves over and off each arm. If your baby has a separate top stretch the neck of the garment after your baby's arms are free and remove it carefully from *front* to *back* over her head so it doesn't touch her face.

Dressing

Put the nappy on first. Once again, stretch the neck of the garment and this time, going from *back* to *front* pull it over her head so it doesn't touch her face, supporting the back of her head raising it slightly as you go. Guide your baby's arms through both arm holes into the arms then her legs into the bottom half. Do up all the fasteners.

Dressing, undressing and bathing young babies is complicated by the way a lot of them cry and appear to be very distressed while it's all going on. After the contained life in the womb where there were limits to their movements and a relatively unchanging environment, even small changes to their bodies and their world will worry them until they become accustomed to new sensations and feelings. Lying naked on a bench top must feel a bit like falling off a cliff to young babies as they have no knowledge of the extent of their new boundaries.

By three months most babies don't mind having their nappies changed and love having a bath. Dressing and undressing is also much easier at this age.

If your baby cries a lot while you are attending to her care when she is young, try to stay calm and do what you need to do. It's a normal way for babies to behave and doesn't mean you are doing something wrong. Individual babies' responses to nappy changing, bathing, dressing and undressing vary enormously. If your baby cries at these times and your friend's baby doesn't, it doesn't mean anything is amiss.

Here are a few tips to help:

- Pick clothes that are easy to put on and take off. For example, front fastening, pop fasteners, stretch or expandable fabric.
- Avoid buttons and bows. Most families are given at least one 'beautiful' outfit which is invariably difficult to get a baby in and out of, especially when the baby is in full crying flight. This doesn't mean you can't ever use it, but save it for a special occasion.
- Have three or four easy changes at the ready.
- When dressing a crying, hungry baby, don't worry about minor details. Get the basics done, then do up buttons and straighten collars while she's feeding.
- Sometimes young babies are calmer and easier to dress and undress while lying on their tummy.

Bathtime

Hospitals usually give parents the opportunity to bath their baby before going home so you know what to do. If you come home early or have a home birth your midwife will show you at home.

Bathing grows into a happy time that becomes lots of fun for you both, but in the early days you might wonder when the fun is going to begin! Lots of new mothers find bathing difficult at first. When you get used to handling a slippery baby and your baby starts to enjoy her bath, things improve dramatically.

If you find bathing stressful during the first six weeks, only bath your baby once or twice a week. 'Topping and tailing' (just cleaning her face and bottom) are quite adequate the rest of the time.

On the other hand, if a deep relaxation bath helps a baby who cries a lot then bathing twice a day is fine. It's all right to bath your baby before a feed, after a feed or in the middle of a feed. You will soon work out what suits you both best.

There are many ways to bath babies. Here is one way.

First, a few safety reminders

- Make sure the room is warm with no draughts.

- If you use a sink, take care that your baby doesn't bump against the taps or burn herself on the hot tap.
- Always put your hand on your baby before turning away.
- Wrap her up and take her with you if the phone rings.
- Put cold water in the bath first, then add the hot. Mix the water before putting your baby in and test the temperature by dipping your elbow in. The water should feel warm to the touch.

Prepare everything before you begin. You need nappies, nappy fasteners, pins, singlet, jumpsuit or nightie, pilchers, cotton wool and soap or a liquid baby bath preparation. Useful but not essential is a moisturiser, petroleum jelly and your favourite nappy cream. You also need two towels or one towel and a hand towel. Here we go!

- Undress your baby. Leave her nappy on. Swaddle her snuggly in a towel. Wash her face with damp cotton wool or a flannel. Pat dry.
- To clean her ears, smear a little petroleum jelly on a cotton wool ball, shape it into a point then wipe firmly inside her ear, lifting out any accumulated wax. Poking cotton buds into her ears or nose is dangerous and never necessary.
- Wet your baby's head then soap it with soapy palms. Use a mild soap. Tuck her under one arm, hold her head over the bath and rinse it well. Babies usually enjoy this part. After her head is rinsed, lie her back on the table and dry her head gently but briskly with your other towel.
- Next, unwrap your baby and remove the nappy. Wet her body with your hands and gently massage in some soapy water or a moisturiser. This is when she is likely to cry. Gently turn her onto her tummy if it makes things easier.
- Now it's time to put her into the bath—here's how to pick her up. If your hands are slippery or soapy rinse and dry them before you put your baby in the bath. One hand supports her head, neck and shoulder. The palm of your other hand supports both legs below the knees. Use your forefingers to separate her ankles. Lift and gently place her in the bath.
- Once she is in the bath, keep supporting her head and neck. You will

find she will float in the water. Use your free hand to rinse off any soap or just to gently splash water onto her body. Unless your baby has an ear infection (unusual at this age) it doesn't matter if her ears are under the water when you bath her.

- When you are ready, lift her out of the bath the same way you put her in. Pat dry, especially behind the ears, between her fingers, under her arms, under her chin and in the groin area. When she is dry, apply some moisturiser if you want to.
- Dress her. Remember, nappy first!

Another variation on the baby bath is the deep relaxation bath. The deep relaxation bath can be used to help babies relax and sleep.

The water is deep and hot (38°C). You lift your baby into the deep bath and hold her on her back in the water. Her head rests on your wrist while your other hand supports her legs with your forefingers between her ankles.

Move her backwards and forwards through the water. After a few glides turn her over onto her tummy, supporting her head on the inside of your wrist. Babies usually relax in the deep, warm water. Some fall asleep, others kick and move about. It is easy to hold her as she is supported by the water.

Keep baby in the water as long as it stays warm. When you lift her out, leave her on her tummy. Place her on a dry towel and pat dry.

Like any practical procedure, bathing is difficult to do from written instructions only. The deep relaxation bath is taught in maternity hospitals, so if you are interested ask for a demonstration. If you miss out, ask your friends who have babies how it is done.

If the deep relaxation bath bothers you, don't feel pressured by well-meaning advisers into feeling it is essential for your baby—it is an option to use if you would like to. Babies also enjoy a shower with their mother or father. A mat in the shower is essential to avoid falls.

Massage

After your baby's bath, if you are both happy and relaxed, try some baby massage. Baby massage is gentle touching using long, firm, smooth strokes. Baby massage is beneficial at any age so wait until you feel confident about handling your baby if you are a bit nervous during the first six weeks. Baby

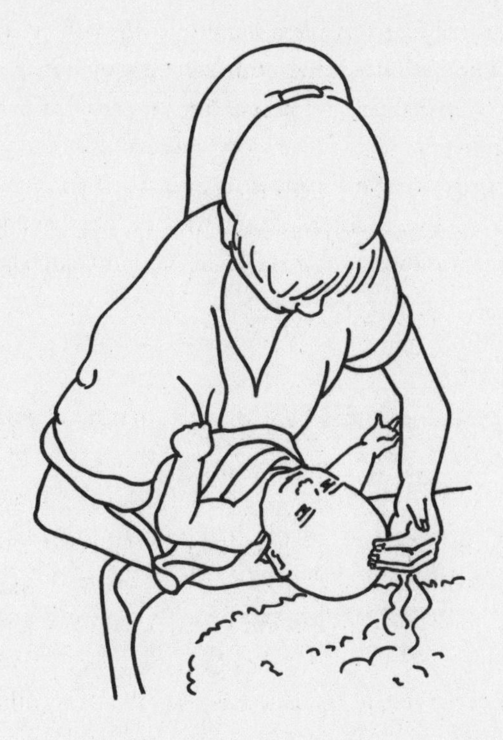

1. Wet your baby's head, then soap with soapy palms.

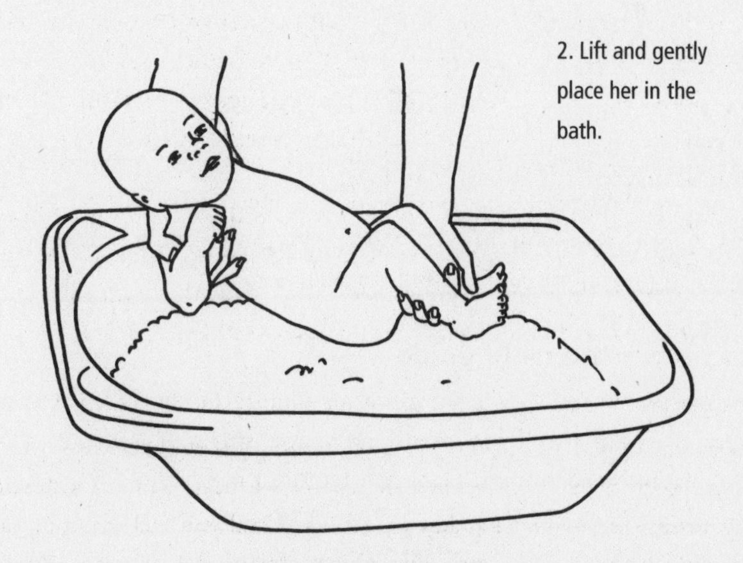

2. Lift and gently place her in the bath.

Two bathing steps

massage is not for everyone, so don't feel it's something you have to do if it's not your scene. It is not the definitive answer to baby crying and sleeping problems but it helps calm babies and it can be very enjoyable for parents and baby alike. Baby massage is never very successful when your baby is very tense and crying a lot or any time you are rushed and feeling anxious or trying to keep an active toddler amused as well. The best time is after a bath as long as she is not hungry. Like all skills, baby massage takes time to learn.

HERE'S A VERY SIMPLE METHOD

Lie your baby on her tummy. Using a little baby oil or a mixture of sorbolene and glycerine and water, rub your hands together. Stroke your baby's back using a hand-over-hand motion, gradually moving downwards, stroking her buttocks and legs right down to her toes. Initially, this is enough to start with, especially if turning her onto her back makes her cry which is quite likely when she is very young. As time goes by and you both become more relaxed, turn her over and continue stroking her tummy and the front of her legs.

If you are interested in baby massage and wish to learn more, try one of the many books or DVDs available which demonstrate this traditional art.

What to wear

Trying to work out what clothes to dress your baby in so she won't be too hot or too cold might cause you some concern. Try not to worry too much. Once again, you'll find as your baby grows you'll quickly get used to working out how much to put on or leave off.

Here is a reasonable guide

- **Summer:** a cotton singlet; a cotton nightie or short-sleeve, short-leg jumpsuit; sun hat if out of doors; nappy; socks; at bedtime, a cotton cuddly and cotton mesh blanket if required.
- **Winter:** one or two singlets or a bodysuit; a warm nightie or a long-sleeve jumpsuit; a warm jacket or sweater; tights or socks, bonnet or

beanie if out of doors; at bedtime, one or two flannelette cuddlies and a shawl and/or a blanket or quilt.

Obviously concessions have to be made for airconditioning and heating (including in cars) and extremely hot or cold climates. As long as your baby's chest, tummy and head are warm to touch, she is comfortably clothed. Hands and feet normally often feel cold so are not a good guide to her body warmth. A good way to check is to put the back of your hand on her tummy; a warm tummy means all is well.

An overheated baby goes very red in the face, sweats profusely and will probably cry vigorously—although a certain amount of sweating and heat rash is normal for all babies and not related to being overdressed.

Out and about

Facing the great outdoors can seem quite daunting in the early weeks after birth and it's easy to be overcome with dread at the thought of going anywhere when you start to think of the effort involved. While you are learning the best way to do the shopping, manage public transport and keep appointments, life before baby suddenly seems very much easier. Despite a few improvements in recent years our society is generally not at all considerate to the needs of mothers trying to negotiate their way around with little ones in tow. Many women tell me they start to understand for the first time the problems disabled people experience in their daily lives, especially those trying to get out with twins, triplets or a couple of babies close in age.

You will find practice makes perfect and the more you go out the more efficient you become at planning how to get where you are going and what you need. Start with simple excursions and build up to more ambitious ventures as you gain confidence. Having a baby bag always packed with the basics makes outings easier. In your bag you need four or more nappies, disposable wipes or damp flannels in plastic bags, cleaning lotion and your favourite nappy cream, cotton balls, extra dummies (if you are using a dummy), muslin squares for mopping up, plastic bags for laundry and used nappies, safety pins, a pair of scissors and an all-purpose baby blanket which can be used as a changing sheet, a cover or to put on the floor so your baby can lie on something familiar and clean.

A lot of women are extremely nervous when they first start to drive with their new baby in the restraint on the back seat of the car. Driving anxiety passes so don't let it put you off going somewhere in the car. If you are worried because you can't see your baby in the capsule attach a mirror to the headrest on the back seat so you can keep an eye on her.

Breastfeeding while you're out is often easy but sadly women breast-feeding in public are sometimes still given a hard time. Wear a two-piece outfit with a top that can be lifted from the waist. If the thought of feeding in public bothers you, check about the availability of a feeding room. If you are bottle feeding, the safest way to transport formula is to take the cool, boiled water and the powdered formula in separate containers and mix them when needed. If transporting prepared formula or expressed breastmilk it must be icy cold when you leave home and carried in a thermal baby bottle pack to keep it cold. If you cannot safely heat the bottle when you reach your destination it's quite all right to give it as it is.

Some mothers plan their outings around their babies' eating and sleeping schedules, others just go when they are ready. Either approach is fine. There's no need to go rushing out every day but you will find that you and your baby are much happier at home and with each other if you spend some time each week out and about.

Take care in the sun

The first and most important line of defence against the sun for all of us, but particularly babies, is to avoid unnecessary sun exposure and cover up as much as possible when in the sun. Babies in the first twelve months should be kept out of direct sunlight. Most babies in Australia don't need daily sun kicks as they are exposed to enough indirect sunlight to get adequate vitamin D. There are some exceptions to this—see the next page. It's fairly easy to keep young, immobile babies away from the sun by providing light covering to exposed parts of their bodies. Use shades on car windows rather than draping a sheet over the infant restraint, as it interferes with efficient air circulation in the restraint. As your baby grows it is vital to keep her covered when out of doors, ideally by a T-shirt with a collar and a hat that provides shade over the face, neck and ears.

The second line of defence against the sun is the use of a suitable sunscreen. As no sunscreen provides 100 per cent protection, babies and toddlers should always be well covered by clothing, hats, shade and kept out of the sun in the danger times (10 am–2 pm and 11 am–3 pm in daylight saving time).

Sunscreen

There is no evidence that a small amount of sunscreen applied to exposed parts of babies' skin is harmful. Allergies to sunscreen are unusual. When they occur it is more likely to be because of other ingredients in the product rather than the sunscreen base. Always do a skin test by applying a small amount on your baby's forearm—if there is no itch or sting the product is safe to use. If there is a negative reaction, try another product.

Some sunscreen now contains insect repellent (Deet). This preparation is best avoided in babies and toddlers, who may ingest it.

The sunscreen you use should be broad spectrum and water resistant and have a sun protection factor of 30. Specially formulated baby and toddler sunscreens are thought to be less allergenic and so less likely to irritate a baby's skin. Use the sunscreen according to the manufacturer's instructions and do not use in place of appropriate clothing and hats. Sunglasses are now advised as well. Older babies often pull off hats and sunglasses, but persist—as they get older they can't remember what it is like to be without them. Be a role model and always wear a hat and sunglasses yourself.

Vitamin D deficiency

Vitamin D is essential for the absorption of calcium. Deficiency of vitamin D prevents adequate mineralisation and calcification of bone and results in rickets (soft, weakened bones). Vitamin D is found in small quantities in cod liver oil and fatty fish, however most Australians get their vitamin D from sunlight. Recently there have been a small but increasing number of women and babies diagnosed with bone problems due to vitamin D deficiency. Those at risk include women with dark pigmented skin, those who have reduced sun exposure for cultural reasons (including veiling) and those with an inadequate dietary intake of calcium and vitamin D. So, while we need to be vigilant about avoiding sun damage, a small amount of safe sun exposure on bare skin without sunscreen is advised for those at risk of vitamin D deficiency.

Care in hot weather

Healthy babies do not suddenly dehydrate when the weather gets hot (think of all the babies around the world who live in very hot climates) as long as a little care and commonsense is used. The fontanelle on all babies' heads pulsates, so there are times when it looks depressed or 'sunken'—this is normal.

Hot weather tips

- Keep your baby out of the sun during the dangerous hours. The sun's ultraviolet light is at its most intense between the hours of 10 am and 2 pm (11 am and 3 pm in areas where there is daylight saving).
- Dress your baby in light, cool clothing—when out of the sun a singlet and nappy is all she needs. Use cotton cuddlies for wrapping.
- Never leave your baby in a parked car.
- Use a fan (not directly on your baby) in the room where your baby sleeps (unless of course you have airconditioning).
- Well-fed, healthy babies (breastfed or bottle fed) do not need to be constantly offered extra water in hot weather. If it is very hot and you think your baby is thirsty, by all means offer some water, but don't get worried if she doesn't drink it. If you are breastfeeding offer extra feeds—there's plenty of water in breastmilk.

Where should she sleep?

What was once a relatively simple matter of personal choice has become somewhat complicated by the need to consider the recommended safety guidelines for co-sleeping, not to mention the pressure exerted from each end of the sleep spectrum about what's emotionally and psychologically best for baby.

It may take you some time to work out what suits you, but once you've made safe sleeping arrangements try not to let the opinions of others pressure you into doing something you're not happy with.

Remember, nothing is cast in concrete. Many families regularly change their sleeping arrangements while they work out what they want. Often a suitable compromise has to be made. You may find the final arrangement is not exactly what you had in mind initially.

What you need to know about safe sleeping

Sudden Unexpected Death in Infancy (SUDI)

The term SUDI is an umbrella term covering all sudden and unexpected deaths of babies. Some sudden unexpected deaths in babies are the result of serious illnesses or particular problems some babies are born with which, sadly, are mostly unpreventable.

MOST UNEXPECTED INFANT DEATHS ARE CAUSED BY SUDDEN INFANT DEATH SYNDROME (SIDS), OR FATAL SLEEP ACCIDENTS:

- **SIDS**

  When no cause for the death can be found by history or autopsy it is called SIDS. It is still not known what causes SIDS but owing to the Reducing the Risk program in place since 1991, SIDS deaths have dropped by 85 per cent. SIDS deaths account for about 140 deaths a year. More boys than girls die of SIDS, more babies die in winter than summer.

- **Fatal sleep accidents**

  Known causes for fatal sleep accidents include: suffocation by a soft pillow; strangulation by a long dummy cord; getting caught under adult bedding; getting trapped between a wall and a bed; falling off a bed; being rolled on by an adult in a deep sleep; overheating from too many coverings, a hot water bottle or an electric blanket.

REDUCING THE RISKS

Most sudden unexpected deaths in infancy are preventable by removing known risk factors and providing a safe sleeping environment.

Ninety-five per cent of deaths from SUDI have occurred by six to eight months of age.

RECOMMENDATIONS TO REDUCE THE RISK FACTORS OF SUDDEN UNEXPECTED DEATHS IN INFANCY:

1. Put your baby on her back to sleep from birth

The risk of SUDI is increased if babies are put to sleep on their sides or tummies. Concerns about increased risks of babies inhaling and choking on regurgitated milk when sleeping on their backs has been shown to be unfounded. Back-sleeping babies are less likely to choke on regurgitated milk than tummy-sleeping babies.

From five or six months onwards many babies roll all over the cot at night and sometimes end up on their tummies. Most SUDI deaths occur under this age so you do not have to try to keep them off their tummies at this time. Put your baby on her back to sleep and let her find her own sleeping position. Follow all the other recommendations for safe sleeping: make sure the mattress is firm and fits securely with no gap between the mattress and the sides of the cot; that there are no dangling blinds, curtains, cords or mobiles within your baby's reach; that there is no bumper, pillows or anything else in her cot that could cover her face. If you use blankets rather than a sleeping bag make sure her feet are touching the bottom of the cot and she is well tucked in under her arms. Sleeping suits with a fitted neck, sleeves and legs are great for babies once they start rolling around as they keep them warm without blankets and allow them to move safely.

It is not necessary at any age to buy a device to keep your baby on her back. One of the problems that inevitably arises out of any recommendations made in relation to SUDI is that there also be corresponding commercial attempts to use these recommendations to sell baby products to anxious parents. There is no scientific evidence that has convinced Sids and Kids that any specific babycare product reduces the risk of SUDI.

2. Sleep baby with face uncovered

Make sure your baby's head remains uncovered during sleep by putting her feet at the bottom of the bassinet or cot so she can't slip down under the covers. Do not use bumpers, quilts, doonas or pillows in the cot. Tuck her in securely so the bedding is not loose, alternatively use a safe sleeping bag with a fitted neck and armholes.

3. **Keep your baby in a smoke-free environment**

   Cigarette smoke harms babies inside and outside the womb. If the mother smokes, the risks of SIDS doubles, if the father smokes as well it doubles again. The risks increase if the baby sleeps with a parent who is a smoker. For reasons that are unclear, the risk of SIDS is increased even if parents smoke outside away from the baby.

   Giving up smoking is not easy but it's worth the effort in terms of your own health and the health of your baby. Call the Quitline on 13 18 48 for help.

4. **Sleep your baby in a cot next to your bed for the first six to twelve months**

   This recommendation has recently been included because there is evidence that it is protective against SIDS and fatal sleep accidents. This recommendation impacts on the options for where to sleep baby.

Here are the where-to-sleep options

Separate bed—sharing your room

You can have the bassinet or cot right near you so you can touch and pat your baby without getting up. Some parents have a three-sided cot arrangement attached to the bed at the same level so the mother has her own space but is still in contact with her baby.

ADVANTAGES

- According to the latest analysis of the research, this is the safest option in relation to SUDI.
- It's easier to do night feeds.

DISADVANTAGES

- If you are among the unfortunate parents who find they can't sleep even when their baby is sleeping because of the noisy breathing, grunting, sucking of fists, hiccoughing, farting and wriggling, all I can suggest is that you try to get used to it. I really sympathise as I found it very hard to sleep when my babies were in the room.

Sharing your bed (or as Sids and Kids put it, sharing a 'sleep surface')

Bed-sharing, co-sleeping—sharing a sleep surface has run the gamut over the decades. The practice was frowned upon for most of last century for weird reasons that seemed to be mostly related to discipline, spoiling and turning baby into a little tyrant although, on consideration, safety was probably an issue as well. In the late eighties and nineties the pendulum swung in the opposite direction when it was assumed that it was super-safe and that all parents secretly longed to sleep with their babies but were being discouraged by bossy health professionals for no good reason.

Many adherents of the practice make over-inflated claims that co-sleeping is a crucial part of 'good' parenting and ensures optimum outcomes in terms of child emotional and social development.

While sharing sleep surfaces can be very pleasant for those for whom it suits, there is no long-term research to support these claims.

IS IT SAFE?

According to Sids and Kids researchers, it is not as safe as having baby in a separate bed in the same room because of an increased risk of SUDI when co-sleeping. This is hotly disputed by the health professionals, researchers and parents dedicated to co-sleeping. You will need to make up your own mind about this.

SUDI researchers have found that:

- Babies who are at highest risk while bed-sharing are babies less than four months of age, babies who are born prematurely and babies who are born small for their gestational age.
- There is a high risk of SUDI if you fall asleep with your baby on a lounge or sofa (or leave your baby alone to sleep on an adult bed or a sofa/couch/lounge).
- Sharing sleep surfaces is not safe in the following circumstances:
  - — Where the baby shares a sleep surface with a smoker
  - — Where there is adult bedding, quilts, doonas or pillows that may cover the baby
  - — Where the parent is drunk, drugged, overly tired or very obese

— Where there are pets in the bed

— Where the surface is a waterbed, beanbag or a sagging mattress.

If you decide to go ahead make sure of the following:

- That the mattress is firm with a tight-fitting sheet.
- Your baby is not close to the edge of the bed where she might fall—the best arrangement is an adult mattress on the floor.
- Place her on her back at the side of one parent—not between parents as this increases the risk of her slipping under covers. The ideal way is facing your baby with your body in a position which stops your baby from going under the sheets or into the pillow. A sleeping bag with a fitted neck and armholes will keep her warm without the need for blankets/sheets.
- Your baby's head stays uncovered.
- Your partner knows the baby is in the bed.
- If you wish to co-sleep it's probably best as a planned strategy. Haphazard arrangements in a daze in the middle of the night may mean that safe sleeping recommendations go by the board.

You think you'd love to do it. Is it worth the hassle?

Some parents find the closeness and convenience of co-sleeping very special. Some parents who start out determined not to bed-share find they actually enjoy it. For others it is an important part of their child-raising philosophy. While setting it up might seem complicated, parents dedicated to co-sleeping find it is not that difficult to arrange.

What is the risk level if all the recommendations for safe sleeping are followed?

If all the recommendations are followed the exact level of risk is difficult to ascertain. The risk of SUDI among non-smoking co-sleepers is slight, and most common in the first eleven weeks. Sids and Kids acknowledge that there is presently insufficient evidence to issue a blanket statement either for or against co-sleeping.

Most studies show that SUDI and SIDS co-sleeping deaths are predominantly amongst smokers. The risk of a fatal sleep accident and co-sleeping is increased because of the potential safety hazards of sharing sleep surfaces with babies—for example, overlaying by an adult, child or animal; entrapment between mattress and wall, mattress and headboard; and suffocation by blankets and pillows. If these hazards are dealt with satisfactorily then the risk is slight—but greater than the separate bed/same room option.

Over to you.

Co-sleeping, the advantages

ADVANTAGES

- It gives great emotional security to know your baby is close to you. Some women sleep better when they sleep with their babies.
- Breastfeeding can take place when you are in a sleepy state which means you get more rest.
- It is especially cosy in the winter months.
- Often a good option with a very young baby who is unsettled at night. Some newborns settle much better in their parents' bed than in their bassinets, which means everyone gets more sleep.
- Sleeping with your baby can be a great aid to getting breastfeeding going and keeping it going.
- Later, when babies and toddlers are older, you may prefer bed-sharing to other strategies, for example the dreaded 'controlled-crying'. I must add here that many parents end up doing neither—lots of babies and toddlers sleep well in their own cots from a young age.

DISADVANTAGES

- Despite the promotion of bed-sharing as a good thing over the last few years many parents in our society are not bursting to sleep with their babies and toddlers because sharing the bed involves a degree of discomfort and irritation they find intolerable. This does not mean they are not 'attached' parents.
- You might find you can't relax and sleep for fear of rolling on your baby.
- Your baby's noises might keep you awake.
- Not all crying, unsettled babies automatically sleep better once they are in their parents' bed. Some continue crying anyway—if your baby is like this it might be easier to settle her in her own bed.

- You'll find the bed-sharing goes on indefinitely unless your baby sleeps mostly in another bed by around three months of age. The bed-sharing arrangement is rarely voluntarily ended by the child until she is three to five years old. Deciding to change the arrangement before your baby or child is ready involves strategies that a lot of parents find painful. There is usually not an easy answer so if you think sharing your bed with your baby is going to worry you in the future, try not to let it go much past three months.

Own bed, separate room

If you secretly think you'd really like to have your baby in another room sometime in the first six months and definitely in the second six months when many babies call and wave and screech their way through the night because they know you are so close, you are not a monster parent. Many parents feel exactly the same way; however, it appears there is higher risk of SUDI when babies are in separate rooms than when they are in separate beds in the same rooms as their parents. This is possibly because in the latter parents can see their babies and check to see that they are safe.

This protective effect doesn't work if the baby shares a room with children. (I wonder how parents get out of bed at all there's so much to worry about.) So, unfortunately, after weighing it all up I can't give the blessing for separate rooms—in the first six months at least. Baby monitors are not the answer because there is no evidence that they protect against SUDI in any way.

Once again the decision is up to you.

Where to sleep baby—a summary

1. The all-embracing term Sudden Unexpected Death in Infancy (SUDI) is now used to cover all sudden and unexpected deaths in infancy due to medical problems, Sudden Infant Death Syndrome (SIDS) and fatal sleep accidents.
2. According to the best information available at the time of writing, the safest way to sleep babies is in their own cot near the parents' bed for the first six to twelve months.

3. If all the recommendations for safe-sleeping are met the increased risk of SIDS or fatal sleep accidents from co-sleeping ('sharing a sleep surface'), or putting baby in a separate room *after the first six months* is small.

Swaddling or wrapping

Swaddling or wrapping babies is a method which has been used by many cultures for centuries to help babies sleep. It makes them feel secure and prevents them from waking themselves up with their startle reflex. Swaddling doesn't suit all babies and as there is no 'medical' reason to swaddle healthy, full-term babies; if your baby doesn't like being wrapped and it doesn't help her to sleep, forget about it.

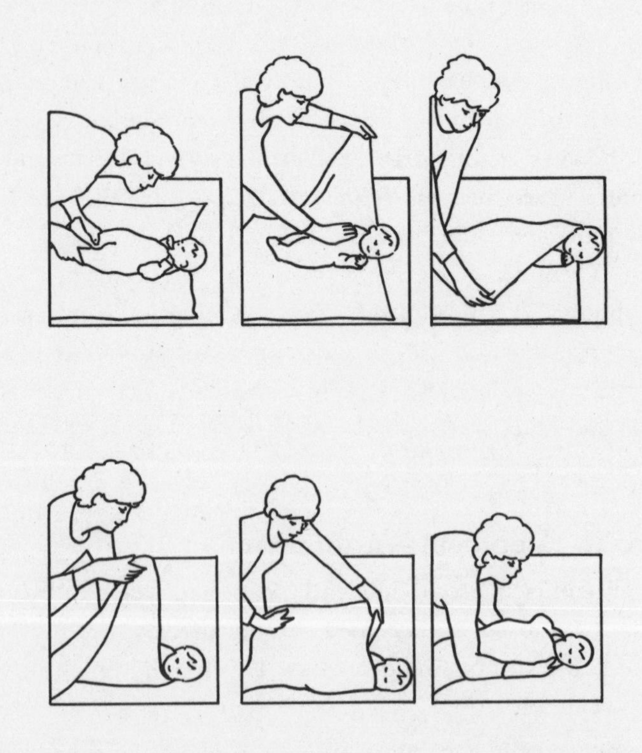

Here's one way to wrap babies. Remember, sleep your baby on her back.

Lotions and creams

A guide to the basic lotions and creams you may need in the first three months follows:

Heads	Bodies	Bottoms
Wash with simple soap	OPTIONS FOR THE BATH Nothing Baby bath lotion	OPTIONS FOR CLEANING Damp tissues Commercial nappy cleaning lotion* Disposable wash cloths* *avoid using if rash present
TO SOFTEN CRADLE CAP CRUSTS Vaseline, Oil 2% Acid Sal/2% Sulphur in Sorbolene and Glycerine Apply overnight—wash out the next day	MOISTURISER OPTIONS Moistened Sorbolene and Glycerine	SOOTHING BARRIER HEALING CREAMS A variety are available—eg Desitin, Amolin, Ungvita, Paw-paw cream, etc. Select one and apply every nappy change
CRUSTY EYEBROWS Apply a little Sorbolene and Glycerine to eyebrows at each nappy change CRUSTS BEHIND EARS Apply a little Sorbolene and Glycerine at each nappy change	RED SKIN BETWEEN SKIN SURFACES eg back of elbow joint, under chin, back of knee joint, under arms, groin area • Zinc and starch powder OR • Cornflour	RED ANUS AND/OR A RED GENITAL AREA *(including bottom)* —choose from • Desitin • Penatin (anus & genitals) • Amolin (anus & genitals) • Bepanthen (genitals)
HEAT RASH AND HORMONE RASH Do not treat	SUNSCREENS (See page 211)	FUNGAL INFECTION (diagnosis required) • Topical anti-fungal
	HEAT RASH No need to treat under three months	HEAT RASH UNDER NAPPY THAT DOESN'T CLEAR SPONTANEOUSLY • Zinc and starch powder OR • Cornflour

The number of creams and lotions available for babies' bottoms, heads and bodies is overwhelming. Skin peculiarities in the first three months tend to be transitory and generally do not need much treatment.

A word about sorbolene and glycerine. Combined sorbolene and glycerine is an inexpensive moisturiser which is great for babies' skin and has a number of uses. It comes as a thick preparation in tubs of various sizes or as a thinner preparation in pump packs. Pump-pack sorbolene is ideal for cleaning the nappy area or using over your baby's body. The thicker variety is good for small areas, such as dry skin patches, behind ears and for cradle cap (see page 165). Don't put sorbolene and glycerine on heat rash and hormone rash as it increases sweating and makes the rash worse, especially on the face. Sometimes too, sorbolene and glycerine stings when it is applied to a raw area, for example a bright red, weeping bottom.

FOR MORE INFORMATION

Chapter 12: Safety *(for safe use of change tables, page 229; nappy buckets, page 227)*

Chapter 13: Growth and Development *(the startle reflex, the Moro reflex, page 253)*

Chapter 16: For Parents *(sudden infant death syndrome, page 361)*

Chapter 14: Sleeping and Waking in the First Six Months *(options for settling, page 270)*

Chapter 12

Safety

I knew a Cappadocian
Who fell into the ocean
His mother came and took him out
With tokens of emotion.

A. E. HOUSEMAN, 'I KNEW A CAPPADOCIAN'

A higher standard of living, improved preventable health care, better health education and major advances in medical technology have all helped reduce the baby and child mortality rate over the past century.

It is sad to note, however, that while the preventable causes of death and disability have largely been eliminated our young are still at risk from preventable injuries. Injury is the leading cause of death for children under fifteen years. The cost in cash terms to the community is estimated at $190 million a year. The cost in anguish, pain and disability can never be measured.

Why do such accidents keep happening to our little ones? It's not because child safety is ignored. Excellent child-safety information is available in books via the media and as part of parent education programs. Major children's hospitals throughout Australia have enthusiastic, knowledgeable staff available for advice and education. Laws are passed in the interest of child safety—for example, the mandatory use of child restraints in cars and bicycle helmets.

It's not because parents don't care. Wanting to keep our babies safe forever is a very strong instinct so it's hard to understand why so many children die or need medical attention as a result of unintentional injury.

The greatest number of deaths and injuries occur in the one-to-four age group and are caused by motor vehicle/pedestrian accidents, drowning (the most common), choking, suffocation, falls, burns and scalds, poisoning and electrocution.

As well as these specific causes, accidents happen for two important general reasons. People believe accidents to be 'fate' or something that happens to someone else. Many parents take it for granted that they will know how to protect and care for their babies and children. In fact, child safety depends a lot on acquiring knowledge, recognising potential hazards, planning ahead and budgeting for safety items as they are needed. Very few adults understand or appreciate baby and child development before they have their own babies. Unless an effort is made to learn about development, parents are not always aware of the potential hazards their babies and children face living in an environment primarily designed for adult comfort rather than child safety.

Babies and children develop dramatically from birth to age five. Children aged between one and five years are at greatest risk of injury and home is the place where they are most likely to come to harm.

Babies in their first year are also vulnerable and need your protection, so it's worth taking a little time to plan a safe environment for your baby before the birth. As well, learn all you can about baby development as you go so it's easier to understand the things babies do at various ages that are likely to lead to unintentional injuries.

Specific hazards relating to development and ways of avoiding injuries are looked at in each section of the book. This section gives you a general guide to making your home safe as well as looking at the special safety needs of babies in the first three months.

The risk of injury is increased when:

- Either parent is unwell but especially when the mother is unwell;
- The baby cries excessively or the toddler is extremely active and never sleeps;

- There's great excitement caused by visitors, a new baby, and so on;
- There's a change of environment such as holidays, moving house or visiting;
- There's nowhere safe for the baby to play;
- The baby equipment doesn't comply to safety standards;
- The parents have unrealistic expectations of baby behaviour and no understanding of normal baby development.

Making your home safe

Once your baby arrives you have much less time for housework, repairs and shopping. The excitement, tiredness and stress can also make you more vulnerable to injuries during the early months so it's a good idea to think about repairs and changes before your baby arrives.

Heart–lung resuscitation

It's an excellent idea to be prepared for emergencies. Think seriously about doing a heart–lung resuscitation course before your baby arrives. If this is not possible, try to set something up after the birth when you are over the initial adjustments. Courses are available in your state from the Royal Lifesaving Society, the Red Cross and St John Ambulance. Single-page charts of basic resuscitation techniques are available from children's hospitals in all states. Pin one on to the back of the toilet door where you will have a constant reminder of what to do.

Kitchen

- Replace electrical appliances and cords if they are old or if you doubt their quality. Short or curly cords are much safer than old dangly cords. If buying a new kettle consider a cordless one.
- Make sure you have plenty of hand towels for quick drying of wet hands before using electrical appliances. A good supply of insulated mittens and pot holders makes handling hot dishes and pots safer.
- Do you know what to do if a pan catches fire on the stove?
  a) Smother the fire with a damp cloth or lid; and
  b) Turn off the hot plate or gas.

NEVER

a) Throw water over the flame, or

b) Attempt to remove the pot.

- Always keep a close eye on boiling fat or oil and never leave the kitchen while using boiling fat or oil.
- Overloading electrical sockets is dangerous. Lighting and appliance switches should be located well away from taps.
- A non-slip floor is always advisable, but especially in the kitchen. It's a good idea to get into the habit of wiping up spills immediately.
- Replace tablecloths with placemats.
- Always turn the handles of your pots and pans inwards. Get into the habit of using the rear hot plates before the front ones.
- Make sure your stove is anchored to the wall or floor, and fit a stove guard.
- A lid on your kitchen bin helps prevent disease and, after your baby becomes active, helps prevent exploratory ventures into the rubbish and the possibility of her inhaling something.
- Keep knives and sharp tools out of reach—the same for matches and lighters. Plastic bags are a great hazard for babies and children so store them well out of reach too.
- Keep all detergents, bleaches, dishwashing detergent and household cleaners locked up. If they are normally kept in a cupboard under the sink install a child-resistant latch on the cupboard door.
- A dishwasher with a safety lock is strongly recommended.

Bathroom

- The hot and cold taps should be clearly marked.
- Never use electrical appliances or heaters near the bath or shower. Electrical heaters should be installed high on the wall. Store and use all electrical appliances in a room other than the bathroom.
- Use a non-slip mat in the bath and on the bathroom floor.
- Install a child-resistant cabinet for medicines, aerosols, hair products and so on.

- Remember to keep the toilet lid closed. Bathroom cabinets installed above the toilet are hazardous—toddlers love to climb onto toilet seats and open bathroom cabinets.
- Nappy buckets are a potential disaster because mobile babies pull themselves up on them, tumble in and drown, so if possible keep them in the laundry or somewhere out of reach in the bathroom.
- Store scissors, razor blades and any other sharp objects out of reach.
- Being able to open the bathroom door from the outside means no one gets locked in. Installing a privacy lock-set is a way of keeping privacy while maintaining access in case of an emergency.

Laundry

- As in the kitchen, keep all cleansing agents, chemicals and dangerous equipment in cupboards with child-resistant latches.
- Keep the washing machine and tumble-dryer closed at all times; again child-resistant latches are a good idea.
- A childproof lock on the laundry door ensures unsupervised babies or children stay out.

Bedrooms

YOUR BABY'S ROOM

- Check cots and bassinets are safe and stable. Don't place cots or bassinets near windows with dangers such as hanging venetian blind cords or curtain ties—these are dangerous.
- Install bars and safety locks on bedroom windows to ensure that windows do not open more than 100mm (4 inches). This will stop little ones falling out. Leave the area around the windows free of furniture.
- Low-power night-lights in your room, the baby's room and the hall makes it safer when you attend to your baby at night.
- A child-resistant lock or handle to your room and/or the baby's room will prevent smaller children making unsupervised visits to the baby.
- Use child-resistant power point plugs.

YOUR ROOM

- Store medications, perfumes, make-up, scissors, earrings, pins, cuff links, coins or breakables away in a safe place.
- Safety catches are simple to install on the window in your bedroom. Don't put anything near your window that a toddler can climb onto.

Halls, living room and stairs

- Keep all doors, passages and stairs free of obstructions.
- Arrange storage for vacuum cleaners and any other major electrical appliances.
- Use child-resistant power point plugs on all power points.
- Avoid slippery floor coverings, loose rugs or highly polished surfaces.
- Special fireguards should be used in front of all fires. The guard should be firmly fixed to the floor or wall.
- Consider installing safety glass if you have large areas of low-level glass. Glass doors should be made more obvious by attaching a colourful motif to them at child and adult eye level.
- Remove small, fragile or breakable items until your youngest child is about five years old.
- Precious possessions, musical equipment, televisions and videos should be kept as high as possible. Store tapes, records and discs well out of reach.
- Alcohol is a poison for a child. Store alcohol and cigarettes well out of reach.
- Indoor plants should be non-poisonous and you might find it easier keeping indoor plants outside until your baby is past the eating dirt stage.
- Loop curtain and blind cords out of reach as they are strangulation hazards.

Pets

Pets who are used to a free run of the house need re-educating. If you can change their habits before the birth you will avoid potential hassles. Always supervise children with pets until they are old enough to know how to behave around animals.

Treating your home for pest control

Find out the chemicals being used and check by calling 13 11 26, which will connect you to a Poisons Information Centre in your state. If possible, arrange to be out of the house when the treatment is being done and to allow some time for airing before being inside again. Always ask if there will be anything left behind (pellets, etc.) and where they are going to be left. Mosquito zappers and coils are safe to use in your baby's room. Care needs to be taken to make sure they are out of reach of older babies and toddlers.

For overall house safety

- Install a smoke detector;
- Lower the hot water temperature to 50°C;
- Install a safety switch or a mains-operated circuit breaker.

Babies aged between birth and three months are not very mobile, but you need to be aware of certain safety measures for even this young age group.

'When eyes are off, hands should be on' is a vital safety rule. It's amazing how quickly babies wriggle off change tables, slip under water or roll off a bed.

IF YOU ARE USING A CHANGE TABLE MAKE SURE:

- It is stable and will not collapse while you are using it;
- The sides are raised so your baby can't roll off;
- It's the right height for you to work comfortably;
- The changing surface is strong, easy to clean and there are no gaps or spaces near the changing surface that your baby's head or limbs can get caught in;
- You never leave her unattended on the change table. A strap to keep your baby in place is useful but she still shouldn't be left unattended even when secured with a strap;
- Everything you need is within reach.

Bottle and dummy safety

- Bottles shouldn't be propped and left. If something needs your attention in the middle of a feed ask for help or, if it's not urgent, delay what needs doing until after the feed. If you have to answer the phone or front door take the bottle with you.
- When buying a dummy, go for a good quality brand rather than a cheap one. Look for a brand approved by the Standards Association of Australia.
- Resist the temptation to dip the dummy in gripe water or honey. There are potential risks of botulism poisoning from giving babies honey in their first year and gripe water is sweet so encourages a habit which may be difficult to break. Dummies dipped in sweet things eventually lead to black teeth.
- Never use anything, for example a rolled-up nappy, to hold your baby's dummy in place as she is unable to spit out the dummy if she has trouble breathing and may suffocate.
- Attaching the dummy to your baby's clothes with ribbon or string is a strangulation hazard. You also risk cutting off the blood circulation to her finger or hand if the ribbon or string gets wrapped around her finger or wrist.
- Keep dummies clean by giving them a good scrub then boiling or steaming for a couple of minutes or leaving them in a disinfecting solution.
- Inspect your baby's dummy regularly and replace it when necessary.
- Adults should not suck dummies before placing them into their baby's mouth. It does not clean the dummy. Sucking the dummy, in fact, is a potentially dangerous practice that can introduce a range of bacteria into the baby's mouth and gut that can cause health problems.

Portable chairs

- Make sure the baby chair has a broad base so your baby can't push back and topple over.
- Always secure your baby with the harness—the best harness is one that covers shoulders, waist and crotch.
- Baby chairs can move off a table top amazingly fast propelled by nothing

more than a baby's gentle movements, so the floor is the best place—don't forget to remind everyone the baby is there! Keep a close eye on other children, pets and adults carrying hot drinks or food.

Cots and bassinets

- Buy a Standards Australia-approved cot.
- Place the cot or bassinet away from windows, heaters and power points.
- Always remember to keep the cot sides up.
- Never use hot water bottles or electric blankets for babies or toddlers.
- Remember to take your baby's bib off before you put her to bed.
- Remove plastic coverings from mattresses and dispose of immediately—don't use them to protect the mattress. Any plastic is dangerous—keep all kinds of plastic bags and film away from babies.

Strollers and prams

- Buy a Standards-approved stroller/pram.
- Make sure the brakes work properly. Test without the baby inside. When you buy, check that the safety harness has both shoulder, waist and crotch straps and that they can be adjusted to be used effectively, even when your baby is very young. Babies falling from strollers and buggies is a very common occurrence and it is often because safety harnesses are inadequate.
- Don't overload the stroller or pram when your baby is in it. Try to avoid hanging shopping bags from the handles.
- Always fit and adjust the safety harness correctly.
- When you change the position of the pram or stroller, make sure your baby's hands or fingers can't get caught.
- Take care when using the pram or stroller on escalators.

Car safety

Cars are almost an extension of the home these days and your baby is likely to spend several hours every week in the car. Here are some safety points:

- Never leave babies or toddlers alone in cars. When you leave the car parked make sure the buckles and seats are covered as babies may be burnt.
- Remove any loose objects or sharp-edged toys from the car before making any journey.

Using a baby capsule or car seat

- Always put your baby on her back and never wrap her in a bunny rug before you put her in.
- Adjust the crotch strap of the harness first, then adjust the shoulder straps until they are firm. The harness shoulder straps should be level with or above the baby's shoulders. Make sure your baby's arms and legs are not caught under the straps and the harness buckle clicks when it is done up. Remember to change the slots for the shoulder harness as your baby grows.
- The rear centre position is the safest place for the car seat, but this has to be weighed up against potential back injury for the mother getting the baby in and out of the car so the left-hand side near the kerb-side door is also a reasonable option. Always take your baby in and out of the car by the rear kerb-side door.
- When your car seat is in the rearward-facing position, check that it is not resting on the back of the front seat, as this impairs the safe functioning of the car seat.
- Ensure that the handles are in the down position once the car seat is placed in the car.
- When you are on a long trip, stop and give your baby a break from the car seat every couple of hours—when your baby is awake. Car seats have been designed to carry babies in cars and are not meant to be used as bassinet substitutes, so avoid leaving your baby in the car seat for long periods of time.

Other general safety tips

- Avoid nursing your baby and drinking a hot drink at the same time. Ask friends to put their hot drinks somewhere safe when they nurse your baby.
- Smoking and nursing a baby is also a health and safety hazard. Give up smoking or if you can't, don't smoke or allow others to smoke near the baby.

- Powder is useful for some skin conditions. When using powder put a small amount into a saucer then apply with your fingertips. Don't shake the powder vigorously into the air—your baby might inhale some.
- Cotton buds need never be used. Cotton wool balls are quite adequate for noses, ears and bottoms.
- Check clothing, especially bootees and socks, for loose threads that might cut off circulation or strangle your baby.
- If you give your baby medication check what it does, what's in it, possible side effects and the correct dose. Always read the label. If you have any doubts, don't give it.

Toy safety

- All rattles, shakers and stuffed animals or dolls should be free of small parts that could be chewed or pulled off and swallowed.
- There should be no sharp edges or harmful ingredients.
- Choose toys appropriate for your baby's age. Toys for toddlers may be dangerous for babies. Check labels, especially when your baby receives a toy as a gift.
- Throw away broken or grubby toys well past their 'use by' date.
- Take care with the packaging. Babies often enjoy the packaging as much as the toy so throw away any plastic and check the box for sharp bits or staples.
- When buying toys look for those that meet the specification of the Australian Standard AS 1647. The Standard covers toys for children from birth to age three years.

Babysitter safety

It may be some time before you feel you can leave your baby and obviously you will feel much more comfortable if you can leave her with a grandparent, family member or a trusted friend when you do take the plunge. If you use an agency, make sure it is one recommended to you by someone whose advice you respect. Inexperienced teenagers are not the ideal babysitters for young babies.

- Show the babysitter how to use equipment such as the stove, heaters and so on.

- Make sure she knows where your emergency list of phone numbers is (see below).
- Always leave your phone number and address and the phone number of a reliable friend or relative in case she can't locate you.
- Your babysitter also needs to know, in writing, what to do in an emergency and where the first-aid kit is kept (see below).
- Leave your babysitter a reliable torch.

Emergency numbers

Have a list of important numbers near the landline and in your mobile:

POLICE
POISONS INFORMATION CENTRE
AMBULANCE
FIRE DEPARTMENT
COUNTY COUNCIL
NEAREST CHILDREN'S HOSPITAL
FAMILY DOCTOR
CHILD AND FAMILY HEALTH NURSE
NEIGHBOUR
RELATIVE
CHEMIST

Your first-aid kit

DRESSINGS

Crepe bandages in various sizes
Gauze squares for cleaning wounds
Non-stick squares that won't stick to wounds and cause bleeding and pain when removed
Adhesive tape
Triangular bandages to use for slings
Cotton wool swabs
Sticking plaster
Clean, non-fluffy cloth or clean plastic film to cover burns until seen by a doctor

CREAMS, LOTIONS, MEDICATIONS

Antiseptic solution
Calamine lotion
Saline eye wash for foreign bodies in the eye

Spray for treating stings
30+ sunblock cream
Paracetamol tablets and liquid with child restraint lids
A bottle of ipecac to induce vomiting only if you live more than thirty minutes from medical assistance. Ipecac should only be used on advice from a doctor or a poisons information centre as it is dangerous to use it for some poisons (for example, kerosene). Ipecac should not be used after its expiration date.

FIRST AID EQUIPMENT
Safety pins of various sizes
Scissors with one sharp end and one blunt end
Tweezers
Disposable gloves

IMMUNISATION

Immunisation is safe, simple and effective and has saved the lives of millions of adults and children worldwide. High levels of childhood immunisation in a community protect not only the children who are immunised but those vulnerable others who are too young to be vaccinated, the rare baby who can't be vaccinated and those few who do not respond to the vaccine.

Immunisation schedules, recommendations and vaccines are continually being revised and vary from state to state. Because it is impossible to keep the information absolutely up to date in a book, I am not including the immunisation schedule here. All parents should receive a copy of the vaccination schedule in the PHR book given to them after the birth of their babies. Immunisation providers will advise you at the time of your baby's immunisation of available vaccine choices. If you are ever in any doubt about aspects of your baby's immunisation, please talk to your child and family health nurse or family doctor.

The following diseases that can all cause serious complications and sometimes death can be prevented by routine childhood vaccination—diphtheria, tetanus, pertussis (whooping cough), polio, measles, mumps, rubella, haemophilus influenzae Type B, hepatitis B, pneumococcal and meningococcal disease, chickenpox and rotavirus.

What is the difference between vaccination and immunisation?

Most people use the words vaccination and immunisation interchangeably but technically the meanings are slightly different. Vaccination is the term used to describe the process of giving the vaccine (by injection or swallowing drops). Immunisation, on the other hand, is the term used to describe both getting the vaccine and then becoming immune to the disease. Immunity follows most vaccinations but not always.

How does immunisation work?

When bacteria and viruses make you sick your body's immune system fights off the disease by making antibodies which either kill the bugs or render them harmless. Sometimes these antibodies continue to protect your body from the disease long term (for example, measles) or the effect wears off more quickly, which means you can become infected again (for example, whooping cough).

Of course, catching a disease also exposes you to all sorts of complications from the disease, including death and disability, so this is not the best way to acquire immunity.

Vaccines are small amounts of a particular bacteria or virus which are scientifically changed so they will not cause a disease but will make your body produce antibodies to protect you from the disease. As the effect of artificial immunity may wear off after a while, booster shots of some vaccines are necessary to remind the body to keep making the antibodies.

Benefits and risks

Despite the fact that modern vaccines provide high levels of protection against a number of debilitating infectious diseases and that serious adverse effects are rare, there are a growing number of people in our community who have reservations about immunisation. The small group of activists who oppose immunisation are very vocal, present their arguments with a great deal of fervour and provide good media copy.

Reports alleging that vaccines causes brain damage, autism, Sudden Infant Death Syndrome (SIDS) and a range of other devastating conditions have naturally caused great concern for parents and made many think twice about submitting their healthy baby to such a perceived risk.

Unfortunately, the age when immunisation is given coincides with the time in early childhood when SIDS and brain damage caused by fits is most likely to happen. When babies are immunised there is a chance that either of these things might happen as an unrelated event following immunisation or the slight possibility the vaccination will bring on a problem that was about to happen.

Understandably, the parents of the small number of babies who appear to have had serious damage as a result of immunisation will have strong concerns about the process for babies in general.

How safe are vaccinations?

No vaccine is one hundred per cent safe, but the unpleasant side effects they cause in some babies are relatively minor and reversible. Serious adverse reactions to vaccines are not only extremely rare but are significantly less common and less severe than the diseases the vaccines prevent.

Good evidence is available showing that vaccines do not cause HIV/AIDS, allergies, asthma, Sudden Infant Death Syndrome, autism or multiple sclerosis.

Babies who are not immunised because of parental choice are protected because the majority of babies are immunised, not because the diseases no longer exist or because the unimmunised have healthy lifestyles and eat the right food.

Homoeopathic 'vaccines'

Homoeopathic vaccines are not effective in preventing childhood diseases. They are also not put through the stringent safety tests the recommended vaccines have to undergo to make sure they work and are safe. The

Australian National Natural Therapists Association does not advocate using homoeopathic remedies as an alternative to orthodox immunisation.

How effective are vaccines?

Most vaccines are not totally protective and become less protective as community rates for immunisation fall. For example, the combined measles, mumps and rubella vaccine is 95 per cent effective, so approximately 5 per cent of babies will not be immune following their vaccination. Three doses of whooping cough vaccine protects about 85 per cent of babies who have been vaccinated and will reduce the severity of the disease of the other 15 per cent if they do catch whooping cough. In general, illnesses are shorter and less complicated in vaccinated babies.

Finding out the facts

We now have generations of children who have been protected from diphtheria, tetanus and polio, so many parents today don't understand the serious threat these diseases once posed. I regularly speak to parents who justifiably feel they need more information before they are prepared to undertake a procedure which they feel may risk the health of their baby. It is outside the scope of this book to list the volume of scientific data supporting childhood immunisation programs. For recommended books please see Further Reading on page 244.

Routine immunisation

Procedures

Some vaccines are combined, meaning fewer injections.

It is recommended that injected vaccines be given in the thigh to babies under twelve months as often as possible and in the top part of the arm if they are over twelve months.

Giving the injection into the buttock is not recommended because of the risk of nerve damage and because the fatty tissue in the buttock may stop vaccines working as well as they should.

It is also recommended that all vaccines due are administered on the one visit. This does not cause problems for the baby, avoids unnecessary expense and inconvenience and makes it easier for parents to keep track of the schedule and make sure no vaccines are missed.

Availability and cost

Immunisation is available from your family doctor, children's hospitals, some local councils and sometimes in child and family health centres. If you are unsure of where to have your baby immunised, your child and family health nurse can give you details of what's available in your local area.

In Australia most vaccines are free. Currently the chickenpox vaccine is not. Some councils charge a small fee and some family doctors charge a consultation fee over and above the Medicare fee.

Maternity Immunisation Allowance

This is a tax-free payment from the Federal Government to parents whose toddlers are fully immunised by eighteen months. The allowance must be claimed before the toddler turns two.

To receive the allowance she must be enrolled on the Australian Childhood Immunisation Register (ACIR) where her immunisation status is recorded. All babies are automatically put on the ACIR when they are enrolled with Medicare at birth. Registered providers (family doctors and others) forward details of immunisations to the ACIR.

Keeping records

It is important to get a written record of your baby's vaccinations in your baby's Personal Health Record as you will need this to confirm your child's immunisation status at various times. Your baby's immunisation status is linked to accessing the Child Care Benefit (CCB). To help increase Australia's immunisation rate the childcare rebate is only available for babies and toddlers who have proof of up-to-date immunisation or have an exemption.

Finding your way around the system

- Phone the Immunisation Hotline on 1800 671 811.
- Visit the Immunise Australia website at www.immunise.health.gov.au

- If your immunisation record is lost, you or your family doctor can obtain the details from the Australian Childhood Immunisation Register by phoning 1800 653 809.
- Two websites full of information about the Commonwealth Childcare Rebate, Childcare Assistance and the Maternity Immunisation Allowance are www.hic.gov.au (Health Insurance Commission) and www.centrelink.gov.au (Centrelink).
- Alternatively, you can phone the Family Assistance Office on 13 61 50.

Schedules

You might wonder about the rationale behind the schedules for immunisation. For example, why start at two months for some and twelve months for others? Vaccines are given at the youngest age at which they will work the most effectively. Delaying vaccination or giving test doses of vaccines is illogical and unsound. It puts the baby at risk of catching the diseases she could otherwise be protected from at an age when she needs the protection the most.

Adverse events following immunisation

Since the introduction of the acellular pertussis (whooping cough) vaccine the number of babies experiencing adverse reactions to immunisation has decreased. The use of the refined vaccine has reduced the incidence of pain and fever associated with the previous whole cell pertussis vaccine by about 30 per cent. In line with this the routine use of paracetamol before vaccination is no longer recommended.

Many babies do not have any adverse reactions to their immunisation. When they do the symptoms are usually mild—local reactions such as soreness, redness, itching or burning at the injection site for one or two days. Systemic reactions include fever, rashes, drowsiness and general discomfort that may make the baby grizzly and unsettled for one or two days. About 5 per cent of babies experience fever, rash, cold symptoms and/or swelling of the salivary glands (under the jaw) five to twelve days after the combined measles, mumps and rubella vaccine (MMR).

Rarely, a baby may become pale, floppy and unresponsive between one and twenty-four hours following immunisation. This frightening event is called a hypotonic episode and happens to only a minuscule number of babies. It is usually associated with either of the pertussis (whooping cough) vaccines, but is less likely with the acellular vaccine. A hypotonic episode can happen with other vaccines, suggesting that the pertussis components are not the only factors contributing to such an event.

Fortunately, follow-up studies show that all babies fully recover from hypotonic episodes and do not have repeat episodes with subsequent vaccines.

Treating adverse reactions

- If necessary, give a single dose of paracetamol to lower fever if the fever goes above 39°C. Paracetamol preparations are now available in a variety of strengths and doses, so it's important to calculate and measure the dose correctly according to the manufacturer's instructions. Paracetamol is not a sedative, but it has a mild sedative effect on some babies the first or second time it is used.
- Give extra fluids.
- If adverse reactions following immunisation are severe and persistent, or if you are worried for any reason about your baby, contact your family doctor or nearest local hospital.
- Serious or unexpected adverse reactions related to immunisation are monitored by the Department of Health and your state or territory Health Department should be notified. Please tell your family doctor about any such occurrences.

Contraindications to immunisation

Instances when immunisation cannot be given are virtually non-existent, but unfortunately sometimes health professionals are nervous about being blamed for times when babies do experience adverse reactions and may unnecessarily delay or withhold immunisation or make it difficult for parents to comply with the schedule. For example, insisting on different visits for different vaccines.

These are not reasons to omit or postpone immunisation

- A simple febrile convulsion or a pre-existing neurologic disease.
- A family history of convulsions or SIDS.
- Asthma, eczema, hay fever, runny nose, snuffles or allergies.

- Treatment with antibiotics.
- Treatment with inhaled cortisone or cortisone cream.
- Recent or imminent surgery.
- If the baby is being breastfed.
- If the baby's mother is pregnant.
- A history of jaundice following the birth.
- Cerebral palsy, Down's syndrome or autism.
- Contact with an infectious disease.

Premature babies

Premature babies should be vaccinated according to the recommended schedule from the date of their birth, not the expected date of birth.

Let the doctor or nurse know the following when you take your baby for her vaccination

- If your baby has a major illness and/or a high fever that day.
- If she has ever had a severe reaction to any vaccine.
- If she has any severe allergies.
- If she has had a live vaccine within the last month (MMR, tuberculosis, oral polio vaccine or yellow fever).
- If she has had an injection of immunoglobulin or a whole blood transfusion in the last three months.
- If she has an immunity-lowering disease (leukaemia, cancer, HIV/AIDS) or is having treatment which lowers immunity (steroids such as cortisone and prednisone or radiotherapy and chemotherapy).
- If she lives with someone who has a disease which lowers immunity or lives with someone who is having treatment which lowers immunity.
- If she has a medical condition which affects the brain or spinal cord.
- If she is living with someone who is not immunised.

Because vaccine combinations and schedules vary from state to state, and change so often, I am not including an immunisation schedule. All parents should receive a copy of a vaccine schedule in their Personal Health

Record book given to them after the birth of their baby. Immunisation providers will advise you at the time of your baby or toddler's immunisation of available vaccine choices.

SUMMARY OF THE MAJOR SAFETY HAZARDS AND PRECAUTIONS: BIRTH TO 3 MONTHS

Most safety hazards remain throughout early childhood. The chart emphasises specific hazards associated with developmental stages at this age.

Age	Developmental stage	Safety hazards	Precautions
0–8 weeks	little motor control—may lift head when on tummy	SUFFOCATION BY: • plastic sheeting • propped bottle • dummy held in position by a rolled up towel • tight clothing around neck	• remove plastic covering from mattress • safe use of dummy and bottle • check baby clothing
0–8 weeks		BURNS AND SCALDS: • bath water too hot • hot drinks spilt on baby	• check water temperature before putting baby into bath • don't handle hot liquids and baby at the same time
0–8 weeks		HEAT EXHAUSTION: • baby left in car on a hot day	• open all car windows • never leave baby alone in a parked car
8–12 weeks	may roll over	FALLS: • from change table, lounges and beds STRANGULATION: • head caught between cot bars	• never leave baby unattended in elevated position • make sure gaps between rails on cots are between 50–80mm wide
8–12 weeks	holds given objects for short periods	INJURY: • babies of this age are unaware of what they are holding and have no control over their fine motor skills	• do not give sharp or breakable objects to baby to hold

FOR MORE INFORMATION

Chapter 13: Growth and Development, page 245
Chapter 5: Choosing Baby Products, page 31
Chapter 10: Early Worries and Queries *(medicating your baby, page 197)*

FURTHER READING

Vaccination: the facts, the fears, the future, Gordon Ada and David Isaacs, Allen & Unwin, Australia, 2000.

Other than this book and the information published by the government and National Health and Medical Research Council, there is little available to parents outlining the objective scientific evidence underpinning immunisation. While I recommend this book for all interested parents because of its rigorous scientific approach, I have to admit it is not an easy read. The material is excellent but, sadly, the style is not particularly user-friendly and the index is terrible.

NH&MRC, *The Australian Immunisation Handbook,* 9th edition, AGPS, ACT, 2008.

The following booklets are available from the Commonwealth Department of Health and Ageing. (To obtain copies call the Immunisation Hotline on 1800 671 811 or go to their website at www.immunise.health.gov.au)

Immunisation Myths and Realities: Responding to Arguments Against Immunisation, Robert Hall, AGPS, 3rd edition, 2000.

Understanding Childhood Immunisation, AGPS, 2005.

(New parents should receive this booklet with their baby's Personal Health Record.)

Chapter 13

Growth and Development

So far as I can see,
There is no one like me.

E. V. Rieu

Watching your baby grow and develop is such a miracle you are bound to find it one of the most joyful aspects of having a child. The rate at which babies grow and develop often causes confusion because of the wide variation in age for achieving a lot of the milestones and because what is a delightful stage for some parents is stressful for others. For example, the toddler years may be a joy for some while others find a certain nightmarish quality about the antics that go on during this time.

Constantly hearing how dreadful the next stage will be from well-meaning friends can get a bit annoying at times. Remember, every parent's experience is different at every age and stage of their baby's development so try not to listen to tales of doom about future stages.

Despite the normal variations in baby and toddler milestones, you will find there is a basic pattern common to all babies. They smile before laughing, hold things before reaching out and grabbing, and usually sit before walking. Babies often achieve milestones then forget about them temporarily. It's not unusual for them to repeat actions like waving, clapping, rolling or making talking noises over and over again only to stop suddenly for a while. As long as they continue to grow and learn new things this is nothing to worry about.

What is growth?

Growth refers to an increase in size. This is easy to gauge by measuring weight, length and head circumference. Most babies who are given the right food grow as they are meant to. Normal growth in healthy babies is quite obvious as they move from bassinets to cots and from restraints to car safety seats.

Health professionals use prepared charts for assessing height, weight and head circumference. These charts are called percentile charts and represent measurements of babies and children of a certain population (for example—all babies in New South Wales in a certain year). As normal variations in height and weight are considerable, the results are drawn on a graph in measurements of a percentage in order to allow for all the variations. The lines on the graph represent the fifth, tenth, twenty-fifth, fiftieth, seventy-fifth, ninetieth and ninety-fifth percentile. Most babies' weight and length fall somewhere between the fifth and ninety-fifth percentile. Allowances have to be made for premature babies.

Understanding the charts

If your baby is on the fifth percentile for height and weight, it means 95 per cent of other babies her age are heavier and taller than she is. If your baby is on the ninety-seventh percentile, 3 per cent of other babies her age are heavier and taller than she is. Both lots of measurements are within the normal range.

Sometimes the concept of percentile charts is hard to grasp. Here's another way: imagine your baby in a room full of other babies her age. If she is on the third percentile, most of the other babies in the room would be bigger than her, but if she is on the ninety-seventh percentile she would probably be one of the biggest babies in the room.

Percentile charts are useful as they are a visual way of understanding your baby's growth as well as seeing the wide range of measurements which are normal. Your baby will follow her own growth pattern which depends a lot on family characteristics. Comments from onlookers such as 'what a big/small baby' are nearly always false perceptions based on unscientific observations. If someone's comments alarm you, ask your child and family health nurse or doctor to plot your baby's measurements on a percentile chart. Ask to see the chart, and if you don't understand it ask for an explanation. It doesn't matter which percentile your baby is on as long as growth is consistent and height and weight are in reasonable balance. (See percentile charts on page 554).

Interestingly, by the time they are three years old, only a small number of babies are on the same percentiles they start out on. Head circumference can also be charted on the percentile chart. Baby heads are measured because their rapid growth in the first year makes it easy to check that they are growing at the right rate.

What is development?

Development refers to your baby's ability to learn all the skills she needs to enjoy a good quality of life. To a large extent development comes naturally to healthy babies who have plenty of love and attention. Development includes things like movement, language, toilet training and play. We tend to take all these functions for granted, but the acquiring of them is amazingly complex.

Developmental achievements are referred to as milestones. Milestones are grouped under the following headings:

Gross motor

- Involves control of large muscles. These skills enable babies to sit, walk and run.

Fine motor

- This refers to the ability to control small muscles. These skills enable your baby to manipulate so she can hold a rattle, pick up objects and eventually scribble with a pencil all over your walls.

Vision

- Vision is the ability to see near and far and interpret what is seen.

Hearing and speech

- Hearing is the ability to hear (receive) and listen (interpret).
- Speech is the ability to understand and learn language.

Social behaviour and play

- These skills enable your baby to learn socially acceptable behaviour. They involve things like eating, communication and personal relationships.

A number of factors may affect growth and development. Some cause delay which may be temporary or sometimes permanent, while some may advance babies in certain areas.

Genetic influences

- Genetic influences can have quite significant effects on growth and development. Small, thin parents are likely to have small, thin babies. A father with a large head may have a baby with a large head. Special talents such as musical and sporting abilities often appear through generations.

Prematurity

- Any baby born at less than thirty-five weeks (compared to forty weeks for a full-term baby) needs an allowance made for prematurity. For example—if birth was at thirty weeks, ten weeks is subtracted from the baby's age from birth in recognition of the fact she is likely to attain her milestones up to ten weeks later than a baby born at forty weeks.
- By the time most premature babies reach their fourth birthday, four out of five have caught up with their peers and many catch up long before this.

Illness and/or prolonged hospitalisation

- If your baby has to spend any length of time in hospital development may be temporarily delayed.

- Babies who have major surgery may be late acquiring a few specific skills. This usually rights itself once they are back in their own surroundings. A long debilitating attack of diarrhoea or the flu can delay milestones temporarily.

Environmental and emotional deprivation

- When home is a place where a baby has plenty of love, stimulation and attention as well as the opportunity for a wide variety of play, a delay in growth and development is very unusual. Delay can happen when there is no love, an unstable, unsafe environment and 'no one cares if you grow or if you shrink'.

Babies born with problems

- A small number of babies are born with specific problems which will greatly affect their growth and development. Babies with conditions such as Down's syndrome, spina bifida, cerebral palsy and so on need special help with their development so they can live the best quality of life possible.

Growth 0–3 months

Average birthweight is around 3175 grams (7lb) but healthy newborns can weigh anything from 2608 grams (5lb 12oz) to 4535 grams (10lb) or more. In general, boys tend to be a little heavier than girls, although there is great variation within this overall trend. Metric weight is still causing confusion, so owning and using a conversion chart helps give your baby's weight meaning if you are unsure about grams (see the conversion chart at the end of the book). Grandparents usually like to know the grandchild's weight in pounds and ounces (unless they were born in Europe).

Weighing babies is just one way of checking on your baby's general wellbeing and by no means an essential part of her care. First babies seem to be weighed much more frequently than subsequent babies, who survive just as well.

Weighing is a useful guide for:

- Working out whether the breastmilk supply is low.

- Working out whether unsettled behaviour in babies under six months is due to hunger or other factors.
- Adjusting the diet of a baby who is underweight.
- Adjusting the diet of a baby who is overweight.

Constantly weighing your baby under the supervision of an unsympathetic health professional can cause great stress, especially if you are breastfeeding for the first time. Weekly weighing is not necessary unless you feel like it or there are specifically defined medical reasons for doing so.

Work out some sort of weighing routine that you feel comfortable with or give it a miss completely if you don't feel like it. It's advisable to weigh your baby on the same scales when possible as different scales give different results.

Weight gains in the first three months

Your baby loses about 10 per cent of her birthweight in the first three to four days. This is caused by loss of extra body fluid, passing meconium (her first poo) and a limited food intake. She will probably regain her birthweight by the time she is ten days old, if not before.

Some babies need extra time to start gaining weight so don't panic if the weight is a little slow, especially if you are breastfeeding. As long as your baby has good muscle tone, is vigorous, sucking well and has six to eight pale, wet nappies a day, relax and carry on. From two to three weeks onwards babies gain anything from 150 to 450 grams (5oz to 1lb). Weight and length never mean as much taken on their own as they do taken together and plotted on a percentile chart so an overall pattern of growth can be seen.

Length

Average length at birth is between 48cm and 56cm (19 inches and 22 inches). You will almost certainly find a discrepancy between the birth measurement and the next visit soon after birth at your doctor's or child and family health centre. Measuring babies accurately needs two people and the right equipment which is not available at birth, so don't worry if it appears your baby has shrunk or turned into a giant on the second measuring.

During the first three months your baby will grow about 1.9cm (¾ inch) a month. Length increases in spurts every few weeks so weekly measuring frequently shows 'no growth'. Measuring every three to four weeks is much more rewarding.

Reflexes

It's a good idea to know a little bit about baby reflexes. Apart from being interesting, it helps explain some of the strange things babies do. Some of the settling techniques suggested for unsettled babies relate to some of these reflexes.

What are they?

Reflexes are automatic responses to nerve stimulation and a number are present in new babies. Some you will be familiar with as they persist to a lesser degree throughout life, such as jumping at a loud noise; sneezing; gagging; yawning; coughing; blinking.

Other reflexes are peculiar to babies and disappear at various times in their first year. Many of the things your baby does happen because she doesn't have control over many of these reflexes; however, recent research suggests some baby reflexes are accompanied by voluntary, intentional movements. Turning the head and seeking the breast, and taking the breast and sucking are thought to be examples of this.

The three main reasons for baby reflexes are:

(a) Survival and protection

Certain reflexes are needed for life outside the womb so babies can obtain nourishment and breathe. Reflexes involved in obtaining nourishment are the rooting reflex, the sucking reflex and the swallowing reflex. (These are explained on pages 252–3.) An example of two reflexes involved with breathing are yawning and the way a baby automatically turns her head to one side to breathe when placed on her tummy. Examples of protective reflexes are blinking, gagging and coughing.

(b) For living life in the womb

Crawling and walking reflexes are directly related to life in the womb. Babies use their feet to push off the side of the womb as they move about inside the womb during pregnancy, so after birth if pressure is applied to the soles of their feet they respond by 'stepping' or 'crawling'. These reflexes have nothing to do with later crawling and walking and are gone by four weeks.

(c) Primitive reflexes

I find the most fascinating reflexes are those thought to be related to early humans. These are called primitive reflexes.

Grasp reflexes in hands and feet are there in memory of an age where it was necessary to clutch onto fur. Your baby will demonstrate the grasp reflex by closing her fingers over your forefinger if you put it in her hand. She will also grasp anything else that comes in contact with her palm such as your long hair, the chain around your neck, the side of the bath or her father's hairy chest.

Touching the soles of her feet will make her toes curl.

Grasping fingers and clenched fists start to lessen after three months. The grasping toes don't disappear until she can stand alone.

Another primitive reflex is the Moro reflex. Any jarring or sudden change in your baby's balance will make her throw out her arms and legs. The Moro reflex is very strong for two months and gone by three to four months.

Here are some other reflexes you are bound to notice.

Sucking

The sucking reflex is a powerful one. Not all the sucking your baby does relates to hunger and food. Babies frequently suck on objects even when they are not hungry, especially when they are overtired or upset. This is called non-nutritive sucking and appears to be an inborn, natural thing that babies do to relieve distress. Some babies need to do this more than others. The sucking reflex is replaced during the first few months of life as voluntary sucking takes over when objects are placed in the baby's mouth.

The rooting reflex

When your baby's cheek is touched either on purpose or accidentally she will turn her head in the direction of the touch and open her mouth to suck. Parents often mistake the rooting reflex as a sign of hunger. Your baby does do this when she is hungry, but she will also behave like this lots of times when she is awake and stimulated, whether she's hungry or not. The rooting reflex is very strong for three to four months and may be present for up to a year.

The startle response

Noise, a sudden movement or your baby jerking herself awake makes her fling out her arms and legs, cry and get quite upset. These reflexes often make it difficult to settle young babies because they keep waking themselves up, which is why some settling techniques involve wrapping or holding your baby firmly to help her get into deep sleep.

The quivering lip

Sudden noise, movement or change of your baby's posture often starts the bottom lip quivering, which in an older child or adult indicates emotion or cold. The quivering bottom lip in a young baby is another reflex and not indicative of either of these things; it is due to external stimuli such as being undressed or disturbed.

The gag reflex

Gagging is an automatic response to stimulation of the lower part of your baby's throat. It is our bodies' natural defence to unsuitable things going down the throat and persists throughout life, but the gag reflex is very exaggerated in babies compared to the gag reflex in adults. It can be quite significant in older babies, who gag a lot when they are given finger food or lumpy food—parents often mistake this for 'choking'.

Development: newborn to six weeks

Gross motor

When your newborn lies on her tummy, you will notice she lies with her arms and legs curled up because of the way she has been lying in the womb. If she was born bottom-first, her legs will not curl up as much.

Most newborns lift their heads while they are on their tummies and turn it from side to side if only for a second. They do this to 'gain their balance'.

If you lie her on her back and pull her gently towards you, her head will fall back behind her body. This is called 'head lag' and is why it's important to support your baby's head when she is being held, fed or bathed.

Fine motor and vision

- **Fine motor:** Your baby grasps objects that come in contact with the palm of her hand.
- **Vision:** Your baby is able to see from birth. Young babies are short-sighted, so brightness and movement will attract your baby's attention and faces and eyes are the things she focuses on best. Hold your face close to her face, move it slightly from side to side and watch how she follows you with her eyes. Do it any time after birth when she is relaxed and alert.

Hearing and speech

- **Hearing:** Your baby is able to detect a loud noise and respond with a startle reflex (a jump) from birth, but you will find her response is not there for every sudden loud noise. When she is sleeping deeply, crying, distracted or feeding, a sudden noise will often make no impression whatsoever. You may find when you try to make her jump by clapping or banging a door there is no response, so don't worry the life out of yourself by continually trying to 'test her hearing'. After a few weeks you will start to notice she does respond to noises such as an adult coughing or sneezing, keys rattling or a dog barking.

  Newborns respond selectively to different sorts of sounds. A soft noise such as a 'whooshing', music or a lullaby can soothe and calm your baby while a loud, jarring noise has the reverse effect. She will also stop crying at times to listen to your voice.

  About one to two babies per thousand are born with significant hearing loss. Early diagnosis and intervention markedly improves their communication and their educational, social and emotional development. Newborn hearing screening programs aim to identify these babies and introduce them to the appropriate services as soon as possible.

  To date, good progress is being made in implementing accurate screening tests for all babies soon after birth across Australia; however, there are still variations from state to state. In New South Wales, the Statewide Infant Screening—Hearing (SWISH) program offers screening for all babies, and Queensland's 'Healthy Hearing' program also offers state-wide screening for all newborns. In the ACT, hearing screening is offered at each maternity hospital. South Australia's program is fully operational in all public and private hospitals, and there are also community-based options. In Victoria, screening is currently available in seven hospitals, and in Western Australia it is available in seven metropolitan public hospitals, in all metropolitan private hospitals and in one regional private hospital. In the Northern Territory, targeted screening for babies at risk (premature babies, babies with a family history of hearing problems and so on) is conducted at the Royal Darwin Hospital, and a territory-wide program is being developed. Tasmania's staged two-year implementation program is well underway.

It is important to remember that, wherever you live and regardless of the screening result, if you ever have concerns about your baby's responses to sound or development of speech and language, you should arrange to have your baby's hearing tested.

- **Speech:** Until your baby starts to coo and make other noises from about six weeks, crying is her only vocalisation, although not her only form of communication. She does have other more subtle ways of communicating such as grasping your finger, staring intently at your face and coming off the breast when she wants to, but crying is the form of communication you're likely to be most aware of in the early weeks. The amount and duration of crying is highly variable between babies. Some babies cry infrequently and only then for an obvious reason, others confuse and bewilder everyone by crying for long periods of time for reasons impossible to work out.

  Baby sign language is very popular. It is a collection of easy to remember simple gestures (signs) that babies can learn to use before they can speak. The aim of baby sign language is to be able to communicate in meaningful ways with babies and so find out what is troubling them and fulfil their every need. The companies involved in selling the baby sign language method(s) claim a host of advantages such as IQ enhancement, an ability with languages and reduction of temper tantrums, tears and frustration. The research cited to support the seemingly amazing benefits of baby signing has predominately been conducted by psychologists who have vested commercial interests in the system. But to be fair, there is also plenty of anecdotal praise for baby signing from parents worldwide. However, as it's difficult to find any objective research by independent researchers to support the claimed benefits, I view baby signing as an unessential option. By all means try it if the idea appeals but before you commit yourself to something you may find not only costly but onerous take note of the following statement by Speech Pathology Australia:

It is the position of Speech Pathology Australia that the best way to successfully stimulate children's speech and language development is by talking to them and sharing joint experiences. Using baby sign is not necessary for successful language acquisition. If parents wish to use baby sign with their children, Speech Pathology Australia encourages its use while accompanied by talking. Research does suggest that the use of augmentative communication, such as sign, is beneficial for children with developmental delays and/or those who are at risk of speech and language difficulties.

Social behaviour and play

Many of your baby's reflexes are outside her control, but you will notice there are times when her response to things is intentional. Research in the last twenty years shows that newborn babies are capable of responding purposefully and making choices. Responding to your voice and being comforted by rocking, sucking, cuddling or skin-to-skin contact are all examples of this. Your baby is aware of differences between tastes—from a very young age babies frequently reject water but drink breastmilk or formula eagerly.

Development: six weeks

Gross motor

By six weeks your baby has noticeably more head control, so you will find you don't have to support her head as much when you lift and hold her.

Hearing and speech

- **Hearing:** Sudden noises will make your baby jump, although there are still times when she doesn't respond.
- **Speech:** Between five and eight weeks she will start to make beautiful gurgling, cooing noises when you talk to her. The first responsive noises babies make are magical sounds.

Social behaviour and play

Along with the cooing noises the first smile appears—and what a moment that is! A small number of babies smile as early as ten days. People love to refer to early smiling as 'wind'. A non-communicative grimace, which is very common for babies to do, especially when they are sleeping, is not a smile (nor is it 'wind'); but when your baby looks at you and smiles in a way that is definitely communicative, ignore suggestions of 'wind'—it is a smile! The average age for the first smile is between five to eight weeks.

Development: three months

Gross motor

At three months your baby has almost full head control with sometimes slight head lag when you pull her towards you from a sitting position. If she doesn't mind lying on her tummy, she will prop herself up on her arms and crane her head around, practising her balancing and getting a grand view of the world. When you hold her standing on a firm surface she may bear her weight, sometimes sagging a bit at the knees. Lots of babies love to stand and bear their weight from as early as eight weeks. If your baby does, you will not cause her any harm by letting her stand as much as she wants to (as long as you have the patience to hold her—some babies like to stand all day). It is a myth that early weight bearing causes 'back problems' or makes babies bandy-legged, so ignore comments suggesting this.

Vision and fine motor

- **Vision:** By three months babies can't get enough to look at. Between three and five months you might find feeding becomes tricky because of the way your baby is constantly distracted by everything around her.

Human faces and eyes still hold the most interest, especially yours. She will now follow your movements around the room.

- **Fine motor:** At around this time you will notice your baby's fists and fingers are never out of her mouth. Continually putting her fists and fingers into her mouth is part of your baby's sensory-motor development and not a sign of teething or hunger. Nor is it a 'bad habit' you have to do something about. There's no need to put mittens on as it's important for your baby to have access to her fingers.

  All babies do this to some degree, replacing fists and fingers with objects when they are old enough to deliberately grasp things to put into their mouths. They have an in-built internal drive that motivates them to explore and find new stimuli so they can learn about the world around them. As well as this, three to four months is the age babies start to do things intentionally. When your baby sees her hands drifting past her face she puts them into her mouth on purpose and keeps repeating the action, at times frantically pushing her fists so far in she makes herself gag. The 'everything in the mouth' stage remains constant throughout the first year and gradually decreases during the second year.

  When you place a rattle in your baby's palm she will grasp it and wave it aimlessly, not really knowing she's holding it. Eventually it just drops out of her hand spontaneously without her being aware that it has gone. She will not look for it. Hand-to-eye co-ordination enabling babies to know they are holding something and to deliberately put objects other than their hands in their mouths starts between four and five months.

  Some time between three and four months your baby will start to clasp and unclasp her hands and to look at them a lot.

Hearing and speech

- **Hearing:** Your baby now responds more consistently to loud noises. In fact, being super-sensitive to loud or sudden noises is normal for a lot of babies this age (especially the noise of the vacuum cleaner). She also gets excited at the sound of approaching voices or footsteps.
- **Speech:** The 'cooing' quickly becomes constant vocalisation (talking noises) which has a delightful musical sound.

  Chuckling and laughing starts at around three months.

Social behaviour and play

Three to four months is a magical age. When your baby wakes she probably makes lots of tuneful noises now instead of crying, particularly in the mornings. Most babies of this age really enjoy their baths—although if your baby doesn't, it doesn't mean anything is wrong. She will love to be tickled, played with, talked to and sung to.

Variations in milestones

Developmental milestones are geared to about the middle 50 per cent of babies. They do not allow for the two extremes of the developmental scale which are still normal. Try not to worry yourself needlessly by comparing babies or expecting a milestone to happen the day your baby turns a certain age.

Normal variations are greatest in the gross motor area. Here are the commonly noticed variations in the first three months.

- **Rolling:** From four weeks to nine months. Involuntary rolling can happen from as early as four weeks, so never leave your baby on an elevated surface and walk away.
- **Head control:** Some babies develop strong head control very early, others still have wobbly heads that bob forwards at three months.
- **Supporting weight when held on a flat surface:** From eight weeks to nine months.
- **Smiling:** Ten days to eight weeks.
- **Responsive cooing noises:** As early as a few weeks to eight weeks.
- **Tuneful talking noises:** From seven weeks to three months.

Stimulating things to do

Parents today are bombarded with ways to provide 'optimum' development. Many find the feeling that they should be constantly involved in stimulating activities, flashcards, musical appreciation, swimming lessons and baby gym overwhelming, especially when there don't seem to be enough hours in the day to do the necessities, let alone endless activities.

Remember, your baby is part of your family. Being part of a family involves times for housework and maintenance, personal time for each family member and times when everyone is together. A healthy baby given the proper food and plenty of attention in a loving home will grow and develop at her own rate as she is meant to. Extra activities are great when you have the time and money or when it provides a social outlet you both enjoy, but there are lots of simple things you can do that are not greatly time-consuming and do not cost much.

Here are some suggestions for the first three months:

- Walking: It's fine to prop your baby up as soon as she is taking an interest in the world at large. Just make sure she is secure and not able to tumble out when you go over a bump.

  At home she will like looking at mobiles hung about 30cm from her cot. Make sure the mobile is always out of your baby's reach. Mobiles can be changed from time to time.
- From as early as two to three weeks your baby can sit in a portable baby chair so she can see what's going on around her.
- Lots of babies enjoy lying on some towels on the floor without their nappies on.
- A selection of inexpensive toys that your baby can start to learn to reach for helps her hand-eye co-ordination. Things that squeak or make an interesting noise are popular, as are dolls with realistic faces and wobbly toys that bounce back when swiped at.
- Your face, your eyes, your voice and your touch are the most important learning and entertaining things for her.

A word about 'tummy time'

My original aim when I wrote *Baby Love* fifteen years ago was to try to give parents less to worry about but as each year goes by this becomes an impossible dream, as the teetering mountain of baby information casts its shadow over every parenting moment and sadly cannot be ignored. The compulsory tummy time advice first hit the decks in the 1980s when some physiotherapists decided that daily tummy time strengthened baby's back and neck muscles, encouraged head control and co-ordination and was a great aid in helping baby learn to crawl. Some even suggested (incorrectly) there was a link between tummy time and baby's future reading ability. Those of us working in the area could see that tummy time was advantageous for babies with specific disabilities or premature babies who need a variety of guided exercises to enhance their development but it was very hard to see that it was necessary for the majority of healthy, normally developing babies who, we observed, learnt to crawl, walk and otherwise develop the way they were meant to without daily tummy time. The push for compulsory tummy time gave mothers yet another job to do, which was frequently stressful because the babies by and large didn't like it too much.

However . . . in view of the flat head concerns (see page 176) and the slight delay in rolling over, pulling up and crawling that is occurring because of sleeping babies on their backs from birth I feel an obligation to go along with the idea. Floor time has always been a good thing for babies as it encourages a range of movements on a nice firm surface. Try for regular tummy time as often as you can. Some babies do enjoy it, others learn to enjoy it ('you vill haf your tummy time') and others, unfortunately, always seem to hate it.

Encouraging babies to get used to tummy time involves lying down with your baby face-to-face and talking to her and amusing her while she lies there. The aim is to try to extend the time each day until she loves it so much you can leave her to her own devices for a while.

Have fun, especially if you've got a toddler who wants to sit on your back while you're down on the floor doing tummy time with baby.

Toys

Toys are very much related to your baby's development. In the first three months toys and activities are centred around stimulating your baby with sounds and small movements. Here are some suggestions for the first three months:

- Rattles, squeakers and shakers.
- Mobiles: Your baby will like to look at a mobile from a very young age. Black and white geometric shapes with pictures of faces create great interest.
- A pull-the-string music box hung out of reach keeps young babies interested and can help them settle.
- One or two soft, washable toys for company.

- Between eight weeks and three months your baby starts to look straight ahead, opens her hands some of the time and starts swiping at things, so a toy frame with dangling bits and pieces is a suitable toy at this age.
- Clear, colourful pictures and/or a frieze or two around the walls creates interest. It's fun to walk around the room with your baby having a conversation about the things and people in the pictures.

You don't have to have wall-to-wall toys at any age. Babies and toddlers do better with a few at a time and no matter how ideal the toy, their attention span is limited, so they will become bored with anything after a period of time which varies from baby to baby. Try not to have too many unrealistic ideas of the entertainment value of toys. A few well-chosen items that suit your baby's age and stage of development are essential, but there is no toy on the market that will keep any baby entertained for hours every day or replace getting out of the house whenever possible or being played with by parents or brothers and sisters.

Developmental summary: 0–6 weeks

Gross motor

- lying on back—head goes to one side
- pull to sit from lying—head falls back
- when held sitting—back curves a lot

Vision and fine motor

- pupils react to light
- follows a face one-quarter of a circle
- can see from birth—short-sighted
- hands usually closed
- grasps a finger placed in palm of hand (involuntary)

Hearing and speech

- startled by a sudden noise
- coos and smiles by six weeks

Developmental summary: 3 months

Gross motor

- lying on back—head stays in the midline
- pull to sit from lying, little or no head lag
- when held sitting back curves slightly
- lying on tummy usually lifts head
- when held standing—may support weight, likely to sag at the knees

Vision and fine motor

- visually very alert
- follows a face and eyes half a circle
- plays with hands—fists constantly in the mouth
- holds a rattle if you place it in her hand but is unaware she has it

Hearing and speech

- sudden noise distresses
- vocalises tunefully

Social and play

- usually enjoys bath
- loves to be talked to and played with

FOR MORE INFORMATION

Chapter 8: Breastfeeding Your Baby After the First Two Weeks *(breastfeeding, low supply, page 121; breast refusal, page 142)*
Chapter 14: Sleeping and Waking in the First Six Months *(startle reflex; crying patterns, page 268)*
Chapter 15: The Crying Baby *(crying patterns, page 286; weighing, page 289)*
Chapter 24: Feeding Your Baby *(gagging, choking, page 447)*
Chapter 12: Safety *(toys, page 233)*

FURTHER READING

From Birth to Five Years—Children's developmental progress, Mary D. Sheridan, revised and updated by Marion Crost and Ajay Sharma, ACER, 3rd edition, Austrália, 2008.

Chapter 14

Sleeping and Waking in the First Six Months

Sister Peters says that newborn babies mostly sleep well. It is only when they get home they start bawling their heads off.

ELIZABETH JOLLEY, *CABIN FEVER*

We are now moving into the trickiest and, in some ways, the most controversial, area in the world of babies—that of baby behaviour. Tricky because it's often hard to interpret what baby and toddler behaviour means before they have the language skills to tell us, and controversial because research into human behaviour is difficult, particularly so with babies, and you are likely to find a variety of opinions from health professional as to why babies do what they do. 'Behaviour' describes what babies do, or don't do, without making value judgements about their characters now or their characters in the future.

Crying, waking and sleep mostly relate to baby behaviour and not to the more tangible things you will keep hearing about like an 'inexperienced mother', food or medical conditions. The term behaviour is not used as a way of describing babies as 'good' and/or 'bad'. 'Good' and 'bad' are meaningless labels based on adult concepts that we persist in giving humans at an age when they have not yet developed any control over their behaviour. A lot of the way babies behave relates to them adapting to a new environment by doing what they have been programmed to do for the last

40,000 years to ensure their survival.

A range of behaviour is observable and common to most babies, which is what much of the advice given to mothers about crying, waking and sleeping is based on, but it is vital to understand that:

- Babies are unpredictable.
- Frequently, clearly defined reasons to explain why the baby's doing what she's doing do not exist, so there are no guaranteed solutions all of the time to difficulties with sleeping, waking and crying.

Information about babies' sleeping and waking often leads parents to believe there is always an answer to making babies sleep and stop crying and only one set of correct guidelines to follow. Unfortunately, experts in babycare often think they have to solve problems and provide answers when there are none, often giving mothers quite unrealistic goals. The word 'should' seems to be used a lot. For example: 'your baby should be sleeping through the night'; 'in the day your baby should be up for one and a half hours then should sleep for one and a half hours'; 'when your baby wakes after twenty minutes she should be put back to sleep' and so on. The mother ends up feeling hopeless when the advice doesn't work and usually assumes it's something she's doing wrong or worse she has a 'bad' or sick baby. Most of the time, just knowing what's normal, how long a particular way of behaving is likely to last and that not that much can be done to change what's happening is the most helpful approach for the mother and her baby.

Looking at all the safe options rather than attempting to 'diagnose', 'cure', or 'make' healthy babies behave in certain ways, especially when we don't know exactly what their problem might be, sums up my approach. Giving a diagnosis or one definitive answer may provide parents with short-term relief but it is also limiting. Providing a full discussion and options allows parents to make their own decisions about what it is they want to do.

Let's look at sleep first

Babies have to learn to sleep; sleeping for long stretches on their own is not something that comes naturally and some learn to do it quicker than others. Babies are all different, so the individual range of sleeping and waking they do varies considerably.

The way we sleep, whether we are babies or adults, is quite complex and consists of various stages ranging from being awake to dreaming to light non-dreaming to deep non-dreaming. Dreaming sleep is called rapid eye movement sleep (REM).

Here is a simple description of the stages of sleep

- Non-REM sleep varies from stages of drowsiness to very deep sleep. When woken from very deep sleep we are slow to respond and confused.
- During REM sleep there is increased brain activity. If we are woken from REM sleep we become quickly alert.
- Brief wakings occur at various times between stages of sleep. During the night the average sound adult sleeper wakes briefly up to nine times a night, returning quickly to sleep a lot of the time unaware of waking, so there is no such thing as 'sleeping through'. 'Sleeping through' is a term used to describe the way a baby sleeps who no longer disturbs her parents during the night. The baby who 'sleeps through' does in fact wake throughout the night but puts herself back to sleep without waking her parents.

When young babies are in REM sleep they twitch, breathe irregularly, sometimes grimace (not a sign of 'wind') and flicker their eyelids. When they are in non-REM sleep they lie very still. Breathing is much more regular with an occasional sudden movement or startle which is enough to wake some babies and start them crying.

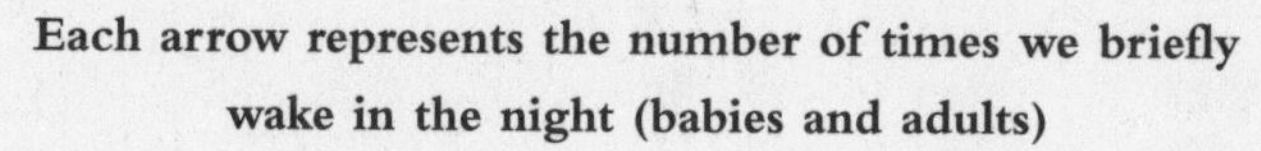
Each arrow represents the number of times we briefly wake in the night (babies and adults)

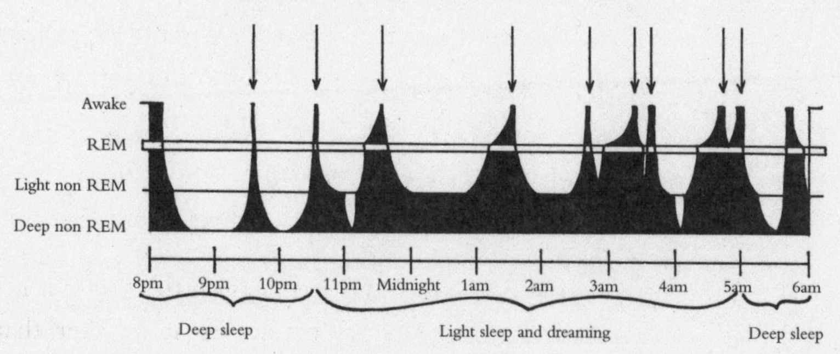

How we sleep

REM sleep takes up to 50 per cent of a baby's sleep cycle compared to 25 per cent in adult sleep cycles. During the first three months babies go into a REM sleep cycle when they first fall asleep. By three months of age this is reversed and the first stage of sleep is non-REM, which continues through life. The entire sleep cycle (that is, passing through the various sleep stages) takes fifty minutes in a baby compared to ninety minutes in an adolescent. Some researchers believe that the increased amount of REM sleep in young babies may be an important factor in brain development.

Just looking at baby sleep cycles alone, without even thinking of the usual reasons given for erratic sleep (hunger, too hot, too cold, 'wind' and so on) gives us some very good reasons why babies have such irregular sleeping and waking patterns:

- The increased amount of REM sleep means they wake more easily and are often alert and 'ready to go' when they do wake and mothers usually find it's very difficult, if not impossible, to get their babies back to sleep.
- As young babies go to sleep via REM sleep it takes longer for them to pass into non-REM and deep sleep, so there are times when helping them go to sleep is also difficult.
- Jerky movements or the startle reflex may wake them suddenly out of deep sleep; this can happen after only an hour's sleep. Again, getting them back to sleep is difficult.
- The brief waking from one stage of sleep to the next brings babies fully awake. Until they learn how to put themselves back to sleep every time it is normal for them to cry some of the time when they wake in between sleep stages.

How much sleep do babies need?

I don't think anyone knows for sure; the range for healthy newborn babies varies from nine to eighteen hours every twenty-four hours. Some babies either do not seem to need much sleep or cannot sleep more than nine hours every twenty-hour hours. This makes them harder to live with as they tend to get over-tired, which makes them crotchety, but it does not harm them in any way.

Rather than look at what 'should' happen, I think it's much more useful to look at what 'does' happen with most babies' sleeping and waking pattern in the first three months.

Sleeping and waking variations in the first three months

The first two to three weeks

Many babies start out eating and sleeping in very regular patterns. When they cry it's easy to work out what the matter is and everyone around the mother says 'what a good baby'. For many this doesn't last long and by week three they are starting to behave quite erratically—sleeping less and crying more at times when no one can work out what the matter is.

After three weeks

THE MOST COMMON SLEEPING AND WAKING PATTERN

One five- to six-hour sleep (if you're lucky, during the night), a couple of three-hourly sleeps, several two-hourly sleeps and up to five or six hours of catnapping, interspersed with wakefulness and crying.

THE UNSETTLED PERIOD

Eighty per cent of normal, healthy well-fed babies have one session of unexplained crying every twenty-four hours. This usually starts to happen around three weeks and continues until they are eight to twelve weeks old. The session of crying behaviour lasts from one and a half to five hours. It's often in the evening but may happen at any time. The other common time is the unsociable hours just before dawn. I call this the 'unsettled period'.

- **Why does it happen?** no one really knows because the baby can't tell us. When your baby is feeding well and sleeping well most of the time, apart from the unsettled period, accepting it and working out ways to manage until she changes is more important than trying to figure out exactly why it is happening. The unsettled period is rarely anything to do with breastfeeding, the brand/type of formula or burping techniques, although fond relatives will almost certainly keep talking to you about 'wind' and 'a little pain'. When such a high percentage of healthy babies behave like this one can only assume it is a normal response to the dramatic change of their environment from the womb to the world as well as an inability to sleep at this time. They become stressed and over-tired and are unable to either get to sleep or enjoy being awake.

- **What can you do during the unsettled period?** Here are the options to think about until the 'unsettled' period stops happening (at about three months, if not before).

OPTION 1. GIVE UNLIMITED BREASTFEEDS: Babies often look hungry when they are unsettled because they seem to want to suck all the time so some women just keep breastfeeding their babies until they eventually settle. Peace is achieved for a while whenever the baby is at the breast. The frequent breastfeeding does not harm the baby in any way but some women find the constant feeding exhausting and notice in the long run their babies fuss and cry whether they are fed a lot or not.

Babies having formula should not be offered unlimited amounts of formula during the unsettled period as bottle fed babies cannot adjust the volume of milk the way breastfed babies can, and may just keep drinking whatever they are given. At best this makes them throw up and at worst makes them overweight. As hunger is not the cause of the unsettled period, try not to offer formula more than every two and a half to three hours; keep to the amount your baby usually drinks at other times.

OPTION 2. LIMIT THE FEEDS, TRY OTHER SETTLING TECHNIQUES: Keep to your normal feeding pattern instead of breastfeeding continuously. Give your baby one feed, offer a top-up an hour later (if you're breastfeeding) then wait the usual two and a half hours before the next feed.

Instead of feeding:

- Wrap, rock and pat: Try swaddling your baby firmly, arms down, put her to bed and wheel or rock the bassinet. If she goes to sleep she is more likely to stay asleep than if you put her to sleep at the breast or in your arms and then put her down. (See helping-to-sleep tips, page 282).
- Keep her next to you (or give her to your partner) in a sling or front-pack for as long as it is acceptable to you (or your partner). When the unsettled period is in the evening, handing the baby over to someone

other than the mother helps. Some women find it upsetting when their partner walks in and calms the baby fairly quickly. This happens because an unavoidable level of stress builds up between the baby and her mother when the baby is unsettled, so another person who has not been with the baby all day can often break the stressful cycle. When the father is the one at home all day the same thing happens to him, so don't feel it's something you're doing wrong or that your baby doesn't like you.

- Try a bath: It doesn't matter if she's already had one that day. If she's been very unsettled and you haven't fed her for a few hours, a bath and a feed often does the trick—sleep descends.
- Dummies: Using a dummy helps some parents and some babies. Not all babies will take dummies and there are some negative aspects to their use (see page 53) but if giving your baby a dummy brings some much-needed relief, go ahead.

OPTION 3. LIMIT FEEDS, ALLOW SOME CRYING (THE BABY, THAT IS, AND MOTHER TOO IF YOU FEEL LIKE IT): Leaving babies to cry is never easy. Some parents find it easier than others and most parents find it easier when it is not their first baby.

There is much confusion surrounding the concept of 'controlled-crying'—the idea of leaving your baby to cry for a while when she is having a long session of fussy behaviour during her unsettled period and can't get herself to sleep and stay asleep.

I prefer not calling it 'controlled-crying' when babies are under six months, as that implies a regime or method that aims to get a permanent, predictable response within a certain time. I don't think that it is possible or even appropriate to attempt to teach babies much less than six months to sleep by leaving them to cry as a planned strategy day in and day out. It is true that sometimes these regimes appear to work quickly with very little crying involved (probably because the baby was going to settle anyway, not because of the particular 'controlled-crying' strategy). However, it is equally true that there are many times when the baby cries endlessly and the mother gets more stressed trying to put the regime in place. Unlike some people, I do not believe that 'controlled-crying' regimes are necessarily harmful for younger babies, but there are too many times when they do not go according to plan and so create stress for the baby and anxiety for the mother.

In general, I find that responding promptly to young babies' crying as often as possible in the first six months is the best way while parents and babies are finding their way. This strategy will eventually get the same results, often more quickly and with less pain, than trying to comply with a 'controlled-crying' regime (modified or otherwise).

I am not suggesting, however, that it is necessary for the mother to wear herself out with constant rocking, patting, breastfeeding and walking the floor. Nor am I suggesting that every parent has to leave their baby to cry when they don't want to. Rather, I believe that allowing a healthy, well-fed baby to cry at times is a safe option in a loving home. Depending on the baby, most parents find that it is impossible to avoid some crying sessions each day and that there are times when leaving the baby to cry for a short period is preferable to the other options.

SUGGESTIONS FOR LETTING A BABY CRY TO SETTLE:

- Leave your baby up for half an hour or so after the feed, sitting in a portable chair or on the floor without her nappy on or keep her next to you in a front-pack.
- After this, give her a top-up if you are breastfeeding then put her to bed. Wrapping tightly helps many babies to go off to sleep; other soothing things are white noise or musical CDs, musical boxes or even a dummy if it helps. If she starts crying, give her five to ten minutes of comforting—patting or rocking—then leave.
- Go back into the room every five to ten minutes depending on the level of distress of the crying. In between visits get on with whatever needs doing to take your mind off the crying. If the crying is really upsetting you, pick her up, calm her down and either put her down again or keep her with you in the front-pack or in your arms. Try to wait around twenty minutes before you do this as she may go to sleep.
- Some mothers find (in relation to the unsettled period) that when they let their babies cry on and off for a couple of hours (in between picking them up and doing some of the other rocking, patting things) then give them a bath and a good feed their babies go sound asleep and stay

asleep; the unsettled period only lasts two-and-a-half to three hours instead of the five- or six-hour stint that happens when babies are constantly walked, rocked, patted and breastfed for hours at a time.

- Tolerating some baby crying does develop better sleep patterns for an appreciable number of babies; however, for some mothers and babies it creates huge tension and makes things worse. Never do anything that doesn't 'feel right' for you. Remember there aren't always solutions to 'sleep' especially in the first six months.

WHAT ABOUT WHEN THE UNSETTLED PERIOD IS IN THE MIDDLE OF THE NIGHT? It's not easy. Letting babies cry in the middle of the night is usually quite an unrealistic suggestion and not particularly useful when they are under six months old, so you either stay up and walk the floor, rock and pat or go back to bed and take your baby with you. Unfortunately, this suggestion is not as simple as it once was as there are now concerns about 'sharing sleep surfaces with babies'. Please read the section on safe sleeping, pages 213–5. As well, if you don't want your baby in your bed for the next few years make sure she's back in her own bed by the time she's three months old. When you are up a lot at night you have to try to catch up on sleep in the day and I know this is difficult, especially if there are other children, but at this stage of your baby's life it is easier to change your sleep habits than to try to change hers.

THE CATNAPPER

A number of babies never sleep soundly for three to four hours at a time. After twenty minutes they stretch luxuriously and become instantly alert as if waking from eight hours' sleep! Many babies can be taught to sleep through the night after six months, but I have never found a way to 'make' babies who don't sleep much in the day sleep more or longer. If your baby catnaps and is otherwise reasonably content and feeding well it's best to accept the fact that her daytime sleeps will be short and frequent rather than longer and fewer. Trying to resettle babies who catnap after they wake is difficult and needs a lot of persistence as well as being able to tolerate a fair amount of crying, with every likelihood nothing is going to change. Most mothers decide it's a pointless exercise. Babies who catnap usually sleep well at night.

THE DAYTIME SLEEPER, NIGHT WAKER

Quite a few babies sleep very well in the day and wake every couple of hours through the night. If your baby does this in the early weeks there's a good chance she may reverse the pattern herself by the time she is a month or so old. It's usually worth waking babies for feeds every three-and-a-half to four hours during the day from about three weeks of age rather than letting them sleep six hours. This will help them to start to learn the difference between night and day.

BAD DAYS

Everyone has bad days with babies and toddlers. Bad days happen when a chain of events leads to everything in the day going from bad to worse with a nightmarish quality descending by evening. The first bad day you have with your baby will come as a shock, particularly if things have been running smoothly until now. Your baby may sleep lightly, wake early, feed poorly and cry a lot no matter what you do.

- **What do you do?** Don't panic—a bad day is exhausting and stressful but rarely a sign of anything major.

  If you feel you need to, ask someone you trust (child and family health nurse, family doctor) to check your baby to make sure she is well. A vigorous baby with good colour and six to eight pale, wet nappies is likely to be just fine despite the fussing and crying.

  During the day get out of the house with your baby if possible. Staying at home and listening to the crying makes everything seem worse. Even sitting in the waiting room of your doctor or child and family health nurse can make things seem better. Alternatively, reassurance from a sympathetic friend or your mother helps a lot, especially if they are able to take over for a while.

  Bad days always end eventually. Everyone has at least one in the first few weeks and several in the first three months.

THE SUDDEN MAJOR CRYING EPISODE

A sudden crying episode which appears to come out of the blue for no apparent reason is quite common in healthy babies at any time in the first year but is more likely to happen in between two and six months. The baby is quite happy one minute and inconsolable the next and it is often difficult to calm her.

- **What can you do?** Stay as calm as you can. The more agitated you get, the more your baby will cry. Sudden crying episodes last up to four hours and all you can really do is see it out. A bath helps. Often after a bath and a feed, sleep will descend.

  If your baby is otherwise well and it doesn't keep happening or go on for lengthy periods (more than four or five hours) a sudden crying episode is usually not a sign of anything significant. If in doubt, see your family doctor.

THE SIX WEEKS CHANGE (SOUNDS LIKE THE MENOPAUSE)

Some babies, whether breast or bottle fed, go through a change around six to eight weeks where they are more wakeful (therefore cry more) and want to feed all the time. When this happens it may last about two to three weeks. This is often referred to as a 'growth spurt' and while such an explanation is certainly reassuring I'm not at all convinced that it is the reason for babies' behaviour around this time. Other researchers feel it has to do with a big leap in the baby's mental development, enabling her to learn a new set of skills that changes the way she perceives the world, causing confusion and bewilderment.

Whatever the reason, an unsettled few weeks is certainly observable in an appreciable number of healthy, well-fed babies around this time. Like a lot of things to do with babies, it's unclear because the baby can't tell us and all we can do is hazard a guess. If your baby changes around this time, remember it's normal and temporary. Give extra feeds and cuddles until it passes.

Night waking under six months

Most babies wake at least once in the night, cry and won't go back to sleep without attention. This is something that is better to accept than try to change when your baby is under six months of age.

As previously mentioned, 'sleeping through' really refers to the stage when babies start to put themselves back to sleep in the night without waking their parents. The age at which they do this varies tremendously and because this is a common topic of conversation between families, mothers often think something is wrong when their babies are still waking at night.

It's important to remember your baby's waking habits at night have nothing to do with your ability as a mother or your baby's development. 'Sleeping through' is not a developmental milestone like walking, sitting, smiling and so on.

Night sleeping and waking variations

- Baby takes a late evening feed (between 8 pm and 11 pm) and an early morning feed (1 am to 4 am). Roughly 60 per cent of babies stop waking for one of these feeds between six and twelve weeks.
- Some babies continue to wake and need attention once a night (between 1 am and 4 am) indefinitely.
- Other babies need no attention for eight hours or longer from as young as eight weeks then suddenly start calling for room service again once or twice a night at about four months.
- About 20 to 30 per cent of babies continue to wake and cry every three to four hours through the night, indefinitely.

For reasons that are not clear some babies do sleep between eight and twelve hours permanently from about six to eight weeks of age. Great though this is, it can also be a dilemma for women who are breastfeeding, especially in the first eight weeks:

HERE ARE SOME SUGGESTIONS:

If your baby is thriving the general rule is 'never wake a sleeping baby.' There are, however, some provisos:

- If your baby sleeps through some nights and not others you are likely to find your breasts waking you even if your baby doesn't. You will probably find you will have to express. As mastitis is a risk you will need to take off as much milk as you need to for comfort. If the night sleeping becomes permanent your breasts will adjust and you will not need to express in the night.
- Most breastfed babies still need six feeds every twenty-four hours to keep

the milk supply going so you will need to make sure that your baby still gets six (or more) feeds in the twenty-four hour period, which might mean some two-hourly feeds during the day and/or evening. Having said that I acknowledge that some breastfed babies do thrive on five feeds for indefinite periods. This is the exception rather than the rule; if you are concerned a quick weigh will give you an idea of what's happening.

HERE ARE THE USUAL STRATEGIES PARENTS TRY, TO ENCOURAGE UNDISTURBED NIGHTS IN THE FIRST SIX MONTHS

- **Waking the baby between 10 and 11 pm for a feed to avoid getting up at 2 or 3 am (the 'roll-over' feed).**

  It's worth a try, but the results are extremely variable. For example, some babies are difficult to wake, don't feed properly and still wake at 3 am. Others wake quite happily, feed well then stay awake for the next two hours! A few wake happily, feed well, go back to sleep and still wake at 3 am. Many parents I talk to find this strategy makes things worse, not better, so don't persist if you find this is the case. Try to go to bed earlier (at least a few evenings a week).

- **Replacing feeding with rocking, patting and dummies.**

  Babies under six months can't really be 'trained' to sleep longer, so this strategy usually means everyone gets less sleep. Occasionally popping the dummy in instead of feeding may bring instant, sustained sleep, but chances are you'll be up and down all night replacing the dummy.

  A feed is usually the best way to settle babies at night when they are under six months, so don't hesitate to start feeding again at night if necessary.

- **Giving extra food.**

  It is often suggested giving extra food in the day or the evening helps babies stop waking at night. Sometimes this appears to do the trick but the relationship between food and babies' night waking is extremely unpredictable. If you wish to try food from a spoon as a way to encourage undisturbed nights, wait until your baby is at least four months old and try not to see it as the magic answer, as 90 per cent of the time it isn't.

  Starting one bottle of formula as a top-up in the evening to improve the nights does work sometimes when you're breastfeeding, for an unfathomable reason, even when there is obviously plenty of breastmilk. Nutritionally it's not necessary for your baby when you have plenty of breastmilk, so whether to try it or not is up to you.

Generally speaking, giving extra food, whether it's formula or food from a spoon, is not going to make any difference unless the baby is not getting enough to eat and is hungry, and even then it may not change anything. I see many instances where an underfed breastfed baby who 'sleeps all night' starts waking again when given more food.

When your baby is still waking a lot at night after six months, strategies can change if it is a problem for you. See Chapter 28, page 482.

Routines and spoiling

It's unfortunate the word 'spoil' is still used when we talk about babies and how to look after them. Spoiling is a negative word which suggests a spoilt baby will grow into an unpleasant child no one likes.

When parents are worried about spoiling their baby it implies babies can deliberately make parents do what they want them to do by acting in certain ways. Conflicting advice from lots of people who are all sure they are right makes it difficult for a new mother to know whether she is 'spoiling' her baby or not—and if she is, does it matter?

The term 'spoiling' shouldn't be used when we talk about babies, especially in their first year. A baby is too young to try to make her parents behave in a certain way by thinking through the results of her actions; for example, 'If I cry a lot they'll pick me up'.

Living with the way a young baby eats, sleeps and cries is one of the hardest things parents have to learn to adapt to. Some babies obligingly fall into a regular eating pattern and learn to sleep on their own very quickly. It is often assumed these are 'good' babies with efficient mothers but in fact these babies just happen to adjust to our way of life a little faster than others. This does not make them grow up into better people.

The 'eat and sleep' babies whose parents proclaim proudly 'we don't even know we've got her' are in the minority. Perpetuating the myth that this is how babies are meant to be causes new mothers a great deal of anxiety.

Generally, working out how best to meet a baby's needs either by trying to organise a routine or simply not bothering is one of the trickiest and, increasingly, along with 'sleep', one of the most polarised areas of babycare.

I'm intrigued to see the resurgence of information harking back to the 'strict routine from birth' philosophy that was all the go for most of last century. I believe this is in part a response to the push of the eighties and nineties to do away with routines and go for 'instinctual' or 'natural' style babycare. The strict routine style is very appealing to mothers who want to be able to structure and plan their days and live and function in a predictable and organised way. There's also the promise built in to these regimes of getting babies to sleep through the night as early as seven or eight weeks. I sympathise with this but I don't offer such routines, as in my experience there are too many times when they caused havoc. When these strategies work I think it's usually because the baby obligingly goes along with the idea. And if this happens with a minimum of distress and crying, fine. There's also the potential for strict routines to mess up the breastfeeding—although again, some women's breastfeeding works well no matter what.

The 'instinctual' or 'natural' style of babycare is appealing to mothers who feel it is more harmonious and close. They are happiest doing their own thing in their own relaxed way and if there's a muddle in the house, so be it. This style of babycare can be taken to extremes where the baby is never put down or separated from her mother at any time. Again, if the mother is happy about this, it's fine; however, some women who start out like this with the best intentions find they can't handle it and collapse under the strain in a heap of guilt.

I believe that mostly mothers do what they've always done—a bit of both. Overall, trying to make a baby behave in a certain way by imposing a set of rules on her before she has developed any control over her behaviour and by trying to eradicate normal baby behaviours and needs—for example, night feeds at a young age—has the potential to make life unnecessarily miserable for the baby and her family.

On the other hand, trying to live up to the ideals of what is known as attachment, natural or instinctive parenting can also take its own toll.

I am aware that some readers of *Baby Love* are disappointed because I don't include charts of routines to follow or make any concrete suggestions about getting young babies to sleep through the night. I am also aware of the disapproval of others because of my suggestions to leave babies to cry for short periods and the use of 'controlled-crying' in the second six months.

So be it.

A reflection of the work I did for so many years helping a diverse range of parents in a diverse range of situations.

A summary of my approach to routines

- During the first six months of a baby's life a routine is more for adult convenience rather than something that is essential for a baby's wellbeing.
- A baby's instinct is to be held and breastfed more or less continuously. It does not come naturally to babies to be fed large amounts less often and put somewhere on their own to sleep, which is what fits in best with our very structured way of life. In many cultures babies are given the breast constantly while permanently attached to their mothers. This probably avoids a lot of the hassles mothers go through in our culture trying to work out how to 'make' babies cry less and sleep longer, but is not a practical approach for life with a baby as most of us live it. Patience and flexibility is needed while our babies learn to fit in with our way of life.
- So, it's much better, if you can, to take a reasonably relaxed approach and try not to get yourself in a knot about four-hourly feeding and sleeping regimes, especially during the first three months. Between six and nine months everything becomes much more predictable and it's easier to follow a more structured routine. By the time babies are toddlers, routines are very important for safety and a sane family life.
- During the first six months it may seem at times that the days and nights with your baby are chaotic, but you will find as the months go by a pattern emerges which tends to become more consistent in the second six months.
- If a routine is important to you, it is much easier to gradually structure eating, sleeping and waking cycles over a reasonable period of time. When possible stick to a consistent way of doing things even when your baby doesn't sleep much.
- On the other hand, if routine doesn't matter at all to you just do what you feel comfortable with.

- All babies and families are different. Babies thrive just as well in families where they are guided into a flexible routine as they do where there is no routine at all—as long as their homes are safe, stable and loving.

And despite what I said about routine charts, below is a very simple one as a guide.

GUIDELINES FOR A FEED–UP–SLEEP DAYTIME PATTERN, BIRTH TO SIX MONTHS

N.B.: *This is a guide only. It will not suit all mothers and babies. You may not always be successful in helping your baby to sleep; however, it is a good idea to always try to put her to sleep an hour or two after her feed or when she shows signs that she is tired.*

- Feed your baby (feeding time usually decreases as the baby grows, whether breast or bottle fed).
- Let her stay up for one to two hours (depending on the age—usually as they get older babies are happy to stay up for longer). When she starts to get grizzly and her movements get jerky, put her to bed and settle for sleep, trying any of the options to settle suggested on page 282.
- Hopefully she will go to sleep and stay asleep for one and a half to two hours.
- Feed again when she wakes, or if she wakes in half an hour and you can't resettle, see if you can delay the feed for at least two and a half hours from the **beginning** of the last feed.

Some ideas for 'up' time:

- A bath.
- Go for a walk.
- Pop around and see your mother, mother-in-law, friend, lover or child and family health nurse.
- Prop her up in the shade outside or inside near a window where she can see the wind blowing the leaves on a tree.
- Sit her in a portable chair where she can see what's going on.
- Let her lie on the floor on towels without a nappy on.
- She may like just lying in her cot looking at her mobile for a while.
- Hold her so she can see your face, your eyes and feel your touch.
- Read her a story.

Summary of sleeping and waking: 0–6 months

There are ways of encouraging babies to sleep, but remember there are no guaranteed solutions all of the time to the problems of crying and sleeping, so don't feel inadequate when you can't help your baby to sleep; baby experts don't know the answers a lot of the time either.

Generally if whatever you are doing (letting cry, rocking and patting, pushing in the stroller) is going to work to get your baby off to sleep, it will do so in about twenty minutes. If your baby doesn't settle within twenty minutes she's probably not going to at this time. It's probably best to keep her up and try again after her next feed when hopefully she will sleep.

There are times in the early weeks when parents may have to change their routines (mother sleeps in the day, father cooks the dinner and maybe sleeps in another room for a while) as at this time it is impossible to change the baby's routine.

Here are some helping-to-sleep tips

- Abolish the words 'good', 'bad' and 'spoil' from your baby vocabulary and encourage those around you to do the same.
- Look for options rather than solutions.
- Make sure your baby is not hungry. Hunger does not play a major role in wakeful babies but if you're breastfeeding a quick check of your baby's weight tells you if there's enough milk; a one-off clothed weight at your child and family health centre or pharmacy is sufficient. Little or no weight gain over several weeks is an indication she might be hungry. If you're bottle feeding, make sure you're making the formula up the way it's supposed to be made.
- Is your baby ready for sleep? From three weeks on, babies start to have regular times when they are happy to be awake. This time increases as they grow older. When they are ready for sleep they start to cry or grunt and suck their fists. Their movements become jerky and they lose eye-contact.

- Babies sleep better on a firm mattress. Dense latex such as maternity hospitals use is fine. There are no particular baby mattresses that are more advantageous than others in relation to SUDI as long as the mattress is firm and well-fitting.

- The following things are options, all of which work some of the time. Remember that when they work (that is, the baby goes off to sleep, hopefully a sustained sleep for an hour or two) they tend to work within about twenty minutes. Some of them are unacceptable to some families, some of them are not possible because of family lifestyle and some may lead to hassles later, but they are all safe:

  – Breastfeed your baby to sleep;

  – Rock and pat your baby to sleep;

  – Sleep with your baby (bearing in mind safe sleep recommendations);

  – Try wrapping your baby firmly so she can't wake herself up when she startles;

  – Carry her in a sling;

  – Give her a warm bath;

  – Play some soothing music;

  – Go for a walk;

  – Give her a dummy.

Unfortunately, if babies only ever learn to associate sleep with these things it often means they don't know how to sleep unless they are present. For example—when a baby goes to sleep on the breast or in her mother's arms she will often wake again soon after being put into her cot and it is very difficult to help her back to sleep. Once she is up again she gets tired very quickly, starts to cry, goes to the breast again, falls asleep, is put into her cot only to wake again a short time later when the cycle is repeated. The reason this happens is because the baby goes to sleep under one set of conditions and when she wakes briefly, as she passes from one sleep stage to the next, is immediately aware her environment is different so comes fully awake and starts to cry instead of slipping into the next stage of sleep.

As time goes by, mothers find it more and more difficult to carry out these routines. So another option is to put your baby down awake and let her cry to sleep sometimes. Like all the other options, sometimes this works and sometimes it doesn't, but letting a well-fed tired baby cry before sleeping can be an aid in helping her to learn how to sleep. Try leaving her for up to twenty minutes some time during the day or the evening, following the guidelines on page 272.

FOR MORE INFORMATION

Chapter 5: Choosing Baby Products *(dummies, page 53)*
Chapter 12: Safety *(dummies, page 230)*
Chapter 28: Sleeping and Waking Six Months and Beyond *(teaching to sleep, page 484)*
Chapter 11: Daily Care *(where to sleep, page 212)*
Chapter 19: Common Worries and Queries *(thumb-sucking, page 409)*

Chapter 15

The Crying Baby

Babies can cry without learning, as far as I know, yet they have to learn to make all other sounds.

KATE LLEWELLYN, *THE MOUNTAIN*

All babies cry. You may find listening to your baby cry is one of the hardest parts of being a parent. From your baby's point of view, crying is an essential part of her survival and not something she does to irritate or upset you.

Why do babies cry?

Baby crying has helped the human race survive; it is a vital way of communicating. It's the most obvious form of early communication but not the only one. Young babies send out communication in other more subtle ways. They gaze intently at an adult face, coo, smile, grasp a finger and indicate when they don't want food by not sucking or pulling away. Mothers respond to all these things and take great pleasure in many of them. Crying, however, is the most powerful way babies have of communicating when they are very young and to some extent during the whole of their first year.

Parents are often unprepared for the crying, believing that as caring people who are only too happy to do the right thing and meet all their baby's needs their baby will not cry. They find it shattering to discover that a certain amount of crying is normal for all babies and for some babies that amount is a lot.

Parents, understandably, start to think it would be much easier if their baby's main way of communicating was not by crying, but crying is the main way babies have of letting their protector know they need something.

A lot of the time what they need is obvious and easy to provide. Obvious causes of crying are things like hunger, over-tiredness, thirst, feeling too hot or too cold, loneliness, over-stimulation, being undressed and bathed, or being alarmed by a sudden noise.

Babies also cry when they are in physical pain. An accident, an injection or a circumcision are clear-cut reasons for distress we can all understand. Medical problems such as an inguinal hernia or a bowel obstruction are other painful experiences. It's very upsetting when a baby gets sick but, once diagnosed, the problem can be treated; knowing something can be done always brings a sense of relief.

When there is no obvious cause, mothers, fathers and even health workers feel helpless, hopeless and distressed, especially when the crying goes on for a long time. I'm sure the baby feels pretty miserable too.

Patterns of crying

The age and times of day babies cry tend to fall into patterns which can be identified.

From birth to three weeks many babies sleep a lot, the crying periods don't last long and are easy to resolve.

From three weeks onwards things may change, sometimes dramatically. Babies tend to cry more and sleep less. The crying, unsettled behaviour can roughly be divided into three groups:

- Explained crying is expected crying and the cause is obvious. It is easy to do something which calms and settles the baby such as feeding, changing or gently rocking. Sometimes a bath, a walk or, if it's in the middle of the night, taking the baby to bed is what's needed.

- Unexplained crying is unexpected crying for a reason which is hard to find. Unexplained crying for a short period every twenty-four hours is normal for about 80 per cent of all babies.
- A small number of babies (about 20 per cent) cry a lot for large parts of the day and night, so instead of having one session of crying they have several which go on for a long time. These babies sleep poorly, wake early, cry and draw up their legs a lot. Days stretch into weeks and into months, with no change. There are bad days and worse days, rarely any good days, until things slowly start to change between three and six months. This sort of crying in healthy, loved, protected babies remains to a large extent a mystery and is what this chapter of the book is about.

Glance at the titles in the baby book section of any book store. You will always find a number of books offering the definitive reasons, cures and ways to help babies who cry a lot. I can only add my point of view to what's already circulating. Like all information related to crying babies, my approach will help some and not others. I do tend to write more about what doesn't work rather than what does, because despite the constant flow of literature and research for the last one hundred years, no causes or treatments have been identified that have made any significant difference to helping crying babies who appear to be otherwise healthy. Ideas change, new theories replace old, but the babies keep crying.

If your baby cries a lot it is important to be aware that:

- The majority of crying babies are healthy babies who do not have a clearly defined, treatable medical problem.
- There is not an easy, single answer that suits every baby who cries excessively.
- Crying babies invariably grow into delightful older babies and toddlers.
- This period of your baby's life is something you have to go through together. Practical help, support and understanding helps a great deal; beyond a certain point, parents are on their own.

I hope the following chapter contributes to your understanding of these babies and helps you and your baby through the crying.

How does excessive crying affect the family?

Even though, in the sum total of a baby's whole life this is a tiny part, living with a baby who cries excessively can have a profound effect on the parents, their relationship and family life. Most people are astounded at how much time any baby takes up even when things are going well. If the baby spends a large amount of time every day crying and unhappy and apparently not responding to all the love and attention she is getting, the mother becomes physically and mentally exhausted.

Mental exhaustion

Feelings of guilt, loss of confidence and loss of self-esteem may come from within or may be triggered off by health professionals, partners, grandparents or the neighbour. Women whose babies cry a lot often become isolated simply because even if they can accept the crying, others can't.

A mother with a crying baby may feel disappointed when a much-loved beautiful baby doesn't come up to everyone's expectations—'not a *good* baby'. Disappointment might turn to anger as the mother tries harder and harder and becomes more and more exhausted.

This is a pretty grim picture and of course not everyone experiences all of these feelings all of the time, but it is quite normal for a mother in this situation at times to wish she had never had the baby and for both parents to see life before the baby as quite pleasant.

Physical exhaustion

Women find so much time in the day is spent with the baby there is little left for anything else and the house becomes chaotic. Well-meaning advisers tell mothers to 'forget about the housework', knowing they themselves would find it stressful living in a mess. It would be more useful to offer practical help.

A constantly crying baby causes a physical response in some women. Chest pain, sweating, palpitations, nausea or light-headedness are all common. Add to this sleep deprivation and often an inadequate diet—is it any wonder women working under these conditions are in a state of physical exhaustion!

Relationships

Relationships are certainly tested in ways they never were before the baby arrived. Sex and social life tend to become non-existent. Couples who previously lived in harmony argue over the best way to look after the baby (pick up, let cry, share the bed, separate room, medicate, don't medicate, stop breastfeeding, keep breastfeeding, change the formula and so on and so on).

Some fathers blame the mother, some ignore the mother's distress and feel sorry for the baby. Others become helpless and hopeless, insisting on their right to sleep, so the mother starts to feel she is dealing with two crying babies, not one.

Another man might want to share the responsibility and give as much support and comfort as he can, only to find the mother shuts herself and the baby off from him. He starts to feel useless and switches off.

Constant crying is doubly difficult when there is no one to share feelings or help decide the best options. Single parents with no one often find they end up using medication or leaving the baby to cry, even when they don't want to do this. There just seems to be no other solution.

A constantly crying baby is likely to give any relationship, good or bad, somewhat of a battering. In general, good relationships stay good after a baby arrives and bad ones tend to get worse—the baby only emphasises how good or bad the relationship is. This is magnified for the 20 per cent of parents who have a baby who cries a lot in the first three to six months; however, many relationships emerge stronger and a new bond forms between the couple.

What can be done?

1. **Rule out hunger and feeding problems.** Very few crying babies cry because they are hungry; the reason for the crying is rarely that simple, but it is important to make sure. If your baby is crying a lot and you are breastfeeding, weighing the baby is the most reliable way of checking the likelihood of hunger. A one-off clothed weight at your child and family health centre or your doctor's is sufficient. Little or no weight gain over several weeks is an indication she might be hungry. If weighing reveals hunger is the cause of the crying, giving extra food will help your baby to be more settled.

- **Breastfeeding:** Check your baby is in the best position to feed well. Worrying, unexplained crying in a healthy breastfed baby who is gaining weight well is rarely a breastfeeding problem. It is suggested that excessive crying in some breastfed babies happens because the baby is only getting the foremilk, which means she is getting too much lactose (the sugar found in milk) and that changing the way the mother breastfeeds solves the problem. If the mother is feeding for relatively short times at each breast she is told to leave the baby on the first breast until the baby decides to come off before offering the second breast. Note that research shows it is not possible for babies to consistently consume only 'low-fat foremilk'. I have not found altering breastfeeding patterns makes any difference to an unsettled baby's behaviour and often raises unnecessary doubts in the mother's mind about her ability to breastfeed and the quality of her milk at a time when that's the last thing she needs.

  Excessive crying happens equally to breastfed and bottle fed babies, so weaning does not mean the crying stops. Some women manage better by weaning, but think everything through carefully before you take this step if breastfeeding means a lot to you.
- **Bottle feeding:** Make sure you are making the formula the way it's supposed to be made. When babies are crying a lot it's always tempting to keep changing the bottle, the teat and the brand and type of formula, but this rarely makes any lasting difference. In general it's best to stick to a cow's milk-based formula labelled 'suitable from birth'.

2. **If you are concerned about your baby's health, have her checked by a paediatrician to rule out the possibility of a clearly defined medical condition.** Persistent crying occasionally does have an obvious underlying medical cause which is possible to diagnose accurately without subjecting the baby to a round of invasive diagnostic procedures. When this is the case, the medical cause can be successfully treated, which brings an end to a lot of the crying.

The main medical causes

INGUINAL HERNIA

A hernia in the groin can become clamped off by the tight muscles in the groin. This is called strangulation, causes intense pain and should be operated on as soon as possible. A similar thing can happen to baby boys who have an undescended testis, although this is rare.

Note, a squashy lump on the navel which 'pops' out when the baby cries is an umbilical hernia. Umbilical hernias are very common, rarely cause pain and are unlikely to be the cause of constant crying.

INTESTINAL OBSTRUCTION

When a baby cries a lot, parents are often worried that 'something is twisted inside' because their baby goes red and draws up her legs when she cries (see page 294 for an explanation about this). Several medical conditions can cause intestinal obstructions in babies but:

- they are very rare;
- babies born with these conditions are nearly always diagnosed soon after birth;
- the other main type of intestinal obstruction (intussusception) is more likely to occur between three and twelve months and is usually a clear-cut diagnosis;
- crying due to intestinal obstruction is accompanied by weight loss, pallor, a sudden change in the baby's poo and an alarming change in the baby's behaviour. Going red, grunting a lot and drawing up their legs is normal behaviour for most babies and not a sign of pain.

URINARY TRACT INFECTION

A small number of crying babies do turn out to have urinary tract infections which, once treated, makes the baby much happier, so testing of a crying baby's urine is now routine. Other signs apart from the crying might be 'thick', smelly urine with obvious discomfort when the urine is being passed by a very irritable baby who might also have a fever.

BABIES BORN WITH PHYSICAL OR MENTAL DISABILITIES

Most of these problems are diagnosed at birth or soon after. Unfortunately some are less obvious and it may be many months before parents know exactly what is wrong.

For example: cerebral palsy—minor degrees of cerebral palsy are difficult to diagnose and can cause tense, crying babies; deafness can cause crying, unsettled babies; undiagnosed heart conditions can also be a cause of miserable, irritable babies who are often difficult feeders who gain weight poorly.

All these things are rare and unlikely to be the cause of your baby's crying, but because they do exist and are sometimes overlooked, make sure your baby is checked by a paediatrician or a doctor.

COMMON INFECTIONS

Illnesses such as head colds, viral diarrhoea, bronchiolitis, sore throats or ear infections are either obvious causes or easily diagnosed and can all contribute to a cross, crying baby. When the baby recovers, the crying behaviour settles, whereas the healthy, crying baby cries on.

Viral diarrhoea, sore throats and ear infections are a much more common cause of 'explained' crying in older babies and toddlers and are not seen very often in babies under three months of age.

THE FOLLOWING THINGS DO NOT CAUSE PERSISTENT, UNEXPLAINED CRYING IN HEALTHY BABIES

'Teething'; cradle cap, heat rash or hormone rash; frothy or loose poo in a healthy breastfed baby; constipation in a bottle fed baby; thrush; nappy rash.

Having ruled out hunger and the possibility of an underlying illness, there remain the myriad theories and unproved diagnoses with their accompanying treatments that parents quickly become familiar with as they try to find an answer. Writing about every theory and suggested cause is a book in itself, so I will look at the major themes in use at the current time to explain and/or 'treat' crying babies under two groups—medical and non-medical.

Medical approach

Unlike the previous medical conditions, these medical conditions are not clear-cut, so the treatment may not be wildly successful. The majority of babies who are treated for the following conditions probably haven't got what it is they are being treated for.

Apart from finding the few babies who have the diagnosed condition and so benefit from the treatment, the other advantages of the medical approach are:

- It helps the mother to feel better and stop blaming herself for her baby's distress.
- Medication often has a valuable placebo effect. A placebo effect refers to a positive result achieved by a non-medical remedy or a harmless medical remedy prescribed for a non-existent condition. The placebo effect should never be ridiculed because no one knows for sure why some babies cry so much in the first three to six months. If harmless remedies and simple diagnoses help parents through a critical period the placebo effect should be encouraged. By understanding that a placebo effect exists, parents are also more aware of the limitations of medications and remedies.
- It gives the mother a concrete plan of action instead of vague reassurances.

The medical approach also has disadvantages:

- It can give parents unrealistic expectations of results.
- A medical diagnosis not properly explained is very worrying for some parents—they may think their baby has a serious long-term illness which is unlikely to be the case.
- Searching for a medical cause can start a merry-go-round of medication and feeding changes which in themselves start to cause problems so it becomes more and more difficult to work out what is going on.
- A medical diagnosis often precipitates unnecessary weaning for breastfed babies.
- Occasionally the medication suggested is unsafe.

The main medically based theories as to why babies cry a lot are all centred around the baby's gastrointestinal tract (the gut).

They are as follows: colic/wind; allergy/food intolerance; reflux; lactose intolerance.

The persistent belief that healthy babies who cry a lot have gut problems has been shown over and over again by observation and research to be incorrect *most* of the time. Despite this, health professionals, who agree it's highly unlikely to be the cause of the baby's distress, continue to diagnose and treat something they themselves think is non-existent *most* of the time.

Why? Partly because of the baby's and parents' distress when there is no explanation, partly because of the time factor (it's quicker to diagnose and medicate than spend a lot of time counselling and comforting) and partly because medication is easily available whereas practical help and resources to help distressed families aren't.

A diagnosis of a problem in the gut is nearly always based on the way the baby behaves, not on medically proven symptoms. All babies go red in the face and draw up their legs at times when they cry. This is an automatic reflex which can be observed in all babies whether they cry excessively or not. It is usually because they are generally distressed, not because they have pains in their bellies. Similarly, an adult stamping his or her foot when upset does not mean he or she has a pain in the foot. The longer babies cry and the less sleep they have, the more distressed they become and the more they repeat this action. Adults quite inappropriately project their own intentions or reasons for actions or behaviour onto babies and so confuse this with adult behaviour which would indicate a pain in the gut. These medically based theories started from this premise.

Colic/wind

Colic and wind are the most frustrating of all the medically based theories as they really are an inaccurate way of describing what the baby does rather than what the baby has. Parents, however, are led to believe that the word 'colic' is a diagnosis of a medically proven condition and so conclude treatment and a cure are just around the corner.

Colic is a general term which means acute paroxysmal pain. Nowhere else in medicine do we use the word 'colic' without describing the site of the pain—example, renal colic, biliary colic or menstrual colic. Calling excessive crying in a healthy baby 'colic' implies a severe pain in the stomach or bowel similar to that experienced by an adult who eats a bad oyster or who has a bowel obstruction. This doesn't make sense when we are referring to a normal baby who is having the correct food. The word 'colic' as a diagnosis for a baby's crying really means 'This healthy baby is crying a lot and we don't know why'.

The myths surrounding babies and 'wind' are second only to that of 'teething'.

Burping and passing wind are normal functions of the human body from birth to death and all babies fart very loudly and very well from the moment they arrive. Some babies do appear to show discomfort associated with eating, digesting and pooing by responding to these normal body functions by squirming, grunting, going red in the face and sometimes crying. I believe this is more a psychological response to the new sensation of all these things happening to their bodies, not physical pain or discomfort the way adults understand it. When babies are generally distressed, overwhelmed and over-tired they are much more sensitive to these internal body movements and exhausted parents looking for answers tend to see these responses as the cause of their baby's crying.

Helping your baby to burp when she is wriggling, squirming and unsettled by holding her over your shoulder or lying her across your lap and applying some pressure to her back may relieve her distress sometimes, but overall 'burping' techniques make very little difference to the behaviour of crying babies.

Gastro-oesophageal reflux disease (GORD): Otherwise known as reflux

Reflux is such a common word used in baby circles that most mothers are aware of it.

WHAT IS MEANT BY THE TERM GASTRO-OESOPHAGEAL REFLUX?

It is normal in humans of all ages for food from the stomach to flow back up into the gullet, especially after meals. This back-flow is called 'reflux'. The technical names of the stomach and gullet are *gastro* and *oesophagus*, hence the term gastro-oesophageal reflux is used to describe this action. In childhood and adulthood we are unaware of it unless it causes heartburn or other problems (nasty taste in the mouth, sore throats, coughing, sleepless nights and so on).

The reason the food-flow goes up and down unnoticed in adults and children is because the gullet is large enough to hold the churned-up food from the stomach and because the muscle, known as the oesophageal sphincter, at the top opening of the stomach works efficiently to keep the food down where it's supposed to be.

Poor co-ordination of the movement of food between the oesophagus and the stomach also contributes to reflux problems in babies. It's still not clearly understood why some babies never regurgitate, some regurgitate all the time and are happy, others regurgitate and scream and are miserable. None of the variations has anything to do with the mother's care of her baby.

It's confusing then to use the word 'reflux' to describe a medical condition in a baby without specifying exactly what the problem is. As with 'colic', it has become a general term used to describe a miserable baby, often with no specific symptoms.

When difficulties arise from this reflux action they can be divided into specific problems.

- **Constant regurgitation:** Almost half of all babies throw up to a degree that makes parents anxious and complicates normal living. Apart from the regurgitation the baby is otherwise well, happy and gaining weight. Unfortunately the constant aroma and mess is never-ending and being thrown up on all day does little for a mother's self-esteem. Regurgitation often increases at around eight to eleven months when many babies are crawling. They are horizontal to the floor at this time and heave themselves around leaving multi-coloured puddles as they go. The regurgitation eventually stops at about a year for all but 5 per cent. A combination of an upright position and improved functioning of the muscle between the stomach and the oesophagus helps stop the flow. For more on regurgitation and vomiting, see page 188.
- **Lung problems:** A tiny number of babies who regurgitate a lot draw some of the stomach contents into their lungs. This causes coughing, wheezing, breathing difficulties or pneumonia. If these problems keep happening, medical care is needed by a specialist doctor. Lung problems due to regurgitation are more common in very premature or sick babies.
- **Weight loss:** A small number of babies may be reluctant to drink because of associated pain with heartburn. This is very unusual as heartburn is uncommon in babies under four months of age and again

is more likely in babies who are premature, sick or developmentally delayed. These babies develop anorexia, do not thrive and need specialist attention. However, weight loss related to regurgitation is not common so other reasons for weight loss should always be investigated before diagnosing failure to thrive caused by regurgitation. Steady weight loss in a breastfed baby who is regurgitating is more likely to be because the milk supply is low than because of the regurgitation.

Limiting a bottle fed baby's intake to try to stop the regurgitation will also cause weight loss. Babies who regurgitate a lot but are otherwise happy should be fed as normal regardless of the regurgitation. Reducing their intake reduces their weight.

- **Heartburn (acid reflux):** When unsettled, crying babies are diagnosed as having reflux, the person making the diagnosis usually means the baby is crying all the time because the stomach contents are irritating the gullet, causing heartburn. In actual fact heartburn in babies is uncommon because babies have such bland diets, especially before they start solids. The condition is very much over-diagnosed and treated.

  Occasionally, however, acid reflux is a problem and may be so severe the gullet becomes ulcerated and bleeds and the baby may vomit blood. Again, this needs treatment from a specialist doctor.

DIAGNOSING GORD

Unfortunately, trying to diagnose GORD in babies is very difficult. Often the diagnosis is made on behavioural symptoms (that is crying, wakefulness, breast or bottle refusal, back arching and so on) and there is a wide range of baby behaviour in the first three to six months which, although worrying, does not necessarily indicate a medical condition warranting drug treatment.

Various procedures can be used to diagnose GORD in babies, but none of them are so definitive that they are appropriate for all crying, unsettled babies.

- **Treatment for GORD problems:** Simple treatment involves posturing the baby when she sleeps so she lies uphill and trying to feed her in a tilted or upright position, which is difficult in the early breastfeeding days but can be done once the breastfeeding is well established and there is less chance of nipple damage.

Frequent small feeds are generally better tolerated than large infrequent feeds when the baby has acid reflux.

Medications are used. See page 301.

Very occasionally, surgery is performed. It is only considered when there is no doubt about the diagnosis and there are continual complications which put the baby at risk and cannot be solved any other way. This is more common in babies with other problems, for example cerebral palsy.

Food allergy and food intolerance

Allergy to protein, which may be cow's milk or soy milk protein, is a possibility in 1 to 3 per cent of babies. Research yields very conflicting results about the incidence of excessive crying being caused by allergy or food intolerance.

For more information on food allergy and food intolerance see page 384.

Here are the usual suggestions:

- **If the mother is breastfeeding, try avoiding a range of food to prevent transfer of antigens to the baby**

  Babies born with family histories of allergies are 50–80 per cent more likely to develop allergic diseases compared to those with no family history (a 20 per cent chance). The risk is higher when both parents are allergic as opposed to one parent. The risk is also higher if the mother (compared with the father) has allergic diseases.

  If you have a strong family history of allergy (food reactions, hayfever, asthma, eczema) it may be worthwhile eliminating milk and milk products from your diet and even, under dietary supervision, try various elimination diets to eliminate foods which are known to cause adverse reactions due to food intolerance—wheat and fish and naturally occurring salicylates, for example.

  In rare circumstances babies have a major reaction in response to a food protein (usually milk) passed through the mother's breastmilk.

  For the majority of breastfeeding women who have very unsettled crying babies, the stress involved with strict special or elimination diets is disproportionate to the results achieved. And, in relation to preventing food allergy in babies, the latest thinking is strongly veering towards there being no benefit in such strategies, see page 387.

The majority of crying babies spontaneously become much more settled between three and four months regardless of what their mothers eat. I have found, overall, that meddling with the mother's diet tends to be unsuccessful and often adds tension to an already stressful situation. For more on food allergy and intolerance, see page 384.

- **If the baby is having formula, change the formula**

Change of formula occasionally makes the baby happier but the change is often short-lived.

If there is a strong family history of allergy it is recommended that babies are given HA formula (hydrolysed formula where the milk protein is artificially partially broken down) for the first four to six months if they are not breastfed. HA formula has been shown to reduce the incidence of atopic eczema and food allergy in high-risk babies. Whether this will calm an otherwise healthy crying, unsettled baby is in the realm of speculation but it may be worth a try.

There's no evidence that changes to low lactose (see next section), soy or goat's milk formula improve the situation—for more on formula see page 96.

Lactose Intolerance

WHAT IS LACTOSE INTOLERANCE?

Lactose is a sugar which only occurs in the milk of mammals, including humans. Babies of all species produce an enzyme called lactase while they are receiving milk which helps digest the lactose. Once weaning occurs lactase is no longer produced in any animals apart from humans.

Not all humans continue to produce lactase. People from Asia, Mediterranean countries, the Middle East and some indigenous Australians do not produce lactase after weaning, which means their guts may be unable to digest the lactose found in dairy products. Caucasian and other people with a history of consuming dairy products usually keep producing lactase into adult life.

TYPES OF LACTOSE INTOLERANCE

1. Primary Lactose Intolerance (congenital)

This is an extremely rare deficiency caused when a baby is born without the ability to make lactase. This is apparent soon after birth. These babies do not gain weight and are very ill. Some researchers question that the condition really exists as it has only ever been indentified in a miniscule number of babies.

2. Secondary Lactose Intolerance

This occurs following damage to the gut due to gastroenteritis, giardia infection, coeliac disease, some medications, cow's milk protein intolerance, and so on. Lactase production is decreased and wind, nausea and diarrhoea keep recurring if milk products are given. Breastmilk, however is well-tolerated by most babies with secondary lactose intolerance despite the fact that breastmilk has high levels of lactose. Some breastfed babies will need a low lactose formula instead of breastmilk (or sometimes as well as breastmilk, depending on the severity of the gut damage) for a week or for as long as it takes their guts to recover at which time full breastfeeding may be resumed.

Secondary lactose intolerance is more common after the first three to four months as older babies/toddlers are more exposed to all the common infections once they are moving around, mixing with other babies/toddlers, and generally out in the big, wide world.

3. Functional Lactase Deficiency

This is the condition most relevant to healthy crying breastfed babies in the first three to six months. It occurs in thriving babies who poo like crazy (watery, frothy poo), often have bright red bottoms, and what appears to be abdominal pain (tricky, often, to work this out). They are also very unhappy (screaming) a lot of the time. If breastfed, it is believed that these babies are receiving more lactose in the breastmilk than they can comfortably digest. I must emphasise here that a considerable number of breastfed babies do poo like crazy—and it's sometimes watery—fart like mad and have a temporary redness of the bum in the first six to eight weeks but are not unhappy and (mostly) sleep well between feeds. This is not about those babies. It is about the babies with these symptoms who are also very unhappy day in and day out over a much longer period.

The recommended course of action is to try the following (if breastfeeding):

- Allow the baby to come off the first breast spontaneously before offering the second breast.
- Space feeds, if possible—allow three hours between feeds. Offer the least full breast in between if you have to feed before the three hours are up.
- Check that the baby's position and attachment at the breast are correct to allow for optimum drainage.

This is thought to maximise the fat content and allow more time for digestion of the lactose. Maybe . . . it's worth a try.

And formula fed babies?

If using formula, a change to a low lactose formula may be advised.

TO SUMMARISE:

- Like other strategies used to try to help healthy, unsettled babies, diagnosing and treating babies for lactose intolerance is mostly guesswork on the part of the person making the diagnosis and usually makes very little difference to how the baby behaves. It is particularly upsetting for mothers to be told to wean and use formula because of 'lactose intolerance'.
- There is no evidence supporting the use of lactase drops.
- Despite research to the contrary and my reluctance to suggest this course of action I am aware that a small number of breastfeeding mothers—at the desperate stage—find that weaning or partially weaning and putting their babies onto a low lactose formula has positive effects on their babies' behaviour.

Medication

Medical diagnoses are usually accompanied by medications. It's tempting for both parent and health professional to believe relief will come from medication, but there are problems when we medicate babies for crying even when we call it 'colic', 'reflux' or 'wind'.

- Most of the time the diagnosis and reason for medicating is guesswork because signs and symptoms are not clear and we can't ask the baby what's happening.

- There is a consistent high failure rate—that is, the baby's behaviour doesn't change for any length of time. Parents find every time they try something new (change the formula, start medication, stop medication and so on) the baby settles for a day or two then goes back to crying a lot again.
- One difficulty in assessing whether medication works is that research shows a placebo effect of between 20 and 30 per cent (see page 292).
- Medications can cause other problems such as heartburn, allergic reactions, vomiting, constipation, rashes and even increased irritability, which makes it more difficult to help the baby. And, over the years, most of the popular wind, colic and reflux medications have been discovered to carry risks far outweighing any possible benefits for the babies. For example, atropine, alcohol, dicyclomine and cisapride (see below).
- Drugs that consistently stop the baby crying usually have a sedative effect rather than doing something that eases the baby's gut. They work on the baby's central nervous system, not on the digestive system, and parents are often unaware of this. Sedating healthy babies who cry a lot seems a risky business and not in the baby's best interest.

  Unfortunately situations happen where daily living becomes intolerable because of a continually distressed, crying baby. Life with a crying baby usually becomes intolerable because the mother is not getting any practical help and support and is left alone day after day with her crying baby. Sedatives are resorted to as a way of easing an intensely stressful time, not because the baby needs them. It is safer for a healthy baby to cry than be sedated.

Here are the main drugs used for babies who cry a lot.

Colic/wind

Colic and wind medications for babies create a profitable market. New ones appear all the time, making extravagant claims about curing babies' gut problems. History reveals that this is not a new practice. Various miraculous potions have been concocted and sold to parents for at least two hundred years, often with the blessing of the medical and pharmaceutical professions. Think things through before you waste your money or buy something potentially harmful to your baby. Potions marketed as 'herbal' or 'natural' need just as much scrutiny as any others.

NON-SEDATIVE

- **Infacol wind drops:** Wholly made up of simethicone in a sugar-free base. Simethicone is an anti-flatulent which supposedly works by joining all the small bubbles together in the intestine so the large bubble will be passed! A dose is given before each feed. Safe to use.
- **Gripe water:** Gripe water has been around for a long time. It consists of dill oil, sodium bicarbonate, water, sugar and alcohol. The alcohol mildly sedates some babies the first few times it's used and babies like the sweet taste. Alcohol-free gripe water is available. If you use gripe water, don't overdo it. Too much sodium bicarbonate (a salt) is not good for your baby's kidneys.
- **Herbal teas:** The use of herbal teas for babies is no longer recommended because a lack of quality control in the manufacture of herbal teas makes them unsafe because other herbs, weeds or seeds may be present.
- **Herbal 'wind' preparations (often also called 'natural'):** These are found in lots of health food shops and pharmacies and contain a variety of different herbs. Parents often report a miracle change in their baby's crying after using one of these preparations; unfortunately the change is usually only temporary. Always find out what is in the mixture—occasionally quite dangerous sedatives are used in 'natural herbal mixtures'.

SEDATIVE EFFECT

Some wind and colic medications contain drugs which work on the baby's central nervous system, thus calming the baby. Although they are promoted as reducing colicky behaviour by easing spasms in the muscles lining the intestines, it is probably the effect on the central nervous system which calms the baby, not the anti-spasmodic effect.

- **Dicyclomine:** The most widely known of these is Merbentyl. Merbentyl is based on dicyclomine, an anti-spasmodic drug.

  Preparations containing dicyclomine have warnings on the labels not to administer them to babies under six months—yet it's the first three to four months when babies are commonly diagnosed as having 'wind' and 'colic'.

Until 1986 preparations containing dicyclomine were used freely for crying babies. Preparations containing dicyclomine were at times quite successful in stopping babies from crying so much, but mostly there was an improvement for a few days then a return to the pre-dicyclomine crying.

As these preparations were freely available, and as parents were hardly ever fully informed about all aspects of 'colic', it meant mixtures containing dicyclomine were frequently over-used and abused. Excessive use can cause drowsiness, a decrease in urine output, constipation and heartburn. Preparations containing the drug were declared unsafe for babies under six months. Looking objectively at all the medications given to healthy, crying babies, dicyclomine is not as potentially dangerous as some others which have no warning.

The problems associated with the use of dicyclomine are similar to those of any medication given to healthy crying babies. Much guesswork is involved, so it's risky to use any medication unreservedly, hoping for something positive to happen. The risks are increased when the drug being used depresses the baby's central nervous system.

If you do use a colic preparation containing dicyclomine:

a) Be aware of its limitations. It is not a miracle cure for crying.
b) Use strictly as directed. When you reach the maximum dose, stop using it and dispose of it down the sink or the toilet.

- **Donnalix Infant Drops:** Donnalix Infant Drops are sold over the counter and contain hyscyamine sulphate, atropine sulphate, hyoscine hydrobromide and alcohol in a flavoured syrup. Use of this drug contributes to reflux heartburn. Atropine can cause dilated pupils, a dry mouth, rapid heartbeat and constipation. Research has consistently shown atropine derivatives to be of no value for 'colic'.

SEDATIVES

The following drugs are sedatives. They work by putting your baby to sleep, not by treating a pain in the tummy.

- **Phenergan:** Phenergan is an anti-histamine that has a tranquillising effect. There are serious risks with using Phenergan, which include extreme drowsiness and depressed breathing or, alternatively, hyperstimulation and poor coordination. Phenergan is available only on prescription. It is not advised for the under twos.

- **Phenobarbitone:** It is unfortunate that preparations containing drugs such as atropine and phenobarbitone are still being prescribed for healthy, crying babies often without the parents being aware of what it is they are giving their baby. Phenobarbitone is a barbiturate which depresses the whole nervous system and causes abnormal deep sleep. It is also dependency-producing, which means babies who are taken off it suddenly may convulse.

  Phenobarbitone has a place when used for babies suffering from drug withdrawal (born to substance-addicted mothers), babies born with severe birth trauma and occasionally for other specific medical problems. It is inappropriate to use it for healthy babies who cry a lot. Never use mixtures containing this drug.

A WORD ABOUT PARACETAMOL AND IBUPROFEN: Tempra, Panadol and Dymadon are examples of paracetamol. Nurofen Junior and Brufen syrup are examples of ibuprofen.

Paracetamol is a medication for babies when they have a fever or are in pain (following surgery). Paracetamol is not useful for crying babies when the cause of the crying is unclear. Parents often resort to a dose of paracetamol when they can't think of anything else to do. Doing this occasionally is okay, bearing in mind that paracetamol has a mild sedative effect on some babies the first couple of times they have it.

Ibuprofen is an anti-inflammatory drug that is also used for symptoms of fever and pain in babies, toddlers and children. Both paracetamol and ibuprofen are equally efficient in reducing fever and pain. Like paracetamol, ibuprofen is not appropriate for healthy, crying babies when the cause of the crying is unclear.

Ibuprofen should not be used when there is a family history of asthma or other allergies. If in doubt check with your family doctor.

The safety of both drugs *depends on them being used correctly*. There is now a multitude of preparations available, all with their own individual strength and dose. It is very important to calculate and measure the dose correctly according to the manufacturer's instructions. If in doubt, check with a second person.

PARACETAMOL AND ASTHMA RISK

A study published in 2008 suggested that giving paracetamol in the first year of life significantly increased the risk of asthma in childhood, however, allergy specialists say that while serious consideration should be given to the study it does not provide clear-cut evidence that paracetamol causes asthma. At the time of publishing (2009) it is still advised to use paracetamol as it is viewed as the safest analgesic drug—ibuprofen, as previously mentioned, can provoke asthma attacks in susceptible children and aspirin can cause a serious life-threatening side-effect in babies, toddlers and children, called Reye's syndrome (children under the age of twelve should never be given aspirin). Parents are, however, strongly urged not to overuse paracetamol. Its main use is for serious fevers—38.5°C or above or for post-operative pain. Neither paracetamol nor ibuprofen should be given routinely prior to immunisation or repeatedly dished out for vague 'sleeping', 'teething' or 'colic' symptoms/problems in otherwise healthy babies.

Gastro-oesophageal Reflux Disease (GORD)

After twenty years of routinely medicating babies with a range of drugs for 'reflux' there is more and more evidence that unless a baby has a definitive diagnosis of acid reflux (heartburn), the commonly used medications do not do anything useful for vomiting/regurgitation, gagging, back arching or excessive crying.

This includes Mylanta, Gaviscon, milk thickeners and 'reflux' formula—see page 190 for a discussion on the use of thickened formula. One commonly used drug, cisapride, has been shown to be not only ineffective but also unsafe.

Acid-reducers such as Zantac and Losic are still routinely used for many crying babies, but as acid reflux is uncommon in the majority of babies these medications should only be used when there is a definitive diagnosis. Occasionally, when there is no doubt about the diagnosis, a tiny dose of an antibiotic is used to hasten the passage of food through the gut to minimise the regurgitation and heartburn.

Unfortunately because of the uncertainty surrounding GORD, it is possible that occasionally a baby with the condition may miss out on medication that would help. At the other end of the spectrum there's no doubt a whole host of babies are getting medication for a condition they don't have.

Non-medical approach

The non-medical approach to excessive crying suggests that most of the time when babies cry a lot it is not caused by an organically defined condition; rather, it is the way the baby is responding to her new environment.

Certainly non-medical reasons are only theories or someone's point of view, but so are most of the medical theories as to why some babies cry so much. Many parents find the non-medical approach helpful as it avoids diagnostic tests, experimental medication and meddling with feeds. This approach looks at ways to help parents adapt to the baby and what she's doing rather than trying to stop or 'cure' it, and involves looking at all the options parents may try and changing them when they don't suit. Like the medical approach the non-medical approach may not stop the crying but it helps the mother feel better about herself and her baby and gives her confidence to carry on without feeling the need to get on the medical roundabout.

Here are some non-medical reasons why some healthy babies cry a lot.

Sleep

I believe an inability to get to sleep and go back to sleep (unrelated to any other factor) is the major cause of distress and crying in healthy babies. Learning to sleep is one of the 'tasks' young babies need to undertake. Learning to sleep involves:

- Learning how to 'hold themselves together' to get to sleep. This is difficult for some babies—not able to get to sleep, they are unable to enjoy being awake. Their movements become jerky, they do not make eye contact and as they become more and more agitated their crying builds to a crescendo.
- Learning how to go back to sleep when suddenly woken from light sleep and dreaming sleep (REM). As mentioned previously, babies have long

periods of REM sleep from which they are easily woken. The reasons for waking might be normal body functions (for example, a poo behind the anus is a strange sensation to a baby, as is passing wind until she gets used to how it feels) or things relating to baby behaviour such as the startle reflex. Once awake, the baby cannot get back to sleep, starts to cry and eventually ends up crying uncontrollably, becoming more and more tense.

- Learning how to go back to sleep following the normal, brief wakings in between sleep stages instead of coming fully awake and crying.

Frustration from over-tiredness

Babies are only able to stay happy and awake for relatively short periods. The less sleep they have, the more crying there is likely to be. For many crying babies it is the lack of sleep causing the crying, not the crying causing the lack of sleep; a situation that is difficult to change until the baby is able to sleep more and longer.

On the subject of 'boredom'

Boredom is often raised as a possibility when considering the reasons why babies might be crying a lot. I have always been reluctant to go along with this idea as I find it a little glib and ultimately not that helpful. Certainly babies can be distracted momentarily from whatever their problem is by showing them moving objects, talking to them, dancing around the room with them, reading to them, showing them the waving leaves on a tree and so on. But as over-tiredness is a prime cause of very unsettled babies I think that pushing boredom as a reason for their behaviour brings the strong possibility of an already exhausted baby being over-stimulated to a degree that will make the problem worse. When babies sleep well, the boredom issue, by and large, is not a consideration because babies who sleep well are generally much happier when they are awake than those who don't. Before searching for endless anti-boredom activities, it's probably better to try to calm your baby and get her to sleep.

Low sensory threshold

A number of all healthy babies respond in an exaggerated way to light, movement, noise and their own normal body functions (burping, startle reflex, intestinal movements, passing urine or having a poo). Babies like this eventually also have trouble sleeping until their systems get used to the 'overload' of sensations and movements. It is thought that babies who have difficult births or sick premature babies are more inclined to have low sensory thresholds, but this is not always the case.

The temperament of the baby

The role of the temperament of the baby comes up time and time again. A small amount of evidence exists that excessive crying may relate to a 'difficult' temperament, but I have a problem with this approach.

Apart from the fact that seeing the baby as 'difficult' might mean a medical problem is overlooked, suggesting that a baby who has only been on the planet several weeks is 'difficult' when we don't know the reason for her distress is somewhat of an insult to a small person at this stage of her life when we have no idea what sort of a person she will be. One of the things I have learnt about being a parent is to be patient and wait for the end of the story.

Other contributing factors

When a baby is very unsettled and crying all the time, everyone unfortunately starts to look for someone or something to blame. Blaming is destructive, not constructive, and great care has to be taken when assessing the possible role the following factors play so that they are not used to make mothers and fathers feel guilty and to blame for the predicament the family is in. I am mentioning them because I do think in some crying baby situations they play a part, and acknowledging them sometimes means they can be changed or help can be obtained from other members of the immediate or extended family. Here they are:

- building extensions to the house;
- moving house;
- money worries;
- a major career change by the parent in paid work;
- overseas visitors who stay a long time;
- relationship problems;
- an unsympathetic partner;

- isolation and loneliness suffered by the parent at home with the baby (usually the mother);
- great emotional stress suffered by one or both parents;
- ill health of one or both parents;
- unrealistic expectations of life with a baby.

Non-medical options for babies who cry a lot centre around helping the baby not cry so much and helping the parents live with the crying. All of these things help some of the time but there is no single option that consistently works all the time for every crying baby. Of course, any of these can be done as well as using medication if the baby has been given a diagnosis and treatment.

Most of these options have already been described in Chapter 14, so please refer to that section if you want more detail.

- A dummy: Distressed babies often need to suck a lot, not from hunger but to relieve their distress. The breast can be used for comfort if the mother is happy to do that.
- Calm handling: Sharp, jerky movements signal distress which makes the baby more alarmed; wrapping her firmly in a flexed position and avoiding over-stimulation by lots of different people helps.
- Carrying the baby in a sling or front-pack.
- A deep, relaxation bath sometimes works wonders.
- Letting the baby cry is quite all right when there is nothing else to do, especially when the parents feel worn out and tense. Well-fed, tired babies often sleep well after crying when left for a short time. I suggest twenty to thirty minutes. Parents shouldn't hesitate to pick up their baby any time they think they should, but there needs to be a balance between constantly picking up and putting down and allowing the baby a reasonable time to get to sleep.
- Gentle rocking, patting, music or going for a walk are all soothing techniques that have been used for thousands of years to calm babies.

Getting help

Health professionals

Unfortunately a lot of health professionals don't get top marks when it comes to helping and supporting families with crying babies. Apart from the fact that there are always unhelpful people in any group of professionals, there are other reasons why this appears to be so:

- Parents caring for a crying baby often expect a miracle answer to safely stop their baby crying. Such an answer doesn't exist.
- Health professionals who deal a lot with healthy, crying babies often just get bogged down in the sheer numbers of difficulties with unsettled babies and take the tack that in the long run the difficulties resolve whether they spend a lot of time with the mother and baby or not. Some health professionals lose interest and look for the quick answer.
- Many parents never give the health professional feedback. They see a health professional once, never think to tell him or her the treatment didn't work and go on to the next health professional. Consequently some health professionals just keep dishing out the same old recipe not really knowing whether it makes any difference to the baby's crying or not.
- Health professionals who have large numbers of clients to see or whose fee structure limits time per client may not be prepared to spend time counselling and comforting a mother and her crying baby once they are confident the baby is healthy and getting the right food.

When looking for professional help the challenge is to find someone you trust to be the major adviser. It is quite reasonable to get a few different opinions, but you need one person who is flexible; someone you like and trust and feel confident with; knowledgeable enough to give you an objective summary of what you are being told so you are fully informed; supportive—this means he or she supports you in whatever action you take even if he or she doesn't agree with it (providing it doesn't pose risks for the baby).

The major health professional may be a child and family health nurse, a family doctor, a paediatrician, a psychologist, a social worker or an occupational therapist.

Help from the family care centres

Family care centres are government-subsidised places which offer help to mothers and babies and frequently play an important role in helping with crying babies. These centres usually give mothers an option of staying for the day or staying overnight for up to a week. Family care centres are found in every capital city—but unfortunately the option to stay overnight is not available in all states.

If you go to one, go with a realistic idea about what can be achieved. Chances are the staff will not discover exactly why your baby is crying so much, but they can help you in these ways: You get some sleep; they can reassure you that your baby is medically fit; you eat properly; you will receive moral support; you will be assisted with basic baby-settling skills and gain some ideas of what to do when the baby cries.

If you are isolated, a family care centre is a way of meeting other women who are going through the same experience. If you are depressed and/or angry, there are trained staff to help you with these feelings.

Family care centres do not suit everyone. Their approach to babycare is fairly structured, some of them do encourage leaving the baby to cry for short periods and they usually attempt to establish some sort of routine. If you don't believe it's all right to let babies cry for short periods and routine is not your style, a family care centre is not for you.

The results achieved in family care centres with young babies are not always permanent. Babies have a sneaky way of sleeping more and crying less in these places only to revert to crying a lot and sleeping less when they go home. This can have a devastating effect on a mother's confidence. Try not to be dismayed if this happens to you. Family care centres have unlimited staff to do lots of rocking and patting on rotating shifts. They are also not trying to run a house and care for a baby twenty-four hours a day, seven days a week.

Other help

Unless you have a miraculous response from seeing a health professional, visiting a family care centre, changing your diet or your baby's formula or by giving medication, you will have to live with the crying.

I have used the word 'parents' a lot in this chapter rather than 'mother' to recognise that fathers as well as mothers have crying babies. I also recognise that men are sharing the ups and downs of parenthood more evenly than was the case in the past, but it still must be acknowledged that it is often the mothers who are caring for and spending the long, often lonely hours with the baby. Fathers have avenues of escape not available to the mother, and the crying baby remains primarily a woman's problem.

Practical help is vital and it is sad to see how few women in our society looking after a crying baby receive any. I am sure there would be far less diagnosing and medicating of healthy babies if more consistent, easily available help and *company* was available for women who need it during the first three to six months after birth. It's amazing what a difference it makes just having someone else in the house who's just there even if they are not directly helping with the baby.

When practical help and company is not available, the following ideas provide limited help if you can arrange it.

- Have you got a trusted friend or family member who doesn't bog you down with endless advice and who doesn't see anything odd about a baby who cries a lot who will mind your baby and give you a break on a regular basis?
- Can you arrange help with the housework? Can you pay someone for a while? What about asking one of your relatives who keeps burbling on about 'wind' to do the shopping or the dishes or something practical instead? Can you put in some earphones and let your baby cry while you clean up? You will feel much better, and chances are your baby is going to cry anyway whether you walk the floor with her or clean the house. If you can restore order you will feel better, more in control and she may go to sleep.
- Send for your mother if this is appropriate. Go to your mother if she is a tower of strength who doesn't mind a crying baby around the house.
- Try to work out what makes you feel better, then *do whatever you feel the need to do until your baby is calmer*. For example, frequent trips to see your major health professional (the right one won't mind) or frequent day visits to a family and baby centre. Mother and baby groups can help if there are any in your area. Don't forget that the Australian Breastfeeding Association (ABA) runs groups. Talking to sympathetic friends on the phone also helps.

Managing angry feelings

At some time or another every parent feels angry or irritated with their baby or with the situation they are in, which directly relates to the fact that they have a baby. Babies bring a lot of pleasure, but they also bring frustrations. A baby disrupts adult lifestyles and limits the mother's independence. She may also throw up, cry a lot and not sleep at the most inconvenient and unpredictable moments. Angry or irritated feelings may range from a fleeting sensation to feelings so intense the parent feels he or she could easily do something they might regret. As the mother is the one with the baby most of the time she is likely to experience this feeling more intensely and more often than the father.

When the baby is crying for a large part of every twenty-four-hour period, angry feelings are normal. So are negative feelings about the baby from time to time. It's important to blow off steam to someone and men should allow their partners to express feelings of anger and to say rude things about the baby without showing shock and horror. Lots of the women I see say all sorts of nasty things from time to time then feel much better because they have been allowed to say them. Nearly all the time these feelings are transient and the parent has no intention of acting upon them. The feelings go away when things improve.

Nevertheless, there may be times when you feel out of control and that there is a chance you might hurt your baby. Put the baby in her bassinet in her room and go as far away as you can. Call someone immediately: your mother; your partner; your child and family health nurse; a twenty-four-hour family and baby centre; Casualty at your nearest children's hospital or local hospital; the nearest child abuse prevention service. And don't feel embarrassed to get help (see page 552).

Can having a baby who cries be prevented?

Probably not. Until we know more about the precise reason why some babies are so unhappy during the first six months of life it is difficult to predict exactly what may or may not contribute.

Care during pregnancy and changing some negative lifestyle habits might help, but there will always be a considerable number of crying babies born to parents who take every care and a number of placid babies born to parents who are very careless about their personal habits. It sometimes seems very unfair but remember, by taking care and providing the right environment you are giving your baby a wonderful life and future which extends way beyond crying difficulties in the first six months.

Care during pregnancy

Eat plenty of fresh food, cut down on takeaways and refined food. Take steps to avoid food you have problems with. *Stop* smoking—research does show a higher incidence of babies who cry excessively in homes where one or both partners smoke. Avoid alcohol and drugs. Try learning relaxation techniques. Even if these things don't make a difference to how much your baby cries you will manage better. Looking after yourself and your body also removes an element of guilt which makes you less stressed.

The non-crying baby of other cultures

By other cultures I am referring to indigenous or traditional cultures as opposed to western or industrial cultures such as ours. Observations and anecdotal stories from other cultures suggest babies don't cry there the way they do in our culture (perhaps none of them have reflux?). I'm never too sure how useful this information is to a woman gallantly doing her best for her crying baby. Suggestions to care for babies here the way they are cared for in peasant communities are for most women in our community unworkable.

Constant references to the 'non-crying baby of other cultures' suggests a superior style of mothering which western women can't quite achieve—so no wonder their babies cry a lot! I find this approach not at all helpful and quite damaging to our women's self-esteem.

It does appear that in some other cultures the work of motherhood is not left entirely up to one person the way it is here, so a baby who cries a lot can be handed around to many relatives. Our society also elevates pregnancy and childbirth to unrealistic heights then leaves women on their own to struggle with the task, making them wonder what they are doing wrong when at times it all seems too much.

However, many things about being women and mothers in our society are wonderful. Few of us would care to live the way women do in other communities so let's stop making our women feel guilty about their education, their independence and their lives and help them care for their babies the way they want to in the context of our culture.

Last hints to help you through

- Try not to blame your baby, try not to blame yourself. This time is part of your life story together. Think how you will laugh about it when she is twenty-one.
- When you can, try to look ahead and make some plans for an optimistic future so you don't feel completely bogged down in the present. Talk about holidays, perhaps schooling and some nights out when the baby is calmer.
- Partners, work together! It is vital. The mother shoulders most of the burden so, father, please support her approach. Organise shift work at the weekends. Don't blame each other.
- Try whatever you think is reasonable. You will not 'spoil' your baby by picking her up all the time, nor will you damage her by letting her cry.
- Never do anything that is suggested that causes you added stress, major inconvenience or goes against what you feel is right. Remember you are in charge, not the health professionals or anyone else who feels inclined to tell you what to do.

Some crying baby stories

My baby was terrible. He screamed all the time and was never happy when he was awake. It started out as wind and I tried all the wind things, none of which helped. Gripe water was the only one that helped a little bit. He kept getting worse, especially after feeding. I only breastfed for a few days.

I went to a family and baby centre where they diagnosed reflux. After that we started Mylanta and thickening the milk and started early solids. This made a slight difference but he was still very difficult and it went on until he was six months old at which time he ate more than he drank and seemed to improve.

I was very tired and depressed and got very run down and sick. I couldn't enjoy him because he was so unhappy. I didn't realise babies could be so unhappy! I hadn't had much experience with babies and other babies I had known before I had my own always seemed happy.

It put a strain on my relationship with my husband because I was always so tired, the baby took up so much time. I felt my husband wasn't understanding enough. Getting practical help with my baby was difficult because he was so hard to look after—no one wanted to mind him or help me.

SUGGESTIONS: Accept all help; prepare for the possibility of a crying baby during pregnancy; the family and baby centre was a great help; try not to take too much advice from friends and never compare babies.

My baby cried constantly. I tried to do everything I could to pacify him but I couldn't. I was reassured by health professionals he was normal and I accepted that. As long as you get confidence from somebody that you're doing the right thing and not hurting the baby you're okay—I managed.

I let him cry, shut the door and put the radio on. As long as they're crying they're fine—it's when they stop you worry.

My husband was very supportive and took him for lots of long walks. He was a baby who constantly wanted to be on the move.

I did not medicate. I tried to stay calm and not get het up. I did not get depressed.

It stopped at four months and it was a great relief when it did—heavenly in fact. He's been wonderful ever since. I felt like weaning because I felt it might help but he thrived on my milk so I didn't and I'm pleased I didn't wean.

SUGGESTIONS: Go for lots of walks; talk about it to the child and family health nurse; make sure you've done everything then leave the baby to cry or go for a walk.

From about six to seven days he started to scream from early morning to 5pm and often at night as well. He didn't just cry, he would scream; his body was like a brick. He'd arch backwards. Occasionally I could rock him to sleep then he would wake again.

I saw the child and family health nurse every week until he was eleven weeks old. We tried gripe water, Infacol and Mylanta but nothing made any difference, although everything worked for a little while.

I was breastfeeding and had sore nipples and one episode of mastitis, however, despite everything, his weight gains were good.

At eleven weeks I went to a family and baby centre and consulted a paediatrician. I continued to breastfeed but started to complement with a soy formula on the advice of the staff and paediatrician. As well treatment for reflux was started. I kept him upright as much as possible. This seemed to help.

By sixteen weeks he was much better. He was fighting the breast so much I weaned at this time but he fought the bottle as well.

I struggled on for another month, at which time he was on three meals a day and whatever he would drink. By then, although he never slept in the day, he did sleep at night.

By six months he had stopped screaming.

How did I feel? Mentally I felt inadequate and as if I was not doing a good job. I felt that I should have been able to manage. I felt that people were talking about me and that it was never going to end. I felt that having a baby was the biggest mistake of my life. I got very depressed and put on a lot of weight. My husband was available and supportive and never blamed me but it definitely put a strain on the marriage. I kept wondering why all my friends' babies were happy and placid and mine wasn't. Why me?

Through it all I did have a special feeling for him even though there were times I thought I hated him. no one is ever prepared for how much a baby can cry. Now I love him to bits. He turned into a fantastic toddler and many of my friends' placid babies have turned into holy terrors.

SUGGESTIONS: It's vital to have your husband's and friends' uncritical support. I found the child and family health nurse and the family and baby centre helped. In the early weeks the lactation consultant helped with the breastfeeding. Overall, none of the medication helped, however Mylanta seemed to when he was four months old in conjunction with keeping him upright. The worst advice for me was to leave him to cry.

The first week was okay, then at two and a half weeks she started to cry a lot. The worst time was from 7 pm to midnight. We couldn't settle her—we tried everything. I tried gripe water, warm water, Infacol Wind Drops and Mylanta. The medication made no difference. We tried baths, car rides and long walks.

I became exhausted and tearful, but not really depressed. Not knowing what to do, I blamed myself. My husband found it difficult because he had to get up early for work but he didn't blame me and our relationship didn't suffer as we worked together.

The child and family health nurse suggested going to a family and baby centre. My husband wasn't keen as he thought we could sort it out. When she was in the family and baby centre she was wonderful. No crying. After three days she was great, so I went home very much refreshed after lots of sleep. At home she started crying again but the time at the family and baby centre made me see things in perspective so I managed much better. I endeavoured to get her to sleep in her cot rather than in my arms. The family and baby centre scheduled her feeds strictly. I tried to do this but it didn't work for me. I then decided to breastfeed her whenever. And to keep her in bed with us at night.

At three months she stopped crying.

IN HINDSIGHT: Medication didn't help and was a waste of money. Nobody told me to 'follow' the baby so I nearly went mad trying to follow everyone's advice, none of which seemed to suit me or my baby. The family and baby centre let me catch up on some precious sleep and gave me a different perspective on how things should be. Support for the mother is vital—before you have a baby you have no idea how hard it can be.

FOR MORE INFORMATION

Chapter 6: Breastfeeding Your Baby For the First Two Weeks *(weighing babies, page 78; foremilk and hindmilk, page 78; burping, page 87)*
Chapter 7: Bottle Feeding Your Baby For the First Two Weeks *(what's in formula? page 96; making the milk, page 105)*
Chapter 10: Early Worries and Queries *(hormone rash and heat rash, pages 164, 165; medicating babies, page 197; growing teeth, page 182)*
Chapter 5: Choosing Baby Products *(dummies, page 53)*
Chapter 14: Sleeping and Waking in the First Six Months *(unsettled period, page 269; settling techniques, page 270)*

Chapter 16

For Parents

A mother, father and baby are in the most vulnerable state of human existence, looking after the future of the world. They need space, time, emotional support and economic security. They need so much . . . And they have a right to it.

NORMA TRACEY, *MOTHERS AND FATHERS SPEAK ON THE DRAMA OF PREGNANCY, BIRTH AND THE FIRST YEAR OF LIFE*

TAKE CARE OF YOURSELF

The first week after birth

During the first week you may have a few concerns and minor discomforts so here is some useful information.

- **Vaginal blood loss:** May be heavy for the first four days, becoming thinner and lighter after this. The colour changes in the first ten days from red to pink-brown and then becomes a creamy white. The creamy white discharge may continue for up to six weeks. It is also normal to have some light bleeding and spotting for up to six weeks. Because of the risk of infection, tampons should not be used until after the first six to eight weeks (a small number of women menstruate at this time).
- **Afterbirth pains:** Are more commonly felt by women who have had previous pregnancies. The pain is caused by a hormone called oxytocin,

which causes the uterus to contract and discomfort may be experienced for three to four days. Use a hot water bottle for pain relief, taking care not to burn yourself or your baby. For severe pain, paracetamol is safe to take while breastfeeding.

- **Stitches:** If you have stitches, a midwife will check them every day for five to seven days to make sure they are healing well. Stitches often feel very tender for the first week or so depending on the extent of the tear or the episiotomy. Most heal quickly, the worst of the discomfort fading in three or four days. The stitches usually dissolve in seven to twelve days. If it is taking longer and you are feeling uncomfortable, it's a good idea to ask your midwife or family doctor to have a look and remove the stitches. Avoid using talcum powder and creams until the stitches have dissolved and the area is well healed. Any pain should have disappeared after two weeks. If your stitches are still painful after this time, see your family doctor.
- **Haemorrhoids:** Are swollen veins just inside the anus and can be very painful and even bleed. They are usually temporary, subsiding without any major treatment, but are troublesome for up to three months for some women. In the first forty-eight hours, cold packs give some relief. Haemorrhoidal ointment is available as well, but be careful not to get the ointment on your stitches. It is important to avoid constipation by drinking plenty of fluids and adding extra fibre to your diet.

  Sometimes it is necessary to take a fibre supplement such as Metamucil.
- **Contact your midwife, maternity hospital or family doctor immediately for any of the following:**

  Increased bright red bleeding;
  Fainting or dizziness;
  A painful, hot, red area in the lower leg;
  A temperature of 38°C or higher for more than two hours;
  Burning or difficulty passing urine;
  Painful breasts and a temperature above 37.5°C.
- **Postnatal check**

  See your midwife, family doctor or obstetrician for a general check of your breasts, uterus and cervix at around six to eight weeks after the bleeding has stopped—don't worry about a small amount of spotting.

Those tired feelings

Mothers find they are often very tired during the first few months after birth. Why? Your body worked hard to give birth and even though initially you feel exhilarated and excited, it takes a while to recover physically, especially while you adjust to night feeds and the normal anxious moments that accompany looking after a new baby. If you had a caesarean section or any birth complications the recovery takes longer. Doing unfamiliar tasks and using muscles not usually used is tiring until your body adjusts. Always putting your baby's needs before your own and not being able to get other things done because your baby interrupts you makes you tired too. If on top of all this your baby is unsettled and cries a lot and is awake a lot at night, the constant lack of sleep will leave you feeling very tired. Breastfeeding difficulties may arise which also contribute to fatigue.

How to help yourself

Remind yourself that time spent with your baby is more important than anything else. Allow yourself time to settle her. Try to lie down at least once a day when she is asleep instead of finding another job to do.

In only a few short months she will be sleeping longer at night and having fewer feeds during the day and all this will be behind you. A lot of breastfeeding problems can be solved or overcome in the first four to six weeks. When this happens you feel a lot less tired.

Remember, you and your baby come first. If you make it clear, others will get the message. Rather than ask your visitors if they want tea or coffee, suggest they wash up or nurse your baby while you have a shower.

Switch off all advice from well-meaning friends and relatives. Practical help from those who want to do something will do a lot more to relieve fatigue than endless suggestions about 'wind'.

Put your feet up when you nurse or feed your baby. Can you learn to relax? If you can it is very helpful as a fatigue buster. Use one of the tapes and the simple suggestions on page 11 or go back to the relaxation techniques you learnt at your childbirth education classes.

Try to eat sensibly. It doesn't have to be a formal meal three times a day. Simple food such as fresh fruit and yoghurt, fresh wholemeal rolls and salad, cold chicken, frozen meals or takeaway is fine. If your partner, lover or friend prepares a meal when he comes home, that's even better.

Your body

Accept how you look for the moment. Please don't buy or read those ridiculous magazines that go into every miniscule boring detail of the cleverness of the celebrity mums who are back to skinny perfection a week after they give birth (most unhealthy). Or even three months after birth (it's their underwear and the airbrushed photography). Be proud of the body that has nurtured your baby (I can assure you your baby doesn't want a celebrity mum as her mother) and be patient about getting back to pre-pregnancy dimensions. Work on about a year—a much more realistic time—to get back to 'normal'. In the meantime wear clothes that are comfortable and bright and make you feel happy. Exercise lifts your mood and makes you feel lighter all over. After the birth, hospital staff or your midwife will show you how to do some recommended exercises without hurting yourself. Ideally it's great to do these exercises, but most of the women I talk to find they are too overwhelmed or too tired to set aside time each day, even if it is only ten minutes, so if you're not doing your postnatal exercises you're not alone.

If you are conscientious about exercise, keep to gentle routines for the first few months. Light yoga which concentrates on passive stretches is excellent. Make sure you have a qualified instructor.

If you find it hard to fit exercises into your new life, just try walking and pelvic floor exercises.

Walking and babies go together. Start slowly and gradually increase the distance.

Pelvic floor muscles support the vagina, uterus, bladder and bowel. Exercising pelvic floor muscles helps your body recover from the birth and prevents stress incontinence. Stress incontinence means that when you cough, sneeze or jump up and down a small amount of urine is passed. You don't have to set aside a special time for pelvic floor exercises. They are easy to do when you are resting, feeding your baby or anytime. Here's what to do:

- Squeeze and hold the muscles around the urethra (where the urine comes out), your vagina and your anus as if you are trying to stop yourself passing urine, hold for three seconds then relax. Do this three times.
- Don't tense your thighs or tummy or hold your breath. Don't overdo it. Start a day or two after birth and build up to fifteen to twenty-five a day doing about five at a time.

Pelvic floor exercises are something recommended for all women throughout life, so after the first three months start increasing the number you do. Do as many as you are able to before the muscle tires. The minimum aim is for 150 pelvic floor exercises a day!

Look after your back. Changes which happen to your body during pregnancy and extra strain on your abdominal muscles mean back problems are common after birth. The extra physical work also makes backache more likely. You are most vulnerable in the first six weeks so avoid lifting laundry baskets full of wet clothes or heavy nappy buckets.

Make sure change tables and bassinets are the right height so you can look after your baby without bending over all the time. When you feed your baby, get into a comfortable position with good support for your back. Ask for help when you need it, especially to empty the baby bath or carry shopping.

If your back becomes painful, physiotherapists, chiropractors and osteopaths offer treatment and exercise, but look for someone familiar with childbirth and postnatal care.

Your head

Expect postnatal drift—not being able to concentrate or remember things is quite normal. Let yourself drift for a while. Take one day at a time; just attend to your immediate needs. Postnatal drift gradually disappears although most of my friends and I think we still have it twenty years later!

As well as postnatal drift it's common to have a wider range of emotions than you normally do. Many women find they burst into tears easily, feel elated one minute and depressed the next. Sometimes you might feel cross and irritated over things others see as unimportant. Feelings like this are a normal response to being tired and the stress and excitement which follow any major change in life. Here are a few suggestions to help you if you are feeling a bit strange:

- Admit it's rotten sometimes. Have a good cry when you need to. You are under no obligation to float in a constant rosy glow.
- A partner who shares the work as well as the joys makes an enormous difference to handling topsy-turvy feelings.
- Think about making contact. The first step might be talking to other mothers at your child and family health centre. Get in touch with members of your childbirth education class. Perhaps you made a friend while you were in hospital—ring her up! Join the Australian Breastfeeding Association.
- If you feel your emotions are out of control it's important to talk to someone like your doctor, your child and family health nurse or staff at a family and baby centre. Constant anxiety and depression can be helped.
- Take time for yourself whenever you can. Having someone mind your baby while you get your hair cut, take a bath or simply stare into space makes a lot of difference to how you feel.

Mothers' Groups

Mothers' groups are usually organised by the nurse at the child and family health centre (maternal and child health centre). Other mothers' groups are run by maternity hospitals, the Australian Breastfeeding Association, churches and various private organisations, some of whom may espouse a particular baby-raising philosophy, for example 'attachment parenting', 'nappy-free' or be tied in to a particular religion.

Mothers' groups provide opportunities to meet other women experiencing the similar joys and dilemmas that you are. You will find that while you maintain contact with your work colleagues and friends, who don't have babies you will make a new circle of friends who are parents. Many women initially view mothers' groups with suspicion but when they take the leap discover that the understanding and support that they get from a mother's group helps immeasurably in adjusting to their new roles. Many people make lifelong friends from their mother's group. Having said that I am aware that some women aren't keen on group activities, some women have unfortunate experiences in mothers' groups and some women have their own circle of support and friends without the need of seeking more. If you feel you'd like to give it a go and don't like the particular group you've fallen in with try another one.

Other odd occurrences

Hair loss

Sudden hair loss is a distressing experience for a number of women. It's upsetting because it comes out in handfuls and seems like baldness is inevitable. The mother feels as if it's excessive, but it is usually not noticeable to others. It happens from two to three months after birth and is not related to breastfeeding, so don't wean! The exact mechanism is unknown, but thought to be related to the major upheaval the body goes through at this time.

Some time after eight months the hair loss stops and twelve months after the birth new, thick hair starts to grow. Beware of myths and wrong diagnoses. It is not happening because of stress, nor do you need hundreds of dollars' worth of naturopathic dietary supplements or an expensive course of hair loss treatment. It bothers me when mothers are talked into expensive, unnecessary remedies which make no difference.

Wrist and arm problems

Wrist and arm problems during pregnancy and the first year after birth happen to an appreciable number of women and to a large extent are unrelated to their previous occupations. Some women find painful wrists and arms most distressing and debilitating. The discomfort experienced may mean they are unable to pick up their babies and have difficulty sleeping.

Problems with wrists and arms can start at the end of pregnancy or appear for the first time six to twelve weeks after the birth and continue for up to a year when it nearly always resolves spontaneously. Many women suffer mild forms of wrist and arm problems and never mention it.

It is usually diagnosed as Carpal Tunnel Syndrome and/or Tenosynovitis according to precise symptoms. Carpal Tunnel Syndrome occurs when a major nerve in the wrist is compressed, in this case thought to be due to excessive fluid. Tenosynovitis is inflammation of a tendon in the arm.

The underlying cause in pregnancy and the first year after birth is unknown, but the old scapegoat hormones may play a part, and the condition is aggravated (not caused) by the physical work involved in caring for a baby. Treatment should be conservative as, unlike Carpal Tunnel Syndrome and Tenosynovitis in the rest of the population, it resolves itself when it happens as a result of pregnancy and birth.

When looking for help, it's important to find a family doctor or hand specialist who is familiar with this phenomenon. This can be difficult; despite the fact that it is not uncommon, very little is known about wrist and hand problems relating to pregnancy. Splinting of the wrists in neutral or slight extension day and night, diuretics, anti-inflammatory drugs or cortisone injections are the usual medical offerings. Most of the women I talk to manage with splints and massage once they know it will go, but it does take some endurance; if you are finding life unbearable, cortisone injections do relieve the symptoms quite dramatically and are safe to have if you are breastfeeding. Needless to say, help with physical chores makes a lot of difference. Surgery is rarely required so seek a second opinion if surgery is suggested.

Night sweats and hot flushes

Symptoms like this are related to breastfeeding and are experienced to some degree by a number of women. The symptoms are quite separate to fevers and chills caused by mastitis, which is sometimes a bit confusing. Mastitis symptoms are similar to the flu, whereas night sweats and hot flushes happen to women who are otherwise well.

The uncomfortable feelings are due to low oestrogen levels. Low oestrogen levels during breastfeeding are normal and essential for efficient lactation. It is thought that the low levels of oestrogen can cause blood vessels to become unstable (sometimes narrow, sometimes wide) which causes the sweating, the hot flushes and sometimes palpitations.

Not much can be done. The symptoms are aggravated by heat, alcohol, obesity, caffeine and hot food. They do not last for the entire time you breastfeed. A dramatic improvement usually happens by twelve weeks, if not before.

Acne

Facial pimples, lumps and bumps can occur in the first six to eight weeks after giving birth. This generally settles with time. Don't squeeze! There has been no correlation found with breastfeeding. The eruptions are most likely due to the hormonal changes that follow the birth.

Headaches

A small number of women get headaches when they are breastfeeding. If they are troublesome it is always important to rule out any underlying causes including dental or ophthalmic problems. Headaches can also indicate impending mastitis. When there are no other causes, headaches due to lactation could be caused by the release of oxytocin when the milk lets down, or very full breasts. Most 'breastfeeding' headaches peak around three to seven days after birth and resolve after a short period of time. Make sure you keep well hydrated by drinking plenty of fluids (water is good).

Anti-inflammatory or paracetamol medications are safe to take if necessary.

Nausea

Nausea related to breastfeeding is reported by some women, usually in conjunction with the let-down. This eases over time and can occur for a few weeks to a few months.

Nausea is often also related to fluid intake (too much/not enough), low blood pressure, fatigue, other illnesses, for example a urinary tract infection, influenza or gastroenteritis, medication (particularly anti-depressant medication) and, as is often common with mothers of new babies, hunger because they forget or are too tired to eat properly.

Relationships

Think about your relationship with your partner. You and your partner have to get to know each other all over again as parents, which takes some thought and effort from both of you. It's very easy to disappear into the mother-and-baby world and lose touch. Your baby is important, but so is your partner. Your partner needs to have access to you and the baby and needs to talk to you about how he feels. Keep in contact with friends and relatives. Your range of friends will change as you start to have more time with people with babies and less with those without. Speaking with other people who have babies is important for moral support and reassurance.

Arrange to go out without the baby when you can—even if it's only for an hour or two, it gives your relationship a great boost.

Bonding

The popularisation of the 'bonding' theory in the seventies and eighties makes bonding seem like the super glue that holds mother and baby together without which irredeemable damage is predicted for the baby.

Advantages have emerged as a result of the emphasis on bonding; it has helped make it possible for women to have as natural a birth as possible; it has changed inhuman, illogical practices in maternity hospitals and helped more women establish breastfeeding successfully, but it gives many women the feeling that there is a critical period where she and her baby must bond otherwise all is lost. As well, there is no mention of a father in all this so the onus is completely on the mother to get it right or else . . .

'Bonding' is falling in love with the baby during pregnancy or at birth, but the normal range of feelings covers strong feelings of instant rapport to numb indifference. When you're in the latter group it does not mean you are abnormal or that your baby will be deprived in some way if it takes time for your relationship to grow. I talk to a number of women who are never really comfortable with babies, but who find that as their babies grow and become 'people' their relationship blossoms.

No evidence exists that premature or sick babies or babies born by caesarean section suffer emotional deprivation because their mother didn't bond or bonded late. When things are difficult in the beginning, worry and distress might overshadow your feelings of love for a while, especially if your baby cries a lot during the first six months, but you will find the mysterious bonding will gently arrive as the weeks slip by.

However, if you are ever seriously worried about your feelings for your baby, talk to your child and family health nurse or your family doctor so you can identify what the problem is and find out where to get help.

Conflicting advice

When you're a new or not-so-new mother, one of the hardest things you invariably find you have to deal with is the constant conflicting advice you get from everyone you come in contact with, whether it's a health professional or someone in the supermarket.

Conflicting advice is a blessing and a curse. It's a blessing (believe it or not) because it allows for the many variations in human nature and experience and provides for flexibility; it's a curse because it raises doubts at a time in your life when you are likely to be very vulnerable, unassertive, sleep-deprived and unable to count to ten let alone work out whose advice you're going to take.

Advice comes from two sources—non-professional experts and professional experts. The mother who is doing all the work is rarely viewed as an expert and usually the assumption is made that she knows very little and everyone else knows lots.

Non-professional experts are friends, family, neighbours and a whole range of people you hardly know like the man on the bus and the woman in the bank. Their advice is usually unsolicited and based on what they did with their own babies.

Professional experts are people such as child and family health nurses, general practitioners, paediatricians, a range of specialist doctors, social workers, psychologists, physiotherapists, dietitians, occupational therapists, lactation consultants, parentcraft nurses, midwives, obstetricians, counsellors who belong to voluntary groups such as the Australian Breastfeeding Association (ABA), staff who work in childcare centres, pre-school teachers and pharmacists, to name a few. Their advice is based on their academic qualifications, their professional experience which varies according to what training they have undertaken, their hands-on work and scientific research.

Having this extraordinary range of people around is the main reason there is so much conflicting advice. Modern-day care of mothers and babies is very fragmented and you are likely to be in the hands of a different expert every step of the way as well as for every different problem that might arise. Other reasons for conflicting advice include tradition, fashion, scientific research and the fact that babies are a mystery and can't tell us what is wrong or how they feel.

Conflicting advice is here to stay—what can you do?

Understand that everyone is different and advice that suits one person may not necessarily suit another.

Unsolicited advice from non-professionals is usually given with the best intentions in the world. You'll probably find yourself doing it once your baby is older and you're feeling experienced enough to offer a few tips to friends about to have their first. Smile and say thanks and forget about it unless it's something you think is useful.

Conflicting advice from health professionals is harder to deal with, especially in the early months. Try to avoid seeing a million different people and find one person you trust.

Here are a few hints on dealing with advice from experts—remember if you're feeling confident and have no problems, you're the expert. Don't worry about the health professionals. Consider these things with regard to advice:

- Is it practical and realistic in relation to your life? Have you been offered some options?
- Is it safe?
- Does the person giving you the advice have any commercial interests which may influence the advice?
- Does the person have a lot of hands-on experience? Quite a lot of written information is done by people who do not work in the field.
- Does the health professional reject out of hand advice from other 'experts' or is he or she happy to help you work out what's right for you?
- Is the advice conflicting or simply a variation on a theme and does your health professional help you to see the difference? What most mothers are looking for is guidance, not instructions.
- Does your health professional make you feel confident and good about yourself and your baby? If not, find someone else.
- Don't assume health professionals know everything—they don't. You are in charge and as the weeks go by you will regain your assertiveness and confidence and learn to trust your own judgment.

For Grandparents

Becoming a grandparent is a big emotional experience that brings heart-thumping excitement and a fresh lease of life. Many grandparents rediscover the intense feelings that they had with their own babies—the unremitting watchfulness, the anxieties, the exquisite pleasure of each small accomplishment. They worry and wonder, bore their friends witless and secretly hope their children know what they are doing. Ideally, grandparents shouldn't have to face the staggering amount of work child-raising demands, nevertheless, their role potentially involves much more than that of interested spectators beaming on the sidelines.

What *is* the grandparent role?

Broadly, grandparents are a vital link to the past. They continue to be a role model to their children and grandchildren. In the ideal world grandparents provide mentorship, emotional support and reassurance, humour and wisdom. Grandparents can provide a counter to the perceived negatives of raising children and bring optimism, enthusiasm and positive support to their children's decisions to create families of their own.

Specifically, the grandparent role is not at all straightforward and varies tremendously from family to family, culture to culture.

While distance, age and health impacts on the extent of their involvement, grandparents can choose how much they are going to be involved with their grandchildren practically, emotionally and socially. Some grandparents are very 'hands-on' which may include regular childcare for parents in paid work and/or taking children during the school holidays. A small but increasing number of grandparents are raising their grandchildren.

Other grandparents are not prepared to take a hands-on role. They may be still in the paid-work force; they may want to use this time of their lives to pursue an interest family life prevented; they may still be raising children; they may be caring for their parents; they may have had so many grandchildren they've run out of puff. Or, they (grandmothers in particular) may feel they simply do not want to face the unrelenting rounds of nappies, sleepless nights and early mornings, temper-tantrums and potty-training all over again in their latter years.

Modern grandparenting—the realities

Becoming a grandparent is a wonderful gift flowing from the years of investment and love that went into raising one of the baby's parents. Reams are written on the joys of being a grandparent but there can be a side hidden beneath the layers of flowery sentiment that is not often discussed.

Grandparents of previous generations had important roles as mentors offering emotional support but, by and large, were not called upon to provide the level of childcare, financial and moral support that is expected by many of today's parents from their parents. For some grandparents, caring for grandchildren is not a burden but a genuine pleasure that brings meaning to their lives regardless of the amount of time and effort involved. Others find providing the level of care their children expect to be a physical and emotional burden. They often don't know how to refuse or how to set reasonable limits. Some—grandmothers in particular—feel pressured by both family and society to present a smiling granny face and constant availability no matter what.

It's a good idea to think beyond the sentiment and take some steps to avoid as many irritations as possible so parents and both sets of grandparents can get the maximum amount of pleasure from their blossoming new relationship—with each other and the little people in their lives.

Preparing for the realities

Most parents look forward to becoming grandparents but there are some important issues to think about. To avoid misunderstandings it's helpful to bring them up before the birth rather than bumbling along, playing it by ear and hoping things will 'work out'.

The biggest misunderstanding is invariably the mismatch between the children's expectations of how much practical help will be forthcoming from the grandparents versus how much help the grandparents are prepared to provide.

For the grandparents who are reading this, here are a few things to think about:

- The amount of practical help grandparents are able to contribute varies tremendously. It's up to the children to accommodate their lives accordingly, not the other way around.

- Ideally, clear guides should be given to the parents right from the start about what grandparents are prepared or not prepared to do. In the heady rush of the arrival of the first grandchild, avoid over-commitment. Step back a little while you reacclimatise to the time, attention and physical demands babies and toddlers need.
- As other grandchildren are likely to follow, bear in mind how disruptive it is to family harmony if one grandchild is perceived to have had more of your time and attention than another has. Likewise, if one adult child has had more access to your services than his or her siblings have had.

General practicalities:

- **The first essential in maintaining a harmonious relationship is to only give advice when you are asked.**

  New mothers often drown in a sea of baby lore lovingly bestowed upon them by anxious grandparents who are likely to have had no close contact with a baby for thirty years. I think this is the single biggest error doting grandparents make and you'd be surprised how much tension it causes. You can trust new parents, mothers in particular, to ask if they want your advice.
- Don't be offended if your daughter/daughter-in-law seems to be mainly getting her knowledge from health professionals or books (or in my case, books other than mine). Read the books she's reading so you are up-to-date with the latest recommendations.
- Accept with a smile names, surnames, manner of birth, naming ceremonies, dietary matters, domestic and childcare arrangements and choice of school. Matters such as these are no longer your concern unless they are illegal or dangerous.
- Most extended families work better when there are structured arrangements about visits. Sudden arrivals on either side—unless it's occasional—can be a source of irritation and inconvenience.
- If you live at a distance, especially overseas, visits need to be carefully planned so conflict doesn't spoil the time together. Long stays can be difficult to manage amicably in small houses. Thought needs to be given about how everyone is going to deal with being in close proximity for

an extended time. Long visits need tolerance, goodwill and organisation to make them positive for everyone.

Specific points in relation to babies

Here are the common things I hear about that cause stress between generations when a new baby arrives:

- Support and practical help are what's needed. Constant suggestions as to why baby is doing what she's doing from grandparents undermine the mother's confidence—it's better to accept the baby the way she is and avoid labels like 'good', 'spoilt', 'windy', 'naughty' and so on.
- There are many day-to-day options (and night-to-night) for looking after babies and your child might choose different options from the ones you chose. For example, she might breastfeed when you bottle fed, she might carry baby all day and co-sleep while you were more into separate beds and routines. Alternatively she might be prepared to let her baby cry to sleep, something you would never have done, and so on. Accepting and supporting her choice without negative comments is important.
- Solids (that strange name we give to the mush babies first eat) are not usually started until four to six months. Giving babies solids before then has no advantages for most babies and doesn't make them 'sleep through the night'.
- Breastfed babies don't need water in between feeds. Nor do formula fed babies unless it's very hot.
- Breastfed babies (and quite a few formula fed babies) generally can't be fed every four hours. Flexible feeding times are needed, which means there may be times when the baby is breastfeeding frequently. Let your daughter do it in peace without constant reference to the number of feeds the baby has had: 'Oh, you're not feeding her again are you?'
- Babies don't automatically start 'sleeping through' at eight weeks—or necessarily at any age up to three. When young babies spontaneously sleep longer at night it's a bonus. There is no safe way you can make young, healthy, thriving babies stop waking at night.
- Regular weighing of healthy babies is not necessary unless the mother wants to do it.

- Older babies often suddenly start to perform when one of the grandparents comes near them. It is normal for babies between nine and twelve months to become very wary of strange faces and places but why it's so often a grandparent is hard to say. It's not permanent, nor is it personal or caused by anything you are doing wrong. If it happens to you, try to take it in your stride, stay calm and don't overwhelm the baby with too much attention. For more information refer to stranger awareness and separation anxiety on page 520.

Grandparents' Rights

The two main areas where legal issues arise are:

- **Grandparents being denied legal access to their grandchildren following family breakdown.**

  Grandparents do have rights. Grandparents are able to seek contact and time with their grandchildren when they have played an active role in their grandchildren's lives.

- **Grandparents as carers**

  Grandparents may become sole carers following the death of a parent, substance abuse, mental illness, family violence or child abuse. Raising a grandchild is done out of love and concern and at great personal cost. Grandparents in this situation face many difficulties with include financial problems, exhaustion and strained family relationships with their own children. Recent changes have recognised the help grandparents need raising their grandchildren and a range of services—financial, childcare, respite—care are available.

For more information—any of the following provide further contacts for legal, financial and other aid:

www.raisingchildren.net.au—an excellent website donated by a grandchild in memory of the grandparents who raised him. It is NSW-based but is a good starting point for grandparents anywhere in Australia.

Council on the Ageing (COTA)—92863860

Family Law Hotline—1800 050 321

Health professionals you may come in contact with

Child and family health nurse

The nurse at a child and family health centre has special training in all aspects of early childhood. She or he (nearly always a she) is usually a midwife as well and has expert breastfeeding knowledge. The service is provided free. The nurse is there to help you with feeding and nutrition, routine growth and development checks, counselling and specific baby and child problems such as rashes, vomiting, crying, temper tantrums, toilet training and sleep problems.

Owing to new government initiatives in Australia, eventually all mothers will receive a home visit by a child and family health nurse or equivalent (maternal and child health nurse and so on—each state has a different name) after the births of their babies. You may find you will be asked what can seem like daunting, even invasive questions. This is to help identify women at risk of domestic violence and serious depression so they can be helped as soon as possible—before there are serious consequences. If you are concerned at any time by the questions, let your nurse know so it can be discussed.

A child and family health centre is a great place to meet other mothers. Most centres offer mothers' groups, which women find an excellent resource for company and the chance to make friends and compare notes. You can also find out what is available in the community for families and babies. The nurse there will tell you about immunisation and where it's available, the best books to read, discuss safety issues as your baby grows, common medications and contraception.

USING THE SERVICE

Maternity hospitals or midwives (if you have a homebirth) notify the centre nearest your home or whichever one you designate shortly after the birth of your baby. This is done with your permission. The decision to attend a child and family health centre is up to you. Most women find it a positive experience, especially with their first babies. If it is not, find another centre, or if you feel confident and self-sufficient you may decide not to go. You should always leave your centre feeling reassured and with a positive plan of action if you have been having a few difficulties.

Telephone numbers and locations of child and family health centres are in the phone book either under government services or in the main part under child and family health centres. Each state has different names for their centres and staff. Please refer to the Resources list on page 546 for more information.

Midwife

Midwives care for women during pregnancy, labour, birth and afterwards for up to a month, sometimes longer. When employed by the government their services are free. Some midwives work privately and charge a fee for service. Fees are not refundable.

Mothercraft nurse

Mothercraft nurses are enrolled nurses with special training in early childhood. They work in maternity hospitals, family and baby centres and childcare centres. When employed by the government their services are free. Some mothercraft nurses work privately for families for a fee. Fees are not refundable.

Lactation consultant

A lactation consultant has an international qualification in human lactation. Lactation consultants may be health professionals (midwives, child and family health nurses or doctors) or people from any background with an interest in breastfeeding who have the qualification. When employed by the government their service is free. Most major maternity hospitals and community services in Australia now have lactation consultants available for help and advice. Some lactation consultants work privately and charge a fee for service. Fees are not refundable.

An Australian Breastfeeding Association (ABA) counsellor

ABA counsellors are mothers who have breastfed. They receive thorough training over a minimum eighteen-month period. ABA has a strict code of ethics which means all counselling is confidential and mothers or babies with possible medical problems are advised to contact child and family health nurses or doctors.

Confidential counselling and breastfeeding information is available from ABA counsellors who work voluntarily on a twenty-four-hour roster. The service is free.

General practitioner

The family doctor. Look for one with an interest in family medicine. Fee for service is refundable.

Paediatrician

A doctor who specialises in the care of babies and children. Fee for service is partly refundable.

Speciality paediatrician

Includes a range of doctors to cover every part of your baby's body from head to toe. Fee for service is partly refundable.

Psychologist

Psychologists help parents understand why babies do the things they do and some parents find their approach useful for specific baby problems. Psychologists are also available to help with personal or relationship problems. A free service by psychologists is offered throughout the government health system in community health centres and hospitals, for which referral is needed and there may be a waiting time.

Alternatively, psychologists work in private practices and charge a fee for service, a proportion of which is refundable from a private health fund.

Your other children

If this is not your first baby, a lot of the things you agonised over the first time around will pass you by. One of your main concerns this time will be how your first baby adjusts to the newcomer. As well, parents often wonder if they can possibly love another baby as much as the one they already have; sometimes even feeling guilty that they are having another baby, especially when the first child's behaviour regresses, sometimes alarmingly, in the first three to six months. If you get an attack of the guilts, bear in mind that learning to live with others in a family is a vital, even essential, part of human development. Most families have more than one child and parents have no trouble spreading their love around many children.

A great deal has been written on this topic and I find the parents I see are very conscientious about preparing the first child; even with the best will in the world, however, things can still be a bit difficult for a while. Difficulties in adjusting are temporary and it does take some children a little longer to accept changes in the family than others. The age when it seems hardest for children to adjust is from fifteen months to about three years. After the age of three a child has more autonomy and is much more sure of her place in the world and your affections. She is also able to look after herself to some degree and has diversions such as friends and kindy. This doesn't mean it's a mistake to have children close, but the closer they are the higher your levels of energy and tolerance need to be to handle the hard work when they are little.

Here are some suggestions for getting your first child ready for the big event in her life.

- Make any changes well before the baby arrives. It's a good idea to sort out sleep problems, bottles, dummies, potty training, bedrooms and starting kindy before your baby is born, but do it well in advance. If you don't get around to it, it's best left until at least six months after the birth.
- Talk about families and how they usually have more than one child. Use your own or your partner's as an example.
- Wait until your pregnancy is obvious before telling her about the new baby, but make sure you tell her before anyone else does. Let her feel the baby and talk to her about babies and what they do as well as telling her some funny, positive things she did when she was a baby. Help her understand that the baby won't be an instant playmate because babies can't walk, talk and so on.
- Expand her life outside the home. Organising a social life for her means she has other houses to visit and places to go. It's also a way of showing her she's different from the baby.
- Plan the arrangements for her care well in advance so she knows what's happening and ideally, knows and loves whoever is responsible for her care.
- Show her the hospital or the birth centre where you will have the baby

(unless you are having a homebirth). Tell her you will be only gone for a short time and she will be able to visit. Let her help you pack your bag. When she's not looking, put in a couple of surprises for her to find when she visits.

After the birth

Things often get off to a smooth start until the first child realises it's a permanent arrangement, at which time negative behaviour is likely to surface. Most negative behaviour in children at this time is not directed against the baby but against the huge adjustment that has to be made, so your child might be very loving to the baby and pretty horrible to you.

Try to keep to your first child's normal routine as much as possible and any time you can spend with her without the baby helps enormously. When you can't do something she wants to do try not to make the baby the excuse too often. Fathers can help a lot by minding the baby while you do something with the older child or by doing something interesting with the older child when you are busy with the baby.

Encourage friends to include your older child when they visit and bring presents. If she is old enough to understand, prepare her for the fact that babies attract a lot of attention—remind her that she did when she was a baby. Let her know she can sit with you if she is feeling lonely or jealous.

Expect changes in your first child's behaviour. Her concentration will be affected by the change in her life. She may be more clumsy than usual so make sure her environment is safe. Young children don't understand concepts of sharing and co-operation, so ignore as much negative behaviour as is reasonable and give her lots of attention for positive behaviour.

Help her not to feel guilty about jealous feelings by talking to her about feelings, how strong they can be and the best ways of handling them. Accept, even suggest that while the baby is a considerable nuisance at the moment eventually she and the baby will be friends and will do lots of things together.

Avoid situations where your older child may hurt the baby as it will make her feel bad.

Try not to leave the baby's belongings all over the house under the first child's nose. Don't talk about the baby in ways that could hurt your child's feelings by saying things like 'thank goodness we have a boy this time' or 'he's a much easier baby' and so on.

It's unrealistic to expect your older child to automatically love the new baby; this will happen in time. Encouraging the idea the baby likes her will help her feel special to her new sister or brother.

Last but not least, remember you are only human and looking after babies and young children is one of the hardest things anyone can do. Blowing your stack sometimes or finding it difficult to manage more than one is completely understandable. Don't agonise over it or waste time feeling guilty. As time goes by it all gets easier; some time between three and seven months the first jealousy passes and your first child will forget what life was like when she was the only one.

Postnatal depression

Many improvements have occurred in recent years in recognising and helping women suffering from depression following the birth of a baby.

Thank goodness the views of fifty years ago have been challenged and found wanting. The widely held belief then was that postnatal depression was a sign of mental illness in women who rejected the role and normal responsibilities of motherhood!

This change of ideas means that women who are depressed feel less threatened and are more likely to seek help. Publicity about postnatal depression, many excellent books, education of health workers and input from feminists have all contributed to a larger number of women feeling able to admit they need help and getting sensitive, effective treatment. Unfortunately, despite these positive advances the reluctance of many women to ask for help, as well as the lack of resources to provide help for every woman who needs it for as long as she needs it, means we still have not come far enough.

I have never been happy with the term 'postnatal' depression. Postnatal is a misleading term in many ways because it implies a condition that occurs directly after the birth of the baby. The term doesn't encompass the women who start to feel depressed further down the track when the excitement and novelty of the baby wears off and when much of the support they started out with is gradually withdrawn. In my work I find most women have some degree of depression in the first two years after birth which, for a few, continues on and off until their children are at school or they are back in paid work. The label 'postnatal' depression also has a tendency to make women feel abnormal when they are reacting in a normal way to situations where they are under a great deal of physical and emotional stress.

Like many mothers you may find that you feel tired and low for some time after the birth because of the lack of unbroken sleep, the responsibilities of being a mother twenty-four hours a day and the natural worry of your baby's wellbeing. Many women today are perfectionists in the workplace and have learned not to make mistakes. The unpredictability of babies, the trial and error that comes with caring for them and the slow realisation that there are not always answers to every problem can be an enormous adjustment that may take six to twelve months to come to terms with. Distinguishing between baby blues, the normal mixed feelings that come with adjusting to life with a baby, and what is known as postnatal depression is an important part of getting the right help if it is needed.

The baby blues

As many as 70 per cent of women experience the baby blues to some degree. They are likely to affect you within a week to ten days after the birth and are strongly associated with hormone imbalance. It can be an emotional and weepy time. The baby blues usually don't last long, don't interfere with your sleep, your appetite or your ability to function and care for your baby. Occasionally the baby blues can be prolonged and traumatic and herald the onset of major depression, but some women find they are a much-needed emotional release.

Postnatal psychosis

Postnatal psychosis can be a severe form of depression after childbirth but is more commonly a different type of mental illness which occurs once or twice every one thousand births. It is a disorder which requires prompt intervention as left untreated there is a high risk of maternal suicide (and less commonly infanticide). With prompt recognition and correct treatment, postnatal psychosis has an excellent prognosis with full recovery in a few months.

Mild depression (sometimes called postnatal disillusion or postpartum adjustment)

I am using 'mild' here as a way of distinguishing one form of depression from another, not to minimise the impact of the depressed feelings. It is common for women at home with small children to suffer from mild depression. The risk of this happening is higher if the woman has a history of depression, but many women who do not have a history become depressed during the early years of their children's lives. If it happens to be the father at home, then he is at just as much risk of becoming depressed as the mother. Most depression suffered by people at home with young children seems to be caused by the demanding nature of the job—occupational depression.

Why does this happen? Looking after a baby can be lonely, constant and unacknowledged work. It's often stressful because of concerns about the baby's feeding, crying and sleeping patterns. A lack of personal spending money, fatigue and a sense of being unappreciated and unrecognised for the job all contribute. Coming to terms with the fact that the babycare is not going to be shared equally with their partners is also a significant factor for many women who had expectations of this before the birth.

Mild depression like this tends to come and go at various times in the first two or three years and is often exacerbated by things such as particular developmental stages the baby is going through, sleep problems, baby illnesses or financial or relationship problems. Mild depression is so common that it is thought by many to be a normal part of adjusting to parenthood and a natural consequence of being at home with babies and toddlers when there is very little in the way of company and support.

This is not to suggest that this is how motherhood should be. The fact that such feelings are viewed as normal is more an indictment on a society that rationalises the miserable experiences of so many in such a way.

The perception that such feelings are the load we mothers have to bear does not make them any less unpleasant or distressing. Nor should it deter you from seeking help if you feel yourself sinking.

Mild depression usually responds to one-on-one counselling with the right person, company (joining in groups), solving baby sleeping and feeding problems, moving on past trying developmental stages and, for some women, going back to paid work—even just half a day a week makes a great difference.

Serious depression (usually called postnatal depression)

About 10 to 25 per cent of women suffer depression more severely during the first months after birth, although it sometimes takes them a lot longer to identify the problem. The causes for this are innumerable and as well as all the occupational and adjustment reasons previously mentioned, other causes may include:

- A family history of depression or a previous history of mental health problems and emotional difficulties.
- Women who do not have a close relationship with the father of the baby are more susceptible, as are women who do not have a circle of friends or relatives they can confide in and express negative feelings to.
- Women who live a highly organised lifestyle and who are used to being in control may be more at risk.
- Disappointment and feelings of failure following a forceps birth or a caesarean section sometimes plays a part.
- A constantly crying baby.
- Life events such as moving house and relationship difficulties can also be contributing factors.
- The role hormone balance plays is unclear, but it seems unlikely it plays a major role in postnatal depression. However, hormone imbalance does not account for the number of women who become seriously depressed months after the birth.
- Women who have a biological vulnerability to feeling highly emotional under stress.

The causes of depression vary for every woman. Some women spiral into depression when none of the above are present in their lives. Other women may experience all these things yet not suffer from serious depression. Postnatal depression affects women from across the whole spectrum of society—the poor, the middle class, the educated, the uneducated, the disadvantaged and the wealthy.

WHAT ARE THE SYMPTOMS OF SERIOUS (POSTNATAL) DEPRESSION?

Here are the recognised warning signs:

- Feeling out of control.
- Low confidence, low self-esteem—a sense of loss of self.
- A continued inability to get anything done and the feeling of being a prisoner unable to leave the house.
- Feelings of frustration, anger and resentment which do not go away. Women I talk to often mention feeling envious of women without babies or women who have older children.
- Alternatively, feelings of numbness.
- Physical symptoms such as constant headaches, palpitations, sweaty hands, sleeping difficulties (even when the baby is sleeping well) or loss of appetite.
- Constant feelings of guilt and shame.
- A fear of going crazy.
- Frightening delusions and fantasies about harming herself or her baby.
- Panic attacks.

WHAT CAN YOU DO?

It is important not to try to carry on in the hope that the distressing symptoms will go away. The first step on the road to recovery is to tell someone. Discuss your feelings with your child and family health nurse, your family doctor or staff at your local community health centre. If you feel you do not get the help you need, try someone else.

The right health professional will:

- Accept you the way you are and not try to 'jolly' you along.
- Respect your confidence.
- Let you express exactly how you feel.
- Help you with any baby sleeping, crying or feeding difficulties or put you in touch with someone who can.
- Give you all the options available to you in the area where you live—there is no single avenue of help that suits everyone, so you need to know what's available and how it will help.

Options for help

- Getting sympathetic one-to-one counselling from a skilled health professional who can help you help yourself is a vital first step. Self-help ideas are things like learning to nurture yourself, learning how to take a break and setting long-term and short-term goals. With the help of the counsellor you can slowly regain a sense of self and start to take control of your life again.
- Many women find joining a postnatal support group where they can talk to other women in confidence who are having the same experience helps a great deal.
- Reading books on the subject is helpful for you and your partner. Those mentioned at the end of this chapter provide guides for self help.
- Your partner requires support and information too. Men often try to solve the problem quickly but end up feeling unappreciated and depressed as well. Your partner needs to understand what you are going through is not his fault and the power to fix the problem does not lie with him. Listening, accepting how you feel and supporting whichever road to recovery you are taking are ways he can help as well as sharing the tasks of caring for the baby and running the home.
- At times psychiatric help and drug therapy is appropriate. Some women may not like this idea, but psychiatrists skilled in the area do not load women up with unnecessary medication and in fact often do not medicate at all after consultation. Medication takes the edges off the symptoms, but is not effective as a quick fix on its own and should always be used in conjunction with counselling and the other supports mentioned above.

Recovery is slow and takes two to twelve months, sometimes longer. A lot of patience is needed from you and your partner as well as commitment from your health worker because time is part of the recovery process. Although recovery can take a while, the result is positive for most women.

Obviously, given a choice no one would choose to suffer from what is known as postnatal depression but many women (and men) acknowledge that in hindsight positive things do come from the experience. By working through the pain of depression they learn more about themselves and about relating to others which has the potential to give a new, positive dimension to their lives.

Post-partum thyroiditis

Occasionally, the symptoms of postnatal depression are confused with a condition known as thyroiditis, inflammation of the thyroid gland. This condition develops in 5–10 per cent of women within the first twelve months after birth. The exact cause is unknown, but it is thought to occur because during pregnancy the immune function is suppressed to prevent antibodies that might harm the developing baby. After birth the immune system rebounds and overproduces antibodies that combat not only infections but the body's glands and organs. The thyroid is one of the glands that may be targeted, causing inflammation and hormone levels to rise or fall.

- **Hyperthyroid phase:** The hormone level rises, which can cause weight loss, loss of concentration, tremors, palpitations, feeling hot and tired, nervousness and insomnia.
- **Hypothyroid phase:** After the overactive stage, the thyroid gland may be unable to make enough thyroid hormone. This stage can begin between the third and eighth month and last for up to eight months. Symptoms here include unexplained weight gain, feeling cold, depression and tiredness. Hypothyroidism is often misdiagnosed as postnatal depression. Hormone levels can rise and fall, so symptoms may swing between the two phases

Diagnosis is by blood test, and thyroid function should always be checked when a woman reports any of the above symptoms following childbirth. For more information visit www.thyroid.org.au or call Thyroid Australia on (03) 9888 2588.

Sex

Despite the fact we live in a time when every bodily function, sexual or otherwise, is openly discussed, analysed, advertised, videoed, filmed or written about, sex between couples in long term relationships remains a big secret especially in relation to what actually happens after childbirth.

For decades we have had broad information about sex after birth, delivered in bland language with a certain amount of coyness but there's been a paucity of honest, in depth, first-hand confessions about the reality of getting together again after the baby comes.

While the matter of sex came up from time to time when I talked to mothers it was a long way from being the leading topic.

So, I decided that I would spark up this section by including some information gleaned from two recent books, in particular because both books have quite a bit to say from the father's perspective. The bloke's perspective has, historically in general baby/breastfeeding books, been brushed aside with the all-encompassing advice that 'practical help for mother is probably going to help her feel more like having sex than watching an erotic video will'. While there is truth in this there is far more involved in sex after childbirth than the delegation of housework.

First some general information:

Some literature suggests it is normal for women to feel wildly sexual as a natural progression of birth and breastfeeding. A number of women do feel like this but many don't. And, of course, many couples have no problems at all—nevertheless I think the following information will be helpful as it's easy to think you are abnormal in some way if your sexual life is not sailing smoothly.

You may be surprised to find out that surveys show the following:

1. The arrival of a baby tends to change a couple's sex life in ways that are seen as negative. Resuming sex at six weeks is not the reality for most. Many couples don't have sex for up to six months after the birth; a lot of couples have sex much less frequently than before the pregnancy for a year, or longer—sometimes much longer—after the birth; at least half of all women are less interested in sex after the birth than they were before the pregnancy and this may last for six to twelve months or longer—again, sometimes much longer. Often, though, this gives way to a new depth of sexuality and, for women, greater ease in having orgasms than before the birth.

2. Couples who pick up where they left off are the exception rather than the rule. This is as much about what's going on inside new parents'

heads, particularly mothers' heads, as it is about the aftermath of birth, fatigue and breastfeeding.

Reasons for this state of affairs are spelled out in some detail in *No Sex Please, We're Parents* (Melanie Roberts-Fraser, lawyer, and Oliver Roberts, journalist) and *From Here to Paternity* (Sacha Molitorisz, journalist)—please see Further Reading page 362.

The information in Melanie and Oliver's book is based on interviews and in Sacha's, blogs. For sure it's not scientific evidence, but there's a great sense of authenticity that in the security of anonymity parents are telling it the way it is. I found it revealing to read what they are saying. You might too.

REASONS WHY SEX MIGHT BE OFF THE AGENDA FOLLOWING BIRTH

From the mother's perspective

- Obviously, first up, discomfort following the birth especially if the birth was long and difficult. Sutures following a tear or episiotomy, haemorrhoids or the after-effects of a caesarean section are all going to influence how a woman feels about having sex.
- Breastfeeding: Data about how breastfeeding affects women's sexuality is conflicting. Some women report enjoying sex in a whole new way while they are breastfeeding and others experience a decrease in libido until they wean or menstruate again. Oestrogen levels are low while you are breastfeeding so the chance of the vaginal wall becoming thinner, less elastic and drier is likely, which can make penetration uncomfortable, even painful.

  There's also another aspect to this: Breastfeeding is a sensual activity once any early problems are solved. Some women find that their physical and emotional needs for intimacy are met by the closeness breastfeeding brings and don't feel the need for anything else at this time in their lives.

  I'm unaware of any research that shows that women who wean soon after birth necessarily feel more like sex than breastfeeding women. As far as I know, the range of sexual feelings and experiences amongst mothers who have weaned is similar to those who breastfeed. I suspect there might be times when breastfeeding is a good excuse for not having sex because women don't feel like it for other reasons.

- The weirdness of what happened 'down there': For many women there's the fear of the unknown, and an understandable reluctance to have sex when it feels like their nether regions have been completely re-arranged. It can be helpful to have a look with a mirror and gently rotate two fingers in your vagina to give you reassurance all is as it should be and an idea of any tender spots.
- Exhaustion is a common state of affairs, not just for six weeks after the birth but on and off for the first three labour-intensive years, especially if there are a couple of small children under three. Many women complain of having to give so much they have nothing left at the end of the day when sex just seems like another demand that's not much different from cooking the dinner.
- Interruptions: Babies (and toddlers) are unpredictable about their waking, sleeping and eating habits and it takes an effort to use the time you might have for sex when you'd sooner sleep or slump in front of the TV.
- Sharing a bed or sharing a room with a third person also takes time for many couples to get used to (some never do).
- Some women are embarrassed by their bodies after giving birth. Everything from breasts to vagina seems to leak or flop which gets in the way of sex both physically and mentally.

From the father's perspective

- A small number of men are so traumatised by witnessing the birth they cannot relate sexually to their partners for some time.
- A small number of men are put off by the change in their partner's body (others love the new 'voluptuousness'). They may find being drenched by breastmilk off-putting (others find it sexually stimulating).
- Exhaustion is also a factor for men.
- Some men have a real problem sharing the bed, even the room, with babies or toddlers or children. And baby monitors can be real turn-offs.
- Men, however, don't have the rigours of birth and its aftermath, the closeness of breastfeeding or, usually, the complete absorption in the baby to the exclusion of everything else in their lives, to get in the way of having sex.

- Some men find sexual rejection a personal rejection and if it goes on for a long time may switch off and stop initiating sex.
- Overall—and I know there are many variations on this—men find sexual abstinence for any length of time more of a problem than women do. Without the physical and emotional connection of sex they tend to feel neglected and sidelined.

What to do, what to do, what to do?

Suggestions (some of which will appeal, some of which may make you hold up your hands in horror)

- Accept early abstinence—depending on the birth, the baby, the breastfeeding, the levels of exhaustion, the support that's around and the temperaments of the parents, this may be for up to six months.
- Sorry to bang on about it yet again, but reliable practical help from their partners does raise women's libidos. As cited in *No Sex Please, We're Parents*, the workload of women has been officially linked to the declining fertility rate in Australia (and other developed countries as well).
- Communication is crucial. If communication was good before the baby arrived it is likely to remain good or re-establish in time. If communication was poor, solving any of the problems babies bring, sexual or otherwise, is much more difficult.
- Start slowly with no pressure. Massages, cuddling and body contact without penetrative sex brings closeness.
- We are so primed to think of sex as a spontaneous earth-shattering event that it's hard to come to terms with organising time for sex the way we organise other parts of our lives. But this is what often has to happen to get sex back again. And it doesn't have to be prolonged, earth-shattering sex. Initially, good enough sex is better than no sex for a positive, emotional connection. Plan ahead and try to remove as many barriers to the event as you can. Turn off the TV.
- Researchers have found that the urge to have sex is not necessarily preceded by feeling aroused. Rather, there are times when arousal and interest in sex follows having it. In other words, do it even if you don't feel like it. Women, especially, should think about taking the plunge

when they feel physically okay even if their heads are telling them something else. There is, I think, some similarity between this and resuming exercise after a break. There's that mental hurdle to cross beforehand but when you do it you feel great and wonder why it took so long.

- At some stage in the first year a mutually agreeable arrangement has to be made in relation to babies and toddlers sharing rooms and beds as these are potential sources of disharmony and sexual discontent. One parent may embrace the bed-sharing arrangement to avoid facing the sex issue.
- When one or both of you are chronically unhappy, marriage guidance or family therapy helps. A dramatic change in the sexual relationship which is not resolved in the first year after the birth may be a sign the relationship has deteriorated with both of you suffering guilt and anger over a variety of things.
- Ongoing lack of interest in sex can be a sign of depression in some women (along with other signs and symptoms, see page 345) and in some men too.
- Women should always seek advice if pain is still experienced deep inside or anywhere around the vagina after six months or later.
- If your sex life is causing problems in your relationship get help from a third party. The longer you wait the harder it is to change anything and it is not worth living in sexual frustration and misery for years or ending a relationship that could be successful.

Ask your child and family health nurse or family doctor for information about sexual counselling, marriage guidance or family therapy. Contacting a women's health nurse through a local community health centre is another option. Alternatively, Family Planning Clinics can help.

Contraception

If you wish to space your children over a period of time you do need to think about contraception soon after the birth if you are having a sexual relationship. Here is a brief rundown of the most common family planning methods. This is not intended as a thorough guide, rather to let you know what's available. You will need much more detailed information on the various methods before use if you are unfamiliar with them, particularly the newer contraceptives. Contraceptive advice and written information is available from your doctor, a women's health nurse (often located at community health centres), the Family Planning Association or a Natural Family Planning Centre. The Family Planning Healthline is 1300 65 88 86.

Barrier methods

- **Condoms and spermicide:** These are particularly useful in the early weeks and while your baby is being breastfed.
- **Diaphragms:** Do need refitting. Wait at least six weeks before refitting, then have the size checked again after three months. Diaphragms must be left in place in the vagina for eight hours after having sex.
- **The female condom:** Is now available in Australia. The female condom is a thin, soft, clear plastic condom that fits inside the vagina with a flexible ring at each end to keep it in place. The female condom is comparable to the male condom as a barrier method of contraception and is more effective than other methods, for example the diaphragm. The female condom cannot be used at the same time as a male condom because if they are used together the female condom could slip out of place or tear and/or the male condom could come off.

Natural methods

- **Exclusive breastfeeding:** *This means breastfeeding without the use of dummies, bottles or any other food.* If you are breastfeeding in this way it is reliable contraception as long as you have not started to menstruate, you feed frequently and your baby is fed at night. Only a small chance of conceiving is possible if you follow these guidelines, but if another pregnancy would cause you problems, other contraception is advisable. If you do use breastfeeding as a contraceptive you are at risk of conceiving once you menstruate, once your baby sleeps through the night or once you start her on formula or food from a spoon.
- **Abstinence:** Abstinence until breastfeeding finishes or until conception is planned is probably practised far more than anyone realises. Abstinence means no penis-in-vagina sex—it does not mean no sex at all. Kissing, touching, oral sex and cuddling are all ways of showing affection.

- **Withdrawal:** Withdrawal means the penis is withdrawn before ejaculation occurs. Withdrawal is not at all reliable but is cheap and readily available.
- **Rhythm, temperature or mucus method:** A combination of all three is the most reliable. The aim of these methods is to know when ovulation is likely to occur and avoid having sex at these times. If this is your choice for contraception, you and your partner need to attend a Natural Family Planning Centre which specialises in the practice.

Hormones

- **The mini pill:** The mini pill is a small dose of progesterone which is not harmful to your baby and should not interfere with breastfeeding. Some women who are breastfeeding report that when they take the mini pill their babies refuse the breast and/or there is less milk. If you find you have difficulties breastfeeding or with excessive bleeding, changing to another brand of the mini pill sometimes helps. If not, other contraception has to be arranged.

  The mini pill works by thickening the mucus around the cervix, which makes it difficult for sperm to penetrate. It is a very satisfactory form of contraception when combined with the added protection of breastfeeding.

  If you wean or if you are only breastfeeding once or twice every twenty-four hours, you need to think about other contraception. It's safe to take the combined pill (see below) and keep breastfeeding once or twice a day, although the oestrogen in the combined pill decreases the milk supply.

  The mini pill's contraceptive effect is best between three and twenty-one hours, so try to avoid having sex for three hours after taking it or within three hours of the pill being due. Therefore, the best time to take it each day is midday or very early in the evening. Make sure it's the same time each day.
- **The combined pill:** The combined pill, known as 'the pill', consists of both oestrogen and progesterone and stops ovulation. It is not recommended for women who are breastfeeding, not because the drug harms the baby, but because the action of the oestrogen interferes with the milk supply. If you wean and wish to take the combined pill, start straight

away. You do not have to wait until you menstruate. Diarrhoea, vomiting and some antibiotics can affect the pill's absorption, so extra precautions might be needed.

- **The contraceptive injection (DMPA):** This is a chemical similar to progesterone. Each injection protects you from pregnancy for twelve weeks. The first injection is best given five to six weeks after birth. It is safe to use DMPA when you are breastfeeding—it does not affect the quantity or quality of the breastmilk. The main side effect from DMPA is irregular bleeding, usually not heavy. Some women also experience weight gain, headaches or depression. It is a very effective form of contraception.
- **Implanon:** Implanon is a small plastic rod containing progestogen which is inserted just underneath the skin of the upper inner arm. It provides protection against pregnancy for the three years it is left in place. It is a very effective method of stopping pregnancy. The most common side effect is irregular bleeding, which can vary from no bleeding at all to troublesome frequent bleeding. A small number of women experience headaches, weight gain and breast symptoms. It is safe to use while breastfeeding. You can have implanon inserted at your nearest Family Planning Clinic or by a family doctor who has been trained in inserting the device.

Intra uterine device (IUD)

IUDs are an effective method of contraception and suitable for some women. An IUD can be fitted by your doctor eight to ten weeks after birth. IUDs do not affect lactation, but there is a slight risk of damage to the womb if a woman is breastfeeding.

Sterilisation

Sterilisation of either father or mother is not usually recommended until the youngest baby is twelve months old. Making such a decision before twelve months is often influenced by a crisis, emotional stress or a lifestyle change. Many people feel differently a year later. Sterilisation of a woman is by tubal ligation and for a man, a vasectomy. These procedures can be reversed but they should be considered permanent contraception.

Returning to paid work and childcare

Many women now work outside the home when their children are young for a variety of reasons, the main ones being:

- They have no choice, owing to relationship problems or real financial need.
- They believe they have no choice because of social and economic pressure related to a high standard of living that has come to be seen as the norm over the last fifty years.
- Paid work brings self-fulfilment and career opportunities. It is unfair that men have unquestioned access to career and family while women have always had to choose. Most professions are structured so a woman's advancement abruptly takes a plunge if she takes time out to have babies and then spends three or four years at home with them. A small number of couples are now arranging their professional working lives so one parent is always at home with the baby. And a tiny number of couples are reversing roles.
- It is difficult for women (or men) to have to depend on another person's income.
- Life at home caring for babies and small children is often lonely because of the way our society is structured. It can be depressing because full-time care of young children at home by their mothers is over-idealised and under-valued, making women at home feel that their work is worthless.

A combination of the above factors is involved for many women. In an ideal world, we would all do what suits us best. There are women in the paid workforce who would sooner not be there and there are women who are at home who would love to go back to their other job.

The main solution offered in Australia for these dilemmas of our times is childcare, and a diverse range of childcare provisions have increased dramatically in the last couple of decades. Informal childcare undertaken by friends, relatives and babysitters has always been around and still is, but services that range from nannies who care for babies in their homes, long daycare nurseries and home-based care are now available for most families. Despite difficulties finding places in suitable geographic areas and the financial burden involved, the majority of parents seeking childcare usually find it.

Childcare has been viewed through rose-coloured glasses for quite some time. A growing social, emotional and economic investment in childcare means that we all want it to be all right so the benefits have been emphasised.

The benefits centre around the right of women to have the same access to careers and economic security as men, and the social benefits to the children—many of whom enjoy the interaction with other children. Some research shows that long daycare experience helps children to become self-reliant, to learn to share and co-operate and have a larger view of the world. In families where there are extreme social problems, long daycare is a vital way of relieving parent stress and keeping the family unit together.

The negatives have been suppressed due to fear of making parents feel guilty and because of the seemingly insurmountable difficulties of other options being made available in this country so parents can combine parenthood with employment. The biggest negative impact is on babies and toddlers who spend long hours in daycare under the age of two.

Concerns about long daycare for children under three have been raised by a number of people such as psychologists Penelope Leach and Steve Biddulph. Two respected researchers, Edward Zigler from Yale University and Jay Belsky from the Pennsylvania State University, both initially staunch proponents of childcare, reversed their positions on long daycare after closely observing long daycare experiences of children under two for over a decade. Negatives centre around the lack of one-on-one care by an adult who has a parent-like commitment to the baby or toddler, the increased possibility of a deprived childhood in a place where there is no privacy, no escape, no place of one's own and a 30 per cent increase in childhood illnesses.

It is still too early to know whether children who spend the first two years of their lives in institutional long daycare will end up with more problems, social or otherwise, than those cared for at home. Chances are, most will not, nor should the prospect of this possibility be used to scare the wits out of parents. Until we know more, I see the main issue being about the quality of life children experience at this time in their lives, which in long daycare centres is far from ideal. Parents themselves often admit this, as do many of the staff who work at the centres. Prospective parents need to be fully informed so they are in a position to make the best decisions for themselves and their babies. Blanket approval and bland reassurances about childcare in the first two or three years are not particularly helpful. Parents who have no other choice but to use long daycare should be aware of the negatives so they can lessen their impact as much as possible.

Many parents do have other options which they may not even consider if well-meaning health professionals keep telling them long daycare is as good as or even better than care at home.

By planning ahead it's often possible to work out ways to minimise long daycare for children under two.

Here are some ideas:

- Lifestyle expenses can often be arranged to allow for one parent to be at home for twelve to eighteen months.
- Part-time work should be negotiated whenever possible.
- Don't assume long daycare for nine hours a day, five days a week is the only option if finances dictate an early return to paid work. Sometimes parents can arrange their work so some of the care can be shared between them. If there is a choice between three days in long daycare and care spread between daycare, grandma and father, choose the latter.
- One-on-one care at home is preferable to long daycare, so if this option is affordable, employ a nanny. Some parents find sharing a nanny between two families is a good compromise.
- Whenever possible, be prepared to change arrangements or find other care any time things are not working out.
- If the need to return to employment is based on career opportunities and self-fulfilment, rather than a financial necessity, try to hold off full-time work for eighteen months. It may be unfair that it is usually the mother who has to make this choice, but the trade-off in terms of peace of mind and the child's quality of life is worth it.

Getting organised

If you are returning to paid work some time in your baby's first two years, it is important to lay the groundwork for a smooth operation. Finding good quality childcare is a top priority and should be organised as soon as your pregnancy is confirmed.

Childcare services available

Childcare services range from nannies who will care for your child in your home, private daycare nurseries, government subsidised daycare nurseries and private or council supervised home-based services (Family Day Care). Some parents make private arrangements with a babysitter who may be untrained but reliable and caring.

When you are choosing, be guided by the cost, the caregiver's ability to be warm and affectionate, the safety and cleanliness of the surroundings, the number of babies or children per caregiver and the caregiver's qualifications. Check what arrangements are made if the caregiver is sick and whether the same person will be there most of the time to care for your baby.

Try to arrange several times when you and your baby can be with the caregiver before you go back to work. See pages 10–11 for more information.

Finding childcare

After you have worked out what it is you are looking for (a nanny, long daycare, family daycare, pre-school/kindergarten, home-based care) try your local council, the Department of Education in your state, the Yellow Pages, the internet, call CareforKids or the Childcare Access Hotline (1800 670 305). To find a nanny try agencies, advertising in your local paper or asking your friends. If you find a nanny yourself, as opposed to going via friends or an agency, it is important to verify references and qualifications. It is also important to have an in-depth interview to make sure, from your point of view that she is suitable, and, for her point of view, that her conditions of work and wages are satisfactory.

Problem times

Babies and toddlers have lots of minor illnesses, especially when they are in care with other children. As they grow older this is less frequent, but it is very common in the first two years.

Mothers in paid employment do get very tired, as few ever seem to get enough help to manage two jobs, either from their partners or their employers.

So, as well as arranging childcare, try and establish a network of friends and family who are prepared to help out in times of emergency.

Have a good talk with your partner so you can make definite arrangements about sharing tasks—for example, picking up and delivering your baby to her carer's, getting up at night, sharing care when your baby is sick and sharing the housework evenly.

Childcare when one parent is at home

The impression that childcare has untold benefits and no disadvantages has been so widely accepted that many parents have come to believe that even if childcare is not needed for paid work reasons, babies and toddlers should be in childcare anyway for 'socialising'. If you are concerned about this be assured that, contrary to what everyone would like to believe, babies and toddlers are not well adapted for social groups. While they are fascinated by other babies and toddlers they are far too young to spend long hours every day socialising. The normal social interaction that goes on between families and friends is all the socialising they need. By age two or three (depending on the child) most children are ready for some limited time in a group setting for educational and social purposes.

This is not to say that children under three cannot be left for short periods in group care or with other caring adults. Parents, especially mothers, need a break and time and space to attend to their own needs. Babies and toddlers often enjoy such a change too but if they don't, are unlikely to suffer when they are not left for long periods.

Sudden unexpected death in infancy (SUDI)

Sudden infant death in infancy is something none of us like to think about but we do; naturally, the time we think about it the most is when our children are babies. Because of my work I am very much aware that parents worry about SUDI as the subject is frequently mentioned when I talk to them. I also come into contact with families who have suffered the shocking event that is SUDI and as I write I am thinking of them and the pain and grief they suffered and are still suffering.

It is normal to think about SUDI after the birth of your baby and at times during the first year or two. It seems at every age and stage of development there is something there to potentially cast a shadow over the joy children bring. Certainly it is hard to find a parallel for the sudden and unexpected death of a healthy baby, but as the years go by there is the fear of 'stranger danger' and the adolescent years bring the worries of car accidents and misuse of drugs and alcohol. These worries are part of being a parent which we tend to be unaware of until we have a baby. Accepting they exist, taking whatever sensible precautions we can and getting on with life is also part of learning to be a parent.

If you find yourself thinking about SUDI, it's better to talk about it with your partner, family, friends or health worker rather than keeping apprehensive thoughts to yourself.

FOR MORE INFORMATION

Chapter 1: Preparing for Parenthood, page 3
Chapter 11: Daily Care *(SUDI, page 213)*
Chapter 15: The Crying Baby *(effect on relationship, page 289; anger and feelings of depression, page 314)*
Chapter 18: Feeding Your Baby *(paid work and breastfeeding, page 389)*
Chapter 22: For Parents *(paid work and night waking, page 430; travelling with your baby, page 433)*
Chapter 32: Becoming a Toddler, page 517

FURTHER READING

Beating the Blues: A Self-help Approach to Overcoming Depression, Susan Tanner, Tower Books, Australia, 1999. (Recommended for its sympathetic, practical advice.)

Postnatal Depression: Families in Turmoil, Lara Bishop, Halstead Press, Australia, 1999.

No Sex Please, We're Parents, Melanie Roberts-Fraser and Oliver Roberts, ABC Books, Australia, 2007.

From Here to Paternity: A User's Manual for Early Fatherhood, Sacha Molitorisz, Pan Macmillan, Australia, 2007; Chapter 16, 'Sex after childbirth . . . three's a crowd'.

PART TWO

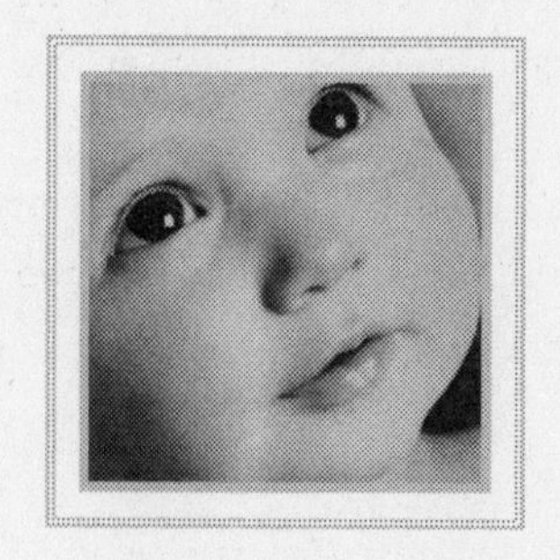

3 to 6 months

Chapter 17

Equipment

Eating equipment

Between four and six months your baby may start eating food from a spoon. Any unbreakable plate and spoon will do, but you might feel like choosing a special baby set from the wide selection available. Don't waste money on sets that include a host of things you don't need. One plate and one spoon is fine. Training system cups that offer a teat, a straw and a spout are a needless expense at this stage. Wait until your baby can use a straw or a spout, then buy whichever one she uses. Buying the three systems is unnecessary, especially when one is a teat—if you're bottle feeding you already have one and if you're breastfeeding you may never use it.

Walkers

A baby walker is a device on a frame with a seat that allows a baby who can sit alone to propel herself around using her feet and toes.

Not only are baby walkers a non-essential item, but overwhelming evidence relating to injuries strongly suggests the supply of walkers should be prohibited.

Walkers are very popular and I can understand why when I talk to parents who use them. Walkers have wonderful entertainment value—babies love them. And if a mother happens to have a baby (or twins) who never sleeps, the time her baby is in the walker may be the only time she gets to do other things.

But walkers do not teach babies to walk, nor do they provide them with any sort of beneficial exercise. The use of baby walkers has no developmental advantages for babies. The only positive feature they have is their entertainment value and the fact that their use gives mothers a break, which has to be weighed up against the following:

- The extraordinary high walker-related injury toll. In Australia it is estimated there are one thousand injuries per year suffered by babies under twelve months while using walkers. The greatest number of injuries are to the baby's head; other injuries include fractures, burns and scalds and broken front teeth. In the United States it is found that up to 50 per cent of babies in walkers suffer a minor walker-related injury. Up to 9 per cent of babies in walkers require medical attention for a walker-related injury.

  Injuries happen when walkers are used because their inherent design is unstable and because babies are able to scoot around unsupervised at great speed. In the process they trip over rugs, fall down stairs, jam their fingers in doors, run into furniture and walls and have access to hot objects and poisons.
- Delays gross motor development (weight-bearing on flat feet, pulling up onto furniture, 'cruising' and walking).
- When babies are propped up in a walker their bodies tend to stiffen and they push back with their feet, which encourages them to walk on their toes and strengthens one group of muscles more than another. This posture is not part of natural walking and can delay walking. Walkers do not

help babies develop their balance the way playing on the floor does. In healthy babies the developmental delay is short-lived and much more likely to occur when babies are left in walkers constantly for long periods.

It is not easy keeping active babies happy all day, especially when they don't sleep much, and I sympathise wholeheartedly with mothers who find using walkers preferable to listening to the grizzling. However, after looking at the injury statistics and the very limited use a walker has, I cannot recommend their use. If you never use one you won't miss it. If you decide to buy one here are some tips for safe use:

- Always supervise your baby while she is in the walker.
- Never use the walker near steps or stairs.
- Check the surfaces are flat with no objects that will cause the walker to tip over.
- Never carry the walker with the child in it.
- If your baby is not bearing her own weight don't let her use a walker. Weight-bearing means that when you hold her standing with her feet touching a hard surface she bears her weight well on both feet without her legs buckling and bounces up and down. Most babies do this by six months. A delay in weight-bearing is not a major problem in a healthy baby who is developing normally, but use of a walker unnecessarily delays weight-bearing even longer; in turn, this delays pulling up, cruising around furniture and eventually walking.
- Make sure that both the baby's feet touch the floor.
- Limit your baby's use of the walker to thirty minutes a day to minimise injury risks and to allow her the full range of movement she needs for her optimum development.

Baby jumpers, battery-operated swings and baby exercisers

Again, these products are non-essential items and have no advantages for baby development. Nor have they any exercising benefit. They are entertaining, offer babies new sensations and give mothers the opportunity for a break, which is never to be sneezed at. Unlike baby walkers their use is self-limiting as babies tire of them in a fairly short period, the risk of injury is minimal and development unaffected when used for healthy full-term babies. They are not recommended for premature babies or babies who have been unwell, as these babies need playing with in ways that enhance their development and this equipment does not offer the best opportunity for this to happen.

Stairgates and safety gates

Once your baby starts to get mobile, gates are useful to block off doorways of rooms such as kitchens, bathrooms, laundries and the tops and bottoms of stairs. Mobility refers to crawling, which happens any time from five to twelve months, walking, which starts between nine to nineteen months, and any time your baby is in a baby walker. Make sure the gap between the bars of safety gates is the same as that recommended for cots—no less than 50mm (2 inches) or greater than 85mm (3 inches), so your baby's head or limbs don't get stuck.

Playpens

Playpens seem to be something used more in the past when women had fewer household aids and had to use playpens to keep their babies away from danger while they worked.

Playpens can still have a use depending on your lifestyle and your baby (lots of babies won't stay in playpens very long). They can be an effective barrier to dangerous areas and I'm sure we all know someone who irons in the playpen while the baby has free run of the room. Playpens are useful to put heaters in. At other times a playpen provides a handy space for toddlers and young children to play in when they are playing with small toys which need to be kept away from the baby. However, wait before you buy—playpens are often bought and never used.

Portable cots

An optional item for families who travel a lot. Take care when buying as portable cots are often badly designed and dangerous. Sadly a number of babies have died following collapse of their cots. Cots that incorporate a rotating lock mechanism which locks the top rails of the cot are the style which cause concern. A number of brands of portable cots have been banned while further enquiries are being made. Contact the Department of Fair Trading or the Consumer Affairs Department in your state for further information. You will find the number in the *White Pages*.

FOR MORE INFORMATION

Chapter 18: Feeding Your Baby, page 370
Chapter 24: Feeding Your Baby *(tips for drinking from a cup, page 454)*

Chapter 18

Feeding Your Baby

We put cereal into his mouth and it kept going in, but it also kept oozing out. My husband said to me, 'Why are we doing this?'

HELEN TOWNSEND, *BABY CRAZY*

Starting new food

The optimum time to start solids changes every decade or so. In the 1920s it was nine months, in the 1970s it was six weeks, in the 1980s it was three to four months, in the 1990s it was four to six months and now it is six months.

Previous recommendations were mostly based on whim, fashion and whatever food was around at the time; now they are mostly based on reliable research and greater scientific knowledge of nutrition, physiology and baby development (we hope). However, cynic that I am, it will be interesting to see what the story is in ten years' time. And since I last updated 'food', sure enough there are rumblings of potential change yet again. I must admit it's hard to take it all *too seriously*!

The confusion (2009) primarily arises in the world of allergy where it is still not certain whether delaying food or certain foods in infancy (as has been the practice for the last twenty-five years) is helpful in allergy avoidance or if, in fact, it might be a factor in the increase in allergic disease so marked in 'developed' countries. In a recent position paper published by the Australasian Society of Clinical Immunology and Allergy on Allergy Prevention in Children (www.allergy.org.au) it is acknowledged that at this stage most allergy prevention strategies are relatively crude with small or unconfirmed effects, and newer strategies are still in experimental stages. Their recommendation is to delay complementary foods (that is food other than milk) for *four* to six months. The paper also says that there is no evidence that eliminating certain foods in babies' diets after six months has any preventative effects and may compromise their nutritional status. On the other hand, avoidance of peanuts, other nuts and shellfish in high-risk babies (babies born into atopic families) for the first two to four years of life is not nutritionally harmful and *may* be beneficial. This strategy certainly eliminates the fear of anaphylaxis (my comment). For more on this see Allergies and food intolerance on page 384.

I happen to be revising my books right at a time when allergy specialists seem to think that there are advantages in starting food other than milk at four months rather than six as a way to halt the steady increase in food allergy. I don't have a problem with this, however, those in the world of lactation continue to believe exclusive breastfeeding for the first six months is best. Many parents by now will be getting advice via their child and family health nurse/maternal and child health nurse and some paediatricians to offer baby food at four months. This confused state of affairs is not very helpful to parents wanting to do the right thing in relation to giving their babies food.

The World Health Organization, which I believe hasn't yet caught up with the latest re the concerns of food allergies in developed countries (a much bigger problem than in developing countries) is still advising exclusive breastfeeding for the first six months because:

1. Studies show that by waiting until six months the risks of infections in babies are reduced. I can't help but think this is more of an issue for vulnerable babies living in areas where there are poor standards of living and low food reserves.
2. Babies' digestive systems are more mature at six months. Their ability to digest starches is limited until then.

3. By waiting until six months a range of food can be introduced relatively quickly—as long as the baby is happy to eat it, of course—rather than stringing the process out over weeks.
4. Until very recently it was believed that there were no advantages to starting food other than milk before six months (providing an exclusively breastfed baby is getting enough milk for proper growth, see below).

What about babies on infant formula?

As infant formula does not have the immune or the anti-allergic function that breastmilk has, it is difficult to see that point one (previous page) is relevant; however, points two, three and four indicate a slight advantage in waiting until six months (as opposed to four or five months). I don't think they are earth-shattering reasons, but if your baby is happy on formula only, why complicate life before you have to?

It is advisable to offer food at six months because:

1. A baby's appetite, nutritional and growth needs are no longer satisfied by milk alone.
2. By six months, babies are starting to chew and bite with their gums. Their hand to mouth co-ordination is more accurate and between six and nine months they are starting to sit on their own, which makes spoon feeding and finger food eating easier.
3. The digestive system is more mature.
4. By six months many babies are interested in trying a range of food of different consistencies. Not all of course, see Some normal variations, page 380.

WHERE DOES ALL THIS LEAVE US?

I wish I knew. We are certainly likely to see a range of opinions about when to give baby her first teaspoon of food as gastroenterologists, breastfeeding enthusiasts, some paediatricians, some food intolerance and allergy specialists, naturopaths and others will almost certainly disagree.

Parents who live in countries where no one gets enough to eat must find all this agonising extremely weird.

Until there are more specific guidelines from those who decide such things, I think it's up to parents to decide. If you would like to get going at four months be my guest. I have always organised the introduction of food in two sections—the first is a beginning food ideas section followed by a second section (after six months) which is a basic plan to include a wide range of family foods.

A variation on the six months 'rule'

BREASTFEEDING WHEN THERE HASN'T BEEN QUITE ENOUGH MILK FOR SOME TIME

There are a number of women whose breastmilk diminishes around four to five months so that there is not enough to match their babies' growth needs. This is shown by slow weight gains or no weight gains over four or five weeks (a very thin baby). Often in this situation the breastmilk does not increase despite increasing breastfeeds and getting extra rest. It is important for babies to be adequately nourished and in my opinion there is nothing to be gained leaving breastfed babies starving until the magic age of six months is reached. As formula in a bottle interferes with breastfeeding and as these babies often refuse bottles anyway, starting them on rice cereal, fruit and vegies is a good way to give them extra food and still maintain the breastfeeding, which may then continue for the whole of the first year and even beyond.

Food from a spoon, whether the official line becomes four to six months or six months, is often advised for a range of reasons that have nothing to do with nutrition or allergies or baby development. Here they are:

- **To encourage 'sleeping through' or because the baby suddenly starts waking at night again around four to six months of age:** Night waking, sadly, is not often related to food. If it were, it would provide a nice simple solution for sleep-deprived parents and hassled health workers. Occasionally, in some specific circumstances, it does the trick, but don't be disappointed if you try it and nothing changes and remember—sleep problems aren't solved by trying to force babies to eat or by searching for the elusive food they will eat.
- **To help prevent regurgitation:** Starting food from a spoon rarely makes any difference to the amount being regurgitated, or to crying

babies. If your baby is a big regurgitator you just end up with technicolour vomit instead of white.

- **Curiosity:** From three months on babies start to become aware of the world around them and start to take a great interest in everyday happenings, including what is going into their parents' mouths at mealtimes. Parents become agog with curiosity to see what their baby will do with food of their own and can't wait to try. However just because babies show interest in the process is not a signal to start giving them food and doesn't necessarily indicate that they want the food themselves. Between four and six months it's fine to offer them occasional small tastes of food if you want to, for example, a suck on a mandarin or a taste of mashed potato, but if your baby is thriving, wait until six months for the main event.
- **The baby starts biting, chewing and sucking on everything in sight including her fingers and hands:** From around three months babies' hands are never out of their mouths. This is part of their sensory/motor development and not a sign of needing food. Between three and six months they all want to bite, chew and suck on anything going—again this is part of their normal development, unrelated to food or eating, and one way they learn about the world and all it contains.
- **Starting food early makes babies good eaters:** I have never seen any evidence that this is the case, including times in the past when babies were started on solids at very young ages. Whether or not babies and toddlers are good eaters seems to depend mostly on temperament, a bit on the parents' management of the eating behaviour and a degree of luck.
- **'Big' babies need food earlier:** Big babies thrive on breastmilk and formula in the first six months the same as any other babies.
- **Pressure from relatives and friends:** As previously noted, the guidelines for starting solids change with every generation so it's usual for mothers to be inundated with a range of suggestions from their nearest and dearest accompanied by what can sound like very valid reasons—'helping them to sleep at night' and 'it didn't do you any harm' are the biggies—however, in light of current knowledge, six months for most babies seems to be the optimum time.

What do you need?

- A spoon without sharp edges. An unbreakable dish. You don't have to disinfect the dish and the spoon.
- Something to grind up the food. If your baby doesn't mind eating food mashed with a fork, a fork is all you need. Many babies like their food smooth to begin with—which means using something mechanical like a Bamix, a hand blender or one of the small electric blenders specifically designed for grinding up baby food.
- Something to sit your baby in. When you start you may find it easier to sit her on your lap. Once you're in the swing of things a portable baby chair is useful until your baby can manage a highchair or a chair attached to a table (six to nine months).
- Plenty of mopping-up cloths.

Which foods?

For those of you who need guidance or would like some homecooking ideas, refer to the recipe section at the back of the book.

- Rice cereal, baby porridge/baby muesli. Rice cereal has been the starter cereal since the early 1980s, especially when given under six months as, it was believed that the early introduction of wheat products could lead to coeliac disease (an inability to absorb gluten, which is found in wheat). Allergy researchers now believe that withholding wheat products is not necessary and may in fact increase—not decrease—the incidence of coeliac disease, so if you would like to try wheat-based cereals instead of boring old rice cereal go ahead.
- Cooked apples and pears;
- Mashed banana;
- Mashed avocado;
- Fruit gels;
- Full-fat yoghurt; ricotta cheese;
- Cooked vegies; chicken soup; vegie broth;
- **Cereal:** Cereal can be purchased at pharmacies or supermarkets or you can make your own.

- **Cooked apples and pears:** You may cook your own and puree them or buy commercially prepared fruit for babies available in tins or jars. Once you have determined your baby likes home-cooked fruit you can prepare and freeze a quantity in the refrigerator. Make sure your baby is going to eat the food first before going mad and filling up the freezer with ice-cube trays of cooked fruit and vegies.

  Cooked food in clean containers or jars of commercially prepared baby food last up to three days in the fridge as long as you always scoop out portions with a clean spoon.

  Commercially prepared baby food is nutritionally sound and convenient but it is more expensive, it has no advantages for babies (advertising often implies it is superior), does not offer the range of tastes home-prepared or fresh food does and when you prepare your baby's food yourself you know exactly what she's getting.
- **Mashed ripe banana:** Mashed or pureed banana with a little orange juice is excellent first food for babies. It does give some babies hard poo, so if this happens you may have to stop the banana for a while. Banana also makes a strange poo sometimes so don't panic if there are a few dark red stringy bits in your baby's poo after she eats banana—it's harmless.
- **Avocado:** Mashed or blended avocado is very nutritious and enjoyed by many babies. For some it is a little rich, which results in a bright green vomit. If this happens wait a few weeks before trying again.
- **Yoghurt:** Yoghurt is an excellent first food for babies, either on its own or combined with fruit or vegetables. Yoghurt is far superior to custard, which is best avoided. Custard is sweet and addictive so give it a miss and try yoghurt instead. If your baby likes and tolerates yoghurt it's a wonderful, healthy convenience food. When served with fresh fruit it makes a good meal on its own for older babies.

  The healthiest yoghurt for babies is natural full-fat yoghurt. If you can't persuade your baby to eat the natural yoghurt try one of the fruit-flavoured yoghurts without added sugar. Stay away from caramel and honey yoghurts—they are sweet and addictive.

  Lactose intolerant people who can't drink milk can tolerate yoghurt because the lactose is partially broken down by the bacteria which cause the milk to thicken.

Commercial baby yoghurt desserts are a diluted version of the real thing. They contain 26 per cent yoghurt which is then sterilised so the yoghurt's culture is destroyed. What's left is mixed with fruit juice. Those are fine to use as an alternative now and then or to start with, but are not as nutritious as full-fat yoghurt.

Yoghurt does make a small number of babies regurgitate, gives a few a red bottom and some a rash around their lips, so wait until your baby is six months and start slowly. If any of these things happen, stop, wait a month and try again.

- **Fruit gels:** Fruit gels are simply pure fruit juice made into a jelly. Babies enjoy them from time to time, especially in hot weather when gels can be a useful way of getting extra fluid into babies who don't have bottles. You can make your own or use commercially prepared gels.
- **Vegetables:** I suggest potato, pumpkin and carrot to begin with as they are all easy to cook and mash or make into a puree. You can try them separately or combine them. Babies often like potato and pumpkin together. Once you establish that your baby is going to be a vegie eater, try the full range of vegies blended up together (broccoli, spinach, sweet potato, zucchini and so on). You do not have to give one little bit of a vegie weekly to test the result—it would take a year to try them all!

  If your family eats meat, when your baby is around six months and eating vegies well, try cooking a little mince meat or chicken and blending it up with the vegies. Grate some cheese and stir it in as well.
- **Chicken soup** is a regular item in the homes of many of the families I see and traditionally in families of European descent this wonderful, nourishing dish is offered as baby's first food. This is fine.

How do you begin?

Pick one of the items from the list. Rice cereal is usually suggested for the first choice but feel free to try one of the others if you would rather. Cereal is convenient and easy to prepare until you work out how your baby takes to this new style of eating. It's a bit frustrating cooking up nutritious fruit and vegies for one little teaspoon which initially may be spat back.

If you are using rice cereal, try one or two teaspoons mixed with 15–30ml of expressed breastmilk, boiled water or prepared formula. Express your own milk if it's easy; if it's difficult, select one of the other options.

Offer one or two teaspoons of food to your baby once a day until you have some idea of how she takes to it. Try any time of the day that suits you. For convenience, offer the food at the same time as the milk. If you offer the food in between the milk feeds you will find you are offering your baby food every two hours—this is time-consuming and unnecessary, but remember there are no strict rules. If you find it suits you and your baby to give the food from a spoon in between the breast or bottle, please do.

A WORD ON THE EARTH-SHATTERING ISSUE OF MILK-FIRST/FOOD-FIRST

There seems to be a push now to give babies their milk before their food for the whole of the first twelve months. I can understand this being advisable in certain situations, however I have a problem with recommending it as a general 'rule for all' for the following reasons:

- Six to twelve months is a critical learning period for eating food—as opposed to sucking milk. Toddlers are renowned for fussy eating and in my opinion this tendency is exacerbated by an over-emphasis on sucking milk, particularly from bottles, in their second six months, which then tends to flow into the toddler years. Excessive fluids negatively alter older babies' and toddlers' appetites for healthy family food. We now have an unacceptable level of tooth decay in the under-fives. Paediatric dentists, confronted with the problem daily, lay the blame squarely on the prolonged use of bottles—and sometimes prolonged breastfeeding—into the toddler and pre-school years.
- It simply doesn't make sense to me to give a nine-month-old baby a big bottle of milk—or a breastfeed—before offering her lunch. In my experience it is unusual for healthy breastfed babies to significantly reduce their breastfeeds because they are eating three meals a day. Most carry on breastfeeding as they were prior to having food unless their mothers purposefully start reducing the breastfeeds with the aim of weaning around twelve months (see following page).

  Babies drinking formula often reduce the amount of milk they drink once they are eating well, which again in my opinion, is a good thing as this means they are not as likely to get hooked on bottles throughout the toddler years.

- Babies who are reluctant to try food are not likely to be remotely interested after a big breastfeed or bottle of milk.
- Many breastfeeding women wish to wean—or to reduce the breastfeeds to two or three every twenty-four hours—by twelve months, which I happen to think is fair enough. The best way to do this is slowly over the second six months in conjunction with offering their babies a wide variety of family foods and water or milk from a cup.

I realise that this flies in the face of information from some breastfeeding advisors so if you are breastfeeding and dedicated to feeding before food please do so. If you are formula feeding I strongly advise offering the milk after the meals.

Other situations where it is advisable to offer milk first:

- When four-to-five month old babies are given extra food because there is not quite enough breastmilk.
- Fussy breastfed or formula-fed babies who are slow to gain weight, especially if they are premature or low-weight babies or have medical problems.
- Breastfed babies who get badly constipated once they start eating food. There are a few different ways to deal with this (see page 410) but breastfeeding before the food until the baby's body adjusts could be helpful.

Initially your baby will probably want to suck when she's hungry—that's what she's used to. Offering her a spoon first will probably frustrate and annoy her. You might like to offer one breast or half the bottle, try the food then give her the other breast or the rest of the bottle.

Once spoon feeding is well under way most babies who enjoy food usually like to eat first then finish off their meal with the breast or bottle, often before having a nap. Sucking at the end of a meal is calming and pleasurable for you both. It is also a nice time for a cuddle.

How to proceed

Sit your baby on your lap or in a portable chair. Take up a small amount of food on the tip of the spoon and place it in her mouth, well back over her tongue before emptying it, to encourage her to swallow. Expect some or all of the food to come back out of her mouth when you first start. Take it slowly, stay relaxed—food is fun, if a little messy.

If you have twins you might find it easier in the beginning to offer the food to each baby separately to see how they take to it. Once it's well under way sit them in portable chairs and use one dish and one spoon and feed them both at the same time unless there's two of you around to do the job. Babies quickly develop individual tastes so don't be surprised to find one baby's eating style is different to the other's.

The same guidelines apply to premature babies as full-term babies, but if your baby was very premature you will probably find she is not ready to start food from a spoon until she is around six to nine months.

It's all experimental until you find out what your baby thinks of this new way of eating.

If after a day or two it's going down with a minimum of fuss, increase an extra teaspoon of cereal every day or two up to a maximum of two tablespoons. If you think your baby is interested but doesn't like rice cereal, try mixing some fruit with the cereal or try one of the other suggested foods. When she is comfortably eating one to two tablespoons of food every day, try a second meal after two weeks. Two or three weeks later offer a third.

Never try to force the food if your baby doesn't want it. If you have an interested eater resist the temptation to try everything on the menu in three days. Try a new food every two or three days.

A word about vegies

Vegies are wonderful. Vegie-eating babies make us all feel good, but I would estimate about half of all babies won't eat vegies so don't let it get you down if you have a non-vegie eater. She will be fine. It's best to stop cooking and offering them after a few weeks if the vegie refusal looks like it's here to stay because you will get angry and your baby will get stressed. Just offer two meals a day or think of something else for the third. A second round of rice cereal and fruit is fine; babies don't look for endless variety.

Some normal variations

It is difficult to be precise about food and babies. They all respond to food in their own way and you must be guided by your baby. Wide variations exist across the eating spectrum which have little to do with the mother's feeding techniques. Here are the main ones I observe:

- **Loves food, eats anything:** Some babies just open up and down it goes! Be careful not to overdo it if you have one like this. Three to four tablespoons of food three times a day as well as the breast or bottle is ample. As babies like this eat anything, they are just as happy with a plate of vegies as anything else so it's easy to give them a healthy diet that won't cause excessive weight gains.
- **Eats well initially then suddenly refuses:** Don't panic. Stop completely and try again in a few weeks. Continue milk only for the time being.
- **Complete refusal:** Not a problem. If, after you try a few different things over a week or two and you are getting nowhere, stop—try again in a few weeks. Continue milk only for the time being.
- **Loves some things, refuses others:** Give her what she likes even when it is the same old boring things each day. Avoid the temptation to try sugary baby biscuits, flavoured custards and added sugar to vary the diet. They are not needed.
- **Keeps refusing all food from a spoon indefinitely:** About 20 per cent of all babies are finger food babies who constantly refuse food until *they* can feed themselves with their fingers. Parents find this frustrating, but it's their baby's decision and respecting this is the only rational approach. If you have a finger food baby, start to allow her two or three pieces of food to suck herself any time from six months onwards. After ten minutes call it quits until around the next mealtime. Sometimes finger food gets eaten, sometimes it gets thrown around the room, but healthy babies who eat like this thrive when left alone to get on with it without a lot of agonising and soul-searching from the parents about the five food groups and so on and so on. Offer the breast or bottle after the food. Here are some finger food suggestions: steamed vegie sticks; grated carrot or apple (because of choking risks do not give whole); small pieces of ripe pawpaw, pear, rockmelon; pieces of home-made rissoles; pieces of home-made salmon or tuna rissoles (after six months); fingers of bread or toast (seedless); crusket biscuits; fingers of cheese on toast.
- **No food at all for a long time:** A number of very healthy thriving breastfed babies have mothers with such an abundant milk supply that

they see no need to eat anything and end up exclusively breastfed for a very long time. They often refuse most food until they are nine to twelve months old. The issue of iron deficiency in babies who are exclusively breastfed beyond six months has been raised in the last few years. There is some evidence that 10 to 30 per cent of babies who are exclusively breastfed after six months may become iron deficient.

Unfortunately, when babies are obviously thriving and look healthy, the only way to monitor this is to take blood tests or give all babies in the second six months who are exclusively breastfed iron supplements. Because opinion is still divided over the age at which iron levels are depleted in breastmilk and the usefulness of such strategies, I suggest feeding on. Try your baby with food in a relaxed way. If you are worried about the possibility of iron deficiency talk it over with your child and family health nurse or paediatrician. If anyone's advice puts you in panic mode, seek a second opinion.

If your baby is not an avid eater, don't be tempted to give food in a bottle instead of off the spoon. Traditionally, parents from some cultures do give fruit, vegies, yoghurt and soup from bottles with big holes cut in the teats.

Whilst recognising that generations of babies have grown into adults where this has been the practice, it is not recommended for the following reasons:

- The baby has no control over the amount of food she is 'drinking'. It just glugs down and weight gains can become excessive.
- Food in a bottle is not teaching your baby the skills she needs to learn to eat in a socially acceptable way.
- Sucking food from teats increases the chance of tooth decay, especially when this way of eating goes on into the second year, which it often does because it is very habit forming.

How do you know if the food causes a reaction or doesn't suit your baby?

It is not always easy to know when food is the cause of problems in babies. Things like runny noses, loose poo, red cheeks, nappy rash, vomiting, grizzling and unexpected night wakings often have nothing to do with diet.

If you are concerned, stop the food, wait a few weeks and try again.

The following things are stronger indications of possible problems:

- Mountainous vomiting one or two hours after the food, especially if your baby does not normally vomit much.
- A sudden bout of loose poo which causes a red, burnt bottom. In older babies who are eating chunkier food, recycled food in the poo is normal.
- Hives. (Food is a common cause of hives but not the only one—drugs and infections also cause hives.)
- Swelling and redness around the mouth soon after the food is eaten.
- A red mottled rash covering the whole body appearing soon after the food is eaten.
- Seek advice if you are worried. A small number of babies need supervised diets because of food allergy and food intolerance (see page 384).

HERE'S A GUIDE TO FOLLOW ONCE YOUR BABY IS EATING WELL

(Offer up to two or more tablespoons three times a day)

Early morning	Breastfeed or bottle feed
Mid morning	Rice cereal with cooked fruit plus breast/bottle ('breakfast')
Early afternoon	Mashed vegies (add meat and chicken after a week or two) plus breast/bottle ('lunch')
Early evening	Yoghurt and fruit or mashed banana or try avocado/cottage cheese mashed or some nutritious chicken soup plus breast/bottle ('dinner')
Late evening	Breast feed or bottle feed (if needed)

The guide above offers four breastfeeds a day. **If you wish to breastfeed more, continue in the way that suits you and your baby.** Water in between meals is optional. Bottles and teats do not need disinfecting after the first six months.

Food allergies and food intolerance

An allergy is an over-reaction of the body's immune system to a foreign antibody, usually a protein. Allergic reactions are often caused by food proteins, but may also be caused by proteins in medication, chemicals, dust, smoke, insect bites, pet hair, pollutants or dust mite poo. Allergic reactions may be immediate, within two hours, or delayed, happening up to forty-eight hours after eating the food. Immediate reactions are more likely to be due to food allergy, delayed reactions to food intolerance.

Some food allergy facts

- The number of children experiencing allergic reactions to food is rising in western society. About 4–6 per cent of babies, toddlers and preschoolers now have true food allergy—egg, milk and peanut protein being the most common. Other foods include the protein in wheat, fish, soybean, nuts, sesame and berries.
- Allergy and intolerance to food is more common in young children because their immune system is not fully developed. Most children grow out of their allergies before starting school—less than 1 per cent of adults have food allergies, usually to peanuts, tree nuts and fish.
- No one is too sure why there is an increase in food allergies, but it is unlikely that it is due to food additives. Some experts think it is because young children are exposed to a much greater range of foods than previous generations were. Others think it may be because modern living and medicine has so dramatically decreased the number of infections in early childhood that instead of fighting off bacteria and viruses, babies' immune systems are now fighting off food proteins. And, as mentioned previously, there is some thought that delaying solids and restricting types of food in babies as has been past practice may be a factor increasing the incidence of allergic disease rather than delaying/preventing it. At the moment all these theories are speculative rather than definitive.

- Food allergy is strongly genetic. Babies who have one family member with asthma or eczema have a 20–40 per cent higher risk of developing food allergy; if there are two or more family members with allergies, the risk increases to 50–80 per cent.

Allergic reactions

NON LIFE-THREATENING REACTIONS

Reactions may be immediate (two hours or less), or delayed (up to forty-eight hours) after the food is ingested. Common allergic symptoms include swelling around the eyes and mouth, flushing of the skin, rashes and hives. Other symptoms include excessive mucus, abdominal cramps, diarrhoea and vomiting.

LIFE-THREATENING REACTIONS

A small number of older babies experience life-threatening reactions to food, peanuts and egg being the most common. This is called anaphylactic shock.

Signs and symptoms of anaphylactic shock—rapid onset

- Noisy/difficult breathing, wheeziness.
- Swelling of throat and tongue.
- Hoarse voice.
- Paleness, floppiness.
- Loss of consciousness.

In some cases anaphylaxis is preceded by the non life-threatening reactions described above. Most babies/toddlers who experience the lesser reaction to food do not go on to have a life-threatening event but a small number do, sometimes the next time the food is introduced.

Steps to follow for unexpected anaphylactic shock (when there is no adrenalin in the home)

1. Dial 000. State that a baby is having an *anaphylactic reaction* and requires rapid transport to hospital via an *intensive care ambulance*. Give full address, phone number and postcode.

2. Lie the baby flat and raise her feet (if possible).
3. Remove the food from her mouth.
4. If she stops breathing, commence heart–lung resuscitation. **N.B.:** Be prepared. Heart–lung resuscitation courses are available in your state from the Royal Lifesaving Society, the Red Cross and St John's Ambulance. Single-page charts of basic resuscitation techniques are available from children's hospitals in all states. Pin one on the back of the toilet door where you will have a constant reminder of what to do.

Tracking down the allergen

NON LIFE-THREATENING REACTIONS

- It can be difficult working out if a rash, runny nose or swelling around the mouth is due to food or a viral infection. During the first three years when babies and toddlers are being introduced to food, many have mild reactions which are not serious. It's simply a matter of waiting a month or two and trying again.
- Toddlers who react to peanuts have a higher chance of reacting to egg, milk or soy as well, although not always. As allergies develop over time the reaction may not occur until a baby or toddler has eaten the food a few times. And sometimes the food is fine in one form but not in another, for example yoghurt may be tolerated when milk is not.
- Laboratory tests are unreliable in diagnosing allergic reactions, although a skin prick test can be a guide. Sometimes the results of laboratory tests are used to inappropriately restrict diets in ways that may not protect against the allergy and may put the toddler's nutritional status at risk. Alternative tests such as hair and saliva testing and kinesiology are of no use—save your money.
- The most reliable way to test for food allergy remains excluding the food for a set period then re-introducing it—this is known as a food challenge. A food challenge may be done on its own or in conjunction with a laboratory test. A food challenge is not as simple as it sounds, because milk, egg or peanut proteins are found in many foods. Guidance from a dietitian, paediatrician or allergy specialist is advisable to find out exactly what foods should be avoided and what substitutes should be used in order to ensure a nutritionally adequate diet.

LIFE-THREATENING REACTIONS

- Identifying the cause of anaphylaxis is obviously very important. Often it appears to be self-evident (for example, it coincides with eating a peanut butter sandwich or an egg), nevertheless you will need to discuss it in detail with your doctor to exclude other conditions that can be confused with anaphylaxis. This may be followed by allergy testing (blood or skin prick) to help confirm or exclude *all* potential triggers.
- Long-term management includes referral to an allergy specialist, education on the avoidance of the trigger(s), which will include advice from a paediatric allergy dietitian, and provision of an Anaphylaxis Action Plan.

Minimising the risks of life-threatening allergic reactions—general guidelines for babies and toddlers

Although the number of babies and toddlers experiencing anaphylaxis triggered by food allergy is increasing, statistically the numbers remain small. Most babies and toddlers tolerate a wide range of food without disastrous consequences.

Because it is nutritionally advantageous for babies (in the second six months) and toddlers to be offered a varied diet, it is not advisable to strictly limit the diet of the general population because of the small possibility of a severe reaction. A life-threatening reaction to food (or medication, bee sting or anything else) is a horrifying event for parents. However, there has to be a balance between protecting vulnerable children while still ensuring that the vast majority of babies and toddlers do not have their diets unnecessarily restricted—which can lead to its own problems.

Here is a list of the latest specific food recommendations to reduce the risk or severity of allergy diseases in high-risk babies taken from the Australasian Society of Clinical Immunology and Allergy's position paper, August 2008:

- High-risk babies can be identified by their family histories; that is by the presence of allergies and asthma in their parents and siblings.
- Dietary restrictions in pregnancy are not recommended for any women, including those from families with high risks of allergies.
- Breastfeeding is recommended for all babies because of the undisputed multiple benefits of breastfeeding. The beneficial effects of exclusive

breastfeeding in relation to allergic disease remains uncertain however **current consensus recommends exclusive breastfeeding as first choice, for at least the first four to six months, for children at high risk of allergy.**

- It is no longer recommended that breastfeeding women avoid certain foods while they are breastfeeding regardless of whether their babies are at high risk of allergic disease.
- If breastfeeding is not possible, high-risk babies should have a partially hydrolysed (HA) cow's milk-based formula in preference to a conventional cow's milk-based formula. Soy and goat's milk formula are not recommended for the reduction of food allergy risk.
- Complementary foods should be delayed for at least four to six months. Interestingly, the allergy preventative effect of this strategy has only been demonstrated in high-risk babies and premature babies, not in the vast majority of babies who have no risk of allergic disease.
- There is no evidence that an elimination diet after the age of four to six months provides a protective effect from allergic disease although this needs additional information. In other words, eliminating dairy products, eggs, fish, berries, soy and sesame products has been shown to be of no benefit beyond six months.
- On the other hand, avoidance of peanuts, nuts and shellfish in high-risk babies (babies born into atopic families) for the first two to four years of life is not nutritionally harmful and *may* be beneficial.

Food intolerance

Food intolerance is more common than food allergy. Food intolerance describes an adverse reaction to chemicals in food. The chemicals may be those that are naturally occurring or additives in processed food.

Food intolerance can occur at any age and reactions usually depend on the amount of a particular food that has been eaten. A baby or toddler may show no symptoms after eating the food in small doses or a one-off dose, but may react after eating or drinking a larger amount following a build-up of the chemical(s) over time.

Commonly recognised symptoms of intolerance are not that different from allergy symptoms and include hives, rashes, itching, migraines, irritable bowel, asthma, nasal congestion, abdominal cramps and diarrhoea, lethargy and limb pains.

Diagnosing food intolerance can only be done by an elimination diet followed by a food challenge. This takes a long time and involves very restricted diets, a difficult feat for young children—not to mention their parents. Results can be ambiguous—it is often hard to know whether a reaction is due to the challenge or to chance.

A tricky business

The issue of allergy, food aversion and food intolerance becomes very confused in relation to babies and toddlers because they can't explain what is troubling them. Many older babies and all toddlers at some time or another suffer from the endless runny nose, the eternal cough, runny poo and mysterious rashes. Toddlers also tend to behave in unpredictable ways, eat like birds and poo like elephants—none of which are symptoms of anything other than being a toddler.

To add to the confusion, research into the relationship between food and common childhood ailments such as asthma, eczema and hay fever is conflicting and the success of dietary restrictions to alleviate these conditions varies tremendously between individuals. As these ailments tend to come and go spontaneously it can be very hard to work out how much of a part food plays compared to cigarette smoke, viral infections, dust and air pollution, pollen, dust mites, the weather and animals.

When problems are suspected it's important to get specialist help so that you are not eliminating, or in the case of babies delaying, the introduction of food unnecessarily.

Paid work and breastfeeding

Organising their return to the paid workforce and arranging the best care possible for their babies is a concern for many women around this time. Combining breastfeeding and paid work is part of this and many women are keen to continue breastfeeding, but unfortunately often feel that breastfeeding has to stop once paid work starts.

Because of this many women who intend returning to work during the first six months often feel discouraged from starting breastfeeding in the first place. Others think that even if they do start, it has to stop once paid work starts.

Many women are also under the impression that they have to either breastfeed or formula feed and that once formula is started they have to wean. This is not the case; breastfeeding and formula feeding can be combined. When you are unable to fully breastfeed, breastfeeding is great for you and your baby whenever you are together, which will still be a considerable amount of the time. Continuing part-time breastfeeding is also a comfort for many women, who find that leaving their babies to go back to work is a very emotional time.

On the following page is a guide so you can get organised before you start work. It can be used for expressed breastmilk or formula or a combination of both. If using formula use a cow's milk-based formula labelled 'suitable from birth'.

Here is some information to help you continue breastfeeding after you go back to your other job.

Get breastfeeding off to a good start

Try to delay returning to paid work until your baby is at least three months old as this gives your baby and your body time to learn to work together to get the milk flowing. It also gives you time to sort out feeding difficulties and overcome any problems.

Planning

Most things in life work a little better with some planning (you may note this seems to be my theme song). Combining paid work and breastfeeding is no exception. In the early days learning to express is of great benefit. You can get help with this from a midwife, a child and family health nurse or an Australian Breastfeeding Association counsellor. Once you have the idea practise as often as you can—it's like any skill, the more you do it the easier it becomes.

Approaches to breastfeeding and paid work vary depending on the age of your baby and the hours of paid work involved, so working out a plan to suit your particular needs *well ahead of time* is very useful. Your child and family health nurse or Australian Breastfeeding Association counsellor can help with this.

A cup instead of a bottle has many advantages, especially for babies who

WEEK ONE

Monday	Tuesday	Wednesday	Thursday	Friday
6am	6am	6am	6am	6am
breastfeed	breastfeed	breastfeed	breastfeed	breastfeed
10am	10am	10am	10am	10am
bottle feed	breastfeed	*bottle feed*	breastfeed	*bottle feed*
2pm	2pm	2pm	2pm	2pm
breastfeed	breastfeed	breastfeed	breastfeed	breastfeed
6pm	6pm	6pm	6pm	6pm
breastfeed	breastfeed	breastfeed	breastfeed	breastfeed

WEEK TWO

Monday	Tuesday	Wednesday	Thursday	Friday
6am	6am	6am	6am	6am
breastfeed	breastfeed	breastfeed	breastfeed	breastfeed
10am	10am	10am	10am	10am
bottle feed	*bottle feed*	*bottle feed*	*bottle feed*	*bottle feed*
2pm	2pm	2pm	2pm	2pm
breastfeed	breastfeed	breastfeed	breastfeed	breastfeed
6pm	6pm	6pm	6pm	6pm
breastfeed	breastfeed	breastfeed	breastfeed	breastfeed

WEEK THREE

Monday	Tuesday	Wednesday	Thursday	Friday
6am	6am	6am	6am	6am
breastfeed	breastfeed	breastfeed	breastfeed	breastfeed
10am	10am	10am	10am	10am
bottle feed	*bottle feed*	*bottle feed*	*bottle feed*	*bottle feed*
2pm	2pm	2pm	2pm	2pm
bottle feed	breastfeed	*bottle feed*	breastfeed	*bottle feed*
6pm	6pm	6pm	6pm	6pm
breastfeed	breastfeed	breastfeed	breastfeed	breastfeed

WEEK FOUR

Monday	Tuesday	Wednesday	Thursday	Friday
6am	6am	6am	6am	6am
breastfeed	breastfeed	breastfeed	breastfeed	breastfeed
10am	10am	10am	10am	10am
bottle feed	*bottle feed*	*bottle feed*	*bottle feed*	*bottle feed*
2pm	2pm	2pm	2pm	2pm
bottle feed	*bottle feed*	*bottle feed*	*bottle feed*	*bottle feed*
6pm	6pm	6pm	6pm	6pm
breastfeed	breastfeed	breastfeed	breastfeed	breastfeed

are reluctant to take bottles. This is possible at any age after four months, but is easier with older babies who are also eating food from a spoon. Starting a cup well before you go back to your other job means your baby is used to it and makes life easier for your carer. Give small amounts frequently throughout the day from a small cup.

Planning is important, but stay flexible as there is usually a period of trial and error during the first month.

Here are the choices

Having your baby looked after at work and being able to feed her there is the ideal way to combine breastfeeding and paid work. Unfortunately, moves to make this option a reality are very slow, so work-based care is only available to a limited number of women in Australia.

Apart from being able to go to your baby for feeds there are three other options.

- Replacing breastfeeds with expressed milk from a bottle when you are not there.
- Replacing breastfeeds with formula from a bottle when you are not there.
- Replacing breastfeeds with food from a spoon and a cup—a possibility from six months onwards. (See Starting new food, page 370.)

OPTION 1

Once your breastfeeding is going well (six to nine weeks) you can replace one of your breastfeeds with a bottle of expressed milk. You will need to express 120–150ml, depending on the size of your baby and her appetite. This amount increases quite quickly as your baby grows. By three months she will need 150–210ml in each bottle. If your partner gives the replacement bottle it leaves you free to express at the time of the missed feed. Starting a regime of expressing and giving one bottle a day well ahead of returning to your other job gives you a chance to learn how to express and helps your baby get used to a bottle. Once you are in a routine with one feed, add another so your baby has two bottles of expressed milk and about four breastfeeds every twenty-four hours. Continue this schedule after you return to work when the bottles of expressed milk are given by your babysitter.

Ideally, to maintain your supply you should express once or twice at work, store the milk in a clean container in a fridge and bring it home with you in a cold storage pack. If it is not possible for you to do this, you will need to express and store the milk during the time you are not at work. This can be done after a feed, between feeds or any time your supply is abundant. If there is neither the time nor facilities to express and store milk while you are at work, you will still need to express once or twice a day for comfort for a week or two until your breasts adjust to missing feeds. Unfortunately in many workplaces the only room to do this in is the women's toilet.

Problems arise with this option either because some women can't express or because the amount they are able to express starts to dwindle after being back at work for a while. It's important to remember an inability to express does not mean you have a low supply; your baby will still get plenty when she goes to the breast. Nevertheless, not being able to express much leads you to option two.

OPTION 2

If you decide to use formula instead of breastmilk before you go back to work it's a good idea to start one bottle of formula a day, then to increase the bottles slowly until your baby is having the number of bottles a day that she will be having once you are back at work. If you are going back full-time you need to start this about three or four weeks before you start work in order to give your breasts time to adjust. The guide on page 391 will help you to organise this and can be used for expressed breastmilk or formula or a combination of both.

If you are already back at work and the amount you are expressing is diminishing, start making up the difference by leaving bottles of formula with your carer as well as any expressed breastmilk you have.

In order to keep your milk flowing, give your baby extra feeds at weekends and in the evenings. Try not to give any more formula than is necessary when you are around to feed as an increase in formula can result in a decrease in breastmilk. Ask your carer to give your baby her last bottle well before you pick her up so she is ready to go straight to the breast as soon as you both get home. A bottle of water will often keep your baby happy until you arrive.

OPTION 3

Babies who start food from a spoon from six months and like it can have food instead of the breast twice a day while you are at work once they are eating well. Fluids such as expressed breastmilk or formula can be given from a cup as well as a little diluted juice for variety. The earliest, realistic age this is a possibility is from about six months as food can only be introduced at the baby's pace and it takes about six weeks for most babies to learn to drink a reasonable amount from a cup. If the time frame fits your return to paid work it's a much gentler option than forcing your baby to take a bottle.

FOR MORE INFORMATION

Chapter 8: Breastfeeding Your Baby After the First Two Weeks *(how to express and store breastmilk, page 114; low supply, page 126; baby won't take a bottle page 150)*

Chapter 7: Bottle Feeding Your Baby For the First Two Weeks *(What's in formula? page 96; equipment, page 101; care of bottles and teats, page 101)*

Chapter 16: For Parents *(Tips for grandparents, page 332; conflicting advice, page 330)*

Chapter 14: Sleeping and Waking in the First Six Months *('sleeping through', page 266)*

Chapter 15: The Crying Baby *(reflux heartburn, page 296; and vomiting, page 295)*

Chapter 24: Feeding Your Baby, page 443

Chapter 19

Common Worries and Queries

Bathing

At some stage between three and six months your baby will grow out of the baby bath and will need to be bathed in your bath. Moving into the big bath goes smoothly for most babies who enjoy the added space and freedom, but a few are not keen. If your baby is like this, take it slowly and gently—bathing her in the baby bath in the big bath or perhaps sharing a bath with her might help her get used to the idea.

Bathing babies in the big bath when they can't sit on their own is not great for adult backs, so if you have a back problem it may be worth investing in a baby bath seat which provides support for your baby until she sits well on her own. *Never* leave your baby unattended while she is in a baby bath seat for any reason as babies have slipped out of them and drowned. If the phone rings take her with you. If you are still using baby bath lotion and it is a drain on your resources, stop using it as it is unnecessary. Avoid bubble bath solutions as they do cause problems for some babies' skin—mild soap and water is fine.

Swimming

Parents often wonder when it is okay to take their baby swimming. Full-term healthy babies can start going for a swim any time after three months.

A few guidelines follow:

- Make sure your baby is well-protected from the sun (see page 210).
- Cold water frightens babies, so test the water yourself first; it should be comfortable.
- Sadly, many of our cities' beaches and natural pools are often polluted so avoid them following heavy rain or if you have any concerns at all about the cleanliness of the water.
- Limit the time to thirty minutes or less to avoid sun damage and over-chilling.
- Inflatable tubes and water wings are not safety devices and do not replace adult supervision. With babies all water activities should be on a one-to-one basis with a responsible adult. Never leave your baby with an older child.
- Be aware that while water play and swimming lessons give babies and toddlers confidence and enjoyment of water they do not give them skills that prevent them from drowning even if they learn to float and dog paddle from a young age.

EARLY CHILDHOOD DROWNING PREVENTION INVOLVES:

Effective, well-maintained fences around swimming pools: Evidence shows that 50 per cent of fences are not properly maintained and that gates are frequently left open and/or have faulty self-closing/locking mechanisms.

Supervision: Lack of parental supervision has been identified as one of the biggest causes of childhood drowning.

Swimming lessons: While teaching babies/toddlers/pre-schoolers to swim is not a guarantee against drowning it is an important drowning prevention strategy. When toddlers/children who have little or no experience of water go under they panic and freeze. If they are used to how it feels being under water they don't panic and have more chance of helping themselves in dangerous situations. Even a minute can make a dramatic difference.

Resuscitation: Prompt, effective resuscitation saves lives. Heart–lung resuscitation courses are available in every state from the Royal Lifesaving Society, the Red Cross and St John Ambulance. Parents (and pool owners) who learn and regularly update resuscitation skills are taking an important step in the prevention of death from drowning in the under-fives. Resuscitation along with the fencing of swimming pools is regarded by many experts to be the two highest drowning preventative measures in this age group.

Formal baby swimming classes

Nowadays it is widely accepted that while the first two to three years is an ideal time for babies and toddlers to learn to relax and be comfortable in the water and ultimately to swim it must be done gently, by degrees, at their own pace.

WHAT IS THE OPTIMUM EARLIEST AGE TO LEARN TO SWIM?

Babies arrive already swimming thanks to their nine months living in the fluid world of the womb, so introducing them back into water soon after birth means they can re-experience the weightless, protective world they were in before they were born. This can be done by getting into a deep bath with your baby and, by using the flannel and a cup, gradually get her used to the sensation of water on her head and face. Early bath time experiences build a good foundation for starting a structured program when they are six to twelve months old.

UNDER WHAT CONDITIONS SHOULD SWIMMING LESSONS TAKE PLACE?

It is important to make sure the baby is happy and comfortable in the water, which means the parent has to be happy and comfortable as well. The water needs to be warm—at least 32°C, still, properly treated and circulated. Unfortunately babies with eczema cannot swim in chlorinated water as the drying effect makes their eczema worse.

It is crucial that group baby/parent classes are conducted by experienced, well-trained teachers in a caring environment where individual differences are respected and lessons are geared to the developmental ages of the babies/toddlers.

SHOULD BABY/TODDLER SWIMMING CLASSES ALWAYS BE ONE-ON-ONE WITH A PARENT?

Definitely, up until at least three years of age. Classes should have a maximum of six. It's just as important for parents to spend time in the water and learn how to handle their babies safely and confidently in the water as it is for the babies to become familiar with and enjoy the water.

WHAT ARE THE MAIN AIMS OF TEACHING BABIES/TODDLERS TO 'SWIM'?

- To learn to love and enjoy the water as a familiar environment whether it be in the bath, under the shower or in a pool, and in the process (at their own pace) develop balance, co-ordination and strength in and under the water in a similar way that babies move from sitting to crawling to walking on land.
- Learning to swim and feel confident in the water is a core part of human development especially in a country like Australia where the climate and easy access to the ocean, rivers and pools means water is very much part of our culture. Swimming helps keep us fit and healthy, is a great social bond, and a source of relaxation and pleasure that lasts all our lives.
- During the baby and toddler years the one-on-one skin contact in the water between the mother or father and baby is close and bonding. It also helps promote good sleep and a healthy appetite—a potential boon in the toddler years when both these areas can be problematic.
- Water safety is a big issue in Australia. Safety is a often a motivating factor for parents in teaching the under-threes to swim and while water skills in this age group may contribute to averting a catastrophe, the ability to float or 'swim' is not a guarantee against drowning. It is crucial that parents are aware of all drowning prevention strategies—see above.

HOW MANY TIMES A WEEK SHOULD BABIES/TODDLERS GO INTO THE WATER?

Ideally, weekly is good. As learning to swim is a long term process it is something that needs to be done consistently to maintain the baby/toddler's comfortable feeling of being in and under the water. When there is a long break, for example, because of illness or during the winter months, parents may find they have to start familiarising their toddler with water all over again.

WHAT ABOUT PARENTS WHO ARE FEELING PRESSURED TO RUSH THEIR UNDER-THREES INTO FORMAL SWIMMING CLASSES ON A REGULAR BASIS?
Often this is not possible for a range of reasons which include illness and, for many families, the cost factor.

Do what you can in the bath, in the wading pool and, as often as possible, swimming one-on-one with your baby/toddler in a pool.

Make it fun, avoid pressure and force.

A little more about routines

I am returning to this because I know it is something that occupies lots of mothers' thoughts.

A reminder—if you are a routine person, don't despair if things are still a trifle chaotic. Once your baby is sleeping all night or most of the night without waking you and eating three meals a day, your days will become much more predictable. This happens between six and nine months for many mothers and babies.

You might find your days are in some sort of pattern now without you realising it. Feeding and sleeping times often vary from day to day. That's to be expected, but if you feel like it, write down your schedule over a weekly period and you will probably find a predictable pattern is emerging. 'Strict' routines are difficult to maintain. Trying to keep to one means structuring your life exactly around the baby's schedule, which limits your movements and usually means putting up with an intolerable amount of baby crying for no constructive purpose when she wakes early for a feed or suddenly varies her sleep patterns. Illness, holidays, moving house or visitors can also play havoc with strict routines.

Here's a flexible guide *if you are looking for one.*

5 AM TO 8 AM: Baby wakes. Breastfeed or bottle. Stays up for about an hour. Bath may be here. Put to sleep—may sleep half an hour to two hours.

9 AM TO 12 NOON: Breastfeed or bottle plus food from a spoon if appropriate. Bath may be here. Up for about an hour. Put to sleep or go out. Baby may sleep half an hour to two hours.

1 PM TO 4 PM: Breastfeed or bottle plus food from a spoon if appropriate. Baby may only sleep for a short period. Awake the remainder of the time. This may be a whingy, grizzly part of the day. Go for a walk.

5 PM TO 7 PM: Bath may be here. Breastfeed or bottle and/or other food if appropriate. Avoid letting your baby have a late 'catnap' if you can as this interferes with bedtime.

7 PM TO 8 PM: Bedtime. Try to keep bedtime regular and consistent regardless what happens the rest of the day. Total sleeping in the day varies from one to four hours. A number of babies only ever catnap. It is usually very difficult to 'make' babies who catnap in the day sleep more or longer. (See page 497 for more on daytime sleeping.)

If some sort of pattern is important to you, follow a similar plan each day and don't keep radically changing the times you feed, bath and put your baby to sleep but stay flexible, because she might radically change what she does from time to time. The main aim is to have a nice time with your baby so don't do anything that doesn't suit your lifestyle or nature.

The crying baby

The majority of crying, unsettled babies are much happier by three to four months. Unfortunately a number of otherwise healthy babies stay the same, which is distressing for the baby and demoralising and exhausting for the parents. Most of the time a definite cause is never found. Living with the baby the way she is until she gets more used to the world is usually the only option. Continued support from a sympathetic health professional you can talk to and uncritical friendship from other parents helps through the difficult times.

If your baby doesn't sleep much during the day go out as much as possible and try to be with people who care about you as much as you can so you are not on your own.

A few babies stay distressed for the first year, but the overwhelming majority are much happier and quite different little people by the time they are six months old.

Sudden crying episodes or a sudden change in behaviour

Babies, like all of us, don't stay the same day in and day out. Sudden erratic changes are quite common. 'Bad' days, sometimes weeks, continue to happen. Most of the time it is difficult to know exactly why the baby is behaving differently. Sometimes it might be because of one of the following:

- **An impending infection:** This may be a head cold and involve an ear infection, a sore throat or a tummy bug which causes diarrhoea and vomiting. Ear infections are not common under six months, but it's always worth having your baby's ears checked if she suddenly starts crying a lot and sleeping less. If the unhappiness is accompanied by a high fever and no other symptoms the urine should be tested. A cross baby may signal a dose of the measles, rubella or chicken pox—not common in the first year, but can happen.
- **Reflux heartburn:** This can be a cause of distress for babies after the first three months when previously it wasn't a problem. Reflux heartburn is always difficult to diagnose and, as in the first three months. probably diagnosed far more frequently than it actually occurs. Sometimes medication for reflux heartburn helps babies who suddenly become unsettled when other causes can't be found.
- **Change in diet:** Starting new food does upset some babies, even when it's only bland old rice cereal, so it might be worth stopping the food for a week if the change in behaviour coincided with starting new food. Go back to milk only and see what happens.
- **Hunger:** Some babies suddenly become irritated or upset if they are hungry. Check your baby's weight. More food might be needed.
- **No obvious cause:** When there's no obvious cause to 'fix' you will probably find your baby settles again in a short time without you doing anything. Sometimes it's boredom (try to go out more), over-tiredness (try staying in more) or some disruption in the home (visitors, moving house or building an extension).

Growing teeth

Many people, of course, will tell you your baby is 'teething' when she is unsettled. 'Teething' is an explanation which supplies a reason at times when it's difficult to know if anything is wrong and replaces 'colic' once babies are over three months old. As babies grow twenty teeth some time in their first three years, there are always going to be times when the emergence of a tooth coincides with developmental changes, normal strange baby habits, nappy rash and illness.

I must admit I'm sometimes tempted to take a less direct approach to the teething issue as I am aware my beliefs seem to upset, even anger, many parents, which is not my intention. I completely understand that on an individual basis it is reasonable to blame teeth for the myriad and often mysterious behavioural, medical and developmental events that come along in the first three years. For example, it is reasonable to see an emerging tooth as a cause of, let's say, diarrhoea and nappy rash if the arrival of a tooth coincides with an attack of diarrhoea. And even more so if your perception is that the arrival of a tooth coincides with *every* attack of diarrhoea. And given that many health professionals have contradicting views to mine, that traditionally teething as the cause of a multitude of baby/toddler problems is an ingrained belief that goes back for centuries, and that it is impossible to prove anything conclusive by research, then I can understand why it is so hard to shift both health professionals and parents on this.

My opinion is based on looking at and hearing about every facet of babies' and toddlers' lives for twenty-five years. During this time I always endeavoured to avoid fobbing mothers off with simplistic answers. For example, 'just let him cry'; 'give him food—that will make him sleep'; 'it's teething'; and so on. It became apparent to me after several years that 'teething' as a reason and/or a solution to baby and toddler problems was a simplistic response which rarely—if ever in my experience—solved the problem. Obviously just shrugging and saying 'I don't believe in teething' is also a fobbing off, unhelpful, simplistic response, which is why I go to some length to explain why I think the way I do and provide other reasons for the behaviours, illnesses or strange activities during these years. It has never been my intention to somehow imply parents are foolish people who don't know what they are talking about, which seems to be how my message is interpreted at times. I acknowledge that there may be occasions, after everything else is ruled out, that 'teething' might be contributing to the concern, however I believe it is helpful to think broadly about this and to keep an open mind. If you are interested in my ideas on teething it's

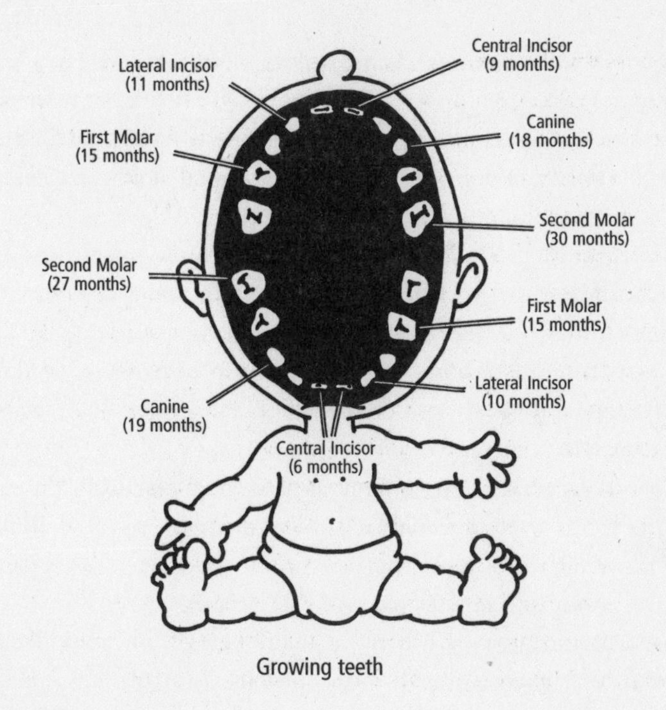

Growing teeth

more helpful to read all that follows rather than just taking bits out of context so you get the whole picture.

Let's look at the growing of teeth.

The first tooth appears some time between fourteen weeks and sixteen months of age. It announces its presence by simply appearing—sometimes a small lump comes first. No secret signs heralding the arrival of a tooth exist, so a health professional cannot peer at a toothless gum and announce that a tooth will or won't appear next week! After the first tooth arrives, others pop up at varying intervals. The central bottom teeth are usually the first to appear and while most teeth do emerge in a set sequence it is not at all unusual for some babies' teeth to appear out of sequence. For example, sometimes the top side teeth come before the top central teeth which gives a gleeful 'Dracula' appearance until the top central teeth appear. Occasionally the top central teeth arrive before the bottom central teeth.

The first twenty teeth arrive during the first two-and-a-half years. They are lost and replaced by thirty-two permanent teeth between the ages of six and twenty years.

Growing and losing teeth is normal for all humans and happens on and off for twenty years or longer. Several hundred years ago the emergence of teeth in babies was frequently given as a cause of death. At the turn of the twentieth century 'dentition' appeared in dental textbooks as a cause of epilepsy. Science has made us realise how illogical these notions are, but to a lesser degree we are still being just as illogical. When seven- and eight-year-old children are growing teeth (some teeth at this age growing for the first time) scant attention is paid. 'Teething' is never a suggested cause for illness or behaviour changes in this age group because older children can communicate and have more predictable behaviour, so it is easier to identify exactly what the problem is.

I understand that on an individual basis there are many times when an emerging tooth coincides with a bad day or night, a nappy rash or an illness, but overall there are many more times when 'teething' is blamed for a variety of conditions and the tooth never arrives.

After observing many babies for many years I am convinced that the perception that growing teeth causes problems in babies is confused with normal development and illnesses caused by other things. While this may not be a popular approach I think it is more useful for parents to understand the many more rational reasons relating to their baby's development, behaviour and health than simply fobbing it all off as 'teething'. 'Teething' also gives rise to the overuse of medications and gels for gums which are sometimes used for months on end waiting for the appearance of the elusive tooth.

Growing teeth does not cause a **fever, diarrhoea, colds, coughs, ear infections, smelly urine or nappy rash**. Persisting with these myths may mean treatment is delayed or a serious illness is not diagnosed.

Funny baby habits such as pulling at ears and constantly putting fists in the mouth are developmental and part of a baby's growing intense curiosity with her own body. I observe or hear about babies doing these things all the time. Most of the time it is not in conjunction with growing a tooth; when it is, I suspect it is a coincidence.

Red cheeks appear a lot and are due to sun, wind, saliva and cheeks constantly rubbing on clothes and sheets. Baby cheeks have sensitive skin, stick out a lot and are easily affected by these things.

Dribbling is a constant feature of babyhood from three months to eighteen months or longer. Saliva first appears around three months in copious amounts and until babies learn to swallow their saliva the dribbling continues regardless of the growing of teeth.

Sleep problems are not caused by teeth emerging and once your baby is over six months if her sleep patterns are causing distress for the family constantly blaming teeth does not solve the problem.

Does teething cause babies discomfort? Certainly not for three months before they are visible! Nor do they cause pain by 'moving around under the gum'. An uncomfortable sensation just before the tooth emerges may worry some babies and if you decide an emerging tooth is causing a problem for your baby, a **one-off** dose of paracetamol is the safest medication to use. If your baby is very distressed and behaving in an unusual way, never assume the problem is simply teething. Look further and if necessary seek a second opinion.

Other teeth titbits

A bluish swelling is often present on the gum when a tooth is emerging. This is normal and not painful for the baby.

Growing teeth is not a developmental milestone and the stage at which they appear has nothing to do with a baby's future intelligence.

Babies do not need teeth for eating a variety of food, for example bread, rusks, fruit, cheese and so on.

Care of teeth

Currently in Australia 40 per cent of children develop avoidable dental caries before their sixth birthday. Up to 8 per cent of these children have serious decay that requires treatment under general anaesthesia.

There are rare genetic conditions, medications and some illnesses that decrease resistance to decay, but most children start out with the potential to have strong and healthy teeth and gums for the rest of their lives.

FOUR INTERACTING FACTORS CAN AFFECT THIS POTENTIAL

1. **An individual's ability to resist decay:** The predisposition of individuals to tooth decay varies. We all know individuals with perfect teeth who eat rubbish, never floss and rarely go near dentists. Similarly some toddlers will not get decay despite lack of teeth cleaning, endless bottles

and sugary snacks. However, it is best not to rely solely on genetic inheritance as it is unknown exactly who these individuals are or why their teeth are unaffected. And—they are in the minority. On the bright side, regardless of the genetic ability to resist decay it is highly unlikely that a toddler will get caries if the next three factors are in place.

2. **The dietary risk factor:** The first line of defence against decay is attention to diet, especially during the toddler years when effective teeth cleaning can be difficult and when prolonged use of bottles is so prevalent.

   Sugar is the main offender. Remember, sugar is sugar whether it is brown, 'natural' (whatever that means), honey or white. Other forms of sugar are found in milk—cow's milk (plain or flavoured) and formula—soy liquid and fruit juice. Dummies dipped in sweet things or sucked by parents before being placed into the baby or toddler's mouth can also cause decay.

   Bottles of anything other than water beyond the first year are a potential cause of tooth decay, especially when they are used through the night or to get the baby/toddler to go to sleep; the longer they continue the greater the risk. There are no nutritional reasons to continue bottles after the first year unless a baby has medical or developmental problems. Constant sipping of juice and milk drinks from spout cups and straws throughout the day also increases the risk of black teeth. Drinks of anything other than water are best given in one sitting.

BREASTFEEDING AND TOOTH DECAY

This is a vexed issue. Research suggests that there is no decay risk from overnight breastfeeding beyond the first year because the milk is taken right into the back of the throat and so doesn't pool around the teeth. As well, the components of breastmilk are thought to protect against decay to some extent. Claims are also made that tooth decay is unknown in traditional societies where babies are breastfed for at least three years. (Do we know though, what goes on at night?) Some breastfeeding researchers believe that when tooth decay occurs in breastfed toddlers it is because of other dietary factors and/or an inherent problem in a small number of individual toddlers' teeth. Statistically there is a much lower risk of decay from breastfeeding overnight than drinking bottles of milk or juice overnight, however, paediatric dentists who treat the problem are adamant that constant breastfeeding overnight much beyond the first year is a decay risk. Taking everything into consideration, I believe there *is* a small decay risk that parents should be aware of if they are to be fully informed.

3. **The teeth cleaning factor:** Baby teeth are important and have many functions. Here are some good reasons why it's important to look after them:

- Baby teeth help the face and jaw develop properly.
- Decayed teeth are unattractive, painful and cause smelly breath. As children grow older they become aware of this.
- Severe infections can cause dental abscesses and affect a child's general health.
- Toddlers and preschoolers need healthy teeth for biting and chewing efficiently. Bad teeth can limit food intake and if severe enough, slow growth.
- Healthy teeth are important for making the correct sounds in speech.
- Baby teeth hold the correct space for the permanent teeth to erupt later as replacements.

CLEANING BABY AND TODDLER TEETH

- Start cleaning your baby's mouth even before the teeth arrive with a washer in the bath.
- Once a few teeth arrive, start using a brush—use a small toothbrush with soft bristles. Toothpaste is not needed until around two years of age.
- It is recommended that children aged between two and six use special low-fluoride toothpaste. Once they can spit, adult-strength fluoride toothpaste can be used.
- Apply a thin, pea-sized amount of toothpaste onto the brush.
- Conduct the teeth cleaning in a brightly lit place.
- Position yourself behind your toddler, standing or sitting, whichever you prefer. This way she can't get away when you put the toothbrush in her mouth.
- Your free hand can be used to support your toddler's head or jaw or to open the lips for better access. It's a good idea to check for hidden decay (a brown line which may be faint at first) by lifting the top lip regularly,

especially if she is still sucking bottles of milk or breastfeeding throughout the night.

- Encourage your toddler to look up at you and to 'open up'.
- Each tooth has five surfaces—a front, back, two sides and a top. The aim is to clean each surface thoroughly. Avoid 'scrubbing'. Use a firm, brushing motion to remove the food.
- Start with the back teeth as with a struggling toddler you may have trouble doing a thorough job. The back teeth remain until age ten to twelve so they need priority.
- Brush twice a day once your toddler is happy to comply. Otherwise aim for every day. Missing a day occasionally is acceptable.
- Regular flossing is advised once the sides of the teeth touch.
- Be prepared to be the main tooth-brusher for quite a few years. Children do not have the manual dexterity to clean their own teeth properly until they are around eight to ten years old. It is recommended that parents make a point of brushing and flossing their children's teeth once a day until that age.

4. **The fluoride factor:** Fluoride protects against tooth decay bacteria, strengthens tooth enamel and minimises the risk of decay. In many areas of Australia fluoride is added to the water supply and the frequency of tooth decay in children in those areas has decreased dramatically over the last thirty years, although as noted there has been an increase again in the last few years owing to other factors.

   If you live in an unfluoridated area or use a water purifier (some water purifiers eliminate all fluoride, others filter out a variable amount) it is beneficial to give a fluoride supplement. For children under four this is best done via the children's low-dose fluoridated toothpaste mentioned above. Once they are over four, check with your dentist about the use of a fluoride tablets or drops. It is important to know the status of your water supply before giving tablets or drops as too much fluoride can cause permanent tooth discolouration.

VISITING THE DENTIST

The first visit to the dentist is recommended at the end of the first year. This may seem over the top to many people, but there is strong evidence that a session with a dentist at this time is good preventative dental care. The dentist will discuss all issues of diet, brushing, fluoride, feeding and first aid for trauma. In Australia this is still a relatively new concept and you may find some dentists are bewildered by a baby visit and are unsure of what information should be covered. Look for a paediatric dentist or a dentist with an interest in paediatric dentistry.

Blood in vomit

Occasionally a breastfed baby damages the nipple after teeth arrive. The nipple bleeds so she swallows a little blood which may then appear when she regurgitates. This is usually only a temporary problem—I have included it because it can cause a moment of panic to suddenly see blood in a baby's vomit.

Thumb-sucking

Thumb-sucking is a normal activity for babies—many do it while in the womb. Thumb-sucking has a few advantages over dummies. Skin is nicer to suck than silicone or rubber, the baby can make her own decisions about when to use her thumb and thumb-sucking doesn't cause sleep problems because babies don't lose their thumbs in the night. Some parents worry about thumb-sucking because they don't like the look of older children sucking their thumbs, they see thumb-sucking as a sign of stress, thumb-sucking in older babies sometimes causes skin irritation on the thumb and of course there's the worry about the orthodontic bill.

Thumb-sucking does not indicate stress and has no effect on a baby's progress if the thumb-sucking continues throughout early childhood. Nor does it affect teeth until the permanent teeth are through, at which time the 10 per cent of children who continue thumb-sucking push their teeth up and out and orthodontics may be needed. I can't help noticing how many children have orthodontic treatment anyway whether they were thumb-suckers or not, so it's not an issue I see as highly significant. If your baby is a thumb-sucker there's not a lot you can do about it. Trying to get thumb-sucking babies to take dummies instead is generally stressful and unsuccessful.

Giving a dummy from birth to avoid thumb-sucking because 'you can throw the dummy away' may introduce your baby to a habit you find as unattractive as thumb-sucking, which is just as hard to break, may interfere with breastfeeding and causes sleep problems to boot. Lots of babies use neither.

If your baby develops a skin irritation on her thumb, try using a tiny dab of diluted Povidone-iodine Sore Throat Gargle on the affected area three times a day.

Some babies are so enamoured of their thumbs they suck them while they eat. This is a harmless habit which may continue into the second year.

More about poo

Poo is a fascinating topic for those involved with babies and promotes endless discussion at each age and stage.

A reminder about breastfed babies: Breastfed babies of this age who are having no other food or milk may go up to three weeks without doing a poo. When they go it will be a very large, soft one—everywhere! They may also do very smelly farts in between poos. You do not have to do anything to make your baby poo, but if you feel better seeing a poo a little more often, try a little diluted prune juice or cooled, boiled water to hasten up the process.

Constipation: Bottle-fed babies and breastfed babies who are eating other food will do firmer poo, which may be a variety of colours. Breastfed babies often get a little constipated when they first start food from a spoon. It is normal for babies to grunt and groan and go red in the face when they do a poo. If your baby's poo gets hard and she gets very distressed beyond the normal grunting, here are a few suggestions:

- Stop banana for a while.
- Stop rice cereal for a while—cooked pureed pears or ripe mashed pawpaw help.
- Increase fluids (extra breastfeeds, water, and in this case fruit juice is helpful).
- Try diluted prune juice. If your baby doesn't drink from a bottle put the prune juice in with her cereal or try prune juice and yoghurt.

- A little added sugar in her cooked fruit or on her cereal helps.
- When your baby is trying to do a poo and it seems difficult, lie her on her back and bend her knees towards her stomach gently for two minutes. Repeat a few times if necessary.

You should not have to resort to medication and suppositories unless the constipation is extreme; the use of these things should be limited to a one-off. Constant constipation that can't be helped by diet needs a trip to a paediatrician.

Recycled food in the poo: Once babies are eating a wide variety of food quite a lot of food appears in the poo in its original state, so don't be amazed to see carrots, crusts or spinach. This is quite normal—no need to change the diet.

Ammonia-smelling urine

Mothers are often amazed at how smelly their babies' urine becomes as their babies grow; this is especially noticeable the first nappy change after a long sleep. As long as your baby is otherwise well and the urine is pale and straw-coloured (although a little darker and concentrated first thing in the morning), there is nothing to worry about. Naturally, if you are at all worried, see your family doctor.

Skin things

Baby rashes in the first three months tend to be a normal response to adjusting to wearing clothes and life outside the womb and generally need no treatment. After three months, rashes and skin things are either caused by medical conditions or because of contact dermatitis caused by the baby's natural secretions coming in contact with her fine baby skin—for example, saliva, urine, sweat or tears—and may need treatment. Let's look at the most common ones.

Eczema

Babies with eczema have dry, easily irritated skin.

WHAT CAUSES ECZEMA?

The exact cause of eczema is still unknown. It is often believed that eczema is due to an allergy and if the allergy can be identified and removed the eczema will be cured. In fact, eczema caused by allergy is rare. Babies who have eczema may also have allergies which give them different symptoms. It is usually not possible to cure eczema by removing a specific substance.

There is a strong hereditary component—when there is a family history of allergic conditions such as asthma and hay fever a toddler has a much higher chance of getting eczema, but one toddler in five who has eczema has no family history of allergies.

Most babies and toddlers outgrow their eczema by age five.

WHAT DOES ECZEMA LOOK LIKE?

Eczema appears as a dry rash, which may become red, moist and itchy. Some areas of the skin can become inflamed and weepy. Depending on the severity it can appear anywhere on the body. Particularly affected areas are the faces of babies and the fronts of the knees and ankles and inside of the wrists of toddlers. It tends not to appear in babyhood until after the first three months. In some babies and toddlers the whole of the body is affected.

DEGREE OF DISCOMFORT

Eczema can be mild, moderate or severe. The more severe, the more widespread and itchy it becomes.

Mild eczema often presents as a round, dry patch which is often confused with a ringworm infection. A ringworm infection, however, has to come from somewhere and if your baby has not been in contact with a person or an animal with ringworm the round dry patches are more likely to be mild eczema.

TREATMENT

The main line of treatment is the use of moisturisers to keep the skin supple and to avoid common skin irritants (see over page). Sorbolene with 10 per cent glycerine is inexpensive and effective, but sometimes stings if the skin is raw. It is available in pharmacies and supermarkets in big tubs. Apply as often as you can, at least twice a day, especially after the bath and at night before bed.

Alternatives such as Eucerin ointment, bath oils or Alpha Keri are suitable if the sorbolene and glycerine irritates or stings the skin. It is important not to use disinfectant preparations on eczema as this will irritate the skin further.

Occasionally a mild cortisone ointment will be needed. This is best used twice a day on the affected areas.

Advice from a dermatologist is advisable for more severe eczema as the treatment is more complicated. Sometimes the skin becomes infected and needs oral antibiotic treatment and/or a period of time in hospital with wet dressings to bring it under control.

Common skin irritants for babies with eczema

- Sand.
- Soap, detergent and bubble baths. Sorbelene and glycerine or aqueous cream is a good soap substitute.
- Perfumed and medicated products, wool and acrylic materials found in clothes, carpets, furniture and car seat covers.
- Chlorinated swimming pools.
- Dry air (air-conditioning and heating).
- Increased sweating due to heat or exercise.
- Occasionally, food.

THE RELATIONSHIP BETWEEN FOOD AND ECZEMA

Research into the relationship between food and eczema is conflicting and the success of dietary measures varies tremendously with individual toddlers. When they work, the eczema is improved but not cured. Before radically altering your toddler's diet, it is a good idea to talk to a paediatric dietitian to make sure the diet is adequate for proper growth.

COMPLICATIONS

Babies with eczema should be kept away from people with cold sores as they are particularly susceptible to the cold sore virus. These babies are also more prone to the contact dermatitis lots of toddlers get from time to time which causes nappy rashes; red, chapped cheeks; rashes around the mouth and eyes; cracking behind the ears; and red, moist areas under the chin.

See page 387—Minimising the risks of life-threatening allergic reactions—for information in relation to food allergies, for example peanuts, and eczema.

Red cheeks

Red cheeks are very common in babies and toddlers until dribbling stops and their cheeks stop constantly coming into contact with clothes and food. Baby cheeks are very soft and chubby and stick out so they catch the wind and sun easily, becoming dry and chapped especially in winter. Red cheeks (or sometimes only one red cheek) are not related to ear infections, 'teething' or diet, although once the cheeks are red and dry, acidic food such as oranges may irritate them further.

Red cheeks are often hard to clear up as the irritants can't be removed but they don't seem to bother babies at all. Try to keep the skin around the area dry, apply sorbolene and glycerine whenever you can (a tricky job—babies don't like it much) and last thing before bed apply a soothing barrier cream. A mild cortisone ointment helps if the redness is very severe. Ointment always works better than cream on moist areas.

Rash around the mouth

Again, very common and caused by saliva, milk and food being constantly on the baby's face. Using a dummy contributes as the fluid gets trapped under the plastic shield which surrounds the teat. Certain food may make the rash worse (orange juice, tomatoes, eggs or yoghurt). This is a frustrating rash as it's often difficult to clear completely until the baby stops dribbling.

Try to keep the area as dry as possible. Apply a soothing barrier cream at night. Experiment a little with food—don't get too uptight about food or you may find your baby's diet is very restricted and the rash is still there anyway.

If this rash gets really bad, check with your family doctor or a skin specialist to make sure there is no underlying bacterial infection (from a snotty nose) which needs antibiotic treatment. If not, the only way to clear it is to apply a mild cortisone ointment (not cream) regularly. This takes some time to clear it but it does eventually.

Red under chin

Another maintenance problem until your baby holds her chin out from her neck and stops dribbling (around twelve months). Here's how to look after it:

Always dry well under your baby's chin. To do this, lie your baby down and firmly but gently pull her chin away from her neck. After you have dried the area apply some zinc and starch powder with your fingers under the chin from ear to ear. The zinc and starch powder absorbs moisture and separates the skin surfaces. The more often you can apply it the better the results, so see if you can do it most nappy change times when you are at home. Your baby might not like it much at first, but she will get used to it quickly.

If the area becomes very inflamed, shiny and weepy, see your family doctor. A combination of a mild cortisone and anti-fungal ointment will clear it. Afterwards, it is better to continue to use the zinc and starch powder. Diet makes no difference to this rash.

Cracking behind ears

This may be related to eczema or simply to moisture behind the ears causing irritation to the skin. It tends to be an on-again, off-again little problem which can go on throughout the first year. It's another maintenance problem—here are a few tips:

Always dry well, but gently, behind your baby's ears every day and check to see what's happening.

Frequent applications of sorbolene and glycerine help keep the area supple, so apply a little every nappy change time while you are at home.

If the area behind the ears becomes very inflamed, cracked and weepy, see your family doctor. A combination of a mild cortisone and anti-fungal ointment will clear it. Continue with the sorbolene and glycerine when it is clear. Diet makes no difference to cracking behind ears.

Heat rash

Heat rash continues to return from time to time, often until the age of three. Heat rash in older babies looks like little reddish-blue separate dots and appears mainly at the back of the neck, on the tummy and the top of the chest, and often arrives with hot weather. It mostly doesn't bother babies, but is sometimes itchy, especially around the back of the neck. Heat rash is not related to diet.

Mosquito bites

Mosquito bites look like a flat red tiny spot almost like a dot from a red felt tip pen. Mosquito bites usually disappear without incident.

Pigeon lice bites

Pigeon lice bites are often confused with chicken pox as they appear as small, raised pink spots which form a blister and a crust. If your baby gets a few lesions like this when she is otherwise well and has not been in contact with chicken pox, pigeons are likely to be the culprit.

Impetigo

Impetigo happens when a lesion on the skin becomes infected, usually because the baby scratches it. The lesion slowly enlarges and spreads. It may be crusty, pus may be present and other lesions may start to appear. See your family doctor—impetigo needs antibiotics.

Baby acne

Occasionally a baby develops inflamed pimples and blackheads on her face which looks very similar to a mild form of teenage acne. It is not related to the hormone rash most babies get in the first three months which is often misnamed 'baby acne'. It is an uncommon condition called infantile acne and tends to happen to babies who come from families where there is a strong history of acne in the teenage years, although this is not always the case. There is no wildly successful treatment, it doesn't bother the baby and goes some time in the first two years, maybe to return in the adolescent years. Baby acne is not affected by diet.

A yellow baby

If your baby is otherwise well but turning yellow before your eyes, it's almost certainly because of her consumption of foods containing betacarotene, such as pumpkin, carrots, spinach, tomatoes, peaches, apricots and prunes. Quite a few babies eat a lot of pumpkin and carrot. Betacarotene is a yellow pigment which is converted by the body into vitamin A.

The yellow skin is harmless; the betacarotene does not have this effect on the skin after age three. There is no need to reduce the offending food items as they are all very good for your baby, however, regular large amounts of carrot juice poses a slight risk of a build-up of vitamin A. This can pose a health risk so avoid overdosing your baby on carrot juice.

Small lump under nipple

It is quite common to be able to feel a lump under the nipple in one of your baby's breasts. This has nothing to do with the swollen breasts that babies under three months develop due to hormones (Red, swollen breasts, page 185). Small lumps in older babies is normal breast tissue and nothing to worry about, but check with your doctor if you are unsure.

FOR MORE INFORMATION

Chapter 14: Sleeping and Waking in the First Six Months *('sleeping through', page 266; 'spoiling' and routines, page 278)*
Chapter 15: The Crying Baby, page 285
Chapter 6: Breastfeeding Your Baby For the First Two Weeks *(notes on using weight as a guide to hunger, page 78)*
Chapter 5: Choosing Baby Products *(dummies, page 53)*
Chapter 28: Sleeping and Waking Six Months and Beyond *(sleep problems and 'teething', page 482)*
Chapter 24: Feeding Your Baby *(tips on using a cup, page 454)*
Chapter 25: Common Worries and Queries *(funny habits, page 458)*
Chapter 29: Feeding Your Baby *(biting the breast, page 506)*

Chapter 20

Growth and Development

Growth

Babies roughly gain 140 to 170 grams (5 to 6oz) a week in the second six months and grow about 2.5cm (¾ inch) in three months. Before you start to worry, here are a few statistics so you can see the wide normal range.

AT SIX MONTHS

	Small/Normal	Large/Normal
Boys	Weight 6.2kg (13lb 2oz) Length 63cm (26 inches) Head circ. 41.5cm (16 inches)	10kg (22lb) 73cm (29 inches) 46cm (18 inches)
Girls	Weight 5.8kg (13lb) Length 61cm (24 inches) Head circ. 40cm (15 inches)	9.2kg (20lb) 70cm (27 inches) 45cm (17 inches)

Development

Gross motor skills

Between three and six months your baby starts a lot of new movements, some at four months, some at five months. By six months you will notice that:

- When she lies on her back she raises her head to look at her feet.
- She lifts her legs to play with her feet.
- When she is on her tummy she takes her weight well on her forearms.
- She has great head control. When you pull her from lying to sitting, she braces her shoulders and pulls herself towards you to sit.
- She might be able to sit on her own. Some babies can sit on their own by six months, for most sitting unsupported happens between six and nine months. It's fine to let babies sit, well supported so they don't fall and hurt themselves, before they can manage to sit on their own—doing this doesn't damage their backs.
- She is probably rolling. By six months a lot of babies roll from front to back and/or from back to front, but the age at which babies intentionally roll is extremely variable. Some do it once or twice and don't do it again for a long time, others still haven't rolled by nine months. Safety is an important consideration in relation to rolling. Never assume your baby can't roll because the very time you leave her unattended on a bed or change table could be the first time she does it—onto the floor!
- She likes to be held standing so she can take her weight and bounce up and down. Most babies do this by six months, however, some still have collapsible legs. If your baby doesn't weight bear, give her some practice when you can, as well as plenty of floor play and no walker.

Vision and fine motor

- Babies of this age are delightful stickybeaks, vitally interested in everything and everyone around them. Eyes should now move together. If they look uneven or crooked, have them checked.
- By now your baby will be reaching out and grabbing everything in sight. She passes toys from one hand to another, usually via her mouth, for a chew and a suck. Exploring things with her mouth and tongue is

her way of getting additional information about all the things she sees and touches. At times she will get quite frantic about this process of discovery. It is important that your baby is able to suck, bite and mouth safe objects without too many inhibitions placed upon her.

- When an object is dropped to the floor your baby will look for it purposefully rather than continuing to stare at the spot from where it disappeared.

Hearing and speech

HEARING

By six months babies turn consistently to a voice or a noise as long as they are not too distracted. This might be a voice from across the room or a quiet noise from something like a rattle behind each ear.

SPEECH

Speech is in the form of tuneful, sing-song vowel sounds. Some babies of this age start single or double syllables (ga-ga, da-da, ma-ma) although most don't start these sounds until a little later. A number of babies go through a 'quiet' stage between five and seven months where they don't make as many talking noises as they did when they were younger. Don't worry—it all starts up again! Laughing, chuckling, squealing and screaming are all part of their speech now.

Social and play

Your baby will now start to bang things together. When you offer her a rattle she will reach for it immediately and shake it deliberately. She will laugh at things and people and especially enjoy games with a surprise element.

Toys

This is the age for movement, kicking, reaching and grasping and chewing. An onion bag full of cellophane makes interesting noises and attracts attention.

Washable safe rattles and shakers are popular. An unbreakable mirror mounted about 18cm (7 inches) away from your baby's face on a wall where she can look at herself is good entertainment value.

Mobiles still attract attention. By six months your baby will be reaching and grabbing so make sure it's well out of reach.

Activity centres manufactured by various companies are a great favourite, especially between six and nine months. Balls are always fun.

Specially designed playmats for babies to lie on give them things to grab and chew and make noises with while they are on the floor.

Books

The first five years are vital for literacy development

Babies come into the world wired to learn language from the time they are born, so parents have a captured audience. Babies and toddlers are eager, almost desperate to absorb the language they hear around them in their homes and their communities.

Before children start school most of their literacy learning comes from within their families. It comes from the way their parents and extended family talk and communicate with them. It comes from family stories, songs and music and from books, magazines, and comics—in fact, from anything in their world that draws their attention to words and pictures.

Literacy learning for most children has the potential to come naturally as part of the close relationship they share with the adults in their lives. You don't have to be an 'expert' to talk meaningfully to your baby or to read to her.

Reading provides a never-ending supply of scenarios, people and possibilities that children can use to create their own pictures and images in their heads. It is a particularly self-sufficient form of entertainment, which is a great bonus for parents.

Initially you may feel you aren't getting far when your baby lunges at the book and tries to eat it, but persevering is well worth the long-term rewards. The earlier you start, the sooner your baby or toddler's attention span increases, and the sooner her interest is sustained.

Reading—when to start

The time to start books is as soon as possible after birth! Babies love bright colours, the rhythm of the words and being held close.

If it is regular, even just for a few minutes a day, by the time your baby is a toddler you will find she will be responding in a most rewarding way.

When babies are at the grab-and-eat stage, give them something to hold and chew to keep them away from the book—a set of keys is good.

How to do it

If you were never read to as a child you may be wondering 'how to do it'. Don't be embarrassed about this—it's more common than you think.

The basic idea is to read expressively and enjoy the story; the more you do it the less inhibited you'll feel. Generally, babies become a rewarding audience the more they are read to.

HERE ARE A FEW TIPS

- Use books with big, bold pictures about things your baby is familiar with. Babies, especially around five months and upwards, love books with flaps to look under. Books with jingles, rhymes and sounds (sheep baa-ing, ducks quacking and cars vrooming) are popular with babies as well. Family photograph albums are also good.
- Sit close and hold your baby on your lap. Point to the pictures and, as well as read the words, embellish a bit—tell stories about what is happening or what the people are doing. Keep going for as long as she is happy, even if at times she doesn't seem to be paying much attention. At this stage you may be sowing the seeds for future interest and enjoyment rather than capturing her immediate interest.
- It is important that the book matches the baby. Libraries are invaluable. If you are in doubt, go to your local library and talk to the people there. If you've never been to your local library, go anyway. Apart from help with choosing books, libraries are wonderful resources and lovely places to take babies to visit. Good bookshops can also advise on suitable books. Bear in mind that the books you choose should be as enjoyable for you as your baby; reading aloud is much more fun when the adult loves the story and the characters as much as the baby does.
- It's a good idea to have books around the house, easily accessible so your baby can learn how to explore books for herself. Your baby will

gradually start to look at the pictures and eventually bring the books to you to look at with her. Books are also a welcome diversion when you are out and about doing routine things that babies find boring.

Developmental summary: 6 months

Gross motor

- on back—lifts head to look at feet;
- lifts leg and grabs foot;
- pulled to sit—braces shoulders, no back curve;
- can roll, front to back (very variable).

Vision and fine movements

- moves head and eyes eagerly;
- a squint is abnormal;
- uses whole hand to grasp objects and passes them from one hand to another;
- watches falling toys.

Hearing and speech

- turns immediately to parents' voices;
- turns to minimal sound;
- makes tuneful talking noises and may use single or double syllables;
- laughs, chuckles, squeals and screams.

Social and play

- puts everything into mouth;
- reaches out and grabs things;
- may be wary of strange faces and places.

Growing and developing—when to worry

It is natural for you to watch your baby closely and to be concerned if she doesn't seem to be growing or is late to reach a milestone. Constant comparisons with other babies and listening to other parents' experiences may increase the worry that 'something is wrong'. Here are some guidelines for action if you are not sure that your baby is growing and developing normally.

Growth

Sometimes parents are concerned or are made to feel concerned because their baby's weight is less than would be expected for her age and height. Family and friends make comments or it might be noted by a health professional.

If you are concerned about your baby's weight, have her weight, length and head circumference taken by someone reliable then plotted on a percentile chart. None of these measurements mean as much taken on their own as they do taken together and plotted on a growth chart so that her overall pattern of growth can be looked at. Her weight should be around the same percentile as her height, but there are always a number of babies who weigh one or two percentiles below their height or one or two above. When they are bright, active and feeding well, there is unlikely to be a problem.

Appearances can be quite deceptive and comments made by onlookers ('what a small baby!') are generally quite wrong, so if you're worried, nine times out of ten this simple procedure is all that's needed to put your mind at rest.

If low weight is a pattern and your baby's weight percentile is a long way below her height percentile, here are the most common reasons which do vary with ages and stages of development:

DIET

Persistent low gains in healthy babies in the first three months are often related to breastfeeding problems. Once these are overcome the weight should increase. Care must be taken before abandoning breastfeeding as some babies continue to gain only small amounts on formula.

Incorrect mixing of formula is occasionally a cause of low weight gains in the early months.

Older babies who are given very restricted diets may not gain weight for long periods. An abundant supply of breastmilk still supplies most dietary needs beyond six months of age, but when the supply is noticeably diminished it is very important to include other fats in the diet such as milk, cheese and yoghurt. Babies do not thrive well on small amounts of breastmilk and fruit and vegetables only. If for some reason dairy products are eliminated, a fortified soy formula is the best choice of extra milk as it has added fat.

It is quite common for babies to start refusing food some time between nine and twelve months, which is a constant source of worry for lots of parents. It is also a time when the weight of many babies, especially breast-fed babies, levels out. As this is normal for most babies, try not to worry. Babies cannot be forced to eat so the best thing you can do is to make sure you offer your baby an adequate diet which includes a range of foods. Health problems in healthy 'non-eating' older babies only happen when they are consistently offered the wrong food or put on crazy fad diets.

ILLNESS

Continuing stationary or low weight gains may be caused by illness. During the first year medical problems such as a urinary tract infection, pyloric stenosis (a narrowing of the passage between the stomach and the small intestine), a heart problem or other rare illnesses may be diagnosed and treated. Acute illnesses such as viral diarrhoea, upper respiratory tract infections, ear infections or tonsillitis can all affect weight gains. Medical problems are nearly always accompanied by signs other than low weight such as strange-smelling poo, apathy, fevers, delayed development, irritability or constant unhappiness.

Most underweight babies and toddlers have nothing at all wrong with them and no one knows precisely why they are underweight. The difficulty always is deciding when the reasons for being underweight need investigating. The approach of health professionals to underweight babies and toddlers varies tremendously so parents find they often receive conflicting advice. Techniques used to diagnose possible medical causes are invasive, often expensive and should not be done as a matter of course on all underweight babies.

When your baby is bright and active, lives in a loving home, is offered an adequate diet, does normal poo and continues gaining some weight every so often, there's unlikely to be anything wrong. Chasing diagnosis after diagnosis is a nerve-racking exercise which rarely changes anything.

If your baby has a sudden weight loss and shows obvious signs of illness or if you are concerned about her milestones, see your child and family health nurse or doctor. Babies born 'small for dates' will catch up, but some won't until their second year. Premature babies of very low birth weight tend to stay small for the first year or two but follow a steady growth pattern of their own.

Height problems, either too short or too long, are not common but do occur. Height anomalies tend to emerge over a period of time and are more likely to be noticed in the second year. When it appears height is outside the normal range, special attention is needed from specialists in the field. As with weight, the first thing to do is to work out whether a height problem exists. Your child and family health nurse or family doctor can help with this.

Development

Remember, milestones are a guide. Listening to other proud parents boasting about their baby's achievements can be hazardous to your peace of mind. Variations in skills and personality differences between babies are just as diverse as they are between adults.

Unless there is a generalised delay in a few areas over several months it doesn't matter if your baby seems slow to do some things compared to other babies. Gross motor skills such as walking, sitting, crawling and rolling have the widest variations and are highly visible. Parents are very aware when their baby sits like a blob at twelve months while their friend's baby of the same age is ready to start Little Athletics.

Delay in gross and fine motor skills can be helped by physiotherapists and occupational therapists if you and your adviser think it's appropriate. Communication skills are very important, so if you ever think your baby can't hear or see, seek help immediately. Here is a general guide about when to go for assessment. Start out with your child and family health nurse, your family doctor or paediatrician, who can tell you where to go next if it's necessary.

SEEK HELP IF

- your baby consistently doesn't respond to sounds;
- your baby doesn't seem to see things or has white or cloudy eyes;
- she isn't interested in what's going on around her;
- she can't hold her head up by three to four months;
- she squints a lot after three months; eyes not focusing;
- persistent and excessive crying continues after three to four months;
- there's no babbling by six months;
- she doesn't use or move **both** arms and/or legs;
- your baby is not sitting well by ten months;
- she doesn't want to weight bear by twelve months.

This is only a very general guide. Always get professional help if you are unsure. You know your baby better than anyone and have a good feel for what's happening. Too many opinions will drive you mad, but a couple of assessments by different people can give you a better idea of whether a problem exists or not, the degree of the problem and the best course of action.

FOR MORE INFORMATION

Chapter 17: Equipment *(baby walkers, page 366)*
Chapter 13: Growth and Development *(understanding percentile charts, page 246)*
Chapter 24: Feeding Your Baby *(fat in diet, page 446)*
Chapter 32: Becoming a Toddler *(not eating, page 518)*

Chapter 21

Safety

The following chart emphasises particular hazards associated with this developmental stage, but don't forget, most safety hazards remain at any age and stage.

Don't forget your baby's second round of immunisation is due at 4 months.

Age	**Developmental stage**	**Safety hazard**	**Precautions**
3–4 months	• rolls over • starts to mouth objects	• falls off heights • inhalation of small, loose pieces of toys or other small objects • scalds by baby grasping and spilling hot drinks while being nursed	• eyes off, hands on is the golden rule • check all toys for small removable parts or household objects or equipment that can be sucked • keep all hot liquids out of baby's reach • think about the way you drink tea and coffee, especially when friends visit

Age	Developmental stage	Safety hazard	Precautions
4–5 months	• may feed self biscuit or rusk	• suffocation by inhalation of food • choking, inhalation hazards as baby has increasing access to small, hard objects	• always supervise with food or bottle • constant supervision and monitoring of bits and pieces left around the home
5–6 months	• increased mobility by crawling and rolling	• falls—from highchair, pram, stroller, change table • burns—exposed fires, heaters, grasping hot objects, sunburn	• safety harness and constant supervision in highchairs, prams and so on • use fireguards, limit exposure to the sun and cover up
6–7 months	• picks up 'tiny' bits • may sit alone • may pull to stand	• drowning—left alone in the bath • falls—from sitting or standing position	• never leave alone in the bath or in the company of older children • close supervision, especially if a baby walker is being used

FOR MORE INFORMATION

Chapter 12: Safety *(immunisation, page 235)*

Chapter 22

For Parents

Contraception

Here's a reminder: Change from the mini pill to an IUD or the combined pill if you wean or dramatically decrease your breastfeeding.

Night waking between 4 and 6 months

It is normal and common for babies to wake at night after three months. Some babies have never slept more than two to three hours at a time, others may have slept most of the night from eight weeks only to start waking frequently again around four to five months.

The amount of distress this causes parents usually depends on the number of times it happens, how quickly the baby goes back to sleep after a feed and whether both parents are in paid employment. Parents' expectations can cause added tension, especially when all their friends' babies are sleeping through. It is also hard to bear if the baby slept well at night for several months and then started waking again.

What can you do?

Unfortunately, contrary to popular opinion, there is no safe, easy way to 'make' (an unfortunate word used a lot in this context) your baby sleep all night.

Here is some information:

- Illness sometimes causes a return to night waking. Wait for a few days and see if something eventuates or ask your family doctor to check her out, including her ears.
- 'Teething', 'hunger' and 'wind' are explanations you will doubtless be given by most friends, relatives, colleagues and health professionals.

Is it teeth? Unfortunately, it's rarely that simple, but if a tooth appears and then she goes back to sleeping—hallelujah! I do not find the growing of teeth relates much to wakeful night-time babies.

Is it hunger? Starting solids is usually the next suggestion. Occasionally this does the trick and if so—great! If your baby rejects the food completely then forget about it; chances are it would not solve the night sleep problem anyway. Most of the time food seems to play a very insignificant role in keeping babies sleeping at night.

Is it wind? When mothers are up a lot at night with babies, in their fog of weariness they often become very aware of their babies' farting and burping habits and tend to see this as the problem. However, babies who sleep all night burp and fart too—it's just that because everyone else is also asleep it passes by (or out) unnoticed. Troublesome wind is not likely to be a reason for night-time waking unless your baby has a defined medical problem which would give her gut pain or is having a reaction to some new food.

- Is your baby too big now for wrapping and being in a bassinet? Sometimes moving the baby into a cot and stopping the wrapping helps. Sometimes it makes things worse; however, give it a try. Put her in the cot on her back with a sheet and blanket over her tucked in tightly around the cot mattress.
- If your baby has been managing without night feeds then suddenly starts

waking again, generally re-introducing a night feed is the best thing to do. You can try replacing the night feeds with a dummy or by rocking and patting, however, most of the time you will find you are up more and get less sleep than if you feed. If you are only getting up once or twice at night and your baby is going straight back to sleep I think it's better to carry on feeding and review the situation when she is over six months old.

- A lot of babies sleep from around seven at night until one or two in the morning, wake for a feed, then wake hourly until the daylight hours. If your baby is doing this, apart from the strategies already suggested, the only other possibilities are: take her to bed, let her cry by following the teaching-to-sleep guidelines on page 484 or live with it and hope it gets better. Waking the baby at 10 to 11 pm and giving her a feed is often suggested as a way of 'making' her sleep through the night. By all means try it, but I find this strategy does not have a high success rate and often makes things worse.
- The dummy. If you find you are getting up frequently to put the dummy in, it's worth thinking seriously about getting rid of it. When the dummy goes there is the dilemma of what to do when the baby wakes. Unless you can quieten her quickly with a feed or a pat the only other alternative is to let her cry.

  Leaving babies to cry at night to teach them to sleep is dealt with in detail in the next section as six months is the earliest most babies and parents can handle this approach. However, if you are desperate and if your baby is well, please refer to page 484 for the best way to do teaching-to-sleep. If you have decided to take this approach it is better to follow these guidelines than just to lie in bed listening to your baby cry.

TO SUMMARISE

Generally babies wake at night as part of normal sleep patterns and do not know how to go back to sleep. Night waking is unlikely to be related to easily explainable things like teeth, hunger and wind. Nor is it usually anything to do with what the parents have or haven't done.

If the night waking is not bothering you unduly, do nothing.

Once hunger and illness have been ruled out the options are to feed and live with it or let the baby cry. Replacing feeds with dummies, rocking, wrapping, patting and so on usually doesn't work. Letting babies cry at any time is fraught and a controversial approach, however, there are times when parents feel there are no alternatives and wish to try.

If you want to do so before your baby is six months old, please follow the guidelines for teaching-to-sleep closely. If there has not been a change for the better in your baby's night sleep patterns within three nights, stop and wait until she is older. Stop before if you find it too distressing.

If you are feeling exhausted and out of control because of your baby's night waking, ask your child and family health nurse about the possibility of going to a residential family and baby centre for four or five nights if one is available.

Travelling with your baby

Travelling with a baby is different from travelling on your own. It is rewarding, exciting and better than staying at home, but it is hard work. Parents' tolerance, expectations and anxiety levels when travelling with babies and toddlers differ greatly from one family to another. Lots of families travel vast distances regularly and thrive on it, other parents find long trips with babies too much to bear and decide to only take unavoidable trips until their babies are older. Don't feel like a wimp if you're in the latter category or feel pressured into taking unnecessary trips when you'd sooner stay home.

The first trip with your baby may seem quite daunting, but the more trips you make the better you become at handling the tricky bits and enjoying yourself at the same time.

To ensure as smooth a trip as possible, planning is essential. Planning includes mental preparation so you don't have too many unrealistic ideas of what's ahead. You will find you are not able to enjoy the same sort of things you did when you travelled before your baby arrived. Leisurely meals, shopping expeditions, fishing trips, extensive sightseeing, late nights and long drives without stopping to get quickly from one place to another tend not to be compatible with babies.

Be mentally prepared for the unexpected so you don't feel too let-down when things go wrong. Illness, crying attacks and diarrhoea are all possible baby events when you're on the road.

Many babies and toddlers find travel disrupting which doesn't hurt them in any way, but you might find their eating, sleeping and behaviour patterns change temporarily.

You may wonder about using a sedative for your baby when travelling overseas. Sedating healthy babies under two is not recommended; most babies in this age group travel well and are, more or less, immobile.

Some parents travelling overseas do take a mild sedative with them in case of difficult times but most find they don't use it. The drugs used for this are usually Vallergan and Phenergan, anti-histamine drugs with a sedative effect available only on prescription. They are not advised for the under twos. You should be aware that there are risks with medications such as these that include extreme drowsiness and depressed breathing or, alternatively, hyperstimulation and poor coordination. It's important to minimise the risks by carefully calculating the dose (check with your pharmacist or doctor) and by using the sedative as a one-off dose only; for example, once only on the plane and/or once only after you get to your destination.

Sedating babies during a long car trip is not advised. It's preferable and safer to structure long car trips to fit in with the baby rather than the adults and not have too many unrealistic expectations about the length and time of your journey.

Try to avoid immunising your baby just before travelling.

Whether travelling by car, train or plane, the all-purpose baby bag is essential. In it you need:

- disposable or cloth nappies depending on the length of the trip;
- disposable wipers or damp flannels in a plastic bag;
- cleaning lotion;
- nappy cream;
- cotton balls;
- extra dummies (if you are using dummies);
- several changes of clothing;

- muslin squares of various sizes;
- safety pins, scissors, masking tape, torch, bandaids, tissues;
- plastic bag for dirty clothes, nappies;
- baby paracetamol, sunblock;
- oral rehydration powder (for example, Gastrolyte). For emergencies only. Unlikely to be needed for exclusively breastfed babies under six months of age;
- a blanket or sheepskin which can be used as a changing sheet or to put on the floor so baby can lie on something familiar and clean.

Plane Trip Tips

Overseas (O) and domestic (D) flights

- You can book a bassinet when you make your initial booking and confirm this when confirming your flight twenty-four hours prior to departure. Availability will depend on the type of aircraft, the class and the number of babies on board. **(O)**
- There is an 11-kg weight restriction on babies in bassinets. Fresh linen is supplied for bassinets at stopovers. **(O)**
- Babies cannot be left in bassinets for take-off and landing. On all Australian airlines they must be restrained on parents' laps. This is done by using a special baby seatbelt with a loop. The baby belt goes around the baby's waist; the adult belt is then passed through the loop and secured. **(O,D)**
- Babies not in bassinets, toddlers and children are not allowed to sleep on the floor of Australian aircrafts as unexpected turbulence can cause severe injury, even death. **(O,D)**
- Depending on the airline, baby/child car seats can be used on board as long as they meet the airline company's requirement for the standard number (all car seats have standard numbers). A seat must be purchased and airline staff will install it for you. Baggage check-in will check your car seat to ensure it meets the standard number. Again it is crucial to confirm this directly with the airline. **(O,D)**
- Special meals must be ordered when making the booking and reconfirmed directly with the airline, not via travel agents, to ensure the

message has got through. If a flight has been delayed or changed unexpectedly a meal order may not be met. **(O)**

- All aircraft have change tables located in toilets and for the sake of fellow passengers it is good manners to use the change table rather than the cabin of the aircraft for the sake of both hygiene and smell. **(O,D)**
- If you have any concerns it is always advisable to check directly with the airline prior to your flight. Different airlines have different rules, requirements and services for travelling with babies so make sure you are familiar with the system of the company you are using. It is also recommended that you reconfirm anything you need to know at each sector of your journey. **(O)**
- Slimline umbrella strollers can be taken on board as long as they are lightweight and compact. If the one you take is too large it may be taken away at the aircraft door but will be available for you again when you disembark, again at the door. **(O,D)**
- If you are formula feeding it's best to take cleaned, disinfected bottles, formula powder and your own *cold* water (in a clear container or bottled still water, not mineral water) and make up feeds as you go. **(O,D)**

  Make sure all your supplies are in see-through containers or they may be removed from you at security—poor baby. You also may be asked to take a sip from the water(!). **(O)**
- Remember that if you ask for bottles or baby food to be heated on airlines it will be heated with boiling water so try to think enough ahead to allow the formula or food to cool down. Most babies don't mind cold/room temperature milk and food. **(O,D)**
- Make sure you have plenty of nappies and supplies of formula. Most airlines carry small supplies of these items but they may not be suitable for your baby and supplies often run out. **(O,D)**
- Babies and toddlers often get distressed on ascent and descent because of the pressure build-up in their Eustachian tubes (the tube that runs from the nose to the ears), which they don't know how to relieve by deliberately yawning. Sucking or crying will relieve the pressure. Sucking is obviously the less distressing option for you and your fellow passengers so the breast, a bottle, a dummy or your finger all fill the bill. If your baby

is really sound asleep and showing no signs of distress there is no need to wake her in order to get her to suck on something. **(O,D)**

- If your baby or toddler has a history of ear infections and/or a mucusy cold prior to departure it is a good idea to ask your family doctor to check her eardrums. **(O,D)**
- When you get to the other end you might find your baby comes down with a minor illness (cough, cold or diarrhoea) which unfortunately often seems to happen when babies leave their usual environment.
- Re-organising sleep patterns might be tricky for a short time. Get your baby back into her normal sleeping patterns as soon as you can by keeping her up when she would normally be up during the day rather than letting her sleep for long periods.

Car trips

Some babies travel well in their restraint or car seat for long stretches. Others only manage two-hourly stints without becoming irritable. Unfortunately a small number of babies go into full roar after departure and continue until the car stops and they are taken out. It's very hard to know why some babies do this—one of my children carried on in this fashion for a year or so which meant our car travel was quite limited until she changed.

Have your baby dry, comfortably dressed, well fed and if possible ready for a sleep before leaving. Make sure she is protected from the sun.

Long car trips are tiring for everyone. Plan to stop every two hours for a break. What do you do if your baby has a sudden screaming attack and you can't pull over?

- Sing a song, play a tape or turn up the radio.
- If someone is available, rub your baby's head, stroke her arm and soothe her as much as possible.
- Give a young baby a finger to suck. Try to distract an older baby with a toy, finger food or a drink.
- Obviously, stop as soon as you can.

It's always worth asking well-travelled friends for tips. Extensive travelling with your baby is best avoided until early difficulties with feeding, crying, sleeping and so on are sorted out, although if it's unavoidable it won't hurt your baby—it just makes things a bit harder for you.

FOR MORE INFORMATION

Chapter 11: Daily Care *(sharing beds, page 216)*
Chapter 14: Sleeping and Waking in the First Six Months *('sleeping through', page 266)*
Chapter 28: Sleeping and Waking Six Months and Beyond *(options for night waking, page 480; teach-to-sleep, page 484)*

PART THREE

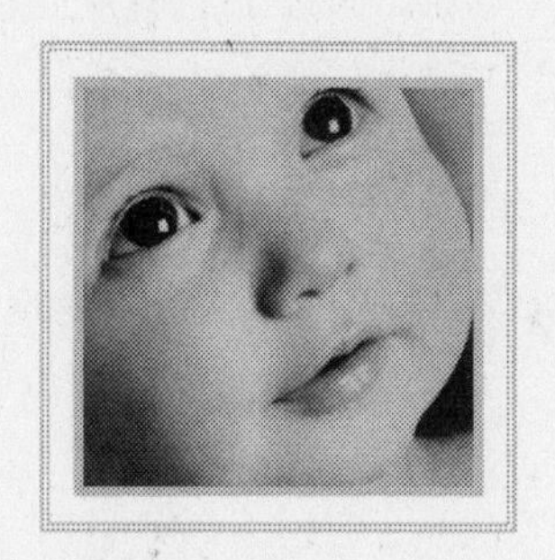

6 to 9 months

Chapter 23

Equipment

Clothes

You are probably noticing now that your baby moves all over her cot at night, rarely staying under the covers, which, if it's winter, is a bit of a worry. As soon as this starts to happen it's a good idea to buy one or two walk-in sleepers (sleeping bags with legs). A walk-in sleeper is worn over pyjamas. It zips up the front and keeps your baby warm without restricting her movements.

A highchair

The major piece of equipment to consider in this age group is a highchair. Types and prices vary tremendously with new styles constantly available.

Here are some guidelines about what to look for:

Safety

Check stability. Highchairs with a narrow base may be less sturdy—this particularly applies to older, secondhand highchairs.

Highchairs come with a waist and crotch harness, but it is advisable to purchase a shoulder harness to use as well so there should be points on the highchair for you to anchor it.

A portable chair that hooks onto a table is a useful accessory for holidays and dining out or to use attached to the family table at home. Portable chairs don't fit all tables, so check when you buy. Babies can't manage portable chairs until they can sit well without support for a reasonable period of time. A harness should always be used and constant supervision is essential while the baby is in the chair because she has access to everything within her reach on the table, so the risk of scalds and inhaling small objects is increased.

The highchair should be made of non-toxic material. The simpler the design, the easier to clean and the less likelihood of small fingers becoming caught. Highchairs which convert to lowchairs should do so smoothly without the risk of pinching fingers or jamming midway.

Practicalities

- The highchair should be light and easy to move.
- Think about the space available—you might need a fold-up model to stack away when not in use.
- The style of highchair that converts to an armchair, swing, potty and table won't be particularly useful unless it converts quickly and you use all its features.

A few tips when using a highchair

- Remember, it's quite normal for many babies to be just beginning to sit on their own around nine months. Until they can sit well independently for any length of time they need support while in a highchair and should only be left sitting supported for a limited time as they do get tired and upset when they start to slide forwards or to one side.
- Always make sure your baby is secure and never leave her alone with food.
- Take her out when she is obviously restless or upset.

Chapter 24

Feeding Your Baby

Alas! What various tastes in food,
Divide the human brotherhood.

HILAIRE BELLOC, 'ON FOOD', *CAUTIONARY VERSES*

More about food—seven to twelve months

Between six and nine months (depending on when you started food other than milk) babies can be introduced to a wide range of food. On the following page is a plan for you to use as a guide if you need one. **Remember, it is only a guide and must be adapted to your baby and your lifestyle. The times given are approximate.**

Here is some information to help you with the diet plan:

- Babies who like eating will be following this plan by nine months. Don't rush things unnecessarily—on the other hand, there's no need to delay introducing a wide variety of food if your baby is enjoying it.
- If allergy is a consideration for you, follow recommendations from your adviser. If you are thinking of restricting your baby's diet in any major way, please seek advice from a knowledgeable health professional so your baby's diet is not nutritionally unsound.

6 am	**Breastfeed or bottle (180–210ml)**					
8 am	**Breakfast suggestions**					
Weetbix Vita Brits porridge baby cereal (add made-up formula or full fat milk)	and/or	stewed fruit	or	full-fat yoghurt	or	egg yolk (whole egg after nine months)
	as well offer bread or toast *drink: water in a cup or bottle*					
10–11 am	**Morning tea (optional)**					
choice of finger food bread cheese fruit rusk	*drink: water in a cup or bottle*					
12:30 pm	**Lunch suggestions**					
any vegies	add	meat or chicken or fish		add		grated cheese (stirred in) or tomato puree or grated hard boiled egg yolk
(mashed or ground up in a handblender or Bamix)						
		drink: breastfeed or bottle (180–210ml)				
2–4 pm	**Afternoon tea (optional)**					
Same as morning tea						

5–6 pm		**Evening meal suggestions**						
(Some time between nine and twelve months cheese on toast, sandwiches, commercial fish fillets, spaghetti or baked beans may also be offered.)								
avocado & cottage cheese mashed	or	mashed banana & yoghurt or tofu & fruit	or	soup	or	jars of commercial baby food or fresh yoghurt & fruit	or	egg (boiled or scrambled) or family food ground up (eg: pasta, rice, casseroles, spaghetti bolognaise)
		drink: breastfeed or bottle (180–210ml)						

- Offer the food before milk from now on if you have been doing the reverse.
- As well as changing from four-hourly feeds to three meals a day, this plan suggests gradually cutting down the breast or bottle feeds to three every twenty-four hours. **This will suit lots of mothers and babies but obviously not all.**

Breastfeeding

If you wish to breastfeed more often, continue in the way that suits you and your baby. Or if you decide to only breastfeed three times a day the feeds do not necessarily have to be given according to the plan—again do what suits you both best.

Bottle feeding

Three bottles of milk a day is all your baby needs once she is eating well. Water at other times is sufficient when your baby is thirsty. Leave your baby on the formula she is already having—changing to follow-on formula is unnecessary, unless it is cheaper.

Night feeding

Night feeding, whether breast or bottle, is related to 'sleep', not food, once babies are over six months.

If you wish to change your baby's night-time feeding patterns, please refer to Sleeping and Waking Six Months and Beyond on page 480. If you are happy with what's happening, carry on.

- If your baby is a 5 am waker, it is easier to give her the breast or bottle at that time than launch into breakfast at the crack of dawn. Often, after a milk feed babies go back to sleep for a while. When your baby has breakfast later after an early feed there's no need to repeat the bottle or the breast—a little water from a bottle or a cup with her breakfast is all that's needed.
- If your baby is a 7 to 8 am waker, give her breakfast as soon as she wakes up followed by breastfeed, her bottle or milk from a cup.
- Some breastfed babies whose mothers have an abundant milk supply do not want breakfast after their morning breastfeed. The breastmilk

supplies all they need so don't worry if your baby does this—she will probably start eating breakfast some time around twelve months.

- Think of your baby now as having family food rather than a special diet. Take a critical look at the family diet; if you have a healthy diet, your baby's diet will be healthy too.

Food to avoid

Avoid junk food and unnecessary sugar (sometimes a little sugar on the morning cereal helps with constipation). On the other hand things like basil, garlic and tomato puree that you use in your food are fine.

Honey is a form of sugar and therefore can be a problem if given too often. It has been known to cause botulism (poisoning by toxins produced by a harmful bacteria) in babies under twelve months, so if you occasionally use honey on bread wait until your baby is over a year old.

Other food to avoid includes whole apple, whole carrot, raw celery, corn chips or popcorn because of the risk of choking. It is now recommended that these foods not be given until children are over four years.

On the rather confusing subject of allergy and food intolerance, see page 384.

A word about fats

Between birth and age two, fat is needed as a concentrated source of energy, and for brain development. Fifty per cent of a baby's energy intake should come from fat during these years.

- **Birth to 2 years:** During the first year use breastmilk and/or infant formula and, after solids are introduced at six months, full-fat dairy products in meals. During the second year, continue breastfeeding and/or full-fat milk as the main drink and full-fat dairy products. Give the milk from a cup instead of a bottle.

  If for some reason you are eliminating dairy food from your baby's diet and you are not breastfeeding, use one of the soy infant formulas as they have added fat.

Salt

Sodium intake should be low in the first year of life as babies have a limited capacity to excrete excessive sodium, which may cause kidney damage. Don't add salt to your baby's food.

Cholesterol

Cholesterol is a fat found in blood and is used by the body to make certain hormones as well as nerve and brain cells. Most blood cholesterol is made within the body from food containing saturated fats or cholesterol. High levels of blood cholesterol can cause fatty plaques to form on the walls of blood vessels that, in adult life, can break down or develop clots on their surface and eventually block off arteries, causing serious disability or death.

Food high in saturated fats, for example, deep-fried food and fatty meat, are the main culprits for raising blood cholesterol. Foods that actually contain cholesterol—for example, eggs and prawns—don't play a major role so it is fine to give your baby an egg a day if she likes them once she is over nine months and is not allergic to them.

Food safety

Food safety precautions are very important as soon as your baby starts eating family food. Small, hard items such as peanuts, pips and seeds are dangerous for babies. This means taking care with pips in fruit and seeds in bread. Offer plain bread and keep all nuts out of your baby's reach. Once your baby starts eating food herself, make sure she is always supervised and not allowed to crawl or walk with food.

GAGGING AND CHOKING

Most parents worry about the way their baby gags at times and the possibility of her choking, and often confuse gagging with choking. It's a normal worry but unfortunately it can lead to a baby's diet being too restricted and the delaying of finger foods at the ideal time to start them (between six and nine months).

WHAT'S THE DIFFERENCE?

1. GAGGING: Babies are born with a strong gag reflex which is part of their bodies' natural defence against food entering the respiratory tract instead of the oesophagus. The gag reflex persists throughout life—for example, if you are forced to eat something you don't like, you will automatically gag. Babies have to learn to inhibit their involuntary gag reflex when they start eating finger foods or food of a lumpier consistency than they are used to. They also have to learn how much food to put in at a time when they feed themselves—biting off more than they can chew is common. The other common thing babies learn to do to confuse the issue is to gag voluntarily when they don't wish to eat something. The 'gagging on purpose' habit can last well into the toddler years, making parents believe their toddler is physically unable to eat anything other than a liquid diet (and forgetting about the times a chocolate biscuit or a packet of chips goes down without a problem).

When a baby gags, the food sits at the back of her throat and ends up either going down where it's supposed to go or coming up again. As long as you are around to make sure she's all right and the food doesn't get stuck, gagging is harmless and part of the way she learns to feed herself and eat lumpier food. Most babies need the main part of their meal ground up until they are twelve months old as the gag reflex remains strong and, to some extent, involuntary until then, so lumpy food from a spoon tends to make meal times stressful because the lumps cause a lot of gagging. Mothers are constantly told to offer lumpy food from a spoon from six months on with dire warnings of babies never learning to chew if they don't. I find this a cause of great stress for many families. Oddly enough when babies feed themselves finger foods they control their gag reflex much more efficiently, so a good compromise is to give your baby the main part of her meal ground up, then offer her some finger food she can eat herself. Obviously if your baby manages chunky food from a spoon without gagging a lot, go for it!

2. CHOKING: Choking occurs when the airway is obstructed, preventing air from reaching the lungs. When it is a small, soft item (a crumb or a soft lump) the baby will usually cough, which removes the object from the airway. Serious obstruction happens when the item is a small, hard object like an orange pip, a peanut, a lolly or a piece of apple which gets 'stuck' in the airway and partially or completely blocks it.

FIRST AID FOR CHOKING: Check first if the baby is still able to breathe, cough or cry. If she is breathing, coughing or crying, she may be able to dislodge the food by coughing.

Do not try to dislodge the food by hitting the baby on the back because this may move the food into a more dangerous position and make her stop breathing.

Stay with the baby and watch to see if her breathing improves.

If she is not breathing easily within a few minutes, phone 000 for an ambulance.

If the baby is not breathing:

- Try to dislodge the piece of food by placing the baby face down over your lap so her head is lower than her chest.
- Give the baby four sharp blows on the back just between the shoulder blades. This should provide enough force to dislodge the food.
- Check again for signs of breathing.
- If the baby is still not breathing, urgently call 000 and ask for an ambulance. The ambulance service operator will be able to tell you what to do next.

These guidelines are from Kids Health at the Children's Hospital, Westmead and Sydney Children's Hospital, Randwick, with grateful acknowledgement to the Women's and Children's Hospital in Adelaide.

N.B.: It is very difficult to learn basic resuscitation techniques from a book. Courses are available in your state from the Royal Life Saving Society, the Red Cross and St John Ambulance and learning and/or updating your skills is always a very worthwhile thing to do.

If you have an emergency and you don't know what to do, take the baby to the phone and ring the Ambulance Service on 000 (everywhere). The trained operator will give emergency instructions over the phone.

It must be emphasised that choking is not a hazard normally associated with introducing a wide range of food to babies over the age of six months as long as you take a few sensible precautions. Don't let fear of choking put you off allowing your baby to try different food and different ways of eating.

Teeth and food

Teeth emerge any time between three-and-a-half and sixteen months. The arrival of teeth has nothing to do with when and what your baby eats. Many twelve-month-old babies with no teeth eat a wide variety of chunky food as they learn to use their gums very efficiently.

Breakfast suggestions

You may give your baby regular cereal (for example, rolled oats, Weet Bix, Vitabrits) after seven months or continue with baby cereals if you prefer, or use both for variety. Whole, full-fat cow's milk is fine to use on the cereal. Cooked fruit may be added to the cereal or yoghurt and fruit can be offered at times instead of cereal.

Egg yolk may be commenced any time after nine months, the whole egg around twelve months. Soft-boil an egg and try the yolk off a spoon or dip a finger of bread or toast into the egg and let your baby suck or chew it. A hard-boiled egg yolk can be grated and mixed into her vegies at lunch or dinner. Try scrambled egg with a little milk. Reactions to eggs include mild swelling of the lips, a rash around the mouth and sometimes vomiting. A small number of babies have life-threatening reactions to egg (usually the white of the egg). See Food allergies and food intolerance, page 384.

Try giving your baby fingers of toast or bread after breakfast.

Morning and afternoon tea

When you are changing from four-hourly feeds to three meals a day you might find a snack and a small drink a handy substitute while your baby is getting used to her new routine. It can also provide distraction from the breast if you are limiting your breastfeeds to three a day. Morning and afternoon tea is optional and if your baby sleeps or is quite happy without a snack at this time, forget it.

Lunch suggestions

The main meal (that is, the vegie one) may be given in the middle of the day or in the evening. There is no truth in the rumour that 'heavy' food shouldn't be given in the evening. If your baby is a non-vegie eater, substitute vegies with some of the breakfast or dinner ideas.

Dinner suggestions

I think everyone has trouble at times working out what to give for the third meal. Babies don't need endless variety and cooking lots of separate little dishes that may not get eaten is time-consuming and stressful. Remember, babies who eat anything will eat easily prepared family foods and babies who are fussy eaters usually won't eat the specially prepared fancy baby dishes made to tempt them, so keep it simple. Your baby may start eating some of your food that is suitable for grinding up such as casseroles, stews, pasta, rice dishes or spaghetti. Obviously avoid hot things such as chilli, pepper and so on.

By nine months some babies are able to eat finger food such as sandwiches and cheese on toast, however, many can't cope with this sort of food until they are around a year. Sandwiches can be made with a variety of fillings such as banana, cream cheese, tomato, paté, vegemite, salmon or tuna, and cheese. Water may be given with dinner and the breastfeed or bottle saved for bedtime if that's what you and your baby prefer.

Juice

Juice is not necessary and an overabundance of juice sipped throughout the day and night in bottles and straw and spout cups in the last twenty years has led to an increase in toddler tooth decay because the juice is being consumed in a way that makes it pool around the teeth, bathing them with sugar that forms plaque, a sticky film that bacteria adhere to. Juice tends to be given to babies and toddlers for a range of reasons that have nothing to do with nutrition—relieving their boredom, getting them to sleep and stopping them from grizzling. Sucking from bottles is extremely habit-forming and hard to stop once it starts. Endless bottles of juice or milk not only cause diarrhoea and tooth decay, but interfere with babies' and toddlers' appetites and prevent them from developing healthy eating habits which are a part of normal weaning.

Occasionally juice is useful for babies who are constipated (see page 410). One drink of juice a day is reasonable in a cup to be drunk in one sitting. If you offer it straight after a meal, the vitamin C helps iron absorption. Juice is problematic when it is offered in bottles or cups with teats or straws over several hours, or worse, overnight.

Water

Water is the ideal drink for babies and toddlers and if they are truly thirsty they will drink it, especially if juice is not immediately offered as an alternative. Town water is best as it contains fluoride and is relatively inexpensive. Bottled water, one of the crazier innovations of the last twenty years, has no fluoride, no advantages over town water and is a waste of money. Mineral water has high levels of salt and other minerals and is definitely not recommended for babies, toddlers or kids of any age.

Whole cow's milk

Unfortunately the issue of milk seems to have got completely out of hand, to the point where it is viewed by many as akin to some sort of nasty poison, drops of which should never pass babies' lips. Manufacturers of infant formulas have a lot to gain from the move to encourage the prolonged use of formula. The general recommendation is to use formula for the first twelve months, but toddler formula designed for the next two years is widely advertised and available. The emphasis on the use of formula means many parents today assume manufactured milk is an essential part of infant feeding for at least the whole of the first year and maybe beyond.

Many babies bypass formula by breastfeeding and, in the second six months, combine breastfeeds with milk from a cup.

WHY THE RECOMMENDATIONS? WHAT ARE THE PROBLEMS WITH WHOLE COW'S MILK?

- When babies under six months are not breastfed or have a combination of breastmilk and formula, formula is the best and safest option to put in their bottles. Whole cow's milk lacks ingredients which are essential for a young baby's proper growth and development when it is supplying their total food requirements. Whole cow's milk is also not suitable for babies over six months as the *major* part of their diet. A large amount of whole milk in conjunction with little or no food is obviously nutritionally unsound for babies and toddlers. This does not mean babies cannot have whole milk as part of their diets, in a cup or on cereal, once they are over six months.
- Allergy/intolerance is a problem for a small number of babies (intolerance

is more common than allergy). Some babies can tolerate cow's milk formula but when introduced to whole cow's milk in any volume may vomit, get cramps and perhaps a shiny red bottom (probably due to the lactose). Other babies may get constipated (probably due to the protein). Some babies with cow's milk allergy/intolerance cannot drink cow's milk (or soy) formula either—naturally it would not be a good idea to give these babies whole cow's milk.

- Research has shown that whole cow's milk plays a part in contributing to iron deficiency in a small number of vulnerable babies and toddlers when it is started early and used excessively. Iron deficiency is cause for concern, but is more strongly associated with poverty, fad diets and ignorance. Whole cow's milk has a relatively low iron concentration and has been found to cause minuscule bleeding into the gut (detectable only by a special test) which increases the chance of iron deficiency in these babies. This information has been used widely to justify the prolonged unnecessary use of infant formula, particularly follow-on formula, for all babies rather than the small number who may need it. Formula certainly contains mammoth amounts of added iron, only 4 to 10 per cent of which is absorbed by the baby. Babies who eat well will get good iron from natural sources such as red meat, chicken and fish, legumes and grains. Citrus fruits, cauliflower, broccoli and melons provide vitamin C to help efficient iron absorption.

So, it's fine to include small amounts of full-fat whole cow's milk in your baby's diet (on her cereal or in her food) after six months. If she is bottle fed, continue to use formula in her bottles until twelve months, when you can change to full-fat whole cow's milk. If she is breastfed and starting to use a cup or straw, whole cow's milk is fine to use in the cup from six months of age—you do not have to go out and buy formula.

Whole cow's milk is preferable to soy drink as it contains naturally occurring ingredients necessary for good nutrition (for example, fat, calcium and iron) that are not present in unfortified soy drink. It is now recommended that soy drink not be used until after age two. If for some reason you are giving your baby soy drink, use a fortified infant formula. Please see page 100 for more information about the use of soy formula.

Babies who will only eat commercial food

This is another cause of anxiety for some mothers. Try not to worry. Remember you can't force babies to eat things they don't want to eat. Commercial food is nutritious and there's an incredible array around now to choose from. Stop cooking your own food if your baby is not eating it and the situation is becoming tense. Give her what she likes, but as soon as she can sit for a while in a highchair follow the jar of food with some finger foods for her to eat herself. Offer some fresh easy food (fruit, bread, cheese) regularly.

Teaching your baby to use a cup

Drinking from a cup is a skill that has to be learned—it is not a developmental milestone that suddenly happens at a certain age. Teaching babies to drink from cups takes time and patience, but there are lots of advantages for you and your baby should you decide to teach her to use a cup during her first year.

- Once she's drinking well from a cup the bottles can go, so there's one less hassle for you to worry about.
- Bottles of milk do interfere with the eating of food and in the second year when lots of babies become fussy eaters, bottles of milk and juice become a quick fix for feeding difficulties at a time when eating should be encouraged, not drinking.
- The risk of tooth decay is increased the longer the bottles are used.
- Going directly from breast to cup is the only option for breastfed babies who don't like bottles.

Here are some tips if you would like to teach your baby to drink from a cup.

N.B.: The definition of a cup is any container that does not have a teat on it.

As all babies are different you need to experiment to find out what suits your baby best—a small cup, a spout or a straw.

A small cup is often the most successful to start with. Start with two teaspoons of fluid only. If you fill up the cup your baby will be drenched and

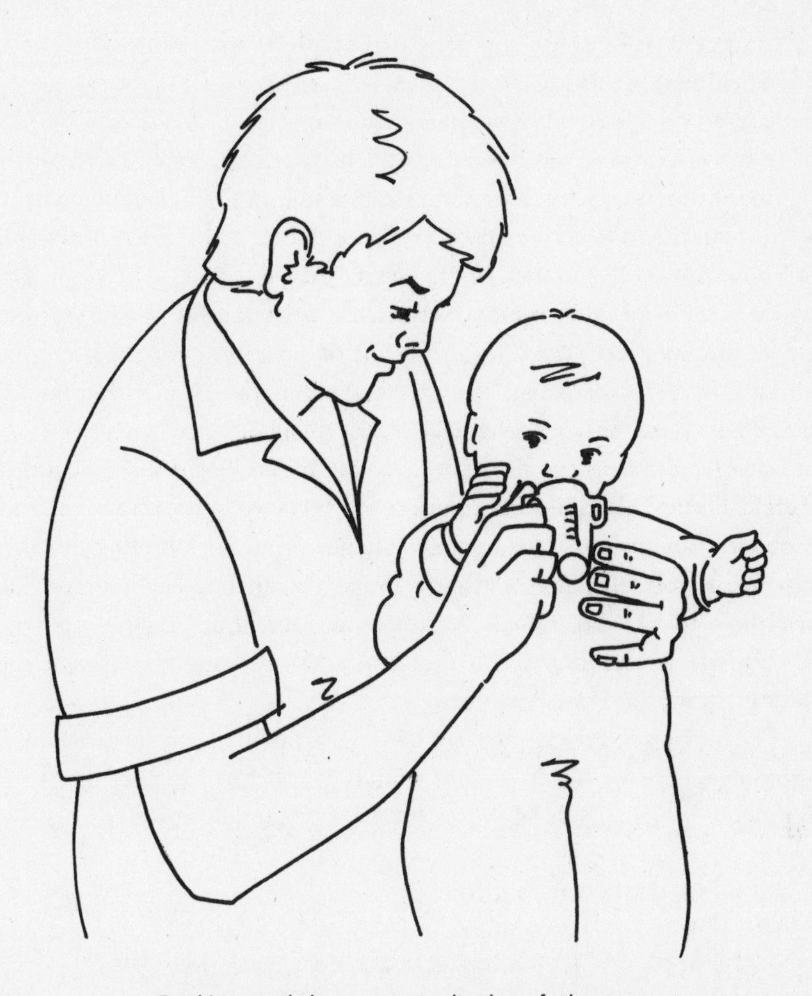

Teaching your baby to use a cup has lots of advantages

you will quickly lose patience. The main aim in the beginning is to gently teach your baby what to do, not to try to get her to drink the same amount she has from the breast or a bottle. Offer her a small amount in a cup at morning or afternoon tea time or after one of her meals. Use breastmilk, milk or water.

The more she has the opportunity to practise, the better she will become at drinking. The amount she drinks steadily increases; it takes about six to eight weeks for a baby to learn to drink 60–80ml in one go. Naturally, you have to hold the cup!

You might like to try a cup with a spout as they are less messy, however I find spouts don't suit a lot of babies because they suck them like a teat and end up coughing and spluttering a lot.

Straws can be very successful once the baby gets the idea. Start by offering one of the water packs that comes with a straw. Show your baby what to do, then put the straw to her lips and squeeze the pack so a little water squirts out to encourage her to suck on the straw. Practise whenever you can. One day she will go 'sip' and get such a surprise she will probably open her mouth and let the fluid drop out. Once she's got the idea of sipping, keeping her mouth shut and swallowing, buy one of the cups available with a built-in straw. These have the great advantage of not spilling everywhere.

Breastfed babies going from breast to cup never consume the quantities of fluid bottle-fed babies consume, so if you have a breast-to-cup baby don't panic about this. There is rarely any need to force a healthy, breastfed baby to take a bottle after six months of age. This includes babies who only have three to four breastfeeds every twenty-four hours. Babies following this plan thrive on their meals, steadily increasing amounts from a cup, spout or straw and their breastfeeds.

While spout and straw cups are extremely useful and help enormously with the mess factor, tooth decay is a risk if your baby or toddler sips at one continuously through the day unless they only contain water.

Vegetarian diets for babies

Many families now choose not to eat meat. A vegetarian diet that includes milk, eggs and other dairy products is fine for babies too.

Vegetarian diets that do not include any animal fats (vegan diets) pose problems for babies and young children as these diets tend to be bulky and offer a very limited range of food, which small people with fussy appetites are likely to have difficulty with. A continuing shortage of protein, vitamin B12, iron, calcium and fat as well as an overall shortage of calories can put a baby or toddler's growth at risk. Some of the problems can be overcome by breastfeeding and/or using a soy infant formula, mixing liberal amounts of smooth peanut butter (not until over one year) and tahini (sesame seed paste) into dishes before serving and giving a vitamin B12 supplement. The use of a soy infant formula (as opposed to soy drinks) should be continued for the second year and when replaced by a soy drink, a brand should be chosen that has added fat, calcium, B12 and iron.

Premature babies

Premature babies can follow the same dietary guidelines, although babies born earlier than thirty-four weeks will take longer to get to the stage of sitting and eating finger foods. Babies born very early may not be ready for the diet sheet on page 444 until about nine to twelve months, but all premature babies should be offered a variety of foods including finger foods by twelve months. It is fine to teach premature babies to drink from a cup any time in their second six months as well as cutting down the number of bottles they have as suggested in the diet chart. The information for breastfed premature babies at this stage is the same as for full-term babies.

Recipes

Not everyone has the time or energy to prepare special baby recipes. Not all babies will eat their delicious home-cooked meals. However, for the mothers and babies who would enjoy the process, please refer to the recipe section at the back of the book.

FOR MORE INFORMATION

Chapter 25: Common Worries and Queries *(flexible sleeping and eating guide for six months and beyond, page 460)*
Recipes, page 526

FURTHER READING

Baby & Toddler Meals, Robin Barker, Pan Macmillan Australia, 1998.

Chapter 25

Common Worries and Queries

Funny habits

Babies have lots of funny little habits that are either related to reflexes which they have no control over or the normal changes happening to their bodies as they grow. Other funny habits are part of babies' inbuilt urges to explore their own bodies and the world around them. Whenever they are tired or bored they become more obsessive and frantic about the particular strange habit they are into. Mothers often notice that the behaviour often stops when their babies are out and about being entertained and distracted.

Here are some examples of a few interesting actions and activities common to all healthy babies—none of them are anything to worry about unless there is a whole range of odd behaviour accompanied by signs of illness.

- Pulling and rubbing ears is a common action from six months and is not a sign of an ear infection or 'teething'. Once your baby discovers her ear it becomes a fascinating pastime to play with it because it makes an interesting sound and it's fun to grab hold of. If your baby is into pulling and rubbing her ears you may notice she does it more when she is bored or over-tired.

- Head-banging is another habit some babies indulge in, especially just before sleep. Try not to get disturbed by head-banging or to get worried by people who tell you it indicates baby anxiety. Try to avoid long hours of boredom on the home front by getting your baby out and about as much as possible. Like all the other actions it stops eventually.
- Sometimes you might notice your baby coughs almost deliberately even though she has no sign of a cold—another funny little habit which shows your baby has reached an age where she imitates and does things on purpose. Often, once a parent realises what's happening, he or she coughs back which encourages their baby to do it again so it becomes a game.
- Babies find their tongues fascinating parts of their equipment and many babies go through stages where they keep sticking out their tongues. Adults often find this amusing and do the same thing back so the tongue-sticking-out game is as popular a pastime as the coughing game!
- Some babies make a peculiar grunting noise deep in their throat. Making a similar noise is quite irritating to adult throats but babies manage to do this continually without any ill effect. Grunting noises in healthy babies is not a sign of constipation, bowel or tummy problems—just another strange habit that passes.
- Another habit is sucking the top or bottom lip, which looks most peculiar but is harmless.
- Babies often find constantly opening and shutting their hands is an interesting occupation which can develop into a habit for a while. Another common hand habit is to sit moving hands and wrists as if driving a motor bike.
- Ear-piercing screeches are fun and often repeated over and over again. If the screeching and squealing gets a bit much, tell your baby firmly and consistently, 'no' every time she does it. Eventually she will stop. If you keep laughing and encouraging her to do it the screechy habit will last longer.

- Rubbing eyes is another common habit. As long as your baby is otherwise well and her eyes are not excessively watery, red or have a discharge, rubbing eyes is not significant.

Babies repeat all sorts of actions. These are just a few normal habits, disappearing as they grow to be replaced by others. Don't try too hard to interpret them by projecting deep and meaningful adult thoughts onto harmless baby habits.

Routines—one last time

Here's a flexible guide for six months and beyond if you are looking for one.

5 AM TO 6 AM: Breastfeed or bottle.

7 AM TO 8.30 AM: If your baby sleeps this late, offer her breakfast as soon as she wakes (choose something from the diet sheet on page 444) before her breastfeed—give her a breastfeed straight after her food.

9 AM TO 11 AM: Bed—after some morning tea (if she wants it—see diet sheet). Baby may sleep from forty minutes to two hours.

12 NOON TO 1.30 PM: Make sure she's up by 1.30 at the latest—it's okay to wake her. Give her lunch—choose something from the diet sheet and give her a breastfeed, bottle or cup after her food.

2 PM TO 3 PM: Bed but make sure she's up by 4 pm and keep her up until bed at 7 or 7.30 pm. Baby may sleep forty minutes to two hours.

4 PM: Afternoon tea (if she wants it). You'll probably need to devote this time to amusing her or going for a walk.

6 PM: Dinner—choose something from the diet sheet.

6.30 PM: Bath followed by breastfeed or bottle.

7 TO 7.30 PM: Bed—if you are having trouble helping your baby to go to sleep read Chapter 28, page 484 and follow the 'teaching-to-sleep' guidelines which will teach her to go to sleep without the breast or bottle.

Total sleeping in the day varies from one to three hours. Changing from two to one daytime sleeps happens any time between nine months and fifteen months and depends a lot on what time the baby wakes in the morning. Babies who catnap (only sleep for thirty to forty-minute stretches) do better having several small sleeps throughout the day. Trying to 'make' babies who catnap sleep for longer periods is usually not possible. For more on sleep see page 480.

'Spoiling' and discipline

Between six and twelve months babies gain skills which make them mobile and keen to explore and this is the time you will find you have to start to set limits, to discipline. Discipline means to guide, to teach, to lead by love and example. Discipline does not mean withholding love, smacking, shouting or imposing rigid rules. Babies of this age need a few reasonable limits so they can begin to understand how their world operates, to develop healthy eating habits and to keep them safe.

At this stage limit-setting is centred around activities associated with normal development. It is not centred on behaviour as babies don't act in a premeditated fashion and still have no control over their behaviour. So, again 'spoiling' in the sense of turning a baby into a nasty person no one likes is a meaningless expression. Not setting a few limits may lead to injuries or, as the baby becomes a toddler, completely unacceptable, exhausting antics which do not contribute to the parent's wellbeing or a loving home atmosphere.

Here are a few tips on limit-setting:

- When saying 'NO', limit it to a few important things. Always say 'NO' in a firm voice that is different from your normal conversational tone.
- Childproof your house and put away as many forbidden objects as you can.
- Try diversion when you want your baby to stop what she's doing or about to do.

- Go out and about as much as possible. Babies quickly become bored at home when they are not eating or sleeping. The need for limit-setting is less when they are stimulated by new sights, sounds and people.
- If your older baby's antics are driving you mad, time out is acceptable for short periods—her cot is the best place for this.
- Work on a united front approach with your partner. Babies don't respond well to chaos and conflict on the home front.
- Repetition and patience are essential, especially between the age of nine months and three years, as it takes this long for children to *start* to develop the ability to make sensible and safe judgments about their behaviour and the possible consequences of their actions. Learn all you can about baby and child development so you know if your expectations and discipline are reasonable.

All babies and parents are different, so the limit-setting and discipline practised will be different for each family. Babies thrive equally well and grow into well-balanced young people whether the discipline is very structured or more easygoing as long as their environment is safe, stable and loving.

Nappy rash

Nappy rashes in older babies usually need a combination of a mild hydrocortisone ointment and an anti-fungal cream to clear them up, so it's always best to seek advice from your child and family health nurse or family doctor before buying out the pharmacy. A sudden bright red shiny bottom can be the result of a dietary change. Whole cow's milk, soy milk or yoghurt can all have this effect and stopping or cutting down the offending food clears the rash up. Antibiotics and a bout of viral diarrhoea can also cause sore red bottoms. Red 'weeping' bottoms caused by food, medication or viral diarrhoea need a good barrier cream thickly applied to help them heal. Here are the two I find the best:

- Ask your pharmacist to mix 1 per cent Ichthyol and 10 per cent zinc in yellow soft paraffin.
- Desitin ointment is made by Pfizer and I find it a marvellous barrier cream for babies with sensitive skin who are prone to nappy rash. It both

heals and prevents nappy rash so it's worth getting some in if your baby has a sensitive bottom.

Common illnesses 6–12 months

Diarrhoea and vomiting

Diarrhoea means that there are a lot of loose, watery bowel motions different from your baby's normal poo. Sudden diarrhoea is usually caused by a viral infection of the gut. It may or may not be accompanied by vomiting. Some gut infections cause vomiting without diarrhoea. It is often confusing sorting out viral diarrhoea and vomiting from loose poo caused by food or medication or other illnesses, so if you are ever in doubt, seek help from your family doctor.

Medication is not a part of treatment for most infectious diarrhoea. Antibiotics are only used occasionally for a specific, diagnosed bacterial infection. Medications such as those adults take to stop diarrhoea are dangerous for babies and should not be used. **Simultaneous diarrhoea and vomiting is potentially serious and needs medical assessment.** Diarrhoea or vomiting on its own usually only needs simple dietary measures.

- The correct treatment for either diarrhoea or vomiting is to give small amounts of clear fluids only for twenty-four hours. If you are breastfeeding, continue breastfeeding—if you have an abundant supply try short, frequent feeds.
- If you are bottle feeding or using a cup, the amount of fluid should not exceed 5–7ml per kilo of the baby's body weight every hour.

SUITABLE FLUIDS

- A commercial preparation such as Gastrolyte: make as directed.
- Non-diet cordial (eg Cottee's): one part cordial to six parts cooled, boiled water.
- Rice water: Boil ¾ cup of white rice in 1½ litres of water until the water is milky—not too thick! Strain the rice and add four flat teaspoons of sugar to every litre of rice water.
- Boiled water: Add four flat teaspoons of sugar to one litre of boiled water.

A FEW IMPORTANT POINTS

- A commercial preparation such as Gastrolyte is not a medication. It is a fluid replacement to be given instead of formula for twenty-four hours. Parents are often given confused messages about using a commercial fluid replacement and give it as well as formula in the mistaken belief it is a medication which will cure the diarrhoea.
- Babies under four months should be given a commercial preparation in preference to diluted cordial, rice water and sugar or boiled water and sugar.
- Older babies with simple diarrhoea or vomiting do not need commercial preparations. Any of the other suggested fluids are fine.
- Follow the guidelines for the addition of sugar closely. A small amount of glucose or sucrose helps the baby absorb fluid more efficiently and makes the fluid more palatable, but too much causes more diarrhoea. Do not give flat lemonade at any age—the sugar content is too high.

After twenty-four hours of small, frequent breastfeeds or clear fluids, reintroduce your normal breastfeeding regime or half-strength formula.

Older babies who are eating food should resume a balanced diet as soon as possible, but continue to give small amounts often for a few days. Make sure some fat is introduced during the second twenty-four-hour period (for example, breastmilk, formula or milk) as constant clear fluids and fruit and vegies alone aggravate acute diarrhoea.

Recommence full-strength formula by day three. Sometimes babies develop a temporary lactose intolerance following gastroenteritis, which means their watery diarrhoea comes back once full-strength formula or milk is reintroduced. When this happens a lactose-free formula is required for two to three weeks until the bowel recovers.

Breastfed babies tolerate breastmilk well following gastroenteritis, and do not need lactose-free formula.

Most babies respond well to these simple measures, but unfortunately there are times when the correct advice is not given or parents and health professionals underestimate the severity of the illness.

Always seek help or a second opinion if:

- You are worried.

- You are given a diagnosis of 'teething' (growing teeth does not cause diarrhoea).
- Your baby is under three months of age.
- Your baby suffers from other illnesses such as diabetes, heart disease, urinary tract infections or is on any medication.
- Your baby is simultaneously vomiting and having diarrhoea, especially if she is not keeping down breastmilk or clear fluids.
- Your baby is lethargic, drowsy, has a dry mouth and is passing less urine than normal.

What about the well, happy baby with mild diarrhoea, no 'burnt' bottom, no vomiting, no weight loss and no fever?

When this happens it is difficult to decide whether or not to start the diarrhoea regime as the baby gets very cross and very hungry. Wait one or two days and see what develops. Continuing loose poo in an otherwise well baby can go on for some time after an episode of viral diarrhoea. It's inconvenient and messy but harmless and eventually stops.

N.B.: endless bottles of juice exacerbate loose poo. Try water when she is thirsty.

Ear infections

Ear problems in older babies are very common.

The problems usually occur in the middle ear because the eustachian tube which connects the middle ear to the throat is short and straight in this age group. This allows easy entry of mucus, milk and germs into the chamber of the middle ear. Older babies and toddlers also catch a lot of colds until they build up some resistance to bugs. The extra mucus that colds create blocks the eustachian tube, which stops the middle ear from draining properly.

A problem with ears is caused by either:

- An acute infection from infected mucus. This is painful so the baby's behaviour may change dramatically. She may have screaming attacks, whinge more than usual or develop a sudden sleep problem. It's always worth having your baby's ears checked when these things happen. Antibiotics and pain relievers are needed;

OR

- A collection of uninfected mucus in the middle ear, called glue ear. Glue ear is generally not painful but transient earaches occur, especially at night, so a change in night sleep patterns may occur even when a baby is happy during the day. Treatment for glue ear ranges from none to medication to insertion of tubes depending on the frequency of infections, the discomfort and the amount of hearing loss.

With universal immunisation of the pneumococcal vaccine there will be a 30 per cent decrease in ear infections and a 20 per cent decrease in the requirement for grommets.

Urinary tract infection

A urinary tract infection (UTI) is caused by a growth of germs—usually in the bladder but sometimes in the kidneys. It is common in babies, toddlers and children. Approximately 30 per cent of urinary tract infections in babies occur because of an underlying structural problem in the urinary system. It is routine for all babies to have investigations (special X-rays) and an ultrasound when a UTI is diagnosed to treat such conditions if they are present to prevent chronic renal problems later in life.

SYMPTOMS

Symptoms in babies and toddlers under three can be vague and confusing, which is why urine is routinely tested when the cause of a fever is not clear. Irritability, vomiting and failure to thrive can also be symptoms of a urinary tract infection.

Sometimes the parent will notice odd-smelling urine or urine that looks cloudy or thick and occasionally the baby may show signs of distress when having a pee.

TREATMENT

A urine specimen is collected and tested and antibiotics commenced if an infection is present. Collecting urine samples from babies can be a challenge. An attempt is made to catch a clean sample of urine in a suitable specimen jar (plastic urine bags are no longer used as contamination causes unreliable results when the urine is tested). If this proves too difficult, or if the baby is very ill, the urine may have to be collected in hospital by inserting a fine tube or needle into the bladder via the abdomen.

With the antibiotics, infections will clear in five to seven days, but the baby may continue a smaller dose of the medication until the results of the investigation are known.

Treatment for underlying kidney and bladder problems ranges from protective antibiotics for a period of time to surgery, depending on what the problem is.

Coughs

Coughing is a reflex we are all born with. Babies cough to clear their throats, which helps clear their air passages. Coughing accompanies many illnesses. When your baby has a cold the reason for coughing is obvious. When coughing is associated with wheezing, a high fever, breathlessness or sleepless nights see your family doctor. It is dangerous to give cough suppressants to a baby or a young child. Worrying coughs should always be investigated.

Croup

Croup is a form of laryngitis that follows a viral infection in the upper respiratory tract and affects the voice box and trachea. It is more common in babies and toddlers than in older children and adults because they have small soft windpipes that collapse easily when inflamed. The baby's cough sounds like a baby seal barking and is accompanied by a crowing noise as she breathes in. Her voice may be hoarse and she may have trouble breathing.

Croup is more severe at night when the air is cooler and the worst period usually lasts about two nights. Some babies have what is known as 'spasmodic croup'—frequent attacks of a small duration. These tend to occur at night lasting for a few hours and occasionally recur the following night.

TREATMENT

The previous treatment of using steam to alleviate symptoms is no longer recommended as the risks of burns and scalds far outweigh any benefits, which have been shown to be negligible. Calm your baby as much as you can by sitting her on your lap while the bout lasts.

Go to hospital immediately if:

- You are worried about your baby's breathing or sucking her chest right in.
- She becomes pale and sweaty or blue.

Croup is usually mild, but it can get worse quickly. If you are worried, seek medical help.

MEDICATIONS

As croup is caused by a virus, antibiotics are not appropriate. The only medications used for croup are steroids and adrenaline, which are administered in hospital.

Wheezing and asthma in babies under twelve months

Accurate diagnosis of asthma in this age group is difficult. Episodes of prolonged coughing are common amongst babies and toddlers under two. The endless cough is usually associated with upper respiratory tract infections and is unlikely to be associated with asthma when there is no wheeze or history of allergic conditions such as eczema, hay fever and reactions to food. Some babies under twelve months have troublesome episodes of wheezing but are otherwise thriving and happy. Most of them lose the wheeze after the first year. Consult your family doctor if you are worried about your baby's coughing or wheezing.

Pneumonia

Pneumonia is a viral or bacterial infection of the lungs that causes swelling and blockage in sections of the lung. It is also often referred to as a 'chest infection'. Pneumonia occurs at all ages but is most common in babies and toddlers.

SYMPTOMS

Pneumonia may follow a mild infection of the nose and throat. It can be tricky to initially diagnose in babies as the symptoms vary greatly and can be very subtle. For example, neck stiffness, lack of energy, fever and loss of appetite (a baby's sudden refusal to feed or disinterest in breast or bottle usually means something is wrong). Other symptoms include rapid breathing, grunting while breathing and a bluish tinge around the mouth. A chest X-ray is usually needed to confirm the diagnosis.

TREATMENT

Antibiotics are used when bacteria is the cause of the infection. Serious pneumonia needs hospitalisation for intravenous therapy to administer fluids and antibiotics (if appropriate). Paracetamol is used for pain and fever. Recovery usually takes seven to ten days.

With universal immunisation of the pneumococcal vaccine there will be a 20 per cent decrease in pneumococcal pneumonia.

Fevers

Babies and toddlers are much more prone to running fevers than older children and adults are. Fever is the body's natural defence against infection (for example a cold, a urinary tract infection). Most fevers in babies are caused by viral infections, but fevers can be caused by things not related to infection such as over-dressing, being kept too long in a hot car or crying for a long time. 'Teething' does not cause fevers. Mild fevers that come and go over a period of time should always be investigated.

A fever is not the only sign of an illness. Some serious illnesses only cause mild fevers. Older babies and toddlers can have relatively high fevers (40°C) and still be active and eating and drinking well.

HOW DO I TAKE MY BABY'S TEMPERATURE?

The regular glass thermometer remains the most accurate way to take a temperature although it is sometimes difficult with a squirming baby. Try to make sure the thermometer is well up into the armpit and surrounded by skin. Hold the top of the baby's arm firmly against her body for as long as you can, ideally at least three minutes. If it is 37.5°C or higher, she has a fever.

Most parents become skilled at estimating fever by touch. The best method is to place the back of your hand on your baby's tummy. You will soon learn the difference between a warm, hot or burning feel.

WHAT IF HER TEMPERATURE IS BELOW NORMAL?

Usually this is because the thermometer is not registering properly—not because there is something wrong with your baby. If her body and head are warm and if she is a good colour with good skin tone and a loud cry, there is unlikely to be a problem. However, if she is pale and floppy and feels cool to touch, seek help immediately.

HERE ARE THE THINGS TO DO IF YOUR BABY HAS A FEVER

- From birth to three months all babies should be checked by a doctor for any fever (37.5°C and over) unless the fever is directly related to immunisation in which case the cause is known and it should run its course and fade. Babies aged from three to twelve months with high fevers (39°C) should also be seen by their doctors.
- Mild to moderate fevers (37.5°C–39°C) do not necessarily have to be treated if the baby is otherwise happy and comfortable.
- If your baby is hot and irritable, undress her down to her singlet and nappy and give a single dose of paracetamol or ibuprofen. Encourage her to take extra fluids and consult your doctor if the fever does not settle or you are worried (see When to call the doctor, page 199).

Fever fits (convulsions)

A fever fit is a convulsion caused by a high temperature. The most common age for this to happen is between eighteen and twenty-four months, but overall it happens to about 4 per cent of all babies and children aged between six months and five years.

WHY DOES IT HAPPEN?

Babies and young children have immature brains that are particularly sensitive to outside stress. Some just can't handle a high body temperature so their brains respond by giving off an abnormal electrical discharge that results in a fit. Having a fit means the baby loses consciousness and twitches all over. It can happen out of the blue when it is not obvious that the baby has a fever, however, there is usually a history of an illness such as a bad cold, an ear infection, tonsillitis or sometimes gastroenteritis. Urinary tract infections are less common, but can cause very high fevers which is why a urine test is done when the cause of the fever is not clear.

WHAT DO YOU DO?

It's very scary but don't panic! The fit usually lasts less than five minutes but that can seem like forever when you're the parent. Stay with your baby. Place her on her side or tummy with her head on the side. Loosen any clothes around her neck and gently support her head with your hands. Don't put anything in her mouth or force open her gums. Urgent medical help should be sought if it lasts longer than five minutes.

When your baby comes around, take her to your family doctor or your nearest children's hospital as it is important to confirm that it is only a fever fit. This may mean some tests being done depending on the age of the baby and how long the fit lasted.

Febrile convulsions can recur. After the first convulsion there is a 30 per cent chance of recurrence (50 per cent if the baby is under a year); after the second convulsion a 50 per cent chance. Guidelines for babies/toddlers with fevers who have histories of fever fits are the same as for any babies or toddlers. Routine repeated use of paracetamol or ibuprofen for mild to moderate fevers has not been shown to be useful in reducing the incidence of febrile convulsions. Frightening though they are, febrile convulsions are usually brief and harmless and when you know one may occur, you can be prepared.

Infectious diseases

These are not common in a baby's first year but do happen. Identifying a rash as a particular disease (for example, measles, roseola, rubella, viral rash or an allergy rash) is often an educated guess in the first year as strange rashes at this time are not always easy to diagnose accurately.

The time between the infection (before the symptoms appear) and the illness (when the symptoms appear) is called the incubation period.

CHICKENPOX

Chickenpox is preceded by a mild fever and a fussy baby. The rash starts as small, raised pink spots which turn into blisters then form crusts. The incubation period is fourteen to twenty-one days so there can be a three-week gap between one family member and another becoming infected. Parents often worry about the likelihood of their very young baby catching chickenpox from older babies and toddlers. New babies can catch chickenpox but their natural immunity protects them to a large extent so it is unusual to see chickenpox in the first six months after birth.

Treatment aims to relieve the itch and fever. Give paracetamol and warm to hot baths. Add some anti-itch solution such as Pinetarsol to the bath water. Calamine lotion applied directly to the spots helps.

A vaccine is now available for chickenpox. You may have your baby vaccinated at your own expense after twelve months of age. See your family doctor.

MEASLES

Measles immunisation is started at twelve months, but a small number of babies do catch measles before they are immunised. If this happens your baby still needs her immunisation at twelve months.

The incubation period is seven to fourteen days. Measles first appear as a cold. The baby is miserable with a runny nose, watery eyes, a cough and a fever. Two days later spots appear on the neck, behind the ears and on her face.

Within hours the whole body is covered. The rash often joins together and becomes one red mass or a series of blotches. Give paracetamol to bring the fever down and encourage extra fluids.

RUBELLA (GERMAN MEASLES)

Rubella immunisation is included with the measles, mumps immunisation at twelve months. Rubella has an incubation period of fourteen to twenty-one days. It is often difficult to diagnose in babies and is frequently confused with measles, roseola, an allergy or a viral rash. The baby may have mild cold symptoms. The rash rapidly spreads over her arms and body. It appears as small, pink separate dots, unlike the measles rash which is red and blotchy.

The most reliable sign confirming rubella is swollen glands at the back of the neck and behind the ears.

Care should be taken to avoid contact with women who are in the early stages of pregnancy as the rubella virus is dangerous to the developing baby.

The introduction of the rubella vaccine as part of the measles/mumps/rubella immunisation, as well as the rubella immunisation in high schools, has done a lot to eliminate the risk, but if there is any doubt about the possibility of a problem your family doctor or obstetrician should be consulted.

ROSEOLA

Roseola is an acute viral disease which is most commonly seen in babies between six and twelve months. The incubation period is about ten days.

Roseola starts with a sudden very high fever which remains for four to five days. Just after the height of the fever a pale pink blotchy rash appears on the chest and spreads to the arms and legs. It is rarely on the face. The rash fades quickly, usually within twenty-four to thirty hours. Treatment involves bringing the high fever down with paracetamol.

WHOOPING COUGH (PERTUSSIS)

Whooping cough is still around; partly because the immunisation only gives 80 to 90 per cent protection, but mostly because there is a rise in the number of parents who are choosing not to immunise their babies.

If your baby has been immunised and does get whooping cough, the illness is much milder and easier to manage. Whooping cough starts as a short, dry cough with a fever developing a short time later. After a few days the whoop develops and vomiting occurs. Small babies tend not to whoop but have difficulty breathing and blue attacks. They are at great risk and need hospital care so they can have round-the-clock attention. Even a mild case lasts six weeks.

FOR MORE INFORMATION

Chapter 10: Early Worries and Queries *(nappy rash, page 167)*
Chapter 12: Safety *(immunisation, page 235)*
Chapter 15: The Crying Baby *(lactose intolerance, page 299)*
Chapter 19: Common Worries and Queries *(recycled food in the poo, page 411)*
Chapter 24: Feeding Your Baby *(diet chart, page 444)*

Chapter 26

Growth and Development

Growth

During the third three months of their lives lots of babies gain around 60 to 90 grams (2 to 3oz) a week and between six months and twelve months will grow 8 to 10cm (3 to 4 inches).

AT NINE MONTHS

	Small/Normal	**Large/Normal**
Boys	weight 7.5kg (17lb)	11.6kg (24lb)
	height 67cm (26 inches)	78cm (29 inches)
	head circ. 43cm (16 inches)	48cm (18 inches)
Girls	weight 7.0kg (15lb)	10.8kg (22lb)
	height 65cm (25 inches)	75cm (28 inches)
	head circ. 42.5cm (15½ inches)	47cm (17½ inches)

Development

Gross motor development

- By nine months your baby will be sitting alone. If she has only just learnt to do it she may only manage ten minutes at a time.
- While she sits she will lean forwards to pick up toys and examine them. If she leans sideways she might fall.
- She may be crawling very efficiently, starting to crawl or still just sitting.
- She may be starting to pull herself up onto furniture. This gives her a new view of the world—suddenly she can see what the top of a coffee table looks like. After standing and holding for a short time she may fall backwards—bump!
- When you hold her she will weight bear and take alternate stepping movements.

Vision and fine movements

- She is visually very eager with a fine eye for detail.
- She will start to pick up fluff, crumbs and small objects with three fingers and may at times have difficulty releasing what's in her fingers. Her forefinger constantly leads the way exploring like a little antenna—poke, poke, poke.
- When she drops things she looks for them. By now she is probably playing the dropping game so you can pick things up for her.

It's important to provide a safe environment so your baby can explore fully without too many inhibitions.

Hearing and speech

- Your baby is very attentive to voices (especially yours), music and everyday sounds.
- She will turn to a tiny sound behind each ear if she is not too distracted.
- She makes talking noises constantly and deliberately, which may be friendly or surprised or noises which show she is upset or annoyed.
- Most babies are now stringing together consonants followed by vowels like da-da, ma-ma, adaba, agaga and so on.

- She will start to imitate noises like a raspberry or a cough.
- She understands 'no, no' (but doesn't necessarily obey) and 'bye-bye'.

Social and play

- Fussiness with strangers and distress when separated from their mothers is common for many babies now in varying degrees.
- Your baby can hold finger food well at this age and eat it without too many mishaps.
- Everything still goes into the mouth for a thorough checking.
- If asked, she will offer you a toy (if she's in the mood) but mostly can't let go of it into your hand.
- She loves playing peek-a-boo and bashing two blocks together. If she has been taught to she can clap hands, although not necessarily on request.
- When you partially hide something and she is interested and watches you do it, she will often find it.

Developmental summary: 9 months

Gross motor skills

- sits alone for 10–15 minutes;
- leans forwards to pick up toys;
- attempts to crawl;
- pulls to stand.

Vision and fine movements

- vision attentive;
- stretches out to grab things;
- pokes with forefinger;
- inferior pincer grasp;
- looks in correct direction for falling toys.

Hearing and speech

- attentive to voice and everyday sounds;

- vocalises (ma, da, ba);
- shouts;
- babbles;
- turns to minimal sound.

Social and play

- holds and chews;
- distinguishes strangers from familiars;
- imitates;
- plays 'boo';
- claps hands (if taught), bangs two blocks together.

Serious developmental delay due to unknown causes

Chapter 13: Growth and Development (page 245) gives a general guide to developmental delays in babies that need investigating. A tiny number of babies appear to develop normally until around nine months, when it starts to become apparent that possibly things are not quite right. Unfortunately it may be a long time before a definite cause or prognosis is established. Needless to say it is an ordeal for parents who face months, even years, of repeated assessments before knowing what the problem is and what the future holds. Parents, understandably, sometimes ignore their secret worries, but if you ever have any concerns it is better to seek advice as soon as possible so you can get all the help and support available. Health professionals can be over-reassuring, so if deep down you feel things are not right with your baby, find someone who is expert at assessing baby/child development. Major children's hospitals in capital cities also have child development units where detailed assessments can be made.

FOR MORE INFORMATION

Chapter 32: Becoming a Toddler *(separation anxiety and stranger awareness, page 520)*

Chapter 27

Safety

The following chart emphasises particular hazards associated with this developmental stage, but don't forget most safety hazards remain at any age and stage.

Don't forget your baby's third round of immunisation is due at 6 months.

Age	Developmental stage	Safety hazard	Precautions
7–8 months	• increasing dexterity at picking up small objects	• greater manual skills increase the risk of swallowing or inhaling foreign bodies • cuts from sharp or breakable objects left within reach	• remove small, sharp and breakable objects from reach • be careful of lotions, creams and equipment on the change table—keep safety pins out of reach

Age	Developmental stage	Safety hazard	Precautions
8–12 months	• may drink from a cup • may walk • increasingly mobile	• poisoning—does not discriminate between food, drinks and other substances • scalds—pulls tablecloth and dangling electrical cords, spilling hot liquids • animal stings, bites, scratches • strangulation—head caught between railings of fence, verandah or banisters • suffocation—plastic bags over airways • electrocution—playing with electrical power appliances and power points • falls—from stairs, porches, beds, highchairs and so on	• store all poisons, cleaning agents, medications, insecticides in a locked cupboard—don't forget alcohol! • take care when medicating your baby • constant supervision • supervision near animals • wear covering on feet out of doors where there is a risk of a bee sting • destroy or tie a knot in unused plastic bags. Don't leave them anywhere near the baby, day or night. This includes shopping bags. • use socket covers on power points • supervision • constant vigilance • stairgates

FOR MORE INFORMATION

Chapter 12: Safety *(immunisation, page 235)*

Chapter 28

Sleeping and Waking Six Months and Beyond

To sleep—perchance to dream, ay, there's the rub.

WILLIAM SHAKESPEARE, *HAMLET*

Night waking—your options

First, a refresher about 'sleeping through'. 'Sleeping through' is a confusing expression as it implies sleeping soundly, without stirring, all night. In fact humans of all ages have brief waking periods during the night following a light sleep and dreaming phase before going into a deep sleep. Babies who disturb their parents at night become fully awake at this time and are unable to put themselves back to sleep so eventually start to cry.

At this stage, they are given a breastfeed, dummy, bottle, are rocked and patted, or are put into bed with their parents. I call these external aids. There is nothing wrong with using external aids to help babies get back to sleep as long as parents remain happy to keep obliging. Many babies will not voluntarily give up their external sleeping aids. As they get older they continue to rely on certain conditions being in place before they get off to sleep. Adults also get used to certain conditions like using the same bed and pillow. If we go on holidays and change our conditions of sleep (the bed and the pillow) we invariably have trouble sleeping but usually get used to new conditions of sleep after a few nights—if they remain consistent—and sleep well again.

Overall, about 40 per cent of babies between six and twelve months continue to wake at night. The night waking varies between waking once for a quick feed and going straight back to sleep to waking every two or three hours.

Many babies start to sleep for longer periods at night without disturbing their parents by the time they are three months old only to start crying again at night between six and twelve months. Some research suggests this is because babies of this age have intense dreaming phases from which they wake easily.

Babies who still share their parents' bedrooms are more likely to wake and want attention more often after six months than babies who are in their own room, although this is not always the case.

All parents and babies are different and parents have their own individual expectations and tolerance of night-time waking. Some are quite prepared for months, even years, of broken sleep, while others hope their babies will sleep all night without disturbing them by the time they are six months old. This expectation is not unreasonable, but unfortunately a lot of information circulating about babies and sleep suggests there is nothing that can be safely done to change an older baby's night waking. Consequently, many sleep-deprived parents live with night waking believing that there is no other safe option.

Night waking under six months

I believe that not a lot can be done about night waking (once any feeding or medical problems are sorted out) until babies are over six months of age for a few different reasons:

- Young breastfed babies need to wake and feed frequently in order to keep breastfeeding working the way it's supposed to.
- Leaving young babies to cry at night instead of feeding them can mean weeks of crying, which is distressing and unkind for everyone and rarely changes what the baby is doing.
- It often takes six months for parents to get to know their baby, work out

which babycare options they wish to follow, learn the difference between food, health and behaviour and gain confidence in caring for their baby.

By six months or so things are different for many babies and parents

- In my opinion between six and twelve months babies are old enough to learn new conditions of sleep. This opinion is based on my hands-on work with families over many years. It is also the opinion of many other practitioners—nurses, paediatricians, psychologists, family doctors and social workers—whose work involves helping sleep-deprived parents to better nights with their babies.
- Parents who wish to change what's happening during the night are more confident about deciding what to do.
- It is also much easier at this stage to separate a sleep problem from hunger or a medical problem. By six months feeding problems are usually sorted out and the majority of babies are thriving. For most babies it's reasonable to assume that they are not waking for hunger, especially when, as is so common, its a strapping nine-month-old baby on three hearty meals a day who has never slept more than two or three hours at a time since birth.

  By six months the early months of worrying about 'colic', 'wind' and 'reflux' have faded, so it's easier now to know if there is actually a medical problem that's causing the night waking (rarely is this the case).

And I know you know it's not teething:

The tendency to view ongoing sleep problems as teething is misleading and unhelpful. Babies get twenty teeth sometime between three-and-a-half months and three years whether they sleep all night or not. Waiting for all the teeth to come through before doing anything about sleepless nights means waiting for three years—interestingly, an age some people on the attachment-parenting end of the sleep spectrum think is about the right time for parents to expect undisturbed nights.

Common causes of night waking apart from sleep patterns and conditions of sleep

- Developmental issues—many things related to normal development have the potential to interfere with sleep: separation anxiety (see page 520); learning about cause and effect; learning new skills—sitting up, pulling up on the side of the cot. And as your baby starts to become a toddler between nine and twelve months you may start to be aware of the beginnings of the negativity, testing limits behaviour and even signs of her working out how much control she might have.

  It must be emphasised that all these things are part of normal development and not a sign of 'naughtiness' or bad behaviour.
- Illnesses (coughs, colds and ear infections are the most common).
- A change of environment (different room, different bed, different house).
- A change of routine (holidays, travel, visitors, separation/divorce, childcare).

Some babies will experience one or more of the above and return to sleeping all night after the drama is over, but for many the ear infection gets better, the visitors leave, but the night waking remains.

What's a parent to do?

Part of deciding to do something about your baby's sleep pattern is to work out whether it is a problem or not. Parents often feel pressured by those around them, so try and learn to ignore uncalled for, unwanted advice.

Lots of advice about night sleeping only emphasises one option, which tends to make parents feel bad if they do something different. For example, 'controlled-crying is harmful and dangerous' or 'sleeping with your baby is wrong'.

There are a few options—the trick is to find what works for you and some parents go around in circles a few times before working out what they are prepared to do.

If you are happy or can live with what's happening, there's no need to do anything.

Try to think things through carefully. Changing your baby's night-time waking usually involves leaving her to cry (yes, 'controlled-crying'). Regardless of how confident or desperate you feel about this, it is painful for most parents to leave their baby to cry. And undoubtedly painful for the babies as well—more on that later.

If your baby is waking once a night for a quick feed and going straight back to sleep I wouldn't recommend changing things. If your baby sleeps for nine or ten hours but doesn't go off until later in the evening I'd suggest you live with it for a while. Nor is it useful to leave babies crying at four o'clock in the morning when they've been asleep since seven at night.

'Controlled-crying' or as I choose to call it, 'teaching-to-sleep', is more a strategy for the two to three-hourly night waker who has not slept all night since birth. I find that teaching-to-sleep is, in general, a successful way to helping these babies learn to sleep without calling for help over a short period of time (three nights).

Most parents ask themselves whether the night waking dilemma could have been prevented. The answer is probably not, and there is very little value in soul-searching, agonising and going back over what you did or didn't do over the last six months. Caring for babies is not always easy and everyone does what they have to do, especially during those exciting, strange and anxious early months.

The four options

Options are limited and despite a multitude of variations on the sleep theme, when you peel back all the layers there are only four. Changing or living with your baby's night-time sleep patterns always involves one of the following:

1. Teaching your baby to sleep (involves stopping all the external helping-to-sleep aids and leaving her to cry).
2. Living with it (continue feeding, rocking, patting and bed sharing).
3. Using a sedative (a very limited option and only appropriate in certain circumstances).
4. The Bhutanese solution.

Let's look at the options:

1. Leave your baby to her own devices: Controlled-crying—otherwise known as 'teaching-to-sleep', 'sleep training', 'control comforting', 'comfort settling', 'responsive settling' and 'progressive waiting'—is the main strategy here. There are many variations on this theme from leaving the baby to 'cry-it-out' after one visit, to complicated regimes that involve going in every one or two minutes to plans similar to the one I offer, to combining controlled-crying with a sedative.

ADVANTAGES OF THIS OPTION

- It has the potential to bring persistent night-time disturbances by a healthy baby to an end when all other strategies have failed and the whole family's mental health and wellbeing is being threatened.
- It has the potential to dramatically improve the relationship of exhausted parents, and between the parents and the baby.
- Solving or at least improving night sleep problems is an aid for postnatal depression.
- It is sometimes the only way to stop evening and night-time bottles and overnight breastfeeding in older babies and toddlers.
- Giving parents balanced information about 'controlled-crying' helps them decide themselves whether this is what they want to do. Some parents need to try it to know they don't want to do it, which then makes it easier for them to go back to learning to live with it.
- Resuming a sexual relationship as well as re-establishing the emotional and social relationship that two adults share is easier for some couples when endless nights of continually disturbed sleep (not just one feed) and bed-sharing are not getting in the way. Most people can handle this for a certain period, but there comes a time when couples may want their babies out of their beds and into separate rooms in the second six months so they can have some time to themselves. This is perfectly reasonable. The quality of the parents' relationship has to be a factor in the overall consideration of what's best for baby.

DISADVANTAGES AND RISKS OF THIS OPTION

- Leaving a baby to cry until she goes to sleep is painful for baby and parents. It sometimes causes so much distress that it is abandoned. Parents may then feel disappointed and let-down, even inadequate in some way.
- It doesn't always work and good results may not be permanent.

- As with co-sleeping, leaving a baby to cry is not safe in certain circumstances:
  - — If the baby is sick or upset by recent events (moving house, starting kindy or childcare, a new baby, divorce and separation).
  - — If there are overwhelming emotional, social or economic family problems. (See page 489, When it's about more than just sleep.)
  - — Leaving babies to cry for weeks on end is unsafe for their physical, emotional and psychological wellbeing.
- Some parents, especially where there is a lot of parental stress, need help and supervision from a committed, experienced health professional to do 'controlled-crying' safely and effectively.
- Unintended negative consequences in some circumstances may include changes in the baby's behaviour such as clinginess and withdrawal. See page 489.
- There have been no studies done which assess the stress levels of babies in association with controlled-crying or its emotional or psychological impact.
- The latest Sids and Kids recommendation to reduce the risks of sudden unexpected death in infancy (SUDI) is for baby to share the room (in a separate bed) for six to twelve months which may cause parents to be anxious about having their baby in a separate room after six months. Teaching babies to sleep on their own is best done with baby in a separate room as the chance of a successful outcome is minimised when the baby stays in the same room as the parents. The Sids and Kids recommendation is frustratingly unclear in relation to the second six months. It is hard to know if room-sharing in the **second six months is an option or a recommendation**. It is also hard to find out exactly what the risk is of a separate room in the second six months if all the guidelines for safe sleeping are met. As 95 per cent of sudden unexpected deaths in infancy have occurred by six to eight months one has to assume the risk is slight, however if this is of concern to you it will affect how you handle doing the teaching-to-sleep. If this is the case I advise you to wait until your baby is twelve months old (or whatever age you feel comfortable about her sleeping in a separate room) before you start a sleep training program.

2. Live with it: Sharing your bed is the main strategy here; other commonly suggested strategies include a three-sided cot adjoining your bed, one parent sleeping with the baby in her room, a cot lined up beside your bed, going to your baby and patting her until she goes to sleep, pretending to ignore, minimal attention, bottles of water instead of milk, free breastfeeding, alternating 'nights on' with your partner, re-organising daytime sleeps, sitting in a chair by her bed until she goes to sleep, a night-light.

ADVANTAGES OF THIS OPTION

- It avoids having to listen to a baby distressed and crying for any length of time.
- Some parents enjoy sleeping with their babies because of the closeness. Some of the other strategies mentioned above are not onerous when the night waking is occasional and when they work quickly to put the baby off to sleep.
- Some health professionals and parents view this option as 'risk-free' in comparison to the various methods of 'controlled-crying' which they believe has the potential to cause harm.
- Some health professionals and parents believe co-sleeping and freely responding to night-time requests from their older babies and toddlers, regardless of what this might entail, is an important part of creating a harmonious family life and being a committed parent.

DISADVANTAGES AND RISKS OF THIS OPTION

- There are identified risk factors to co-sleeping. However, these can be dealt with. Please see page 216.
- Dental decay is a small risk for some toddlers when co-sleeping includes continuous breastfeeding throughout the night over several years. Decay is a considerable risk when bottles of milk or juice are used throughout the toddler years to help get the toddler to sleep in the first place and back to sleep during the night.
- Co-sleeping, endless broken nights feeding and/or patting babies to sleep, constantly replacing dummies and playing musical beds is not everybody's idea of family nirvana. It has the potential to eventually negatively affect the parental relationship and the emotional life of the whole family. In my work I find that it is not what the majority of adults

wish to do, which has a lot to do with my approach to routine sleep problems. There is no evidence, either way, that there are any long-term advantages for children based solely on where they slept as babies and toddlers (as long as basic safety measures are in place).

3. Sedation: A very limited option and only appropriate under certain circumstances.

ADVANTAGES OF THIS OPTION

- If it works, a sedative can give everyone a night's sleep.
- It is occasionally helpful for sick babies or babies recovering from jet lag.

DISADVANTAGES AND RISKS OF THIS OPTION

- Sedatives have a relatively high failure rate.
- Long-term use of a sedative is dangerous and if overused may have a negative impact on the baby's development.
- Sedatives do not solve night sleep problems.

4. The Bhutanese solution: In her book, *A Baby in a Backpack to Bhutan* (Pan Macmillan, Australia, 2004), Bunty Avieson and Kathryn, her nine-month-old baby, join a stream of Bhutanese mothers and babies visiting a local deity for help with sleepless babies—apparently 'sleep' is an issue for Bhutanese mothers too. In an ancient Bhutan temple, on a high ridge in the Himalayas, a smiling Buddhist monk lights incense, chants and gently taps Kathryn's head with an ancient relic. The results are excellent, Kathryn and Bunty enjoy nine glorious uninterrupted hours of sleep in separate beds thereafter.

Sound good to me. I wonder if there's any possibility of arranging for Bhutanese monks to spend some time in Australian child and family health centres.

If you are considering making the trip, as well as your baby you need to take a large quantity of butter, sweet biscuits, top quality incense and strong beer. Bhutan is a tiny nation nestled in the Himalayas ruled by a king who has decreed that Gross National Happiness is more important than Gross National Product. Enjoy your journey.

When it's about more than just sleep

Sometimes ongoing sleep problems are about more than just sleep. There are times when baby sleep problems are an indication of more deep-seated family problems which need to be addressed before dealing with the sleep problems on a practical level. It is impossible when writing a book to cover every reader's individual experience, so, if you are aware of such a possibility in your household I recommend that you seek professional advice and help.

A quick rule of thumb is that if you feel that you are continually distressed about your baby's night-time waking and you can't put a teach-to-sleep plan into action or come to a suitable compromise, then further help is advisable. Further help involves counselling to resolve other issues that may be affecting your ability to deal satisfactorily with the sleep hassles.

Controlled-crying, teaching-to-sleep—proof of harm/proof of no harm

One of the problems you may be facing is whether strategies to teach babies to sleep at night by leaving them to cry is harmful. Here is some information to help you decide. Please peruse the Further Reading list as well.

PROOF OF HARM

Concerns about harm are based on selective information related to sleep, childhood development theories, and theories on emotional and psychological stress in children. Critics of controlled-crying strategies often use extreme examples of emotional deprivation to support their claims of harm, for example Romanian orphanages, which bear little relationship to much-loved babies in good homes.

The majority of critics are mostly (I acknowledge not always) people who are not hands-on practitioners and do not have the day-to-day experience hands-on practitioners have with normal families. They do not have to come up with suitable, practical ways of helping all families rather than a relatively few like-minded people.

Proof of harm would have to show that there were long-term, sustained emotional and psychological problems *solely* related to doing a safe version of controlled-crying with older babies and toddlers over a short period of time. There are no studies to show this is the case. As a hands-on practitioner of twenty years who helped and followed up around ten families a week with older baby and toddler sleep problems, I never found there to be any long-term emotional or psychological ill effects. In fact for most of the families the whole issue became a minor blip on the horizon once the sleep problem was sorted out. Similar anecdotal reports are made by the majority of hands-on practitioners whose work entails a never-ending flow of sleep-deprived parents.

PROOF OF NO HARM

It is true, however, that despite the fact that versions of controlled-crying (long before it was called that) have been around for decades there has never been any assessments done to determine the impact of the stress of it on babies and toddlers or the impact of it on their emotional and psychological development. In other words, we do not know for certain that it is 100 per cent safe.

I acknowledge that because I found 'no harm' in my practice does not mean that there is no risk and that, in some situations, there may be unintended negative consequences. There may also be unintended negative consequences when parents feel they are forced to sleep with their baby or toddler or put up with night-time shenanigans over many years because there is no safe alternative, not to mention the increased risk of tooth decay from long-term overnight feeding; breast or bottle.

In the context of a healthy baby in a loving home I believe, based on my professional experience, that if there were negative consequences due *solely* to controlled-crying they would be short-term.

Some babies experience negative consequences from childcare, from hospitalisation, from giving up their bottles and dummies and from having their hair washed. To put it bluntly, with help from confident, stable parents, they get over it.

Children are damaged by war, malnutrition, neglect, emotional deprivation, abuse, poverty, saturated fats, refugee detention camps, fighting parents . . . let's get a bit of perspective into the issue of 'sleep'.

Here's a plan to teach your baby to sleep

As leaving babies to cry is never easy, it's best to teach your baby to sleep in the most efficient way possible so it's all over quickly and everyone can start enjoying a good night's sleep. This means planning. The more haphazard you are, the more exhausting and drawn-out the whole thing becomes, with little chance of anything changing.

ONE PROVISO

As I am not around to give personal guidance I recommend that if you are following my guidelines for 'teaching-to-sleep' and there is any negative impact on your baby that bothers you or if you do not feel right about it, please stop. (See page 495, What if it takes longer than three nights?).

BEFORE YOU BEGIN

- Your baby must be in a room on her own. This may mean temporarily moving family members around.
- If your baby shares your room and there is no other bedroom, I suggest you and your partner sleep in the lounge room for a week. Once your baby is sleeping all night, move back to your bedroom. Unfortunately, shared accommodation sometimes means a return to disturbed nights. But if you're getting desperate for sleep it's certainly worth a try. If you are about to move to a bigger apartment or house wait until you move before teaching your baby to sleep.
- If you have an older child in another room and the baby shares your room, bring the older child into your room for five nights (move the cot in or put a mattress on the floor). Make sure you tell your older child this is a temporary arrangement as well as explaining what it's all about. Put the baby into the room on her own. Once she's sleeping all night, move your older child back in with the baby. I find this works very well. Often older children sleep better when their baby brothers or sisters are in the room with them. As well, babies do not wake and call for room service when they share the room with their siblings the way they do when they share the room with their parents.
- As the aim is to teach your baby to sleep on her own, all external aids must stop. Remember, swapping one for another will not stop the night waking—all must be stopped.

  Here is a list of all the external aids I can think of: Breastfeeding; bottles of milk, water or juice; dummies; rocking and patting;

walking the floor; driving around the block in the car; playing games or watching late-night television; flipping your baby over from front to back or changing her position; rewrapping. Videos taken of babies who 'sleep through the night' show that these babies wake, sit up, talk to themselves and roll all over the cot, often ending up in some very strange postures and positions, yet they do not call for attention. Getting up every few hours at night to change your baby's position quickly becomes an external aid. Babies can learn to sleep where they land without any harmful effects.

- You and your partner must co-operate, so talk over your plan of action well in advance. Teaching your baby to sleep is easier when partners agree on the course of action and both take part. However, this is not always possible. In the situation where one is prepared to follow the plan and the other isn't, the non-participator must either bury their head under the pillow or if this is too difficult, sleep somewhere else for three to five nights. Listening to a baby cry is not easy, but it's doubly difficult when one partner undermines the other's actions.
- Let your neighbours know so they don't give you a hard time. Impress upon them that you are up with your baby—she is not being left to cry on her own—and that you would appreciate their patience for a few nights.
- Pick a time that suits you, bearing in mind things like work commitments, visitors, holidays and moving house. It's important to make sure your baby continues to sleep in the same bed, in the same room for at least a month afterwards.
- Your baby must be well (ignore teething).
- You and your partner must be well and not under too much other stress when you decide to teach your baby to sleep. Babies respond well as long as their parents stay calm and confident—if you become visibly upset and worried, your baby will get distress signals from you and take much longer to go to sleep.

THE FIRST EVENING

Here are three key words for you to remember while you are teaching your baby to sleep. Write them in capital letters and put them on the fridge: Stay: **calm, confident and consistent**.

It's a good idea to start from bedtime so your baby learns how to go to sleep without breast, dummy and so on. Put her to bed at about 7.30 pm without any of the external aids. Make sure she has been up since 4 pm at the latest—a late catnap after 4 pm makes it very difficult for her to go to sleep before 9 pm or 10 pm.

As she is used to having help to sleep she will cry as you leave the room. This is the hard part—do not linger, leave. Wait three minutes then go back in and give brief comfort. Brief comfort means telling her you love her and a gentle stroke on the cheek. Brief comfort does not include picking her up, replacing the dummy, a breastfeed, a bottle, rolling her over or a rock and a pat. If you keep doing these things she will not learn to sleep on her own. Remember, it is not your job to get her to go back to sleep any more—it is hers.

After a brief time with your baby leave the room. Do not linger.

Continue to go to your baby but make the intervals longer—wait five, ten, fifteen, then every twenty minutes until she falls asleep. It may take one or two hours before she sleeps. Remain calm and confident; she *will* sleep.

Before going to bed mentally prepare yourself for a stint of night duty. When your baby wakes next, leave your bed and stay up until she sleeps. It is much more stressful scrambling in and out of bed than staying up. Make a cup of tea, perhaps turn on the TV or some calming music. Think of greener pastures. Repeat the evening procedure.

There is likely to be a fair bit of crying the first night—maybe up to two or more hours. Each night there is less and by the third night there will only be a little bit of crying and lots of sleeping. Your baby should be sleeping well within five nights with a small cry of about ten minutes before she falls asleep at 7.30 pm. This pre-sleep cry may go on for a few weeks. It's best to ignore it. Whatever you do, don't start any of the external aids again.

TIPS

- It is often hard to accept that the dummy must go, but if you continue to use it the night waking will start up again—the dummy is a problem, not a solution. I find that once parents make the commitment to follow the teaching-to-sleep guidelines, throwing the dummy away does not cause any added disruption, in fact it often turns into a non-event. Put your baby to bed without the dummy on the first evening you start teaching-to-sleep and never reintroduce it. The day-time sleeps may not be great for about a week because the dummy has gone, but once your baby sleeps all night without the dummy the day-time sleeps will improve. For more on daytime sleeping after six months see page 497.

- There is no need to change the nappy—if she slept all night you would not get up at 2 am to change her nappy.
- A good vomit is certainly distressing but remain calm, clean your baby up with a minimum of fuss and continue from where you left off. Whatever you do don't start going back to the old sleeping aids because of a vomit. Unlike healthy adults, healthy babies and toddlers vomit very easily and providing they are otherwise well, it is not a sign of anything drastic. I find babies who throw up when left to cry as part of teaching-to-sleep stop quickly as long as their parents stay calm and consistent so the baby gets a clear message.
- Once babies are able to pull themselves up they often stand at the side of the cot and cry until they are ready to fall asleep. If your baby is at this stage there is no point in lying her down as she will stand up again before you can blink. Just gently stroke her cheek and leave. It does not hurt her to stand at the side of the cot until she is ready to lie down and go to sleep.
- There is no advantage in picking your baby up each time you go into her room—it simply makes it harder for both of you.

WHAT ABOUT TWINS?

It's a little harder with twins, but the procedure is exactly the same. When both babies are waking leave them in the same room, plan things carefully around work schedules and so on and be mentally prepared for a stint of night duty. You will probably get less sleep than parents with one baby while you are following the guidelines, but the end results are excellent—both babies will learn to sleep within the same time frame as one. It's much easier when both parents participate so try and arrange a time when this is possible or if you are a sole parent perhaps your mother or a friend can help you.

If only one baby is waking it's better to put her in a room on her own then move both babies in together again as soon as she's sleeping.

AND PREMATURE BABIES?

You can start any time six months after birth, but if your baby was sick as a newborn and/or premature please wait until you feel confident and sure that teaching-to-sleep is what you want to do. When the beginning is difficult it's often harder and takes longer for parents to come to terms with leaving their babies to cry. Thinking it all through carefully and waiting until you are ready rather than stopping and starting is much less stressful for you all.

TEACHING YOUR BABY TO SLEEP MAY NOT BE AN OPTION IF

- You think it is wrong to leave babies to cry.
- You are uncertain about putting your baby into a separate room.
- Your living arrangements involve a shortage of bedrooms, paper-thin walls or sharing a house with others who may object.
- You and your partner cannot come to an agreement over what you should do.

Some parents would like to change things but cannot bear the thought of leaving their baby to cry. This is not a sign of weakness and is quite understandable. It is possible to get help to teach your baby to sleep from family care centres located in some capital cities throughout Australia. Services vary from state to state and you may find there is a waiting time.

Commonly asked questions

WHAT IF IT TAKES LONGER THAN THREE NIGHTS?

Sometimes it takes up to seven nights. As long as you are following the guidelines and the level of the distress is not markedly increasing, keep going. It should not take longer than five to seven nights. If it does, perhaps you are not ready for this option yet—you may be combining teaching-to-sleep with rocking, patting, a dummy and so on.

Or perhaps your baby is not ready. Some babies need to be a little older (nine to ten months).

Here are some other reasons why it might not be going to plan:

- Lack of support from your partner.
- A lack of confidence due to disapproval from extended family members; fear of doing the wrong thing after reading of the dangers of 'controlled-crying'; or fears that the baby won't love you any more and that the attachment is threatened.
- Inadequate planning or it's the wrong time (sick baby, moving house, visitors).
- Doing it for the wrong reason—'it's time I taught her to sleep now she's six months old'.
- A basic child-rearing philosophy that is at odds with this strategy.
- Unknown (it doesn't always work).

If the teaching-to-sleep is not going to plan it is best to forget about it for the time being. Consider the above points. Are you able to do something about any that may be causing you problems? Try leaving it for a month and start again if you haven't come to a suitable compromise in the meantime.

WILL MY BABY BE UPSET AND CLINGY DURING THE DAY?

Most aren't, but a few are. The ones who do become clingy are fine after about a week. Stay calm and consistent throughout—avoid guilty behaviour that might upset your baby.

MY BABY SEEMS TO BE MORE UPSET WHEN I GO IN AND OUT OF THE ROOM

Going in and out of the room is optional. If you prefer not to or want to make the times in between visits longer, that is up to you.

WILL THE RESULTS LAST FOREVER?

Unfortunately, maybe not. Illness, holidays, a change in routine and so on can change babies' sleep patterns and you might find she starts crying again during the night. If this does happen, and you know that you don't want to go back to regularly getting up at night and/or sharing beds, start teaching her to sleep again as quickly as possible.

MY BABY STILL WAKES BETWEEN 4 AM AND 5 AM. LEAVING HER TO CRY MEANS SHE CRIES AND CRIES UNTIL IT'S TIME TO GET UP AND WE'RE ALL WRECKS

Unfortunately, a number of babies only manage to sleep from around 7 pm until 4 am after teaching-to-sleep (which is a vast improvement from waking every two hours) and there usually isn't an answer to this. Leaving them to cry in the early hours of the morning for weeks on end is not recommended. I suggest giving them a quick feed, after which most will go back to sleep.

SHOULD I PUT HER TO BED LATER SO SHE'LL SLEEP LONGER IN THE MORNING?

As a general rule, no. She will almost certainly still wake at the crack of dawn. Babies sleep very well in the early part of the evening. Putting them to bed late means they get less sleep and you miss your quiet time in the evening.

SHOULD I TRY TEACHING-TO-SLEEP IF MY BABY SLEEPS THROUGH SOME NIGHTS AND WAKES OTHERS?

This is a tricky situation. Teaching-to-sleep is really a strategy for the two-hourly night waker who has never learned to sleep for longer periods without calling for help. If your baby sleeps through more nights than she wakes and goes to sleep quickly after minimal attention, carry on with what you're doing. If the night waking starts to cause you serious sleep deprivation, you might like to think about starting teaching-to-sleep. It is difficult when babies are not consistent because the very night you get yourself ready for action she will probably sleep all night. By the time the next bad night comes around you may find you have lost the plot. It's a dilemma I have no answer for.

Daytime sleeping—six months and beyond

The range of daytime sleeping that babies and toddlers do varies from almost nil to three hours a day and the range of variations in daytime sleep patterns and habits are similar to those in babies under six months except that many babies now sleep more predictably.

When babies are not sleeping much day or night it is possible to help them sleep longer at night by stopping external aids and teaching them to sleep (see page 490). It's always best to *do teaching-to-sleep during the evening and night* and forget about the day because helping them to sleep better during the night is achievable. Babies always eventually go to sleep at night—during the day they don't and may cry for two hours, after which time a distressed mother picks up a distressed baby and nothing is achieved. This can go on day after day for an unlimited time. Often when the nights are better the daytime sleeps improve, but even if they don't it's much easier to manage because at least everyone is sleeping at night.

Unfortunately I have found no sure way to encourage consistent daytime sleeping in babies who don't sleep much or who have twenty- to forty-minute catnaps during the day. It doesn't hurt a baby not to have much sleep but there is much more of the day to fill in so the baby has more time to get bored, cross and over-tired, which in turn makes life more difficult for the mother who never gets much of a break.

If this is happening to you I think it's more stressful trying to keep 'making' the baby sleep more or longer day after day. It's probably better to accept what's happening, try for three catnaps (make sure the last one starts no later than 3.30 pm), go out as much as you can, put your baby to bed by 7 pm and if you haven't yet done so, follow the teaching-to-sleep guidelines so you are all sleeping at night.

Babies who sleep more and longer will have one or two hours in the morning and/or one or two in the afternoon. Daytime sleep times depend a lot on what time the baby wakes and goes to bed. Some time between nine and eighteen months lots of babies stay up all morning and have one sleep of one, two or three hours after lunch.

Early-morning waking

Early morning waking is part of the baby package. Not all babies wake at the crack of dawn but lots do, and most of the time there's not much you can do about it. Leaving babies to cry from 5 am onwards doesn't teach them to sleep longer and when they have been asleep since 7 or 7.30 pm it's not really a fair or reasonable thing to do.

If you have an early-morning waker, whatever you do don't start putting her to bed later. Babies tend to wake at the same time in the morning regardless of when they go to bed so keeping her up means she gets less sleep and you don't get your time off in the evenings.

Here are the usual strategies to deal with early-morning waking

- Get up and start your day. It's unfair when it's always the same person so some sort of roster system should be worked out so both parents get a chance to sleep in at times. If you're a single parent there's not much you can do unless you've got a friend who will step in sometimes.

OR

- Bring your baby into bed and give her a breastfeed or a bottle and see if you can all get some more sleep together.

OR

- Give your baby a breastfeed or a bottle or a drink from a cup and put her back to her bed for another sleep.

OR

- Some parents try to slowly extend the time by going in five minutes later each week.

FOR MORE INFORMATION

Chapter 14: Sleeping and Waking in the First Six Months *(stages of sleep, page 267; 'sleeping through', page 276; 'spoiling', page 278)*
Chapter 5: Choosing Baby Products *(dummies, page 53)*
Chapter 11: Daily Care *(where to sleep—guidelines for co-sleeping, page 216)*
Chapter 10: Early Worries and Queries *(vomiting, page 188)*
Chapter 16: For Parents *(conflicting advice, page 330)*

FURTHER READING

The following two books centre on leaving babies/toddlers to their own devices to teach them to sleep.

1. Richard Ferber, *Solve Your Child's Sleep Problems,* Fireside, USA, 2006.

   A revised, expanded ('sleep' is taking over everybody's life) edition of this famous book. Dr Richard Ferber is an American paediatrician whose speciality area is 'sleep'—what a hero. His book is based on his hands-on work at the Children's Hospital in Boston.

2. Tweddle Child and Family Health Service, Victoria, *Sleep Right, Sleep Tight,* Random House, Australia, 2000.

   Good info for parents and health professionals based on years of hands-on experience from the nurses at Tweddle Child and Family Health Service in Melbourne.

The following books promote bedsharing and other strategies to avoid controlled-crying.

1. W Sears, MD, *Nighttime Parenting,* Plume, USA, Revised edition, 1999.

   William Sears is a Californian paediatrician with years of hands-on experience in a wide-ranging practice.

2. Pinky McKay, *Sleeping Like a Baby,* Penguin, Australia, 2007.
3. Anni Gethin and Beth Macgregor, *Helping Your Baby to Sleep*, Finch Publishing, Australia, 2007.

   McKay, Gethin and Macgregor's information is based on their own experiences, selected research, sleep and child development theories but limited wide-ranging hands-on practice over many years.

And finally:

If you are in sleep-deprived limbo but are worried about the safety of controlled-crying and feel it's worth pursuing every avenue to help make a decision, you might like to read the position paper on controlled-crying published by the Australian Association for Infant Mental Health (AAIMH). The Association certainly does not approve of controlled crying but the position paper is balanced and presents its view without over-the-top scare tactics.

Go to www.aaimhi.org or call (08) 8303 1566 for a copy of: *Position Paper 1: Controlled Crying*, issued November 2002, revised March 2004.

PART FOUR

9 to 12 months

Chapter 29

Feeding Your Baby

Breastfeeding

Late mastitis

Mastitis (see page 135) mostly happens in the first three months, but it can happen any time while you are breastfeeding. Signs and symptoms are the same as previously described, as is the treatment. A sudden change in night feeding, a baby who suddenly loses interest in the breast, return to paid work, ill health or trauma to the breast (perhaps from sport) are all possible reasons. Sometimes the flu-like symptoms appear first, making the diagnosis uncertain until the breast symptoms appear. If it doesn't settle in six to twelve hours, you will need antibiotics.

Breastfeeding into the second year and beyond

Some women are happy to continue breastfeeding for as long as their baby or toddler wants to. Night waking is not an issue and, for them, the rewards of this option outweigh any disadvantages. As well, the thought of getting their babies/toddlers to sleep by leaving them to cry is unacceptable.

Unfortunately mothers who do this often get a hard time from all and sundry and can be made to feel as if they are doing the wrong thing. If this is your choice, continue to enjoy your baby, your breastfeeding and sharing your bed for as long as you feel like doing it—some view this approach as the optimum.

There is, however, the small risk of tooth decay to consider (see page 406).

Weaning older babies

Weaning can happen at any time from soon after birth up to three or four years of age. It might be your decision or your baby's or it might be mutual. **All the benefits of breastfeeding are there for as long as you and your baby wish to continue, so if you are happy with what's happening, carry on.**

The following information is for women who wish to stop breastfeeding at night and/or slowly wean between six and twelve months. If your baby is breastfeeding a lot day and night and you wish to do fewer feeds or wean, here are some guidelines to follow.

ADDRESS THE NIGHT WAKING FIRST

Babies who are still breastfeeding frequently during the second six months usually breastfeed a lot at night and a number of women find they become increasingly frustrated and depressed because of the constant night waking.

If this is happening to you, waiting for your baby to decide to feed less or wean might mean waiting until she is a lot older. It's fine for you to make the decision to wean and/or stop night feeding rather than leaving it up to your baby.

Stopping breastfeeding at night involves teaching your baby to go back to sleep without the breast. Swapping the breast for a dummy, a bottle, a rock and a pat and so on is not the answer—it simply teaches your baby to rely on something else and will probably take even longer to get her back to sleep. Trying to make older breastfed babies take bottles when they don't want to is usually a catastrophe and does not teach them to sleep at night.

Teaching your baby to sleep without the breast involves letting her cry which is never easy, but by reading Chapter 28 and following the guidelines carefully you can help her sleep all night without the breast within three to five nights. It takes three to five nights for your breasts to adjust to not being used at night so don't forget to hand express for comfort once or twice a night for three to five nights. If they are really uncomfortable cold cabbage leaves (see page 156) and a firm bra help.

DAYTIME—DIET AND FLUIDS

Once your baby sleeps all night without needing the breast to go back to sleep, only breastfeed her three times during the day with meals. Be firm and consistent and don't give her the breast at sleep time. Changing your daily activities helps until she forgets about the breast.

If your baby takes a bottle you can then replace each daytime breastfeed with a bottle of formula or milk over the next month or two at a pace which suits you. If your baby will not take a bottle, forget about bottles; give her three meals a day and gradually replace each breastfeed with milk from a cup. Once your baby is not drinking all night and only having a few breastfeeds during the day you will find she will drink more and more from the cup.

Some mothers worry about their babies' fluid intake when they use a cup instead of a bottle as it seems so much less than the amount babies have who drink from bottles. Try not to let this bother you—babies who drink from bottles drink more than they need a lot of the time. When the weather is hot extra fluids can be given in the form of fruit gels, fruit iceblocks or by putting extra fluid in the food. Letting your baby sit in the bath and suck the flannel is another way of giving extra fluid in hot weather.

Once you decide to breastfeed less or wean, be consistent so your baby gets a clear message. If you do one thing one day and something else the next she won't know what's going on. Never re-introduce a breastfeed once it's gone.

Babies who wean themselves

A number of babies take themselves off the breast some time between six and twelve months. This can be upsetting whether you planned to breastfeed indefinitely or planned to wean around a year. Unfortunately it's usually something you have to accept unless the breast refusal is temporary because your baby is unwell, in which case she might go back to the breast when she is better. When it's permanent, talk about it to someone sympathetic and have a good cry—the sad feelings will pass.

Again, there is no need to start bottles if your baby is happy to drink from a cup. Give her small amounts of milk or water frequently throughout the day. The amount she drinks will gradually increase.

Biting the breast

Mostly, the arrival of teeth makes no difference to breastfeeding, but a few babies do start to bite which is very painful indeed. Deliberate biting in older babies (whether it's a breast or a shoulder) is part of their development and one way they find out about the world and what their bodies can do. It is nothing to do with 'teething', nor is it intentionally done to hurt; however, they have to learn that biting another person hurts, is not a game and it is unacceptable behaviour. Here are a few tips to help with biting:

- Playing with the nipple rather than sucking it for food or comfort is a diversion for older babies and a time when biting may occur, so try not to let yourself get distracted while feeding and allow the feed to go past the time your baby is really interested. Older babies are able to drain the breast in two or three minutes and may not be interested in extra sucking time when other things are attracting their attention.
- Try not to overreact to a bite (easier said than done, especially when the first nip takes you by surprise) as a major response from you may mean your baby refuses all breastfeeds. The minute she bites, a quiet but firm 'no' is required. Take her off the breast immediately and don't breastfeed again for several hours. Resist offering her your breast every time she starts to whinge—try diversionary tactics such as a snack, a drink from a cup or going out.
- Like everything to do with babies, try to stay consistent. If you laugh sometimes, go 'ouch' sometimes and keep letting her play with your breast, the biting is likely to go on indefinitely.

When should a baby feed herself with a spoon?

Sometimes there is no choice about this because a number of babies won't eat unless they can feed themselves. If your baby is an independent eater and you don't mind the mess, by all means let her use a spoon and her fingers to feed herself mushy food as well as the less messy finger foods.

If your baby is happy to let you be in charge of the spoon there is no urgency about teaching her to do it herself until she is older and has better co-ordination. Most toddlers can use a spoon reasonably neatly around eighteen to twenty months.

Bottle feeding

When you are breastfeeding, it is fine to use full-fat cow's milk in your baby's food, on her cereal and to drink from a cup from six months of age. There is no need to go to the expense of using formula when you are following this plan. If you are breastfeeding and for some reason don't want your baby to have cow's milk it's better to use a soy-based infant formula on cereal, in a cup and so on until she is a year old rather than soy drinks.

When babies are not breastfed or if you wean between six and twelve months, infant formula is recommended. 'Follow-on' formula (labelled 'suitable for babies over six months') is an unnecessary product designed by formula companies to bypass the advertising restrictions placed on standard formula (labelled 'suitable from birth'). Follow-on formula has no advantages for healthy babies who are eating a wide variety of food unless it is cheaper than standard formula. An unlimited amount of formula is not part of a well-balanced diet in the second six months when it's best to encourage babies to eat a wide variety of family food. Three bottles of 180–200ml daily is sufficient.

Teach your baby to use a cup and aim to bid the bottles farewell soon after the first birthday. Prolonged use of bottles in the second year is a risk for tooth decay, interferes with good eating and is nutritionally unnecessary. Toddler formula is a marketing ploy aimed at the anxious parents of fussy eaters (see page 518). Cow's milk, and water, ideally from a cup, are the best drinks during the toddler years and beyond.

FOR MORE INFORMATION

Chapter 28: Sleeping and Waking Six Months and Beyond *(options for night waking, page 480)*

Chapter 24: Feeding Your Baby *(particularly information on the use of whole cow's milk, page 452)*

Chapter 30

Growth and Development

Growth

Lots of babies are three times their birthweight by twelve months. From nine to twelve months onwards weight gains are often slow and irregular, but length continues to increase steadily. The weight of breastfed babies in particular can level out quite dramatically. As long as they are otherwise fit and healthy this is rarely a sign of anything being wrong.

AT TWELVE MONTHS

	Small/Normal	Large/Normal
Boys	weight 8.2kg (18lb)	12kg (26lb)
	height 72cm (28 inches)	80cm (32 inches)
	head circ. 45cm (17 inches)	50cm (20 inches)
Girls	weight 7.8kg (16lb)	11.2kg (25lb)
	height 70cm (27 inches)	79cm (31 inches)
	head circ. 43.5cm (16½ inches)	49cm (19½ inches)

Development

Gross motor

- By twelve months your baby will be sitting well, on her own, indefinitely.
- She will probably be crawling (some babies still just sit).
- Lots of babies are 'cruising' (walking around the furniture) by twelve months.
- Many are walking on their own.
- If you have stairs, your baby may be able to crawl up the stairs but not down.

Vision and fine motor

- She now uses her index finger and thumb to pick up anything she finds (crumbs, fluff off the carpet, paper clips and so on).
- She can drop objects or release them deliberately (if she wants to). She can give you a toy willingly (if she's in the mood).
- Both hands are used to play, eat and manipulate objects.
- Pointing at everything starts at about a year. It is often not noticed much because obvious skills like walking and crawling attract much more attention.

  Pointing is a way of communicating found only in humans, and babies start to point around twelve months, some as early as nine months, but intentional pointing is never any earlier.

  Pointing is a clear communication signal and the way a person singles out an object as being important enough to consider and contemplate. By pointing, the person draws someone else's attention to the object to get them to consider and contemplate the object as well. Pointing is always done with someone, not alone. I find pointing a fascinating part of the development of baby communication skills which happens long before babies have the verbal skills to draw their parents' attention to objects in the astonishing world around them.
- Your baby can recognise you from a distance of six metres (twenty feet) or more.

Hearing and speech

- She knows and turns to her name immediately and will also turn to a quiet noise behind each ear.
- Vocalises constantly as if having a conversation using lots of vowels and consonants; a few babies may have one or two words.
- Your baby shows by her behaviour and response that she understands conversation and simple instructions like 'Come to Mummy', 'Don't touch' and so on.

Social and play

- Loves to empty cupboards and tip things out of containers.
- Likes having a cuddle, although if you have a 'busy' baby, cuddles may be few and far between at times.
- Offers a kiss to people she knows and trusts.
- Waves 'bye-bye', plays pat-a-cake and 'boo'.
- From twelve months on things tend to go into the mouth less often.
- Lots of babies start being able to put shapes into the correct hole, particularly if encouraged and given help.
- Your baby will now examine things much more closely before waving them about and dropping them. She will also start to use things like a hairbrush or a small broom appropriately.
- It's now quite obvious what mood she's in—sad, happy, cross and so on.

Bottom shuffling—a normal variation

Bottom shuffling babies are normal late walkers. Babies who bottom shuffle move about in a sitting position by extending their legs and then moving their bodies forwards by pushing with their hands behind them.

Bottom shuffling often runs in families and babies who move around like this are late to pull themselves up onto furniture as it's much harder to pull up onto furniture from a sitting position than a crawling position. This means they are also later to walk (usually around eighteen months), but this is no cause for concern.

Non-crawlers—a normal variation

A number of babies bypass crawling. There is no evidence that this causes problems and opinions vary as to whether some sort of intervention makes any long-term difference. Like many areas in babycare, the decision whether or not to give your baby therapy is ultimately yours. Ask a few different people for their opinion before becoming committed to time-consuming exercises and activities for your baby which will make you feel guilty when you don't do them.

Developmental summary: 12 months

Gross motor

- sits well, indefinitely;
- crawls;
- cruises, walks.

Vision and fine motor

- pincer grasp;
- watches toys fall to the ground;
- points with index finger;
- recognises familiar people from six metres away (twenty feet).

Hearing and speech

- knows own name;
- vocalises—vowels and consonants;
- understands the meaning of many concepts and words as well as simple instructions.

Social and play

- may drink from a cup;
- holds a spoon;
- helps with dressing if in the mood;
- tips things out of containers;

- likes having a cuddle;
- demonstrates affection;
- plays 'pat-a-cake';
- waves 'bye-bye'.

FOR MORE INFORMATION

Chapter 32: Becoming a Toddler *(toys and activities, page 523)*

Chapter 31

Safety

Holiday safety

It's essential to be aware of the added hazards to your child's safety when the family leaves home for a while.

Holidays with babies are different from holidays on your own. Parents often feel there's no such thing as a holiday with babies and toddlers; it's simply a change of scenery with fewer conveniences and more work. Despite this, everyone still does it. Parents enjoy the change of scenery and the opportunity to spend time with their babies without having to worry about the demands of life in the suburbs and the routine of the working week for a while.

The hard work of holidays does centre around keeping little ones safe. Constant vigilance is essential.

Going to live in an unfamiliar environment is the first hazard. Whether you are renting a flat or house or camping, check the surrounding areas to make sure they are safe for playing. Ask about potential drowning hazards such as pools, spas, ponds, septic tanks or post holes. Find out the whereabouts of any barbecues or incinerators. Make a note of driveways and which way cars come and go (especially in camp sites) so your baby or toddler plays in a safe spot.

A rented house or a flat is unlikely to have any of the safety features around that you have in your home, so pack some of the equipment you use at home to make the surroundings safer.

Appliances such as the stove, the hot water system, the kettle, the toaster or the washing machine may not be as safe or in as safe a place as they are at home. Also, check baby furniture such as the cot if it is supplied with the house. Watch out for flimsy curtains near the stove or for venetian blind cords that may hang over the cot. Old-style holiday cottages often have strange containers of liquid in outside toilets or laundries that need putting out of reach.

Access to windows may be easier, which increases the risk of a toddler falling out. Look in the bedroom your baby is going to occupy and remove any mirrors, heaters or fans which might be broken or played with.

Camping holidays

These need to be planned very carefully. Camping usually means a confined cooking, sleeping and living area. The combination of this and active young babies can lead to tensions, especially in wet weather, which makes accidents more likely to happen.

Keep cooking, sleeping and lighting equipment simple and safe. If you are in a tent it is much safer to have equipment without a flame. When sleeping bags are dry-cleaned you should allow at least a week before they are used. After dry-cleaning they need to be aired for four to five days. Children have died in un-aired sleeping bags due to breathing fumes from the dry-cleaning chemicals.

If you are staying with friends or grandparents who normally do not have babies or children around, there are likely to be many hazards within easy reach of curious minds and fingers, not to mention potential damage to prized possessions in your host's home.

Check where medicines are kept and poisons are stored. I remember leaving my son to sleep on his grandparents' bed only to find when we went to get him up that he had emptied out every drawer and cupboard in the bedroom and liberally applied every bit of make-up he could find to himself and the cream wool carpet. Luckily there were no medications in their bedroom.

Water plays a big part in summer holiday fun. Unfortunately drownings keep happening. Remember small children fall into water with so little sound it cannot be heard above normal conversation. There is no such thing as a 'drown-proof' child, even those who have been to swimming lessons.

HERE ARE SOME GENERAL GUIDELINES TO FOLLOW FOR WATER SAFETY

- Never leave your baby alone in water such as the bath or a wading pool while answering the phone or door. Take her with you when you go if there is no other adult around to supervise her in the bath or pool.
- Don't leave younger children in the care of older children at bath time or when they are playing at the beach, near a creek or near a river.
- Flotation toys and swimming aids are not lifesaving devices and do not replace adult supervision.
- Alcohol increases water hazards. During the holiday season there is likely to be more risk of being in situations where there is both water and alcohol. If you are taking your baby to a pool party, decide beforehand which parent is going to drink and which parent is going to drive *and* take care of their baby in a hazardous environment.
- Remember to drain wading pools after use and remove the access ladder from above-ground pools when swimming is over for the day.
- See page 396 for more on water safety.

The following chart emphasises particular hazards associated with this developmental stage but don't forget most safety hazards remain at any age and stage.

Don't forget your baby's immunisation which is due at twelve months.

Age	Developmental stage	Safety hazard	Precautions
12–18 months	• watching • learning • imitating • absorbing • exploring • finding out • mastering gross motor and fine motor skills • very mobile	• scalds—pulls protruding handles on the stove • burns—clothing catches alight (open fires and barbecues) • drowning—in bath, buckets of water, fish pond, wading pool, swimming pool • poisoning—medication, confuses tablets with sweets. Drinks fluids from bottles (especially soft drink bottles) • cuts—from knives and sharp utensils • suffocation—airtight spaces such as old fridges, wardrobes	• turn handles away from edge of stove or bench. Fit a stove guard. • non-flammable clothing such as wool or treated fabrics. Fitted nightwear. • always supervise near water. Do not leave older child in charge. Cover fish ponds, empty bath, buckets, wading pools when not in use. Safe storage of nappy buckets. • keep poisons in locked cupboards. Don't take medication in view of small children. Store poison in correct containers (not cordial or soft drink bottles). • keep tools and knives out of reach. • remove doors from old fridges and lock wardrobes—put key somewhere out of reach.

FOR MORE INFORMATION

Chapter 12: Safety *(immunisation, page 235)*
Chapter 19: Common Worries and Queries *(Swimming, page 396)*
Chapter 22: For Parents *(travelling with your baby, page 433)*

Chapter 32

Becoming a Toddler

You used to lean
on that cot rail
and wait
with the vigour of a flame
to leap into my arms
two feet tall and two years old.

KATE LLEWELLYN, 'THE FLAME', *THE MOUNTAIN*

The toddler age is from about twelve months, when toddling starts, to three years. It is a time of tremendous development when babies discover they are able to use their minds and bodies to do things and make things happen.

Learning to do things and make things happen can be quite frustrating for the toddler as well as for her parents. Children of this age have a strong desire to be independent but still need a great deal of help and security. As they learn to do things more efficiently and to understand the world around them more, they experience less frustration and lots of the exasperating things they do fade away. So it's important to realise that the things your baby or toddler does to assert herself and her attempts at independence are by no means indicative of her future temperament or character. Toddlers do many things that adults find exasperating and some toddlers do them more than others.

Temper tantrums, not eating, not sleeping, biting, thumping other toddlers, not wanting to poo in the pot and whingeing are some of them, to name a few. All of this sounds very negative—a lot of the time, of course, toddlers are rewarding and delightful and parents find they are well compensated for the exasperating times by the enormous amount of pleasure they get watching and helping their baby through this stage.

Some babies don't get into the full swing of toddlerhood until they are fifteen months old; others start to change from the easy, cuddly baby stage as early as nine months. When your nine-month-old suddenly refuses to eat lunch or launches into a mini temper tantrum by flinging herself backwards when something upsets her, it marks the beginning of a new era for you both.

Here are some of the things you might find your baby starts to do any time from nine months onwards. They are all normal and the suggestions to help are aimed at managing your life together and not making things worse, rather than providing solutions as in time they disappear.

Difficulty dressing, undressing and changing nappies

And very frustrating this is! Suddenly you find your baby does not lie peacefully while you attend to her daily care and it all becomes a monumental struggle. Changing a pooey nappy is a major catastrophe which is particularly trying if your baby poos four or five times a day, not to mention if you are on holiday somewhere in the back blocks with no decent changing facilities. Your baby's resistance to dressing and nappy changing may last well into the second year.

What can you do? Not a lot, unfortunately. Distract your baby as much as possible with toys and music and obviously have everything at the ready to do the job as fast as you can. Holding and distracting a determined baby is much easier with two than one so always get help if help is around.

Not eating

Faddy appetites in healthy babies and toddlers aged between nine months and three years are quite normal and often start to happen between nine months and twelve months. Some babies of this age have never eaten happily from a spoon so not eating is not new. Others who used to eat with gusto suddenly start refusing all their lovingly prepared nutritious meals, particularly vegies.

What can you do? Remember your job is to offer your baby food, not force her to eat it. This means a change in your behaviour and may take a little while to come to terms with. Leaving the job to your baby will probably give you a feeling of neglecting her, but babies understand from a very early age that the decision to eat is theirs and they will exercise this choice in a very human way. When healthy babies are in a loving environment and are being offered the right food they do not suffer.

There are several reasons why toddlers lose interest in food and why their bodies still function efficiently even when they appear to eat very little:

- After the first year their growth rate slows down, they do not need as much food and they are not as hungry.
- Most have accumulated stores of fat and other nutrients which stand them in good stead.
- Their bodies use what they do eat very efficiently.
- Food becomes relatively unimportant for many toddlers compared to other things in their lives.

As so many older babies and toddlers have little interest in food yet remain active and healthy it is reasonable to assume this is a normal state of affairs for the human body at this time.

Here are a few tips

- A lot of babies will not eat unless they can feed themselves with their fingers. There's no doubt it's not nearly as rewarding to have finger food thrown around the room as to have a nice plate of pureed vegies disappear neatly into an open mouth, but if this is your baby's choice save yourself a lot of angst and accept it.
- Resist the temptation to keep replacing meals with extra bottles of milk and juice. This only fills your baby up and makes her less inclined to eat. Three bottles of milk a day is more than enough for babies aged between nine and twelve months. If you are breastfeeding do what suits you and your baby. Three breastfeeds a day are plenty for babies in this

age group; if you want to breastfeed more frequently, that's fine, but if your baby is having a lot of breastfeeds she may not eat much.

- Give breast or bottle after the food and avoid any drinks an hour before the meal if you can.
- Nourishing snacks throughout the day are quite acceptable. Make sure they are nutritious, not chips, lollies and biscuits. But if your baby snacks a lot don't expect her to eat three formal meals a day as well.
- If your baby is or has become a fussy eater, try not to let it turn into a major issue. Avoid cooking and preparing a million nourishing meals which do not get eaten. Your efforts will be unappreciated, you will become angry and upset—and probably overweight when you keep polishing off what your baby doesn't eat. Keep the food simple, stay calm and pretend you don't care whether she eats or not. As faddy food behaviour frequently lasts at least until three years of age, constant confrontation and stress about eating can unnecessarily turn these years into a nightmare.

Separation anxiety and stranger awareness

Part of a growing baby's mental development is all about learning how to tell the difference between things, places and people and how to compare and judge them. Separation anxiety and stranger awareness refers to the time in a baby's life when she realises the difference between her mother and a few other close acquaintances and the rest of the world. When this happens lots of babies start to make a fuss when unfamiliar people look after them or even just pay them attention. Glasses and beards put some babies off, others shriek whenever a particular person comes near them (which is unfortunate when it's a grandparent). They also become distressed if they are taken to unfamiliar surroundings even when their mother is with them.

Stranger awareness and separation anxiety happens any time from three to four months to nine to twelve months. It is most common and intense around nine months. Not all babies show signs of being upset while they are learning to tell the difference between faces and places and it's difficult to come up with reasons why some do and some don't. Lots of exposure to new faces and places from a young age doesn't necessarily make any difference. In the same family where the environment is similar for all the children, one baby may be incredibly clingy and another won't.

Becoming clingy, anti-social with unknown people and distressed in strange places is normal for many healthy babies at this time and to a large extent outside your control. If your baby is like this it does not mean she is spoilt or insecure. On the other hand if she mostly doesn't give a hoot who she is with or where she is it doesn't mean she is not attached or hasn't bonded. The normal range of separation anxiety varies tremendously. Some babies pass through it quickly. Others are unsure about being away from their mothers or meeting strangers until the age of two or even older.

Separation anxiety often puts women in a turmoil when they are trying to work out aspects of their lives—especially in relation to paid work, occasional care (for much needed time off) and solving night-time sleep problems, particularly when older babies are still being breastfed frequently through the night.

Remember, if your baby is clingy and gets distressed at being somewhere strange, it is normal. In a good, loving environment it will not harm her to start learning to separate for short periods such as:

- Occasions when you want/need some time off to go to the dentist, shopping, classes or part-time paid work.
- When it is essential for your sanity (moving your baby to her own room and teaching her to sleep) or leaving her somewhere safe while you attend to household chores or to your own personal requirements (showering, dressing or going to the toilet).

Some guidelines to help with separation anxiety

- Make whatever arrangements you need to and stick to them, including having a shower and going to the toilet alone. It doesn't matter if your baby performs for thirty minutes as long as she is left in a safe spot.

TIPS FOR REGULAR OCCASIONAL CHILDCARE

- A sensible babysitter and quality childcare is crucial. The carer needs to be someone who is very patient, understands the baby's distress is normal and temporary and is willing to mind her without giving you a blow-by-blow description of the drama when you return.

- Babies will usually settle with a carer in occasional care after about seven weeks. If they are not happy within seven or eight weeks chances are they are going to continue to be unhappy indefinitely. If the hours in care per week are short and you desperately need a break, it's difficult to see that it will cause any long-term harm as long as your carer is willing to continue. Long daycare is another matter (see below).
- Spending time with her at the centre or the carer's until she becomes familiar with the place and the people helps.
- Try not to leave your baby at her carer's in a great disorganised flurry. Make sure she has her security items (lambskin, dummy, blanket, cuddly or special toy).
- When you are leaving her, leave decisively. Don't stop and start and hang about. Remember, lots of babies and toddlers cry initially, are fine for the period you are not there then cry again as soon as they see their mother.
- Resist the temptation to sneak off to avoid the fuss that occurs when she knows you are going. Overall this will only make her more anxious. Painful as it may seem it is better for her to learn to trust you and know that when you go, you will always come back.

LONG DAYCARE FOR PAID WORK PURPOSES (LONG DAYCARE CENTRES OR FAMILY DAYCARE)

A small number of babies never settle. If this happens you do have to look at things again. You may decide an unhappy baby outweighs the benefits of paid work. If possible other options have to be looked at which may include arranging one-to-one care at home with a nanny (obviously not an option for many families), a relative, your partner or giving up the paid work temporarily.

Feet and shoes

Many babies start walking between nine and twelve months and their feet often go in all directions when they first start to walk. This is quite normal and rarely needs any special treatment or equipment. Feet turning in, feet turning out, bow legs and flat feet are all common variations of normal posture that worry parents. Another interesting one is the baby who bends her outer ankle so the edge of one foot rolls over.

All these things are seen frequently in many babies from the time they start to walk (nine to nineteen months) until the time their legs straighten and their feet point ahead (between two and five years). Plasters, night splints, inserts and special shoes are generally not needed, but if in doubt ask a specialist such as a paediatric physiotherapist or a paediatric orthopaedic surgeon.

Shoes

Babies need shoes for warmth and protection, not for development. They learn to walk and run more efficiently in bare feet so leave your baby barefoot whenever it's warm enough and she is not in danger of hurting her feet.

Wait seven to eight weeks after she starts walking before buying shoes. Until then let her stay barefoot or use socks. Slipping and sliding can be a hazard—bootees with a non-slip sole are available for older babies.

The first shoes need not be expensive. Bear in mind that they don't last long.

- The fit should be the same size and shape as the foot with sufficient room for the toes.
- Rounded toes are preferable but sandals with a firm heel are fine for the summer.
- Shoes should be flexible, not too heavy and have a firm heel. Ankle support is not required. The only advantage to expensive leather ankle boots is that they are more difficult for your baby to keep removing.
- Sneakers, preferably with a firm heel and ventilation holes, are fine.

Toys and activities

This is a watching, learning, imitating, absorbing, exploring and finding out stage as well as being a time when your baby is mastering her gross motor and fine motor skills.

A few suggestions for toys and activities

- Continue books—babies love books.
- Short bursts of screen-time watching shows such as 'The Wiggles' and 'Playschool' are fun for her but resist the temptation to use the TV as a babysitter.
- Toys that give her practice with her hands are things like: nesting cups; peg boards with pegs and string; pull-along-string toys (for practising her pincer grasp); blocks (for building up, knocking down and banging together); a collection of things in a container that can be taken out, examined and put back; babies love keys—organise a safe set for her; they also love old telephones.
- Bath toys; once she sits alone in the bath tipping and pouring bath toys will interest and delight her.
- Toys that help her to practise gross motor skills are things like a weighted trolley she can push around when she is at the cruising stage. Balls are always popular. A big cardboard box she can crawl in and out of is lots of fun—make sure there are no sharp edges or staples.

  She will enjoy an obstacle course made of cushions, blankets and boxes.
- Music is important; babies are musical and enjoy any music from birth. Your baby will quickly pick up simple nursery rhymes and repetitive tunes.
- Household items. Babies often prefer things in cupboards to things in their toy boxes, such as: a torch; cardboard egg containers; old magazines and junk mail; pots and pans with lids; measuring cups and spoons; bandaids; wooden spoons; safe cutlery; cardboard tubes (toilet rolls, foil and plastic wrap rolls); playing cards; funnels, strainers and a colander; a pastry brush.

  Don't forget to check everything for safety.

Playgroups

The Playgroup Association of Australia is a voluntary organisation whose main aim is to provide regular, informal groups of babies, children and parents in local areas so the children and parents can learn through play and get to know each other.

The association also publishes written material for parents, runs conferences and is a wonderful resource for information about children's development, their educational and emotional needs as well as things to do and places to go. Joining a playgroup is a good way to get to know other parents and if you are lonely you can join at any time, even when your baby is quite young. If you don't feel the need to seek company but would like your older baby to mix with other babies and toddlers, wait until she's about fifteen months.

Playgroups don't suit everyone and it's important that you enjoy it as well as your baby. There are usually a few different groups in any area so it's worth looking for one that suits you. If you decide a playgroup is not your style, that's fine. While it's a great resource it's by no means essential for your baby's optimum growth and development.

FOR MORE INFORMATION

Chapter 19: Common Worries and Queries *(care of teeth, page 405; recycled food in the poo, page 411)*
Chapter 25: Common Worries and Queries *('spoiling' and discipline, page 461)*

FURTHER READING

The Mighty Toddler, Robin Barker, Pan Macmillan Australia, revised edition, 2009.
The Emotional Life of the Toddler, Alicia F. Lieberman, Simon & Schuster, 1995.

Recipes

We live in a wonderful country with a fantastic variety of foods available. Use them, experiment with them and mix them so that your baby learns to enjoy the delicious flavours and textures of good food.

4–6 MONTHS

For all the following first foods add breastmilk, formula or boiled water to get to the consistency that you want. Start with one or two teaspoons of food and gradually increase the amount to one or two tablespoons at a pace to suit your baby. Freeze the remaining amounts in icecube trays.

You can use a fork, food processor, blender or mouli to puree the food.

Rice Cereal

For commercial rice cereal just follow the directions on the packet. Home-made rice cereal is amazingly easy and tastes delicious—parents may want to eat it too!

¼ cup rice powder (Made by grinding raw rice in a food processor or blender, do it on a high speed for a few minutes. Do two cups of rice and store the rest in a sealed jar in the fridge.)
1 cup of made-up formula

Mix rice powder and milk together in a small saucepan. Bring mixture to the boil whilst stirring. Continue to stir and cook gently for about four minutes or until it is creamy. If it is too thick, add more formula and mix through. Take out the amount that you require and refrigerate the rest. Reheat with a little formula if it needs to be thinned down.

Banana

1 ripe banana

Mash banana with a fork until smooth.

Apple

2 medium apples (try the many different varieties available)

Wash, peel, core and slice apples. Put in a microwave dish with 1 tablespoon of water. Cover and cook on high for 5–7 minutes. Remove and mash with a fork or other appropriate equipment.

OR

Put apples in a saucepan with ¼ cup of water and cover and cook on a low heat until soft. Mash with a fork or other appropriate equipment.

Pear

2 ripe pears

Use same method as for apples.

Potato

2 potatoes

Wash, peel and cut the potatoes in pieces. Microwave, steam or boil until soft. Mash with a fork or other appropriate equipment.

Sweet Potato

1 small red or white sweet potato

Same method as for potato.

Pumpkin

300–400g of any variety of pumpkin

Same method as for potato.

Carrot

1 carrot

Same method as for potato.

Avocado

½ a ripe avocado (you eat the other half mashed with garlic and lemon juice or just splash in some balsamic vinegar)

Mash avocado with a fork.

Yoghurt

Plain, full-fat yoghurt

Yoghurt is very versatile. You can mix it in with any of the above foods for new flavours.

Peaches

1 ripe peach

Peel, remove stone and slice or cut the peach. Microwave, steam or boil until soft. Mash with a fork or other appropriate equipment.

6–9 MONTHS

Now it gets more interesting as you can begin to mix foods together. Add yoghurt to fruit, and grated cheese to vegetables, and you suddenly have several new meals for your baby to try.

Try different vegetables individually and mixed together in all sorts of combinations. Buy vegetables in season so that they are at their tastiest and cheapest. This is the time to try a range of vegetables such as celeriac, beetroot, taro, artichoke, Jerusalem artichoke, bok choy, choy sum. Your greengrocer should be a wealth of information as to when vegetables are available.

Grains can now be introduced, such as pasta, rice, cous cous and bread, and these can be served individually or mixed with other food. Use fresh or dried breadcrumbs to add variety.

Lean beef, lamb, pork, chicken and fish can be introduced now, along with egg yolks.

Use a variety of cheese to add different flavours to dishes e.g. edam, cottage, gruyère, cheddar, mozzarella, gouda, haloumi, fetta and Swiss.

Vegetables

Peel and chop vegetables. Steam, boil or microwave until soft. Mash roughly with a fork or use a food processor or blender if appropriate.

SUGGESTIONS FOR VEGETABLES

Vegetables in the 6 months section as well as the following: beans; beetroot; broccoli; capsicum (red, green, yellow); cauliflower; celeriac; choko; eggplant; fennel; green leafy vegetables like spinach; Chinese vegetables; leeks; parsnip; peas; squash; taro; tomato (peeled and de-seeded); turnip and zucchini.

SERVING SUGGESTIONS

Serve each vegetable individually or use your imagination to mix any combinations together.

- Mix two vegetables together, e.g. pumpkin and potato, capsicum and sweet potato.
- Add grated cheese to cooked hot vegetables and stir through.
- Add cottage cheese to vegetables and mix.
- Mix cooked rice with any vegetables.
- Mix cooked pasta (use different shapes) with any vegetables.
- Mix any vegetable with cooked red lentils. (See recipe for Lentil and Meat Hotpot* for how to cook lentils.)
- Mix through some hard-boiled egg yolk with any vegetable.
- Mix cooked lean beef mince or chicken mince with any vegetables.
- Mix cooked lean mince with rice or pasta.
- Mix tinned fish such as tuna or salmon (remove bones) through any vegetable.
- Mix cooked, flaked fresh fish* (remove all bones) through vegetables.
- Mix any vegetable with cous cous*.
- Mix vegetables with cooked or tinned mashed legumes, e.g. three-bean mix, baked beans.

Experiment with different flavours. Moisten food with tomato paste, tahini (sesame seed paste), hommus (chick pea paste), lemon juice, white sauce*,

cheese sauce★ or soy sauce. Small amounts of finely chopped fresh herbs like parsley, basil, coriander, dill, chives or spices such as nutmeg, paprika and ginger can be mixed through dishes to vary the taste.
★Recipes follow.

Cous Cous

Pour 1 cup of boiling water onto 1 cup cous cous. Stir and then leave for a few minutes and then fluff up with a fork. That's it. Use stock instead of water for a change.

To cook meat

It's easy. Puree up a leftover casserole (cheaper cuts of meat can be used for a casserole such as blade, chuck, gravy beef or round steak). Puree or mince leftover roast beef (use the inside bit as it is more moist). Blend grilled or pan-fried meat—use suitable cuts like fillet steak, rump steak, sirloin steak, veal, trim lamb, lamb loin chop or lamb cutlet. Don't overcook the meat. Puree meat with gravy, stock, vegetable water, water or milk.

To cook chicken

1 chicken breast fillet (about 250g), remove skin

ON THE STOVE: Put chicken fillet in a saucepan and cover with water. Bring to boil. Reduce to low heat, cover and simmer for about ten minutes or until chicken is cooked. Remove chicken.

TO MICROWAVE: Place chicken in a suitable microwave dish and pierce chicken a couple of times. Toss in 1 tablespoon of lemon juice to coat chicken breast. Cover and cook on medium-high for 3 to 3½ minutes. Stand for a few minutes.

Mince in a food processor or blender or cut very finely and add water, vegetable water, stock or white sauce to make it moist.

To cook fish

1 fillet of fish (about 150g)
lemon juice
½ teaspoon butter

TO MICROWAVE: Put fish in a suitable microwave dish. Add a few drops of lemon juice. Dot with butter. Cover and cook on high for about three minutes or until the fish is soft and can be flaked easily.

TO BAKE: Place a piece of fish on a sheet of foil. Add a few drops of lemon and dot with butter. Wrap the fish in the foil and then cook for about ten minutes on 180°C.

White Sauce

2 tablespoons butter
2 tablespoons plain flour
300ml full-cream milk

Melt butter in a small saucepan. Remove from heat. Stir in flour and then cook over a low heat for one minute. Gradually add milk, stirring constantly over a medium heat until boiling. Simmer for two minutes. Makes one cup of sauce.

Cheese Sauce

1 quantity of white sauce
½ cup cheese, grated

After making the white sauce, remove saucepan from heat and mix through the grated cheese.

Mix the sauce through cooked minced chicken or flaked salmon or tuna and cooked pasta.

Mix the sauce through some mashed vegetables.

Lentil and Meat Hotpot

200g red lentils (about 1 cup)
4 cups water
1 tablespoon olive oil
½ onion, chopped
100g lean beef mince
1 tablespoon tomato paste
½ cup water

Boil four cups of water and add lentils. Simmer for about thirty minutes or until soft and then drain. (When cooking lentils for another use, try cooking in stock and a bay leaf. Remove bay leaf after cooking.)

Heat oil. Add onion and cook until soft. Add meat and stir to break up lumps and then cook for ten minutes stirring occasionally. Mix through tomato paste. Add lentils and water, boil and then cover and simmer for ten more minutes, stirring occasionally.

Makes about 2½ cups. Serve on its own or with cous cous or rice. Suitable to freeze. Cook double this amount of lentils and freeze half of them for another use.

Fruit

It's time for your baby to enjoy a wide selection of ripe fruit, served separately or mixed up in all sorts of combinations. Fruits may have to be peeled, cooked and mashed depending on the fruit. Some fruits can be grated, e.g. apple and pears.

Fruits that are inherently soft like bananas and mangoes do not need to be cooked first. Fruit should be ripe. Please take care with the seeds and pips in fruit.

Fruits to try: Those in the 6 months section as well as the following: apricots; grapefruit; honeydew melon; kiwi fruit; lychee; mandarin; nashi pears; nectarines; oranges; pawpaw; pineapple; plums; rhubarb; rockmelon; sugar bananas and watermelon.

TO SERVE FRUIT AND ADD VARIETY

- Mix through some plain, full-fat yoghurt.
- Top some cooked fruit like apple, peach or pear with a mixture of baby muesli and butter and bake for a delicious crumble.
- Toss different fruits together, e.g. apple and peach or banana and grated apple.

Fruit Gel

1 cup juice (fresh or use a commercial juice that is labelled with no added sugar)
2 teaspoons gelatine

Heat half of the juice and gradually stir in the gelatine to this hot juice. Add the rest of the juice and stir. Refrigerate until set.

Finger Foods

Around 9–12 months you can start to offer your baby finger foods.

OFFER

- Steamed or microwaved vegetables cut into the shape of chips, e.g. carrots, swede, zucchini and green beans.
- Cubes or slices of cheese.
- Grated cheese mixed with grated vegetables, e.g. cheeses and carrot.
- Pieces of suitably prepared fruit, e.g. sliced mango, sliced ripe peach or apricot, tinned apricots, pears or peaches.
- Slices of cooked tender meat or pieces of cooked chicken. (Dip into yoghurt, mayonnaise, tahini or hommus to make it moist.)
- Cruskets.
- Cooked pasta.

Polenta Fingers

1 cup milk
¼ teaspoon vanilla essence
⅓ cup polenta

Heat milk with vanilla until nearly boiled. Slowly add the polenta whilst stirring. Turn down heat and cook and stir for five minutes. When it is the consistency of mashed potato, spoon the mixture into a greased, small baking tin, sprinkle with cinnamon and refrigerate until cold. Cut into fingers.

Rusks

Make rusks yourself as they are easy to prepare and much cheaper than commercial rusks. Cut day-old bread into four pieces. Put in microwave uncovered for one minute on high. Leave for five minutes to harden or bake in a 150°C oven for about one hour. For a change, spread a smear of Vegemite on the bread before cooking.

9 MONTHS AND OVER

Now we are talking real food here. Look for recipes that the whole family can enjoy that are suitable for baby as well. This need not be difficult. Try risottos, pasta and sauce, gnocchi (plain, add sauce or mix with grated cheese), frittatas, rissoles, meat or fish or lentil loafs and meat balls. Many family recipes are suitable for a baby. Be adventurous. When in doubt babies usually love pasta; just add grated cheese or bolognaise sauce.

- **Avoid hard foods such as nuts, whole apple, carrot.**

The serving size of the recipes are for two adults and one or two small children unless otherwise stated, and recipes use standard cup and spoon sizes.

Basic Tomato Sauce

1 tablespoon olive oil
1 clove garlic
1 × 400g can tomatoes (or nearest size)
a few fresh basil leaves, chopped or shredded
¼ teaspoon sugar
pepper
pinch salt

Heat oil in a big frying pan. Add garlic and stir for a few minutes but do not brown it. Add tomatoes with the juice and crush tomatoes with a spoon in the pan. Add sugar, pepper, salt and basil. Cover and simmer for about fifteen to twenty minutes.

N.B.: Double the mixture to serve four, or freeze half of it for another meal.

VARIATIONS: This tomato sauce can be used as a foundation for many dishes. Turn it into different meals by adding onion, mushrooms, eggplant, capsicum, seeded olives, chopped ham or tuna. Or brown some mince meat and then mix through tomato sauce and cook.

It can be used for the sauce on a pizza (use English muffins or pocket bread as a base) or served over pasta. Turn it into lasagne by layering lasagne pasta with sauce and grated cheese. Bake until cheese is golden, or for an easy meal spoon over baked potato. Add a tin of kidney beans to the sauce and spoon into tacos with some chopped lettuce, tomato and grated cheese.

Chicken Risotto

1 tablespoon oil
1 small onion, finely chopped
1 clove garlic, crushed
300g chicken mince
100g mushrooms, finely sliced
1 large tomato, peeled, seeded and chopped

½ medium capsicum, chopped
1 tablespoon tomato paste
a generous pinch of oregano
1 tablespoon parsley, chopped
1 cup short-grain rice
2 cups chicken stock

Heat the oil in a saucepan, add onion and garlic and cook for a few minutes. Add chicken mince and brown, stirring occasionally for a few minutes. Add mushrooms, tomato, capsicum, tomato paste, oregano and parsley and mix through and cook for a minute.

Stir in the rice then add the stock. Bring to the boil and then cover and simmer for about fifteen minutes, stirring occasionally or until all the liquid is absorbed and the rice is tender.

Polenta with Tomato Sauce

1 cup polenta
3 cups stock or water or half-and-half
2 tablespoons parmesan cheese, grated
1 tablespoon parsley, chopped

Grease and line a lamington tin. Boil stock and/or water and then gradually add polenta while stirring.

Turn down heat and cook for about ten minutes and keep stirring until the polenta has the consistency of mashed potato. Remove from heat and stir in cheese and parsley.

Spoon mixture into the baking tin and cover and refrigerate until cold. Cut the polenta into eight pieces and then grill (brush with a little oil), or bake (brush with a little oil) or fry in about two tablespoons oil or butter until golden. Top with tomato sauce.

N.B.: Cooked cold polenta makes great finger food.
Serves four.

Pumpkin and Bean Casserole

1 tablespoon oil
1 stalk celery, sliced
1 small onion, chopped
250g pumpkin, peeled and chopped into small pieces
250ml canned tomato soup (use the rest for another meal of soup and add rice)
1 × 300g can (or nearest size) 3- or 4-bean mix, washed and drained
grated cheese to serve

Heat oil in a saucepan. Fry celery and onion for about five minutes on a medium heat. (If the vegetables begin to stick add a few drops of water and stir.) Add pumpkin and pour over tomato soup and mix through. Cover and simmer for about thirty minutes or until vegetables are soft.

Add beans, mix and cook for another five minutes. Top with grated cheese. Serve as a meal for baby and a side dish for adults. Put in a jaffle or mix through some pasta. Suitable to freeze.

Basic Frittata

1 tablespoon olive oil
300g small zucchini (about 3 zucchini), sliced thinly
4 eggs, lightly beaten
100ml full-cream milk
pepper, optional

Heat oil and sauté zucchini over a low heat for about fifteen minutes or until soft.

Mix eggs, milk and pepper and then pour over zucchini. When set on one side either skilfully turn it over or put it under a grill for a few minutes until golden.

Serve with a salad and bread.

VARIATIONS
Add sliced onions, leeks, mushrooms, tomato, capsicum or any other leftover vegetables and cook with the zucchini.

Add grated cheese to the egg mixture or when grilling the frittata. Use tasty cheese or parmesan cheese.

Pasta with Avocado Sauce

300g pasta
½ ripe avocado, deseeded and peeled
2 tablespoons parsley, chopped finely
2 tablespoons plain, full-fat yoghurt
2 tablespoons parmesan cheese, grated
1 tablespoon lemon juice
1 teaspoon chives, chopped
3 tablespoons ricotta cheese

Cook the pasta in a large saucepan of boiling water. Mix the rest of the ingredients together by hand or use a food processor and toss the pasta through the sauce. Season with pepper.

VARIATION: Add a 100g can of drained tuna.

Basic Hearty Meat Casserole

500g lean meat, chopped into cubes (use blade, chuck or gravy beef)
1 tablespoon oil
1 small onion, chopped
1 carrot, chopped in small pieces
1 capsicum, chopped
1 × 400g can tomatoes (or nearest size)
½ cup stock
2 tablespoons parsley, chopped
1 bay leaf
pepper

Heat oil and brown meat in two batches in a large saucepan. Return meat to pan and add onion, carrot and capsicum to meat and cook until onions are transparent. Stir occasionally.

Stir in the can of tomatoes with juice, stock, parsley, bay leaf and pepper. Cover and simmer for 1½ to 2 hours. (Depending on your baby, you may need to chop the meat finely after it is cooked.)

Serve with rice, pasta or cous cous. Serves four. Suitable to freeze.

This casserole can be varied by changing the vegetables, liquid or flavourings. Add different vegetables, e.g. potato, pumpkin, zucchini, eggplant, mushrooms, pitted olives. Add herbs and flavourings like basil, oregano, paprika, coriander, lemon rind, garlic and tomato paste. Liquids such as coconut milk, a dash of wine or vegetable juice, depending on the flavours you like and the nationality of the dish, can also be added.

Throw in a can of 3-bean mix or kidney beans at the end of cooking for another change.

Salmon and Vegetable Slice

4–5 slices wholemeal or white bread or a mixture, spread with butter and crusts removed *(use the crusts for finger foods or make into breadcrumbs and freeze)*
3 teaspoons butter, additional
1 leek, washed and sliced
1 small zucchini and 1 small carrot, grated *(or use any vegetable to make up 1 cup of grated vegetables)*
½ cup tasty cheese, grated *(grate a bit extra vegetable and cheese and use this as finger food)*
210g can pink salmon (or nearest size), drained
2 eggs, lightly beaten
1 tablespoon self-raising flour
1 tablespoon parsley, chopped

Heat butter in a frying pan and sauté leeks until soft, about ten minutes. Mix grated vegetables, cheese, leeks, salmon, eggs, flour and parsley together.

Put buttered slices of bread in a greased baking dish and then spread the salmon mixture over the bread. Bake in a 180°C oven for thirty minutes or until golden. Delicious served hot, warm or cold. Serve with a salad.

Desserts

You can't beat delicious, juicy, choice fruit as a dessert. It is the best, easiest and quickest dessert. Use any sort served at a texture suitable for your baby. At this stage fruit may just need to be cut up or sliced. Serve unadorned or with a dollop of yoghurt.

If you want fancier desserts look for desserts based on fruit (e.g. fruit crumbles), bread, rice (e.g. creamy rice puddings) or pasta, milk (e.g. custards) or yoghurt.

Baked Noodle Pudding

125g long life noodles, cooked and drained
3 eggs, lightly beaten
1 tablespoon sugar
2 tablespoons melted margarine or butter
¼ teaspoon cinnamon
¾ cup crushed tinned pineapple, drained (*mix the leftover pineapple with grated carrot for an easy salad*)
¾ cup tinned pie apple (*use the leftover apple for another dessert—serve as is, or with yoghurt or custard*)

Set oven to 180°C. Mix butter or margarine and sugar with eggs. Add fruit, noodles and cinnamon and mix together. Pour mixture into a greased baking dish and cook for thirty-five to forty minutes. Serves 4–6.

Bread and Butter Pudding

continental loaf (about 4 to 5 slices)
butter or margarine
cinnamon
2 eggs

1½ cups milk
1 tablespoon sugar

Heat oven to 180°C. Slice enough fruit loaf to fit in a small baking dish. Butter the bread and place in the baking dish. Sprinkle over cinnamon.

Mix eggs, milk and sugar and pour over bread. Set aside for thirty minutes. Cook for about thirty minutes or until mixture is puffed and golden. Serve hot or cold.

Simple and healthy meal ideas for when you don't have much time

- Jacket potatoes (easily made in the microwave—pierce one medium potato, wrap in paper towel and microwave for about three minutes on high). Top with baked beans, cheese, leftovers, avocado and cheese, tuna.
- Baked beans or spaghetti on toast or in jaffles.
- Cheese or ham and tomato on toast or in jaffles.
- Mashed avocado mixed with cottage cheese on toast.
- Tuna on toast.
- Eggs—scrambled, boiled, poached, omelette.
- Rissoles—meat or fish.
- Spaghetti bolognaise.
- Fruit—fresh or tinned with yoghurt.
- Cooked vegetables topped with grated cheese or cheese sauce.
- Rice, pasta, quick-cooking or long life noodles with grated cheese.
- Cous cous mixed with chopped vegetables.
- Sandwiches, plain or toasted, or as a jaffle with a variety of fillings.
- Baked or grilled fish fingers with vegetables or salad.
- Quick-cooking or long life noodles with a splash of sesame oil and soy sauce. Add some shredded barbecued chicken if you have it.
- Home-made pizzas made on pocket bread, halved English muffins or Lebanese bread, spread with tomato paste and herbs with favourite toppings.
- Leftovers.

Snack foods for toddlers

- Fruit—sliced or cut up in pieces or mixed together as a fruit salad.
- Cheese slices or cubes.
- Grissini sticks.
- Yoghurt.
- Fromage frais.
- Cereal—plain or with milk.
- Toasted crumpets, lightly buttered.
- English muffins with cheese, Vegemite, peanut butter or avocado.
- Plain biscuits.
- Vegetable sticks (raw or steamed if too hard, e.g. carrot).
- Raisin loaf or sliced continental fruit loaf.
- Scones.
- Pikelets.
- Wedges of hard-boiled egg.
- Meat balls, kibbeh, felafel.
- Quick-cooking or long life noodles, plain or with cheese, or a splash of soy sauce and sesame oil.
- Frozen fruit, e.g. watermelon pieces, grapes, orange quarters.
- Sandwiches.

What's It All About?

(THE LAST WORD)

The end of your baby's first year is only the beginning of a never-ending story that flows through generations. When our children are babies it is hard to see the whole picture, as the change to our lives is so immense and, often, the physical and emotional demands so overwhelming that we wonder what *is* it all about?

My babies are now two delightful adults, one of them the father of two hilarious, clever, entirely adorable grandchildren and my pride and joy in all of them equals that of what I imagine a writer or a painter feels after completing a great work. If I have one message to today's overly-anxious parents it is to 'lighten up' and try not to get ground down by things that don't matter. Raising children is fun if you let it be. All parents go through an incredible mix of emotions and hard work, at times one step forward and two steps back, but it's a rare parent who doesn't look back and think every minute was worth it.

And I guess that's what it's all about.

Resources

Australia has many resources available for families, although there never seems to be quite enough. Some are constant, others wax and wane according to government funding or how much voluntary support is around to keep them going. Services also vary between urban and rural areas and from state to state.

Agencies come and go, as do phone numbers, websites and name changes, so it is not practical to have detailed resource lists in books as it's impossible to keep such lists up-to-date and relevant. The aim of the following is to let you know the main services that are available.

I would also suggest you use the following resources to find out what's around in your area and how to contact the service you need.

YOUR CHILD AND FAMILY HEALTH CENTRE

This service is also called Maternal and Child Health and Child and Adolescent and Family Health depending on the state you live in.

The child and family health centre is the first step for any concerns relating to your baby's development, health or behaviour.

YOUR FAMILY DOCTOR

THE MATERNITY HOSPITAL

YOUR NEAREST COMMUNITY HEALTH CENTRE

Free services from nurses, psychologists, social workers, counsellors, speech pathologists and psychiatrists can be accessed from community health centres, but there can be long waiting lists. Information about private services is available from community health centres, your family doctor and child and family health nurses.

YOUR NEAREST CHILDREN'S OR LOCAL HOSPITAL

A variety of free services can be accessed via the public hospital system including paediatric dietitians, occupational therapists, speech pathologists, psychologists, physiotherapists, optometrists, audiologists and so on. Again, depending on the urgency and the service there can be long waits. Some children's hospitals have twenty-four-hour helplines to answer questions about childhood illnesses.

YOUR LOCAL COUNCIL

YOUR LOCAL LIBRARY

THE PHONE BOOK OF THE CAPITAL CITY OF YOUR STATE

Helping organisations

Here are the contact details of the helping organisations mentioned in this book:

AUSTRALIAN MULTIPLE BIRTH ASSOCIATION (AMBA)

A great resource for parents with twins or more. See the *White Pages* of your nearest capital city or their website at www.amba.org.au
National phone number: 1300 886 499

BREASTFEEDING EDUCATION, INFORMATION, ADVICE AND SUPPORT

Australian Breastfeeding Association (ABA)
General Office Phone: (03) 9885 0855
Telephone Counselling: All capital cities and some other areas run a Breastfeeding Helpline on a roster system. You can also look under Australian Breastfeeding Association in your local White Pages. The helplines are available seven days a week. Counsellors answer calls on a voluntary basis in their

own homes so please take this into account when calling.
Internet: www.breastfeeding.asn.au
Email: info@breastfeeding.asn.au
Local groups: Information about contact for local groups can be obtained from the website, from the hospital where you gave birth (or your home-birth midwife) or your child and family health nurse.

CHILDCARE/IMMUNISATION

Childcare Access Hotline 1800 670 305.
Family Assistance Office 13 61 50.
Immunisation Infoline 1800 671 811.
Australian Childhood Immunisation Register (ACIR) 1800 653 809.
CareforKids, a privately run resource for finding out about all aspects of childcare (02) 9235 2807.

WEBSITES

www.immunise.health.gov.au (Immunise Australia).
www.hic.gov.au (Health Insurance Commission).
www.centrelink.gov.au (Centrelink).
www.careforkids.com.au

CHILD SAFETY

Child safety centres, now called names like Child Health Promotion Units, are found in the capital city of most states and are usually based in a hospital. The units actively promote child health and safety issues and provide information to parents, carers and health professionals.

Kidsafe is the Child Accident Prevention Foundation of Australia. It is a non-profit non-government organisation dedicated to the prevention of unintentional injury and death to children. Kidsafe can be contacted on (02) 9845 0890 or via their website www.kidsafe.com.au

DEPRESSION FOLLOWING CHILDBIRTH

The resources are out there for help with depression but there is no national organisation for postnatal depression, and organisations, state by state, seem to change all the time so I don't think it is useful putting addresses and phone numbers into a book.

Panda (Post and Ante Natal Depression Association Inc) appears to be well established and permanent. Panda is located in Victoria. It is not a national body but may be a starting place if you are having problems finding a specific organisation in your state.

PANDA phone number: 1300 726 306
PANDA mensline: 1300 789 978
Internet: www.panda.org.au

DIETITIANS ASSOCIATION OF AUSTRALIA

If you need an accredited dietitian and don't know where to go, call 1800 812 942 to obtain names and contact details. Make sure you let them know it's for paediatric advice. The website is www.daa.asn.au

DOMESTIC VIOLENCE

Advice and resources vary from state to state. Look in the front of the *White Pages* for contact numbers in your state. Numbers include emergency help, advocacy services and local community services.

A national confidential domestic violence help line is available on 1800 200 526.

PARENT EDUCATION

The availability and range of parent education varies widely across Australia. It is often available via child and family health centres, community health centres, long daycare centres, schools, children's hospitals, churches, residential family and baby centres, associations such as the ABA, AMBA, Playgroup Association of Australia, and local councils.

Finding out what is available is usually a challenge. Local newspapers often advertise parent education courses/functions. Try a Google search if you are on the net. A good resource is the website of the Children's Hospital at Westmead, where fact sheets are available on childhood health and safety: www.chw.edu.au/parents/factsheets

PLAYGROUP ASSOCIATION OF AUSTRALIA

The Playgroup Association of Australia has contacts in all states of Australia. See the *White Pages* of your nearest capital city. Alternatively, child and family health centres usually have contact numbers for playgroups.

POISONS INFORMATION CENTRE

Phone 13 11 26.

RELATIONSHIP HELP

A number of other organisations offer relationship support services including Relationships Australia, Unifam, Anglicare and Centacare.

RESIDENTIAL FAMILY CARE CENTRES

Residential services are only found in capital cities and are not available in all states. Information about these services can be acquired locally through your maternity hospital, child and family health centre or community health centre.

SEPARATION AND DIVORCE

For information about mediation or parenting-after-divorce courses, contact your nearest family court registry.

To contact a mediator in private practice look in the *Yellow Pages* under 'mediators'.

Information for men on parenting after divorce is available through MENDS (Men Exploring New Directional Strategies). Call 1300 363 361 or go to www.mends.com.au

SINGLE PARENTS

The two main support groups are:

Single Parent Family Association (SPFA), phone: 1300 300 496, or visit their website www.users.bigpond.com/spfa

Parents Without Partners: Phone (03) 9852 1945, email pwpvicine@bigpond.com or go to www.pwp.freeyellow.com

SPEECH AND LANGUAGE

Speech Pathology Australia is the official body representing speech pathologists and is happy to answer questions and supply fact sheets.

Phone: (03) 9642 4899

Email: office@speechpathologyaustralia.org.au
Internet: www.speechpathologyaustralia.org.au

SUPPORT FOR SUDDEN UNEXPECTED DEATH IN INFANCY (SUDI), STILLBIRTH AND NEONATAL DEATH

Sids and Kids provides Bereavement Support Services for parents following the death of a baby, a stillbirth or a neonatal death.

The organisation also provides the latest information on safe sleeping, including specific statements on a variety of issues in relation to SUDI (for example, the use of dummies, breastfeeding, immunisation, wrapping babies, mattresses and so on), and recommendations to reduce the risks of SUDI (an umbrella term that refers to all unexpected deaths—medical, sudden infant death syndrome (SIDS) and fatal sleep accidents).
Phone number national office: (03) 9819 4595
Contact for state branches: Call 1300 308 307 or go to www.sidsandkids.org
Information statements can be downloaded from the website or requested from the Sids and Kids organisation in your state.

SUPPORT FOR PARENTS WHO THINK THEY MIGHT HURT THEIR BABIES

Phone 1800 688 009 or 13 21 11. Sympathetic listening and suitable referral for help is available. Don't be afraid to call. Include the numbers in your mobile and on the emergency list by the landline.

REFLUX INFANTS SUPPORT ASSOCIATION (RISA)

A volunteer group for parents of babies with gastro oesophageal reflux disease (GORD).

Phone contact: (07) 3229 1090

Internet: www.reflux.org.au

BOYS: BIRTH TO 36 MONTHS PHYSICAL GROWTH PERCENTILES

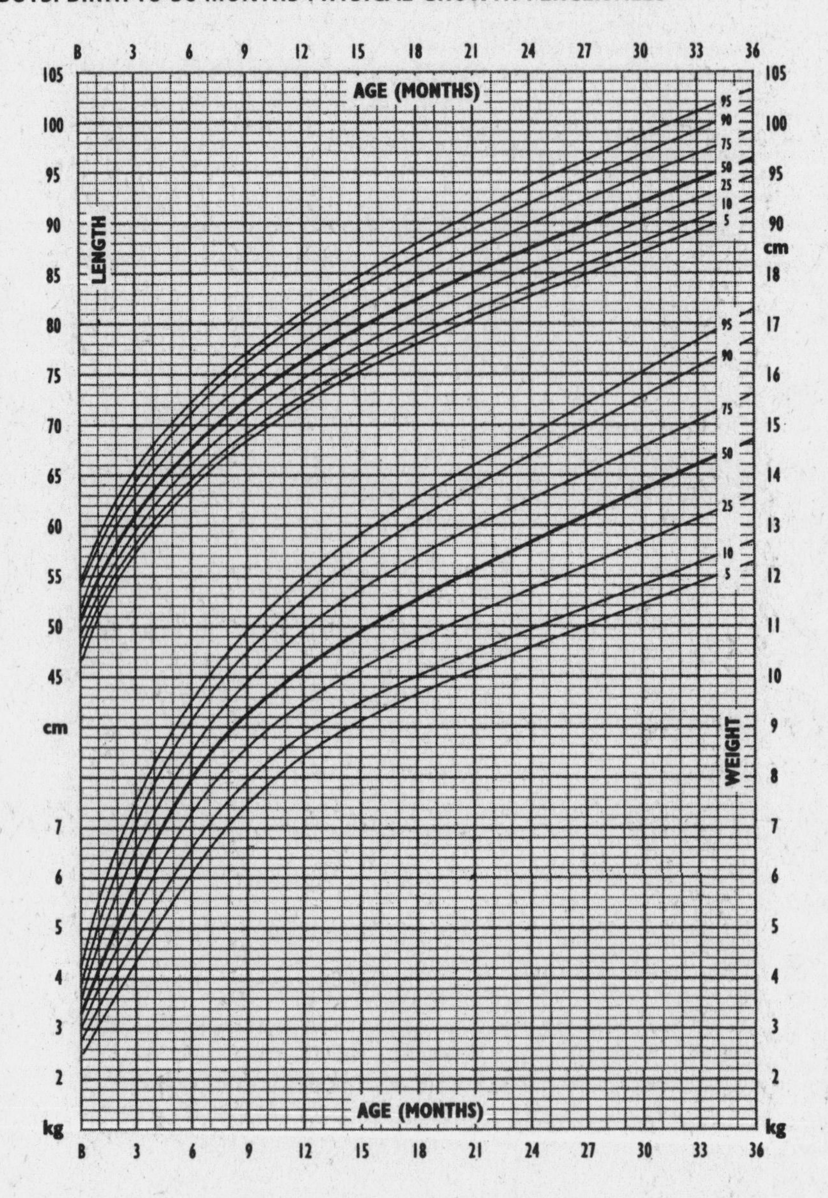

GIRLS: BIRTH TO 36 MONTHS PHYSICAL GROWTH PERCENTILES

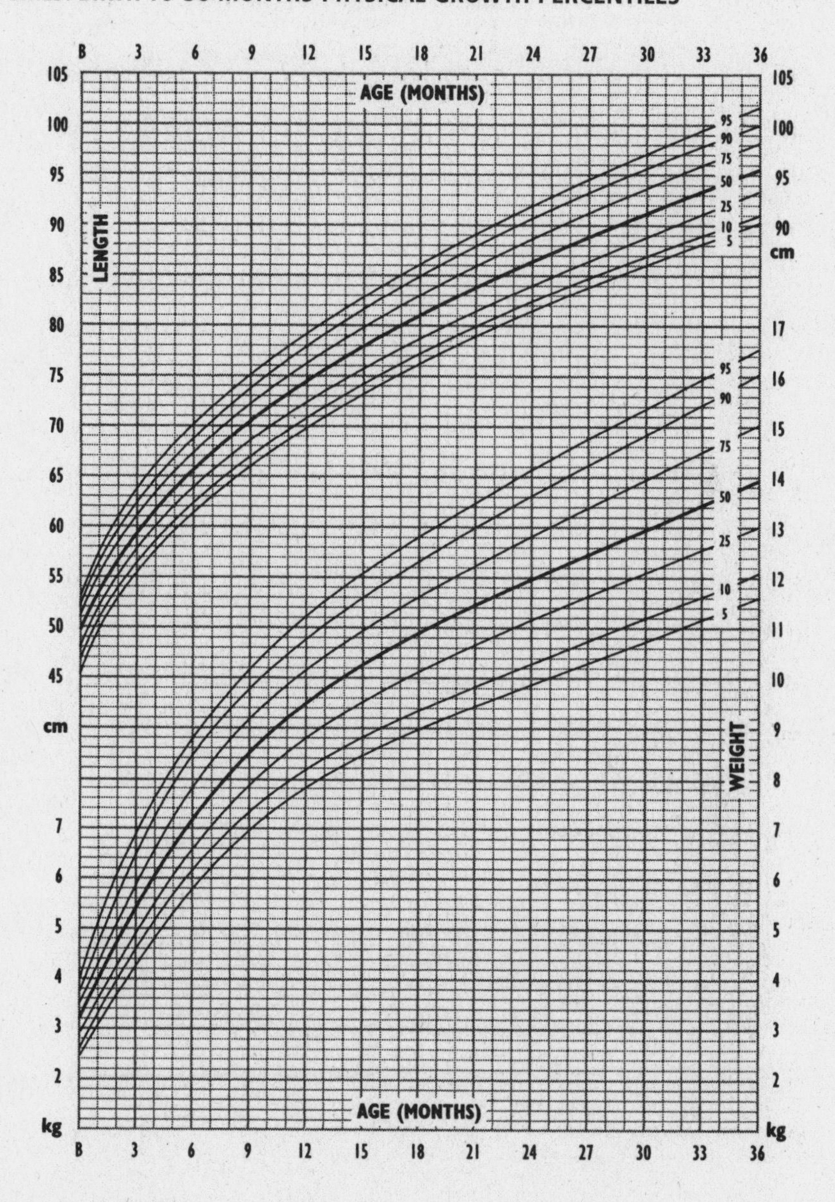

Pounds and Ounces	Metric Grams	Pounds and Ounces	Metric Grams
3 lb	1360.8	6 lb	2721.6
3 lb 1 oz	1389.1	6 lb 1 oz	2749.9
3 lb 2 oz	1417.5	6 lb 2 oz	2778.3
3 lb 3 oz	1445.8	6 lb 3 oz	2806.6
3 lb 4 oz	1474.2	6 lb 4 oz	2835.0
3 lb 5 oz	1502.5	6 lb 5 oz	2863.3
3 lb 6 oz	1503.9	6 lb 6 oz	2891.7
3 lb 7 oz	1559.2	6 lb 7 oz	2920.0
3 lb 8 oz	1587.6	6 lb 8 oz	2948.4
3 lb 9 oz	1615.9	6 lb 9 oz	2976.7
3 lb 10 oz	1644.3	6 lb 10 oz	3005.1
3 lb 11 oz	1672.6	6 lb 11 oz	3033.4
3 lb 12 oz	1701.0	6 lb 12 oz	3061.8
3 lb 13 oz	1729.3	6 lb 13 oz	3090.1
3 lb 14 oz	1757.7	6 lb 14 oz	3118.5
3 lb 15 oz	1786.0	6 lb 15 oz	3146.8
4 lb	1814.4	7 lb	3175.2
4 lb 1 oz	1842.7	7 lb 1 oz	3203.5
4 lb 2 oz	1871.1	7 lb 2 oz	3231.9
4 lb 3 oz	1899.4	7 lb 3 oz	3262.2
4 lb 4 oz	1927.8	7 lb 4 oz	3288.6
4 lb 5 oz	1956.1	7 lb 5 oz	3316.9
4 lb 6 oz	1984.5	7 lb 6 oz	3345.2
4 lb 7 oz	2012.8	7 lb 7 oz	3373.6
4 lb 8 oz	2041.2	7 lb 8 oz	3401.9
4 lb 9 oz	2069.5	7 lb 9 oz	3430.3
4 lb 10 oz	2097.9	7 lb 10 oz	3458.6
4 lb 11 oz	2126.2	7 lb 11 oz	3487.0
4 lb 12 oz	2154.6	7 lb 12 oz	3515.3
4 lb 13 oz	2182.9	7 lb 13 oz	3543.7
4 lb 14 oz	2211.3	7 lb 14 oz	3572.0
4 lb 15 oz	2239.6	7 lb 15 oz	3600.4
5 lb	2268.0	8 lb	3628.7
5 lb 1 oz	2296.3	8 lb 1 oz	3657.1
5 lb 2 oz	2324.7	8 lb 2 oz	3685.4
5 lb 3 oz	2353.0	8 lb 3 oz	3713.8
5 lb 4 oz	2381.4	8 lb 4 oz	3742.1
5 lb 5 oz	2409.7	8 lb 5 oz	3770.5
5 lb 6 oz	2438.1	8 lb 6 oz	3798.8
5 lb 7 oz	2466.4	8 lb 7 oz	3827.2
5 lb 8 oz	2494.8	8 lb 8 oz	3855.5
5 lb 9 oz	2523.1	8 lb 9 oz	3883.9
5 lb 10 oz	2551.5	8 lb 10 oz	3912.2
5 lb 11 oz	2579.8	8 lb 11 oz	3940.6
5 lb 12 oz	2608.2	8 lb 12 oz	3968.9
5 lb 13 oz	2636.5	8 lb 13 oz	3997.3
5 lb 14 oz	2664.9	8 lb 14 oz	4025.6
5 lb 15 oz	2693.2	8 lb 15 oz	4054.0

Pounds and Ounces	Metric Grams
9 lb	4082.3
9 lb 1 oz	4110.7
9 lb 2 oz	4139.0
9 lb 3 oz	4167.4
9 lb 4 oz	4195.7
9 lb 5 oz	4224.1
9 lb 6 oz	4252.4
9 lb 7 oz	4280.8
9 lb 8 oz	4309.1
9 lb 9 oz	4337.5
9 lb 10 oz	4365.8
9 lb 11 oz	4394.2
9 lb 12 oz	4422.5
9 lb 13 oz	4450.9
9 lb 14 oz	4479.2
9 lb 15 oz	4507.6
10 lb	4535.9
10 lb 1 oz	4564.3
10 lb 2 oz	4592.6
10 lb 3 oz	4621.0
10 lb 4 oz	4649.3
10 lb 5 oz	4677.7
10 lb 6 oz	4706.0
10 lb 7 oz	4734.4
10 lb 8 oz	4762.7
10 lb 9 oz	4791.1
10 lb 10 oz	4819.4
10 lb 11 oz	4847.8
10 lb 12 oz	4876.1
10 lb 13 oz	4904.5
10 lb 14 oz	4932.8
10 lb 15 oz	4961.2
11 lb	4989.5
11 lb 1 oz	5017.9
11 lb 2 oz	5046.2
11 lb 3 oz	5074.6
11 lb 4 oz	5102.9
11 lb 5 oz	5131.3
11 lb 6 oz	5159.6
11 lb 7 oz	5188.0
11 lb 8 oz	5216.3
11 lb 9 oz	5254.7
11 lb 10 oz	5273.0
11 lb 11 oz	5301.4
11 lb 12 oz	5329.7
11 lb 13 oz	5358.1
11 lb 14 oz	5386.4
11 lb 15 oz	5414.8
12 lb	5443.1
12 lb 1 oz	5471.5
12 lb 2 oz	5499.8
12 lb 3 oz	5528.2
12 lb 4 oz	5556.5
12 lb 5 oz	5584.9
12 lb 6 oz	5613.2
12 lb 7 oz	5641.6
12 lb 8 oz	5669.9
12 lb 9 oz	5698.3
12 lb 10 oz	5726.6
12 lb 11 oz	5755.0
12 lb 12 oz	5783.3
12 lb 13 oz	5811.7
12 lb 14 oz	5840.0
12 lb 15 oz	5868.4

Inches	Centimetres
12	30.5
13	33.0
14	35.6
15	38.1
16	40.5
17	43.2
18	45.7
19	48.3
20	50.8
21	53.3
22	55.9
23	58.4
24	61.0

Acknowledgements

I am indebted to my family and the many friends and health professionals who have been involved in *Baby Love* and helped bring it to life.

Roger Barker has been my partner, lover and friend for many years. Unbeknown to me when we started this arrangement, he had another hidden talent—that of being a great father to our children. I have never worked out whether it was instinct or if he reads father books on the sly, but I give thanks daily that my partner in life is not only a great lover and friend but a truly great father. As well, Roger has given me unlimited emotional and financial support for this never-ending project and even (most of the time) shown avid interest in its progress. Thank you Rog.

Thanks to good friends Narelle and Peter Black, who let me take over a portion of their house to write the final draft and who continue to show genuine interest in all my projects, be they mad or sane, successful or not.

Several nursing colleagues let me use their ideas. Thank you to Jann Zintgraff for her delightful observation, '. . . the uncircumcised penis needs the same care as the elbow' and for her thoughts on sibling rivalry, to Sally Keegan for her ideas on 'looking after yourself', to Patrizio Fiorillo for help with the relaxation exercise, to Liz Flamsteed for her expertise on the immediate post partum area and to Jan Annson for her help with the ever-important breastfeeding positioning.

Thanks too to Murray Cox for his insights into fatherhood which made me think again about what it means to be a father. And to Diane Temple for the wonderful recipes.

I am grateful to an enthusiastic band of readers for their encouragement and forthright comments. Thanks to Carolyn Parfitt, Tina Matthews, Sally Zwartz, Janine Goldberg, Jenny Miller, Leah and Doug Shelton, Michelle Maxwell, Ruth Sainsbury, Jann Zintgraff, Maureen Fisher, Dasha Gilden, Mary Lynch, Laureen Laylor-Smith, Peter Hartmann, Hilary and Ian Jacobson, Mark Ferson, Lorraine Young and Anthony Samuels.

Special thanks to four people who are the sort of friends who give our lives that extra dimension—Helen Wilmore, Margaret Sheens, Jann Zintgraff and Fay Macartney-Bourne.

During the course of *Baby Love*'s history I have developed a deep appreciation of the skills of editors and publishers. Oddly enough hands-on contact with the *Baby Love* manuscript seems destined to produce babies. The following women had no children when I first knew them. I am happy to report that they now have five babies and toddlers amongst them despite exposure to a manuscript full of sleepless nights, crying babies, sore nipples and endless poo. Well done team! Thank you to Julia Stiles and Cath Proctor for their excellent editorial guidance and unflagging encouragement and support for my labours and to Jane Curry, publisher at Pan Macmillan, for believing in the author and the book and making sure neither sink.

A special mention to Carolyn Parfitt for a thorough and vigorous job of copyediting, to Susie Baxter-Smith for the great illustrations magically produced in between caring for two toddlers, to Elspeth Menzies, editor at Pan Macmillan, who helped me look at the material yet again with a fresh eye for this edition and to Margaret O'Sullivan, friend and agent.

Finally, to all the mothers, fathers and babies who have allowed me for a short time to share your lives—this book was born out of conversations with you and your experiences provide a great deal of the material throughout the book—thank you.

Fourth Edition Acknowledgements

Many thanks to Dr Lisa Amir, inspired researcher into the problems that beset breastfeeding women and babies, and for help with the ubiquitous Candida and other fungal infections.

I'm most appreciative of the mighty effort made by Donna Walsh, mother of the gorgeous Jonathon and Layton, and Kim Carruthers, mother of my darling granddaughter, Sage, for a not *too* stressful photographic session spent getting the look just right for the covers—thank you all for your time and patience.

Thanks to the great crew at Pan Macmillan—can't believe it's over ten years since we first met over the baby scales at the Bondi Junction Early Childhood Centre, James. This time round, special thanks to Anna McFarlane, publisher, mother of a *Mighty Toddler* and a *Baby Love* baby (it's no wonder we get on so well); to Tom Gilliatt, publisher and mutual friend of Bluey the Groper; and to Brianne Tunnicliffe and Karen Ward, for seamlessly rearranging my add-ins and erasures. And a big hug to Anyez Lindop for your smiley face, all the fun and for looking after me so well in the publicity arena.

Fifth Edition Acknowledgements

A fifth edition—wow!

This time round thank you to Alex Craig, publisher, for your support and enthusiasm for this baby tome, which is growing so rapidly it's almost out of control. Where will it end?

Thanks to Kylie Mason, editor, for seamlessly gluing in the additions (many) and joining up the gaps left by the deletions (few).

Thanks as well to Brianne Tunnicliffe for your intelligent insights and suggestions; Marissa McInnes, flight attendant, for the update on flying with babies and toddlers; and Christine Rhodes, Nurse Manager, Statewide Infant Screening Hearing (SWISH), for the latest on newborn hearing screening around Australia.

A very special thank you to Alison Black for agreeing to let me be photographed cuddling her delicious newborn James for the photo on the back cover.

Finally, thanks to all the readers who write and email, and give feedback—positive and negative—via the web; I enjoy reading what you have to say.

Index

B

C

D

I

J

K

L

M

N

R

T

Y

Z